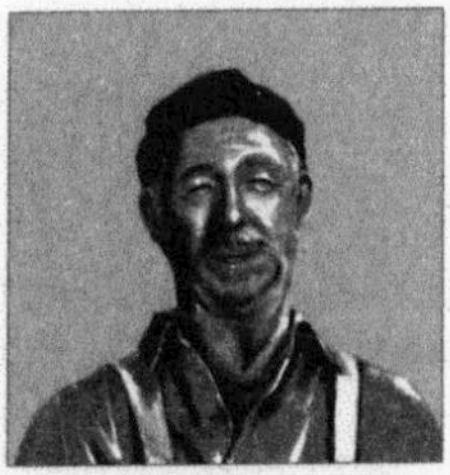

尾田栄一郎

...ation for chapter 233 is framed in black ... llow manga artist Gin Shinga. Someone ... artists live on in their characters ar... blessed to be in this profession.

...2



Eiichiro Oda began his manga career at the age of 17, when his one-shot cowboy manga **Wanted!** won second place in the coveted Tezuka manga awards. Oda went on to work as an assistant to some of the biggest manga artists in the industry, including Nobuhiro Watsuki, before winning the Hop Step Award for new artists. His pirate adventure **One Piece**, which debuted in **Weekly Shonen Jump** in 1997, quickly became one of the most popular manga in Japan.

# ONE PIECE VOL. 25
# SKYPIEA PART 2

## SHONEN JUMP Manga Edition

### STORY AND ART BY EIICHIRO ODA

English Adaptation/Lance Caselman
Translation/JN Productions
Touch-up Art & Lettering/Steven Rhyse & HudsonYards
Design/Fawn Lau
Editor/Yuki Murashige

VP, Production/Alvin Lu
VP, Sales & Product Marketing/Gonzalo Ferreyra
VP, Creative/Linda Espinosa
Publisher/Hyoe Narita

Printed in the U.S.A.

Published by VIZ Media, LLC
P.O. Box 77010
San Francisco, CA 94107

10 9 8 7 6 5 4 3 2 1
First printing, January 2010

www.viz.com

THE WORLD'S MOST POPULAR MANGA

www.shonenjump.com

SHONEN JUMP MANGA

# ONE PIECE

## Vol. 25
## THE 100 MILLION BERRY MAN

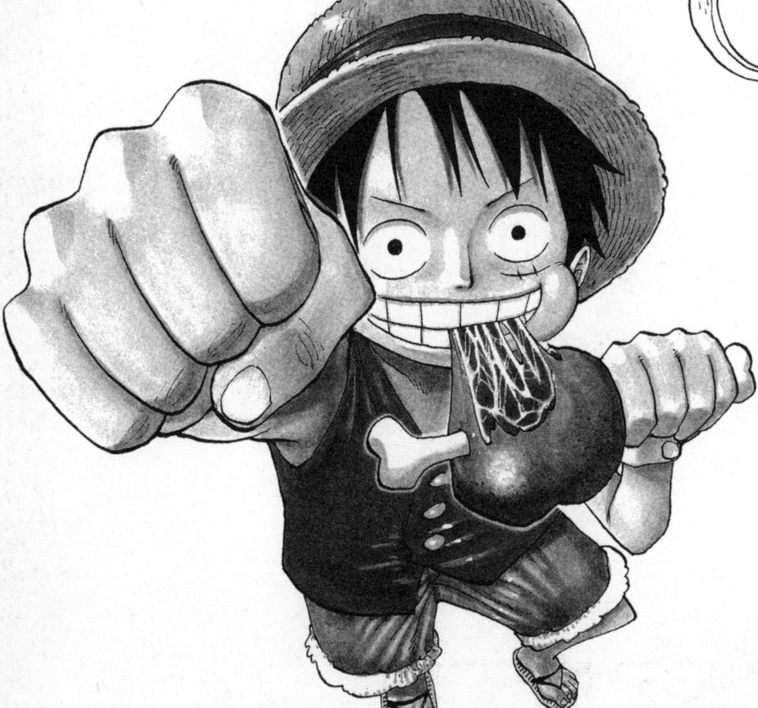

STORY AND ART BY

**EIICHIRO ODA**

Masira

Shoujou

Boundlessly optimistic and able to stretch like rubber, he is determined to become King of the Pirates.

**Monkey D. Luffy**

A former bounty hunter and master of the "three-sword" style. He aspires to be the world's greatest swordsman.

**Roronoa Zolo**

A thief who specializes in robbing pirates. Nami hates pirates, but Luffy convinced her to be his navigator.

**Nami**

A village boy with a talent for telling tall tales. His father, Yasopp, is a member of Shanks's crew.

**Usopp**

The big-hearted cook (and ladies' man) whose dream is to find the legendary sea, the "All Blue."

**Sanji**

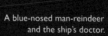

A blue-nosed man-reindeer and the ship's doctor.

**Tony Tony Chopper**

A mysterious woman in search of the Ponegliff on which true history is recorded.

**Nico Robin**

# THE STORY OF ONE PIECE

Volume 25

Monkey D. Luffy started out as just a kid with a dream—to become the greatest pirate in history! Stirred by the tales of pirate "Red-Haired" Shanks, Luffy vowed to become a pirate himself. That was before the enchanted Devil Fruit gave Luffy the power to stretch like rubber, at the cost of being unable to swim—a serious handicap for an aspiring sea dog. Undeterred, Luffy set out to sea and recruited some crewmates—master swordsman Zolo; treasure-hunting thief Nami; lying sharpshooter Usopp; the high-kicking chef Sanji; Chopper, the walkin' talkin' reindeer doctor; and the mysterious archaeologist Robin.

Having defeated Sir Crocodile and restored peace to the Kingdom of Alabasta, Luffy and crew bid Princess Vivi a tearful farewell and set sail once more on the Grand Line. They soon discover they have a stowaway—none other than Nico Robin, formerly Crocodile's partner, Ms. All Sunday! She surprises them even more by asking to join their merry crew. After some initial hesitation over her sudden turn of allegiance, they welcome her aboard. As they follow the course set by their Log Pose, it suddenly starts pointing up to the sky. When Robin tells them of a legendary island in the sky, Luffy becomes determined to go there. They sail to the island of Jaya to gather more information, but there they are bullied and beaten by the pirate Bellamy the Hyena, who has no tolerance for dreamers. Hearing of an eccentric man named Mont Blanc Cricket, "the man who speaks of big dreams," they decide to visit him, hoping he holds the secret of how to get to the mysterious island in the sky...

**Bellamy Pirates**

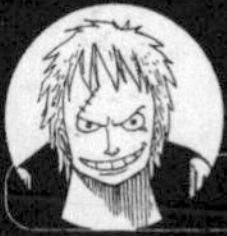

**Bellamy**

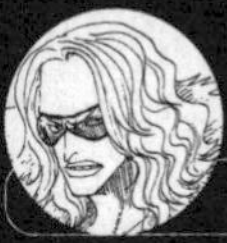

**Sarquiss**

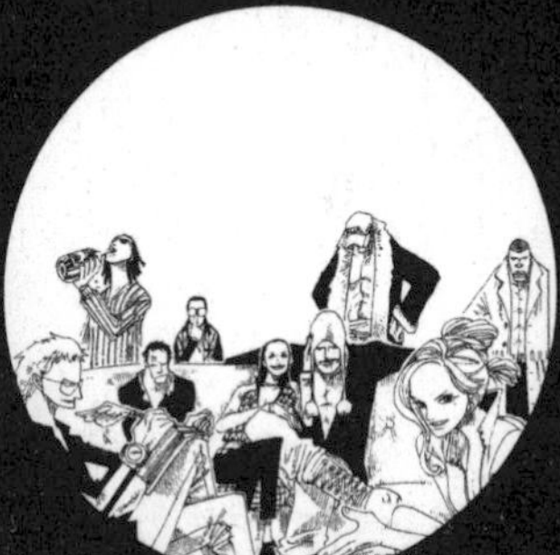

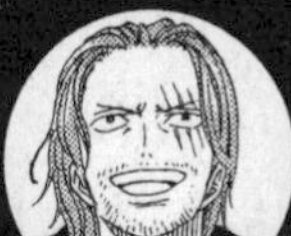

A pirate that Luffy idolizes. Shanks gave Luffy his trade-mark straw hat.

**"Red-Haired" Shanks**

## Vol. 25
## The 100 Million Berry Man

## CONTENTS

Chapter 227: Noland the Liar 7

Chapter 228: Mont Blanc Cricket, the Last Boss of the
Monkey Mountain Allied Force 27

Chapter 229: Let's Eat 47

Chapter 230: Pursue the South Bird! 67

Chapter 231: Bellamy the Hyena 87

Chapter 232: The 100 Million Berry Man 107

Chapter 233: The World's Greatest Power 127

Chapter 234: Please Remember 147

Chapter 235: The Knock Up Stream 167

Chapter 236: The Ship Sails to the Sky 187

# Chapter 227:

# NOLAND THE LIAR

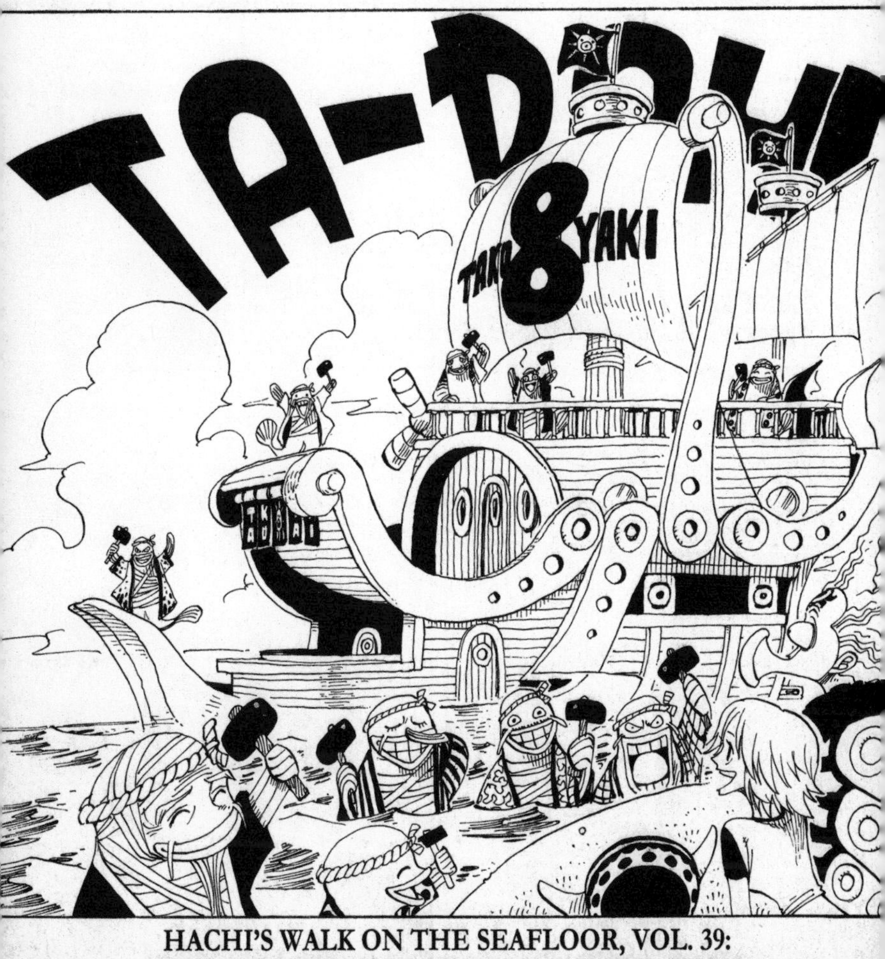
TA-D
TAKO 8 YAKI

HACHI'S WALK ON THE SEAFLOOR, VOL. 39:
"THE CATFISH VILLAGE REPAYS THEIR DEBT"

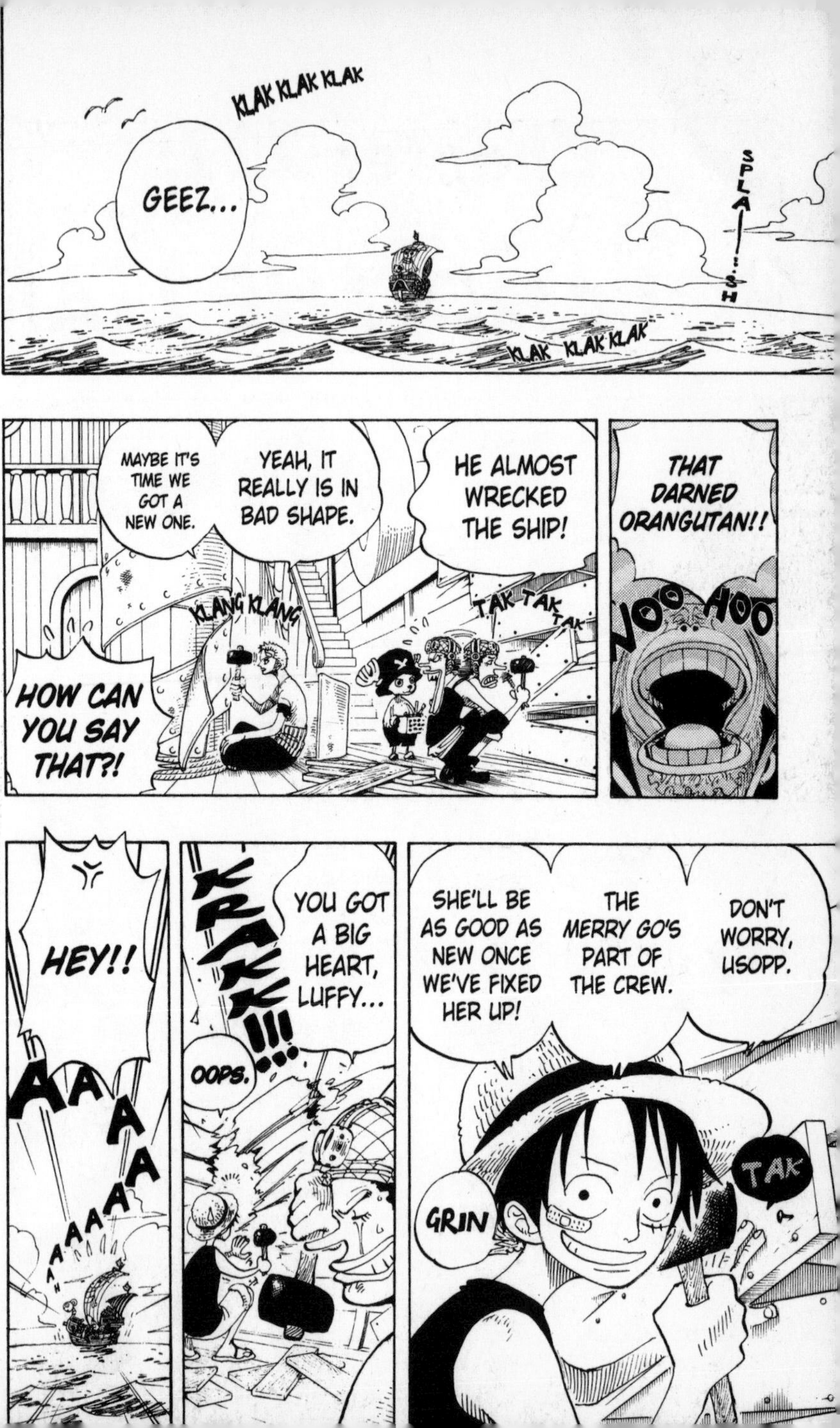
KLAK KLAK KLAK
SPLA!!SH
GEEZ...
KLAK KLAK KLAK
THAT DARNED ORANGUTAN!!
HOO HOO
HE ALMOST WRECKED THE SHIP!
YEAH, IT REALLY IS IN BAD SHAPE.
MAYBE IT'S TIME WE GOT A NEW ONE.
TAK TAK TAK
KLANG KLANG
HOW CAN YOU SAY THAT?!
DON'T WORRY, USOPP.
THE MERRY GO'S PART OF THE CREW.
SHE'LL BE AS GOOD AS NEW ONCE WE'VE FIXED HER UP!
TAK
GRIN
YOU GOT A BIG HEART, LUFFY...
KRAKK!!!
OOPS.
HEY!!
AAAAAAAAAH

READ THIS WAY

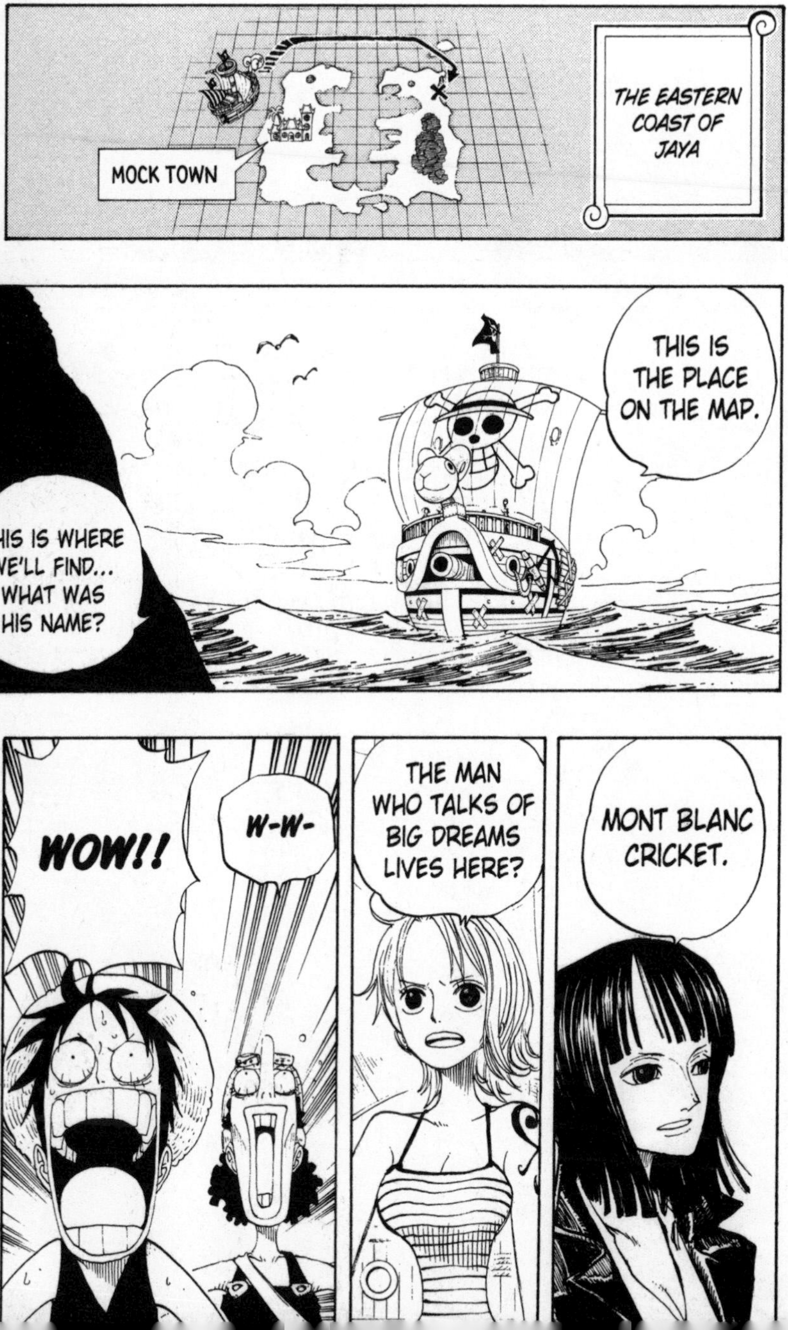
THE EASTERN COAST OF JAYA
MOCK TOWN
THIS IS THE PLACE ON THE MAP.
THIS IS WHERE WE'LL FIND... WHAT WAS HIS NAME?
MONT BLANC CRICKET.
THE MAN WHO TALKS OF BIG DREAMS LIVES HERE?
W-W-
WOW!!

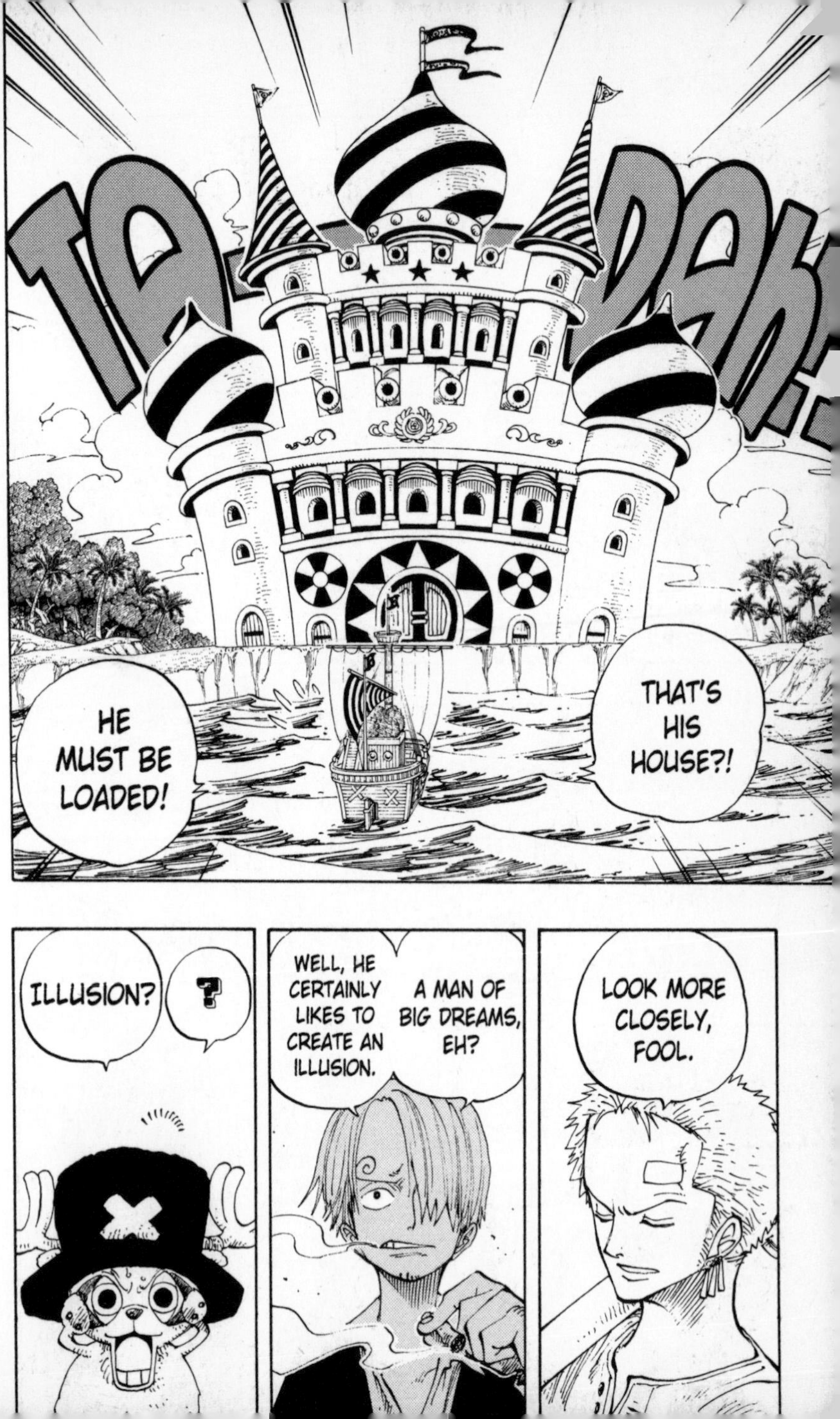
TA-DAH!!
THAT'S HIS HOUSE?!
HE MUST BE LOADED!
LOOK MORE CLOSELY, FOOL.
A MAN OF BIG DREAMS, EH?
WELL, HE CERTAINLY LIKES TO CREATE AN ILLUSION.
?
ILLUSION?

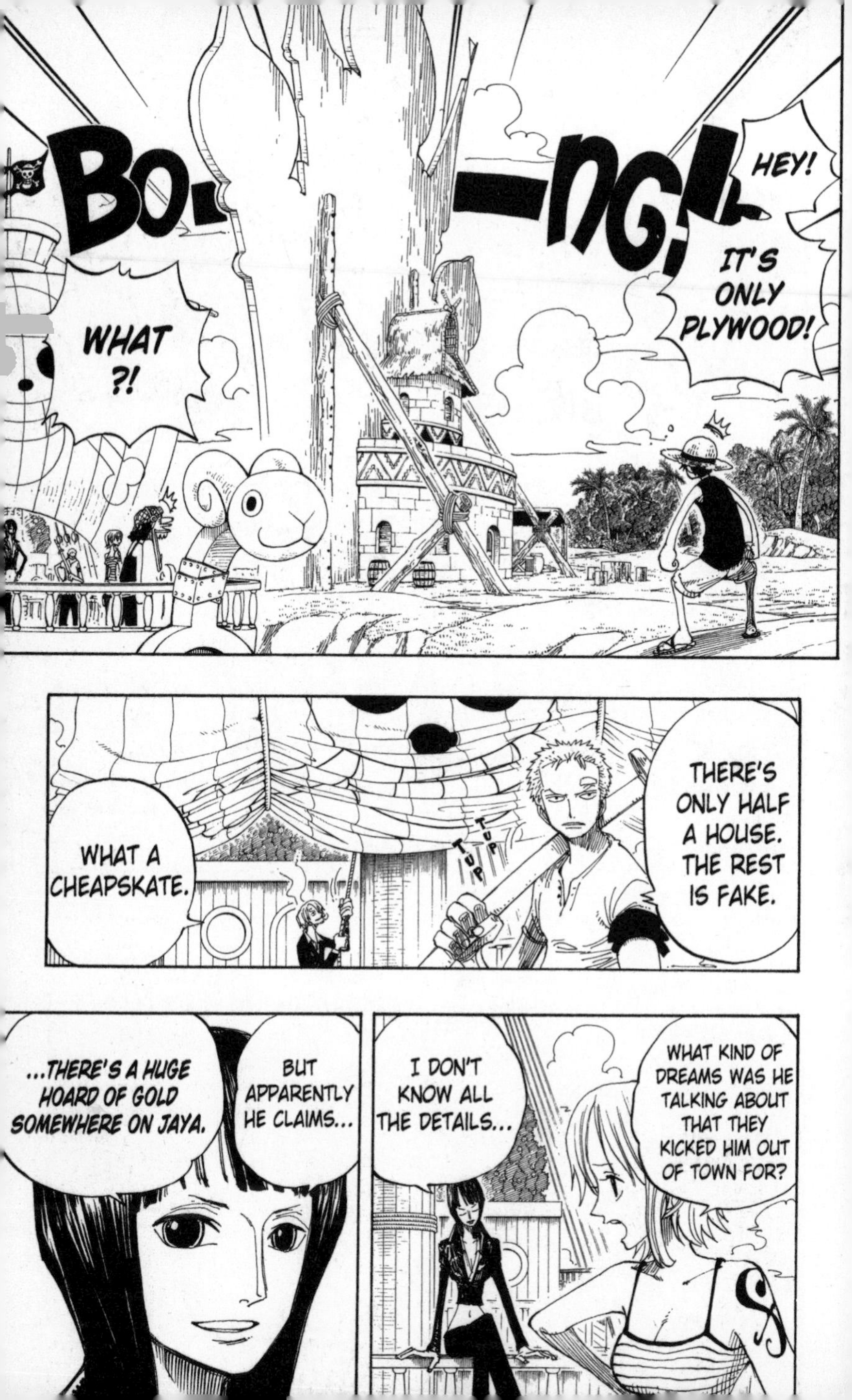
BO—NG!
HEY!
IT'S ONLY PLYWOOD!
WHAT ?!
THERE'S ONLY HALF A HOUSE. THE REST IS FAKE.
TUP TUP
WHAT A CHEAPSKATE.
WHAT KIND OF DREAMS WAS HE TALKING ABOUT THAT THEY KICKED HIM OUT OF TOWN FOR?
I DON'T KNOW ALL THE DETAILS...
BUT APPARENTLY HE CLAIMS...
...THERE'S A HUGE HOARD OF GOLD SOMEWHERE ON JAYA.

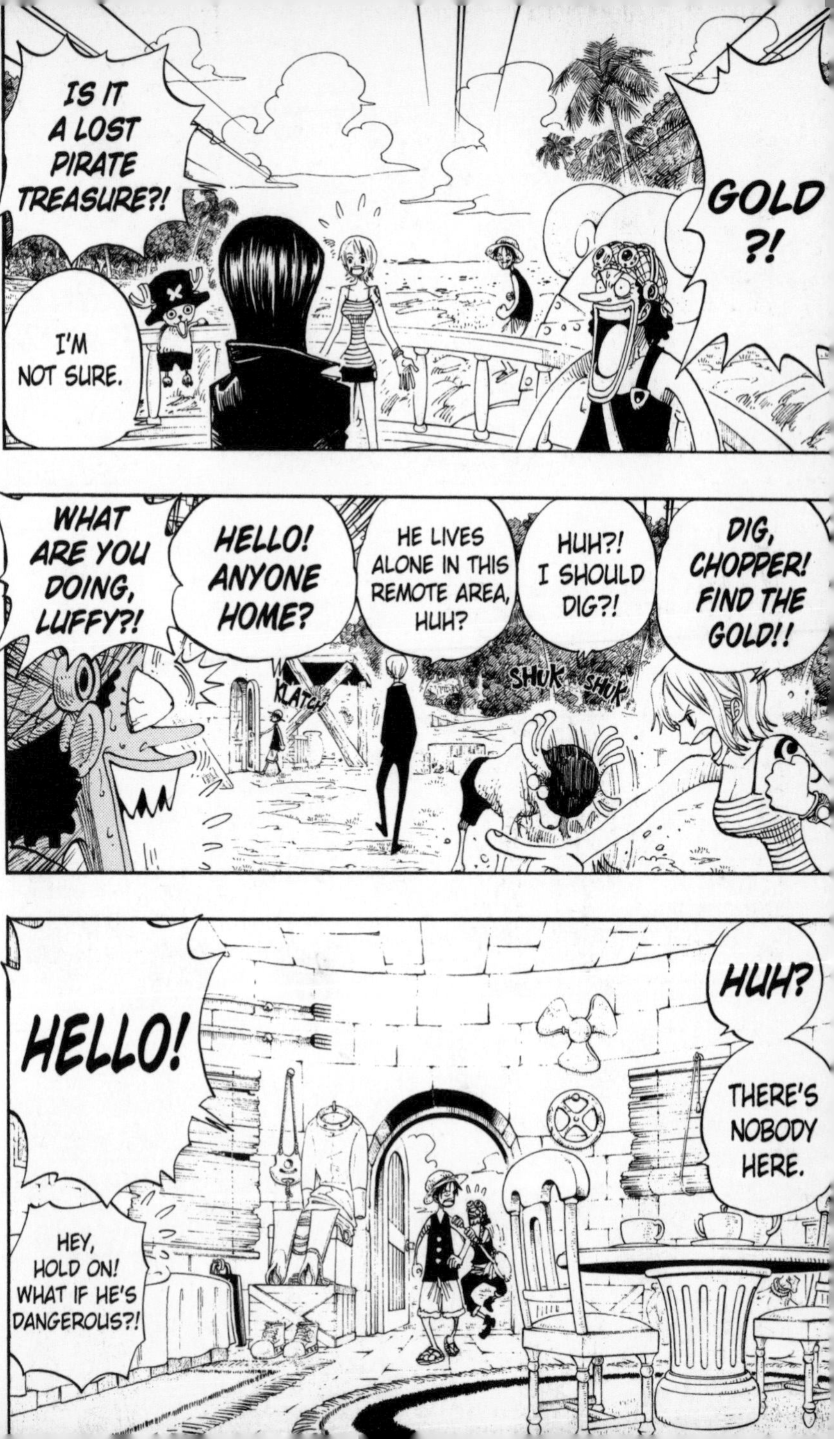
GOLD ?!
IS IT A LOST PIRATE TREASURE?!
I'M NOT SURE.
DIG, CHOPPER! FIND THE GOLD!!
HUH?! I SHOULD DIG?!
SHUK SHUK
HE LIVES ALONE IN THIS REMOTE AREA, HUH?
KLATCH
HELLO! ANYONE HOME?
WHAT ARE YOU DOING, LUFFY?!
HUH?
THERE'S NOBODY HERE.
HELLO!
HEY, HOLD ON! WHAT IF HE'S DANGEROUS?!

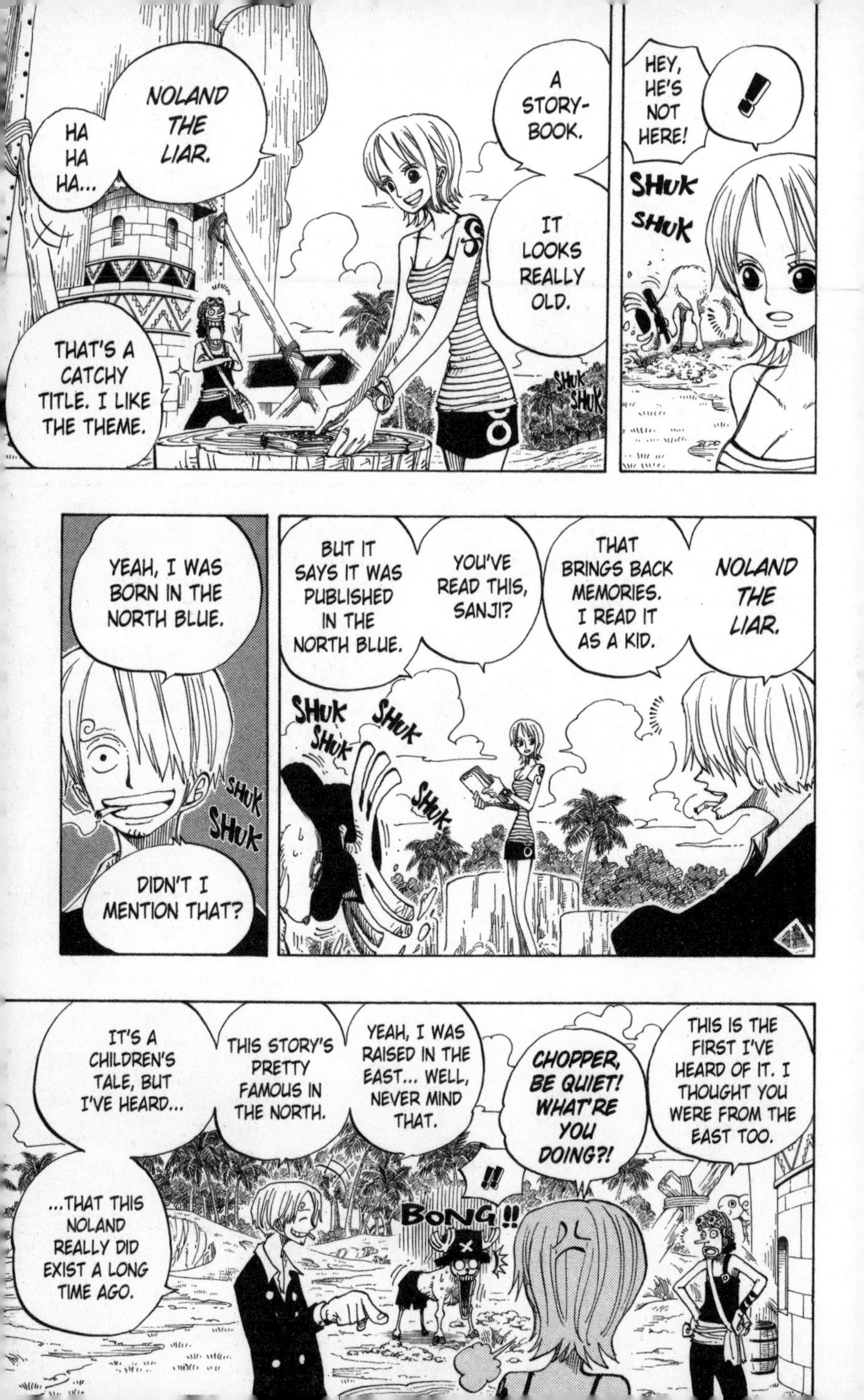
!
HEY, HE'S NOT HERE!
SHUK
SHUK
A STORY-BOOK.
IT LOOKS REALLY OLD.
SHUK SHUK
NOLAND THE LIAR.
HA HA HA...
THAT'S A CATCHY TITLE. I LIKE THE THEME.
NOLAND THE LIAR.
THAT BRINGS BACK MEMORIES. I READ IT AS A KID.
YOU'VE READ THIS, SANJI?
BUT IT SAYS IT WAS PUBLISHED IN THE NORTH BLUE.
SHUK
SHUK
SHUK
SHUK
YEAH, I WAS BORN IN THE NORTH BLUE.
SHUK
SHUK
DIDN'T I MENTION THAT?
THIS IS THE FIRST I'VE HEARD OF IT. I THOUGHT YOU WERE FROM THE EAST TOO.
CHOPPER, BE QUIET! WHAT'RE YOU DOING?!
!!
BONG!!
YEAH, I WAS RAISED IN THE EAST... WELL, NEVER MIND THAT.
THIS STORY'S PRETTY FAMOUS IN THE NORTH.
IT'S A CHILDREN'S TALE, BUT I'VE HEARD...
...THAT THIS NOLAND REALLY DID EXIST A LONG TIME AGO.

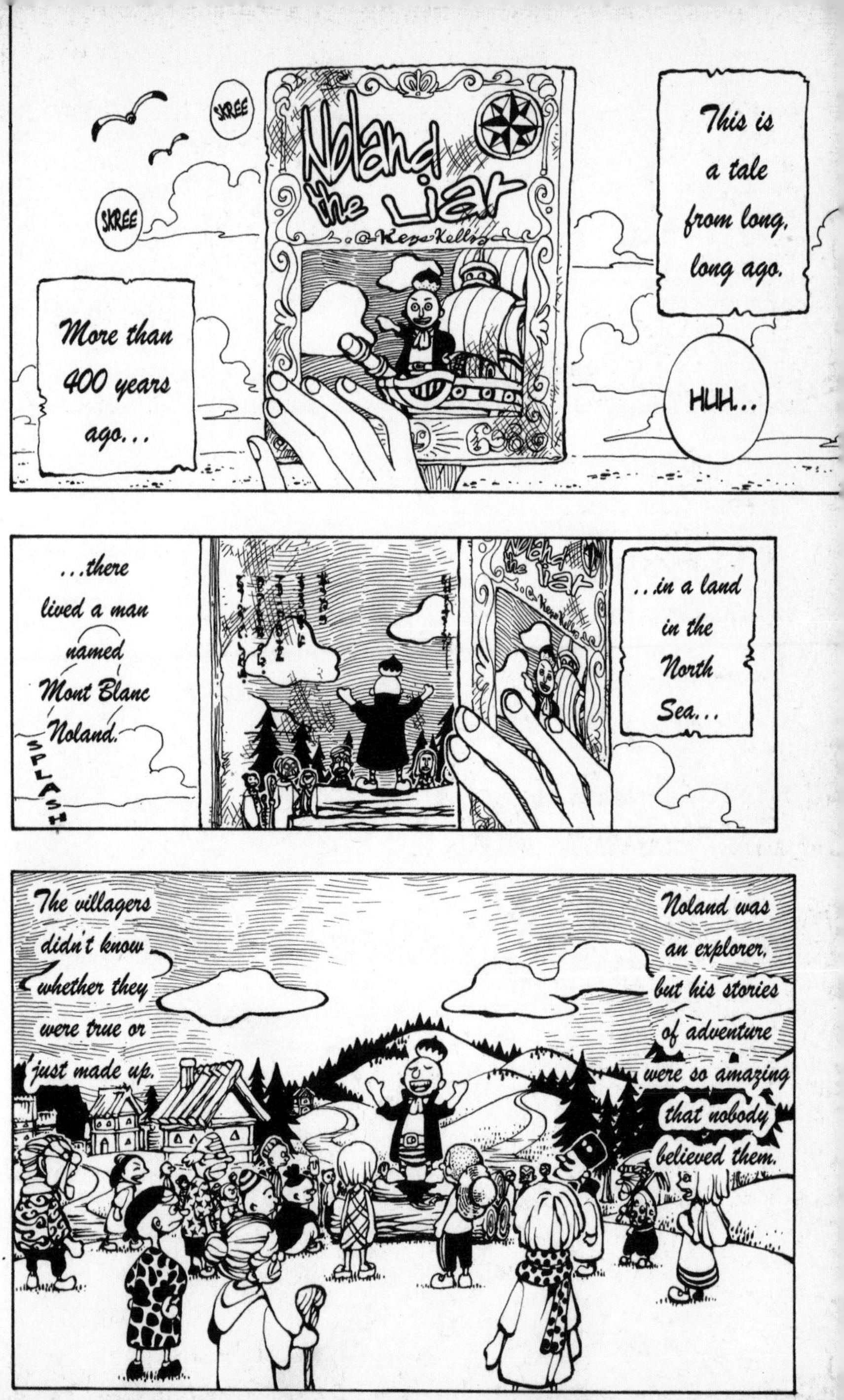
This is a tale from long, long ago.
HUH...
Noland the Liar
SKREE
SKREE
More than 400 years ago...
...in a land in the North Sea...
Noland the Liar
...there lived a man named Mont Blanc Noland.
SPLASH
Noland was an explorer, but his stories of adventure were so amazing that nobody believed them.
The villagers didn't know whether they were true or just made up.

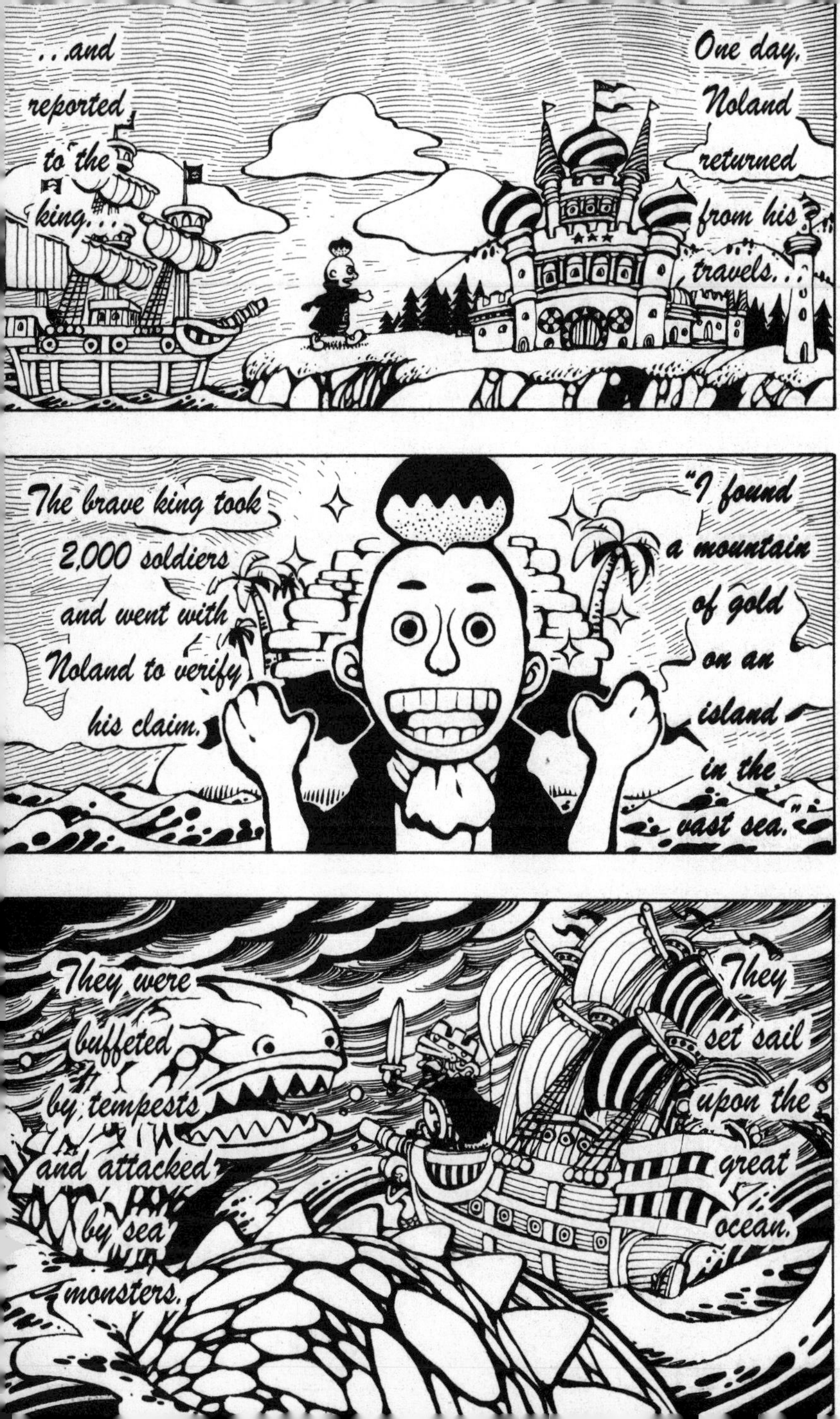
One day, Noland returned from his travels...
...and reported to the king...
"I found a mountain of gold on an island in the vast sea."
The brave king took 2,000 soldiers and went with Noland to verify his claim.
They set sail upon the great ocean.
They were buffeted by tempests and attacked by sea monsters.

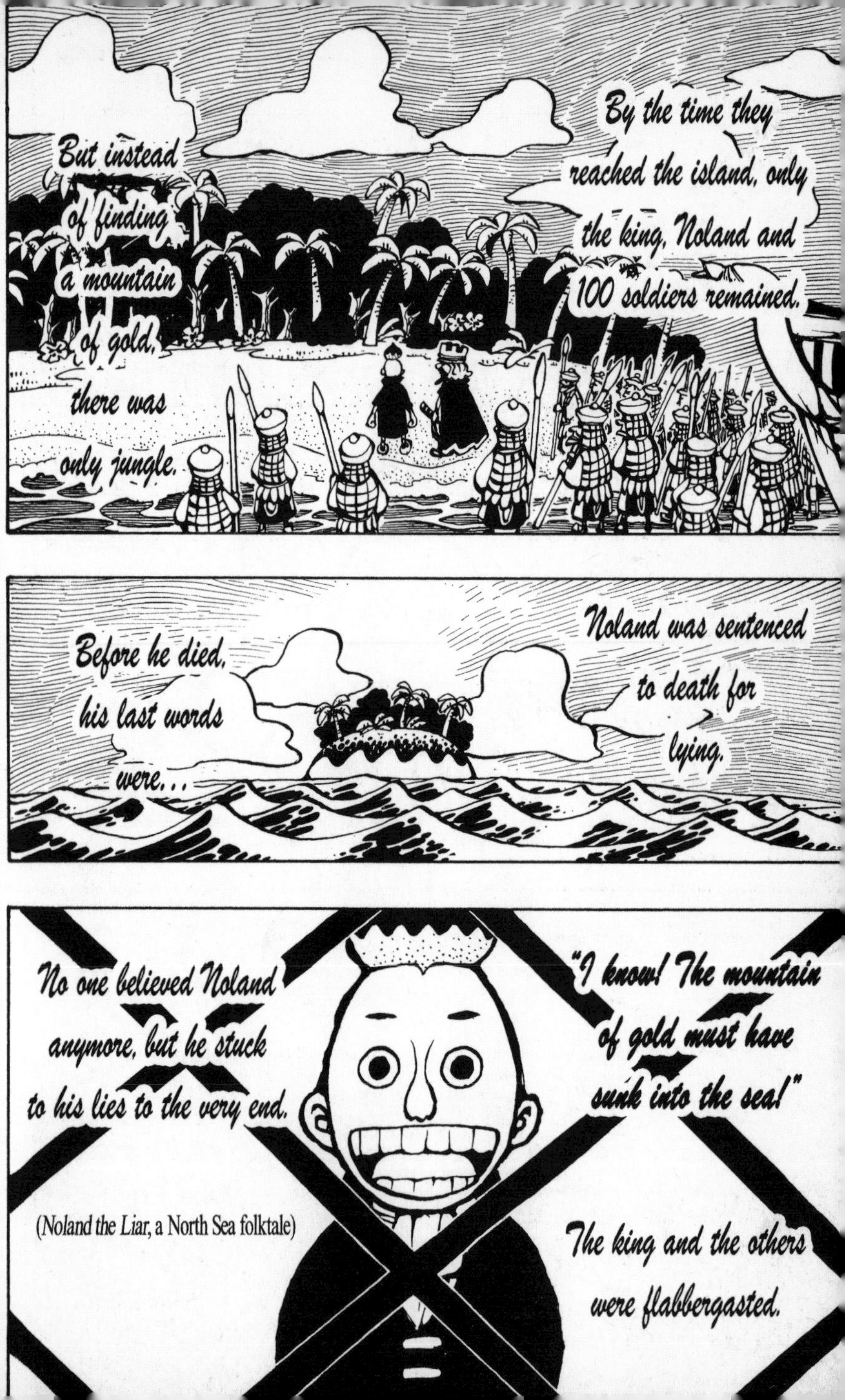
By the time they reached the island, only the king, Noland and 100 soldiers remained.
But instead of finding a mountain of gold, there was only jungle.
Noland was sentenced to death for lying.
Before he died, his last words were...
"I know! The mountain of gold must have sunk into the sea!"
The king and the others were flabbergasted.
No one believed Noland anymore, but he stuck to his lies to the very end.
(Noland the Liar, a North Sea folktale)

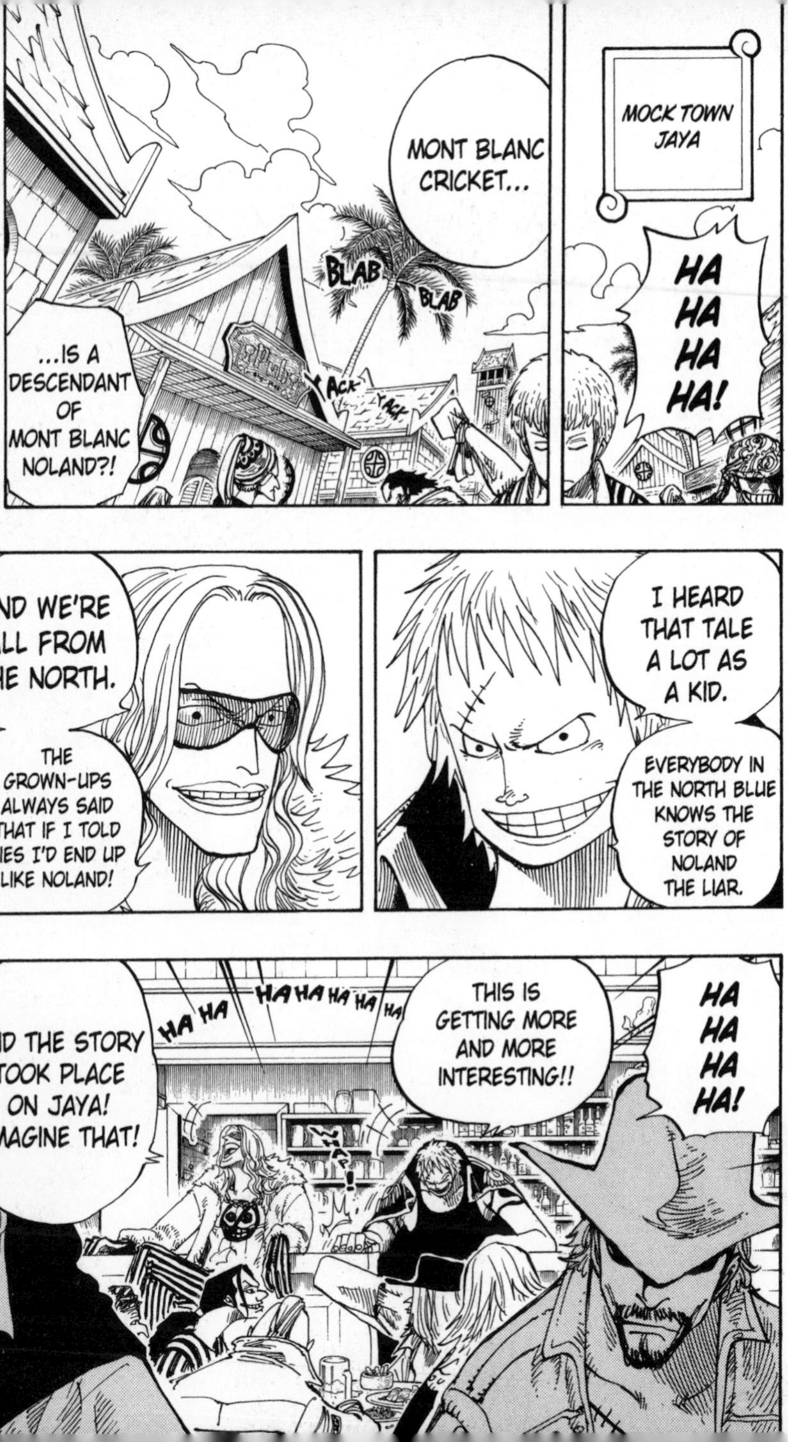
MOCK TOWN JAYA
HA HA HA HA!
MONT BLANC CRICKET...
BLAB BLAB
YACK YACK
...IS A DESCENDANT OF MONT BLANC NOLAND?!
I HEARD THAT TALE A LOT AS A KID.
EVERYBODY IN THE NORTH BLUE KNOWS THE STORY OF NOLAND THE LIAR.
AND WE'RE ALL FROM THE NORTH.
THE GROWN-UPS ALWAYS SAID THAT IF I TOLD LIES I'D END UP LIKE NOLAND!
HA HA HA HA!
THIS IS GETTING MORE AND MORE INTERESTING!!
HA HA HA HA HA HA HA
WHAP!
AND THE STORY TOOK PLACE ON JAYA! IMAGINE THAT!

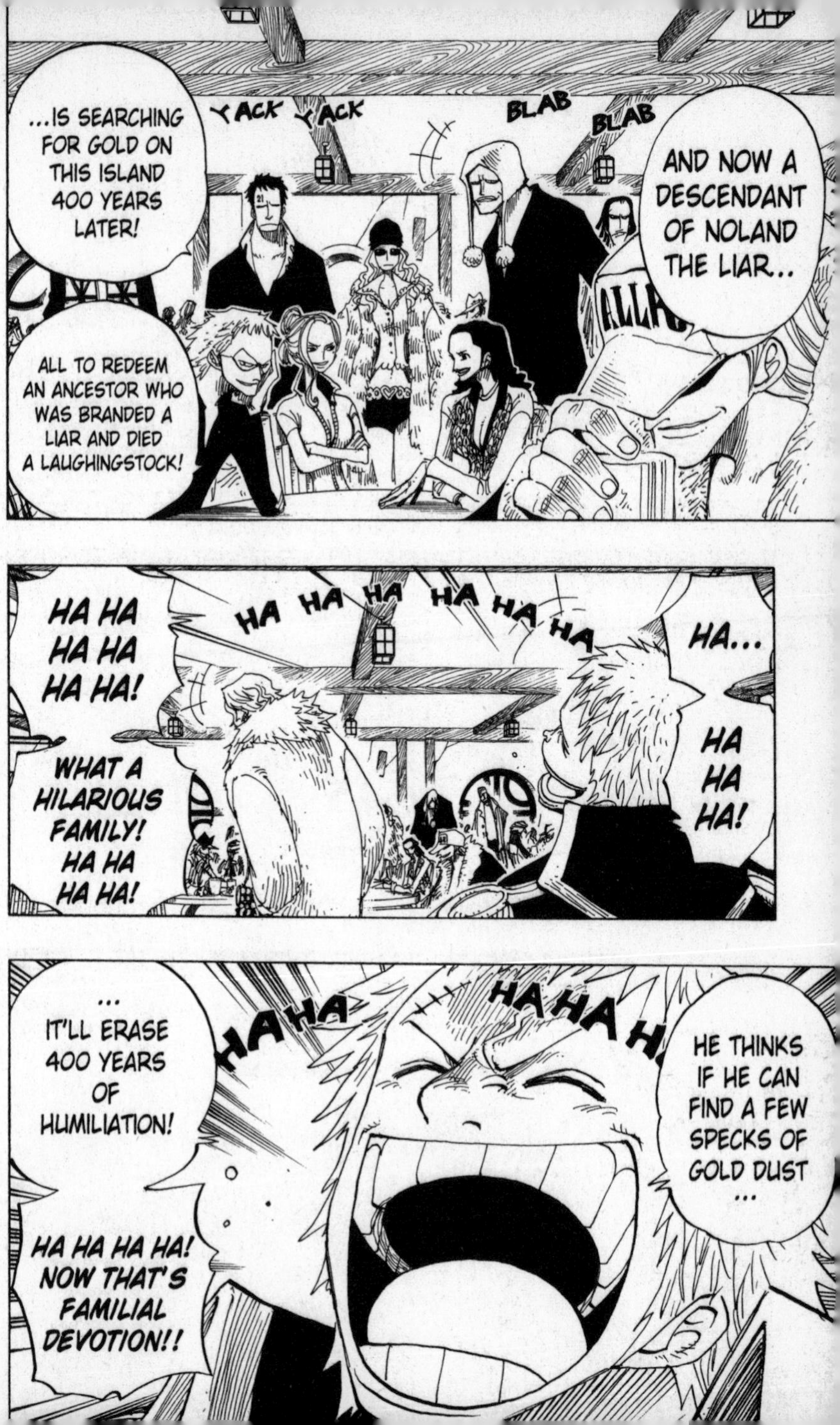
BLAB BLAB
AND NOW A DESCENDANT OF NOLAND THE LIAR...
YACK YACK
...IS SEARCHING FOR GOLD ON THIS ISLAND 400 YEARS LATER!
ALL TO REDEEM AN ANCESTOR WHO WAS BRANDED A LIAR AND DIED A LAUGHINGSTOCK!
HA...
HA HA HA!
HA HA HA HA HA HA HA
HA HA HA HA HA HA!
WHAT A HILARIOUS FAMILY! HA HA HA HA!
HE THINKS IF HE CAN FIND A FEW SPECKS OF GOLD DUST ...
HAHAHAH
HAHA
... IT'LL ERASE 400 YEARS OF HUMILIATION!
HA HA HA HA! NOW THAT'S FAMILIAL DEVOTION!!

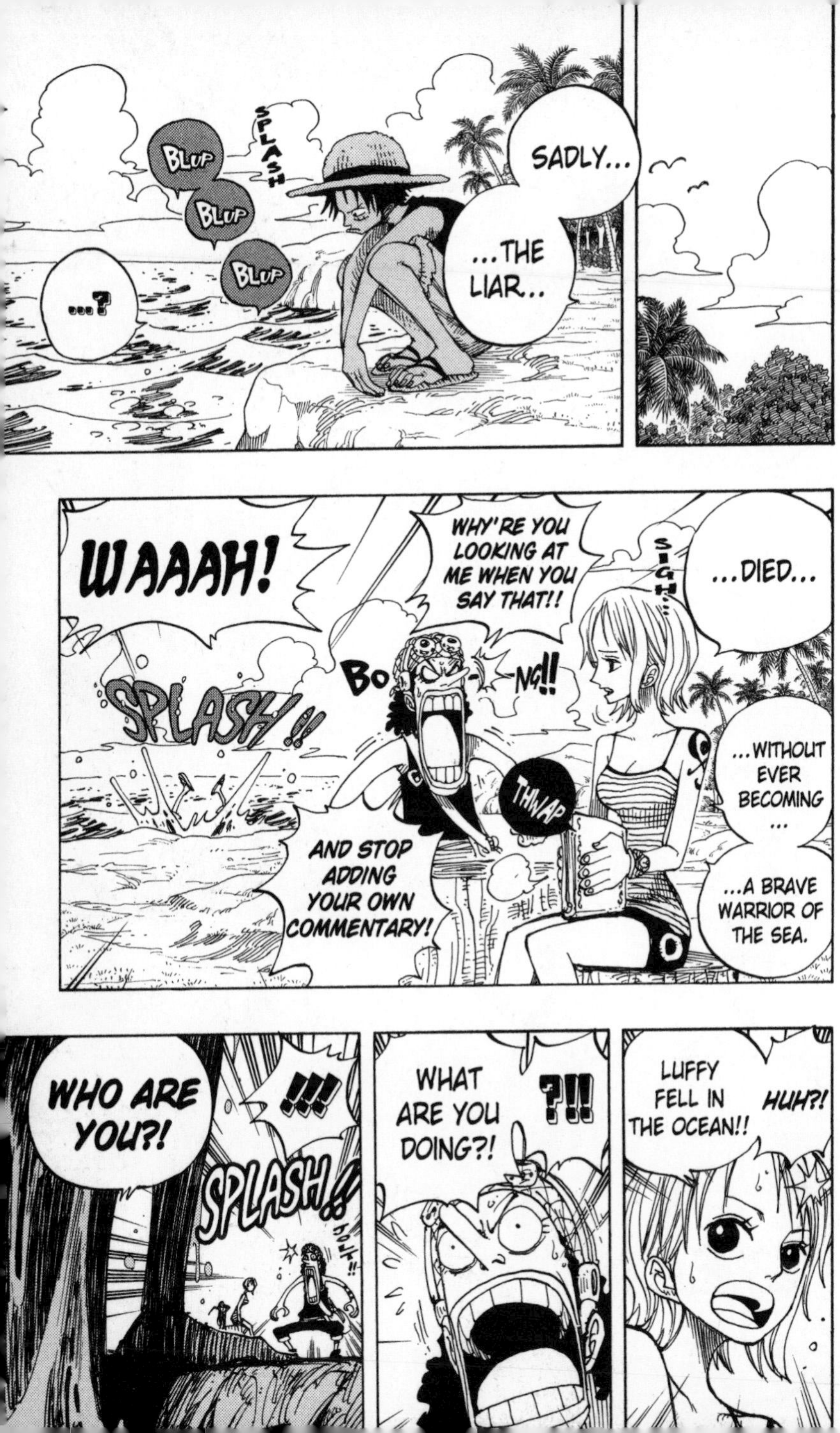
SADLY...
...THE LIAR...
SPLASH
BLUP
BLUP
BLUP
...?
...DIED...
SIGH...
...WITHOUT EVER BECOMING ...
...A BRAVE WARRIOR OF THE SEA.
WHY'RE YOU LOOKING AT ME WHEN YOU SAY THAT!!
BO-NG!!
THWAP
AND STOP ADDING YOUR OWN COMMENTARY!
WAAAH!
SPLASH!!
LUFFY FELL IN THE OCEAN!!
HUH?!
?!!
WHAT ARE YOU DOING?!
!!!
WHO ARE YOU?!
SPLASH!!
JOLT!!

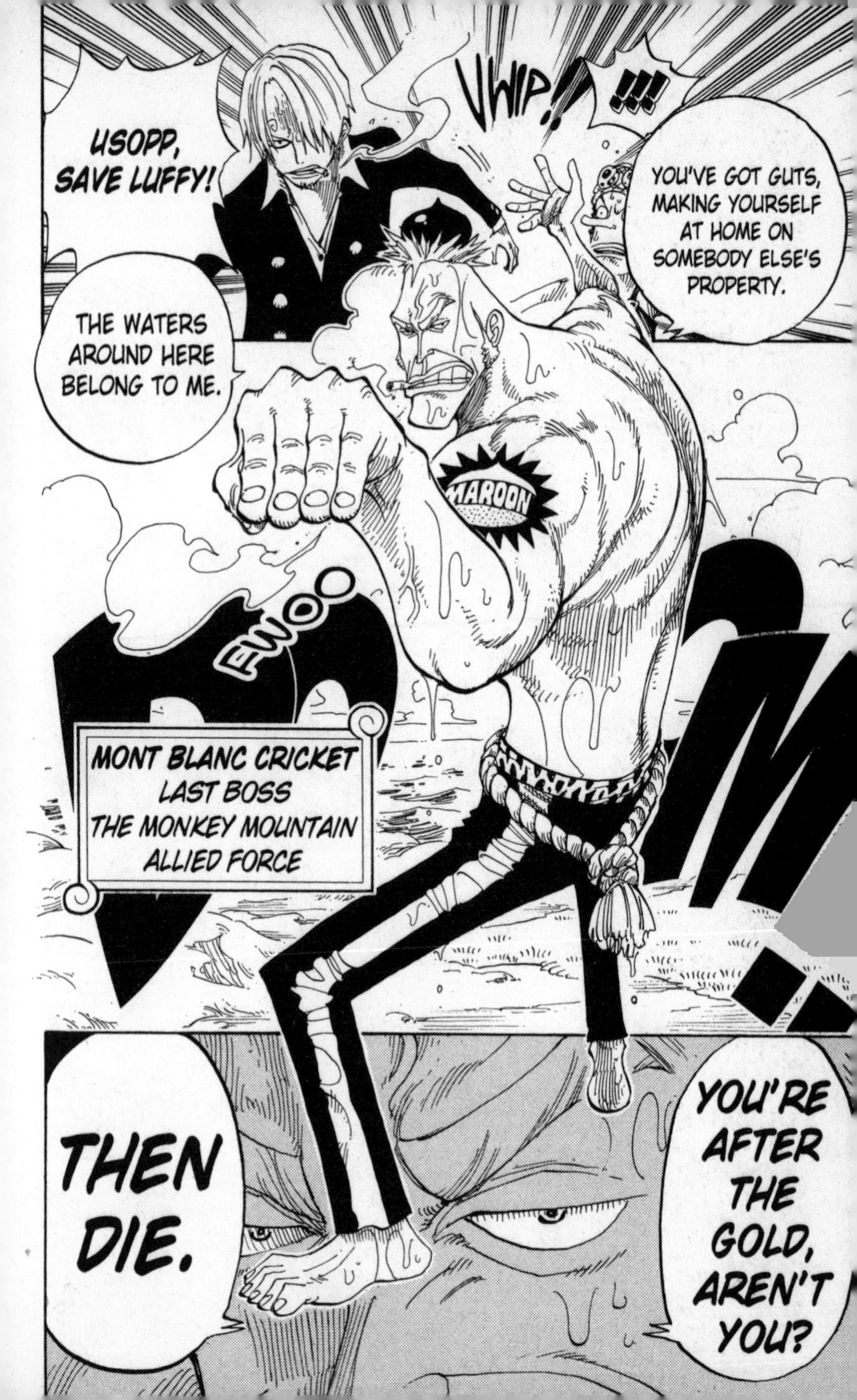
WHIP!!!
YOU'VE GOT GUTS, MAKING YOURSELF AT HOME ON SOMEBODY ELSE'S PROPERTY.
USOPP, SAVE LUFFY!
THE WATERS AROUND HERE BELONG TO ME.
MAROON
FWOOM...
MONT BLANC CRICKET
LAST BOSS
THE MONKEY MOUNTAIN ALLIED FORCE
YOU'RE AFTER THE GOLD, AREN'T YOU?
THEN DIE.

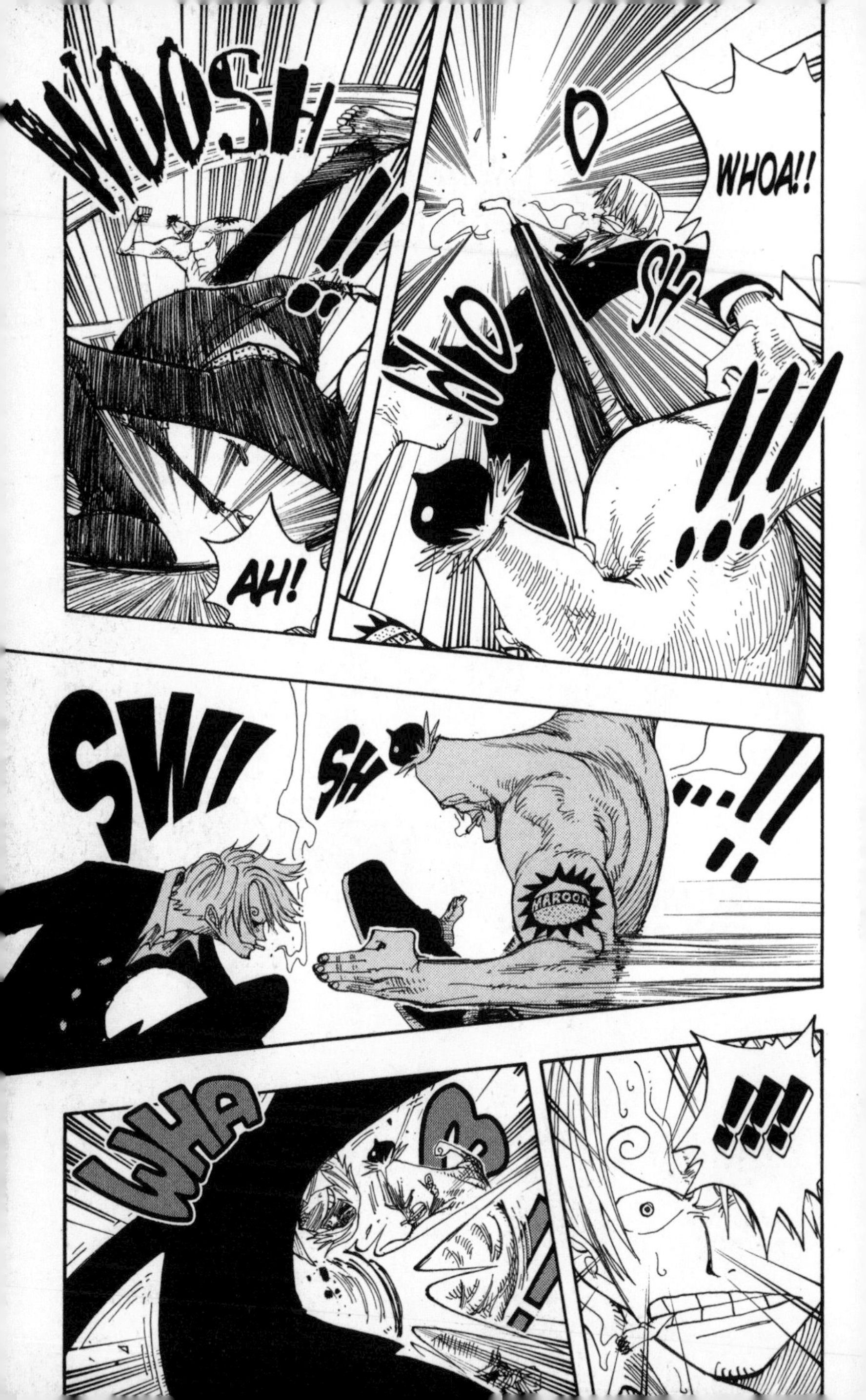
WHOA!!
!!...!!
WHOOSH
!!...
AH!
SWISH
...!!
!!!
WHAM
!!

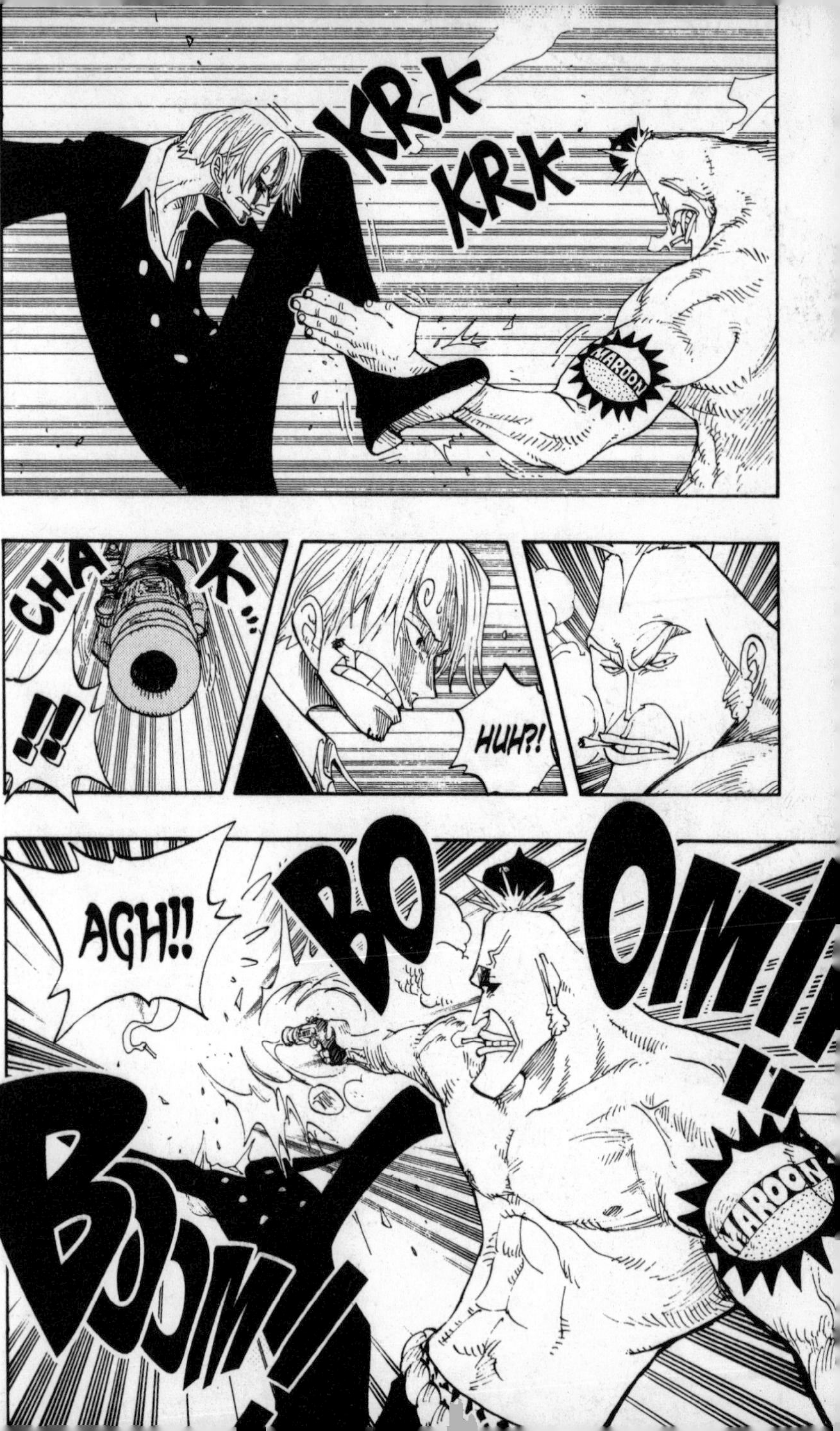
KRK KRK
MAROON
HUH?!
CHAK...
!!
BOOM!!
AGH!!
MAROON
BOOM!!

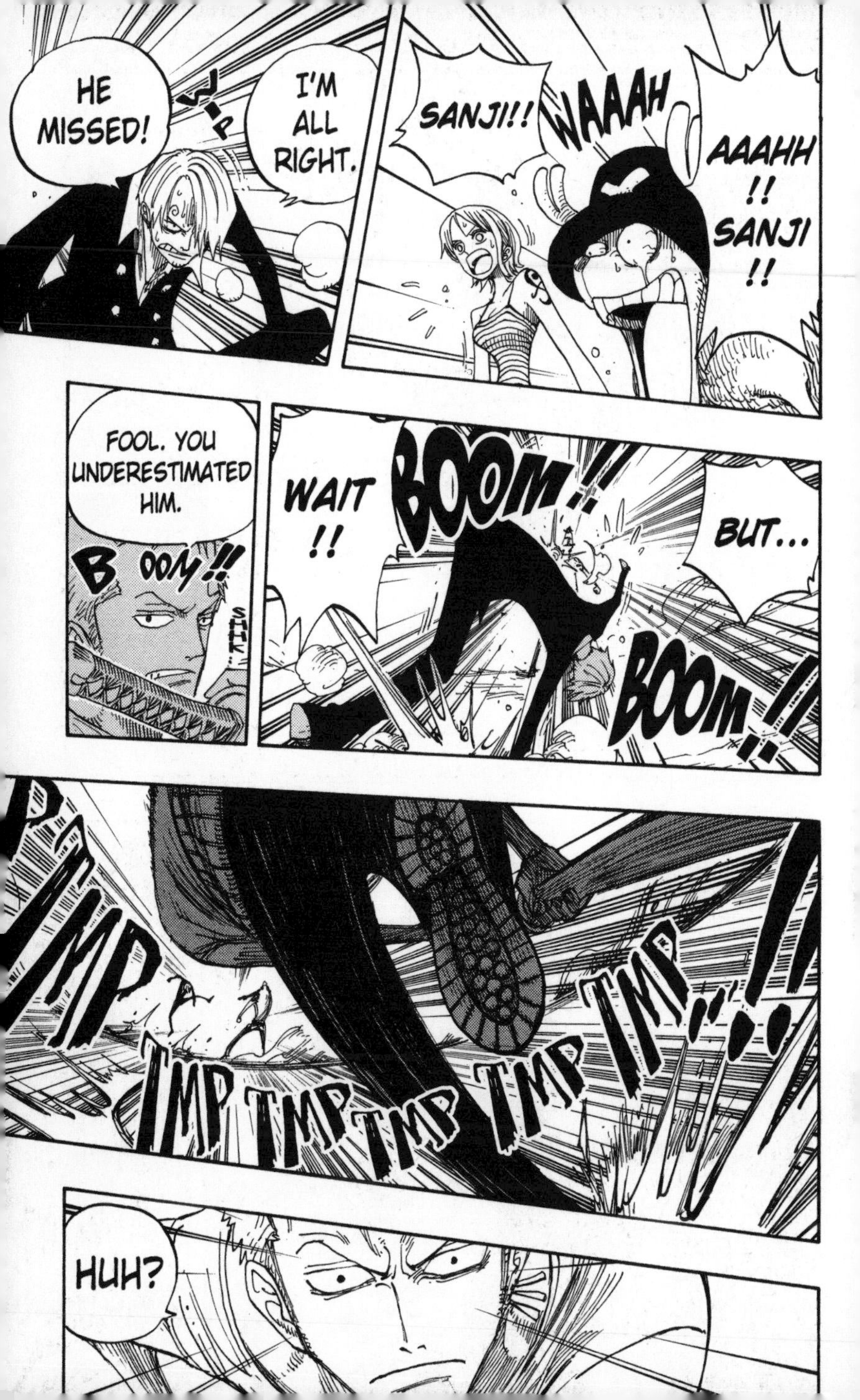
AAAHH!! SANJI!!
WAAAH
SANJI!!
I'M ALL RIGHT.
WIP
HE MISSED!
BUT...
BOOM!!
WAIT!!
BOOM!!
FOOL. YOU UNDERESTIMATED HIM.
BOOM!!
SHHK...
TMP TMP TMP TMP TMP!!
HUH?

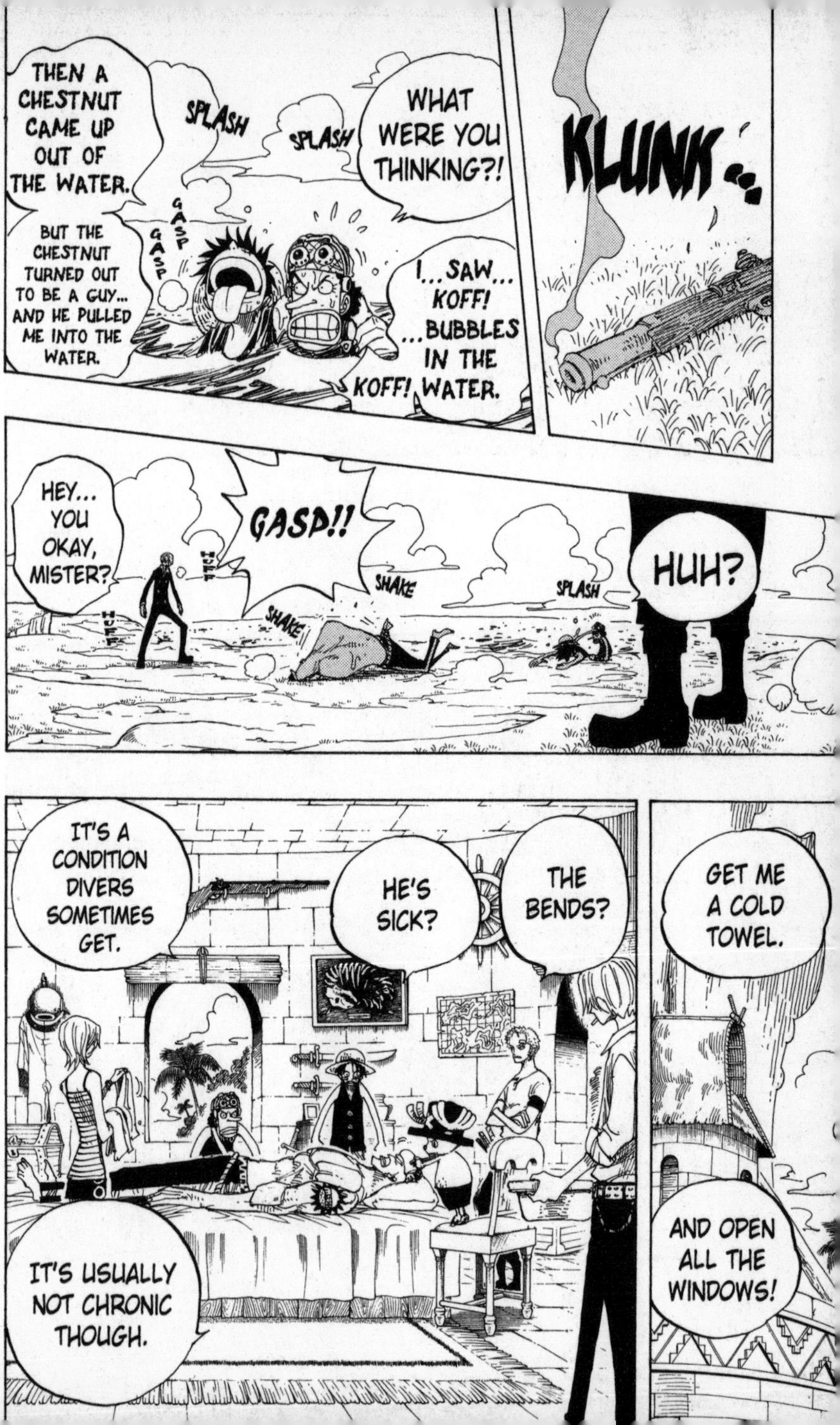
KLUNK
WHAT WERE YOU THINKING?!
SPLASH
SPLASH
THEN A CHESTNUT CAME UP OUT OF THE WATER.
I... SAW... KOFF! ...BUBBLES IN THE WATER.
KOFF!
GASP GASP
BUT THE CHESTNUT TURNED OUT TO BE A GUY... AND HE PULLED ME INTO THE WATER.
HUH?
SPLASH
SHAKE
SHAKE
GASP!!
HUFF
HEY... YOU OKAY, MISTER?
HUFF
GET ME A COLD TOWEL.
AND OPEN ALL THE WINDOWS!
THE BENDS?
HE'S SICK?
IT'S A CONDITION DIVERS SOMETIMES GET.
IT'S USUALLY NOT CHRONIC THOUGH.

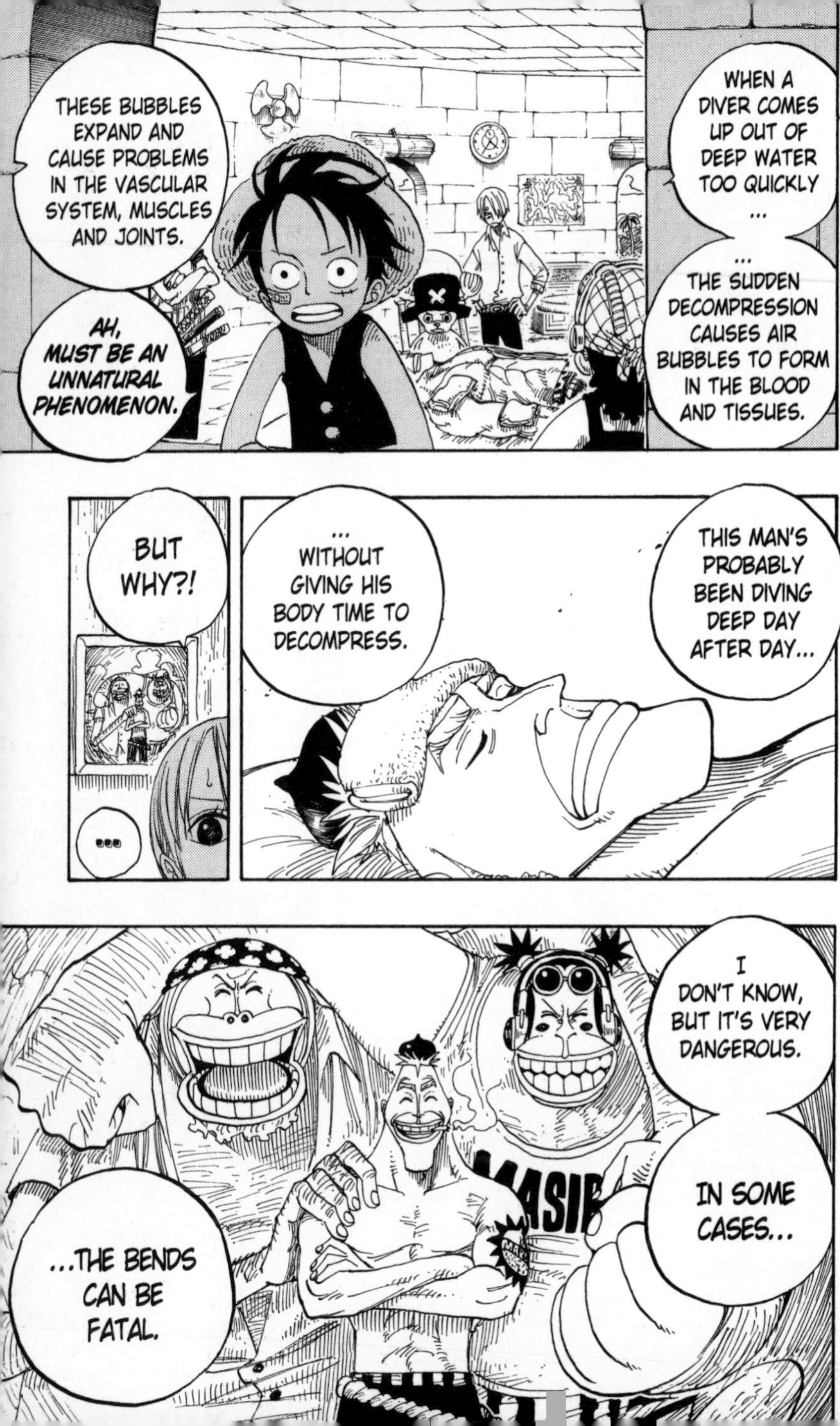
WHEN A DIVER COMES UP OUT OF DEEP WATER TOO QUICKLY ...
... THE SUDDEN DECOMPRESSION CAUSES AIR BUBBLES TO FORM IN THE BLOOD AND TISSUES.
THESE BUBBLES EXPAND AND CAUSE PROBLEMS IN THE VASCULAR SYSTEM, MUSCLES AND JOINTS.
AH, MUST BE AN UNNATURAL PHENOMENON.
THIS MAN'S PROBABLY BEEN DIVING DEEP DAY AFTER DAY...
... WITHOUT GIVING HIS BODY TIME TO DECOMPRESS.
BUT WHY?!
...
I DON'T KNOW, BUT IT'S VERY DANGEROUS.
IN SOME CASES...
...THE BENDS CAN BE FATAL.

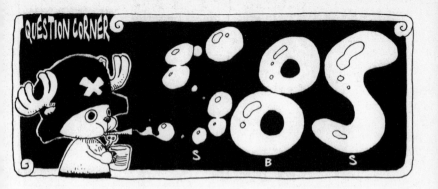

**Reader:** Boys and girls, gather around! Who will start the Question Corner today? All right... You! Little Eiichiro! Huh? What? Everyone wants to say it? All right, gotcha! Then let's all say it together! Ready?

**Let's start the Question Corner!!**
(Okay, this is fair. ☆)

**Oda:** Let's start the Quest--! Hey! Hey...! I flubbed. And it was my big chance...

**Q:** Hello, Oda Sensei! In volume 18 on page 28, is the Sea Cat wearing an earring in its left ear? Why is that? Tell me!
--Ms. White Day

**A:** Uh... That's just ear hair. Okay, everyone, try saying it three times as fast as you can. Ear hair, ear hair, ear hair. Hard, huh?

**Q:** Hello, Oda Sensei! This is regarding Nico Robin's birthday. I think February 6 (NI-co RO-bin*) would be nice.
*In Japanese, ni=2 and ro=6. --Editor

**A:** Oh yes, I agree.

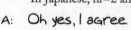

# Chapter 228: MONT BLANC CRICKET, THE LAST BOSS OF THE MONKEY MOUNTAIN ALLIED FORCE

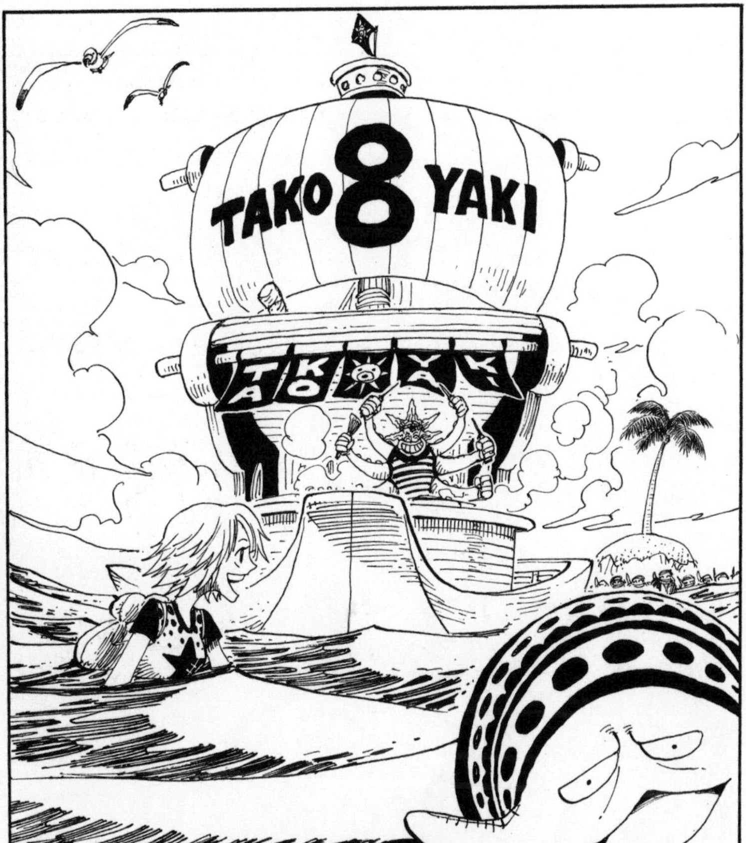
TAKO 8 YAKI
TAKOYAKI

HACHI'S WALK ON THE SEAFLOOR, FINAL VOLUME: "GRAND OPENING! TAKOYAKI 8, AN OCTOPUS FRITTER SHOP ON THE HIGH SEAS"

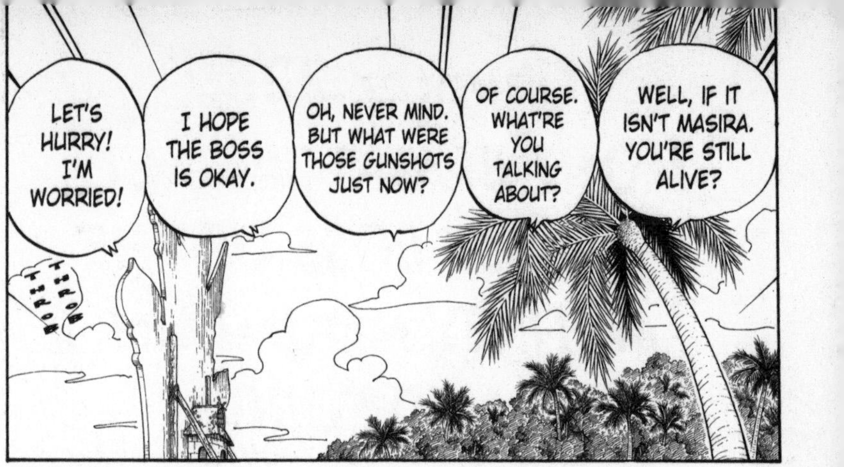
WELL, IF IT ISN'T MASIRA. YOU'RE STILL ALIVE?
OF COURSE. WHAT'RE YOU TALKING ABOUT?
OH, NEVER MIND. BUT WHAT WERE THOSE GUNSHOTS JUST NOW?
I HOPE THE BOSS IS OKAY.
LET'S HURRY! I'M WORRIED!
THROB THROB

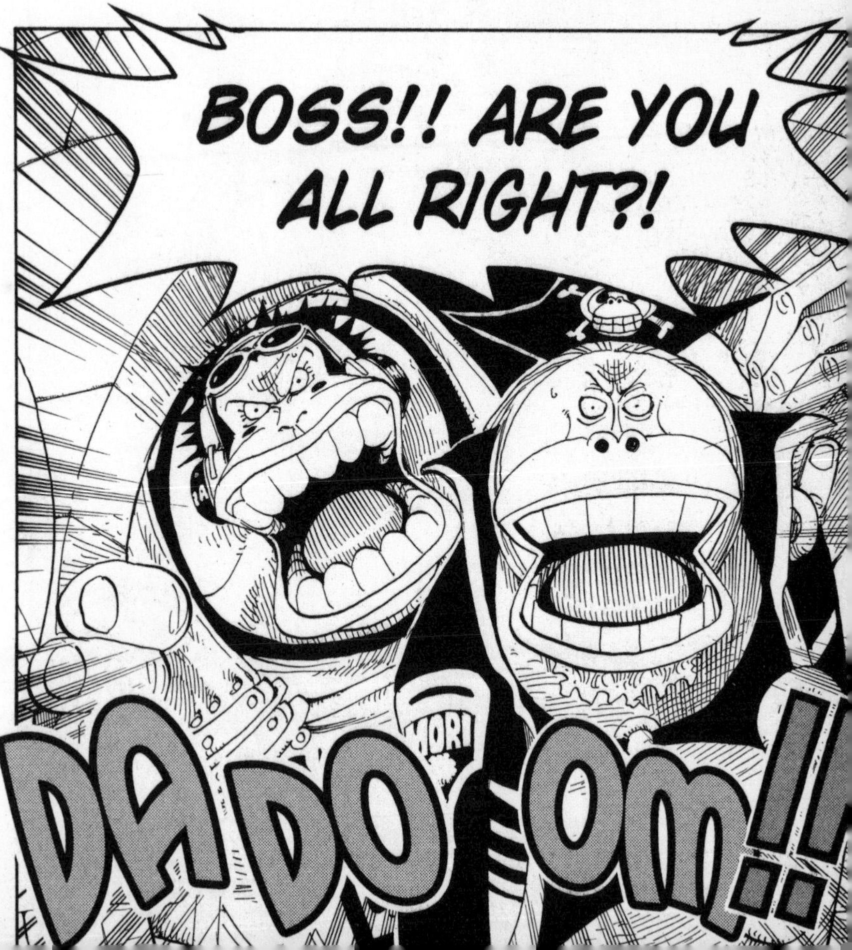
BOSS!! ARE YOU ALL RIGHT?!
DADO-OM!!

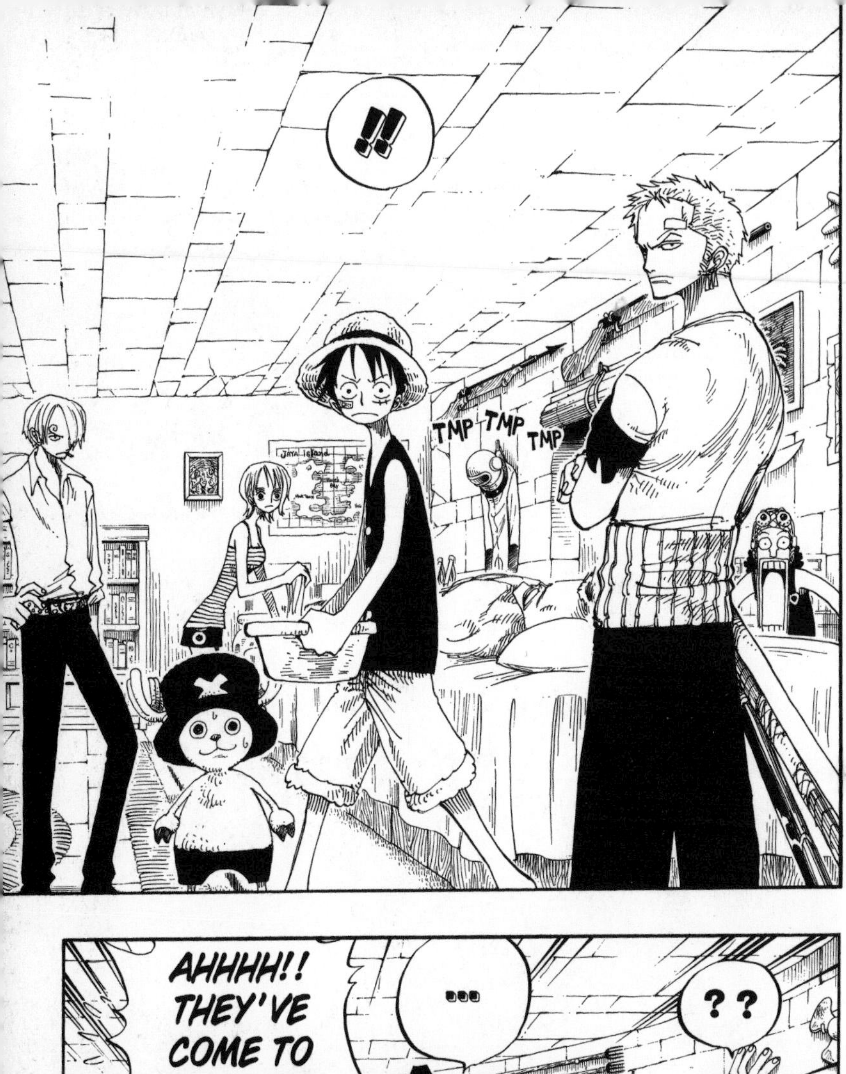
!!
TMP TMP TMP

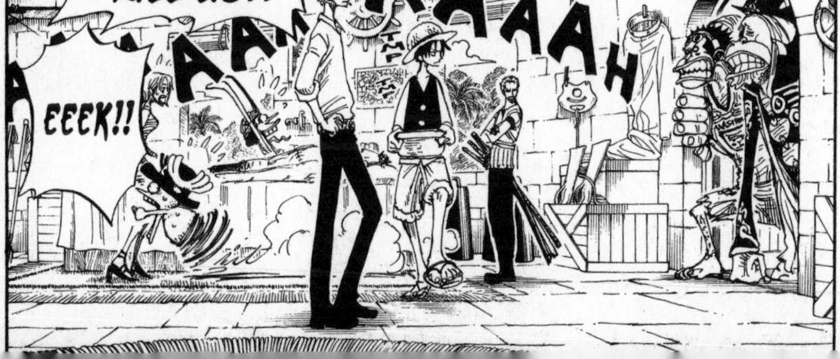
??
...
AHHHH!! THEY'VE COME TO KILL US!!
TMP
AAAAAAAH
EEEK!!

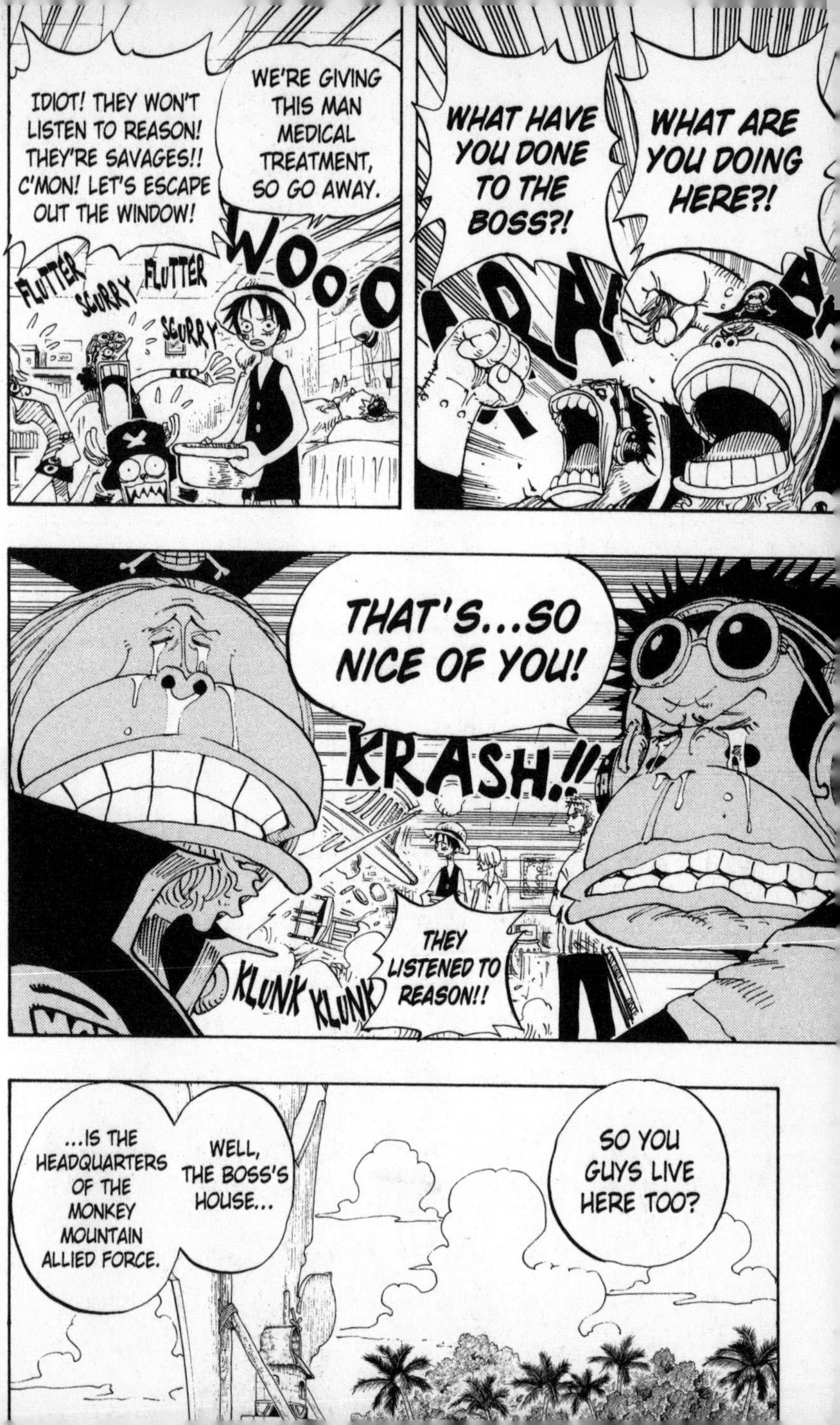
WHAT ARE YOU DOING HERE?!
WHAT HAVE YOU DONE TO THE BOSS?!
WE'RE GIVING THIS MAN MEDICAL TREATMENT, SO GO AWAY.
IDIOT! THEY WON'T LISTEN TO REASON! THEY'RE SAVAGES!! C'MON! LET'S ESCAPE OUT THE WINDOW!
WOOO
FLUTTER
SCURRY
FLUTTER
SCURRY
THAT'S...SO NICE OF YOU!
KRASH!!
THEY LISTENED TO REASON!!
KLUNK
KLUNK
SO YOU GUYS LIVE HERE TOO?
WELL, THE BOSS'S HOUSE...
...IS THE HEADQUARTERS OF THE MONKEY MOUNTAIN ALLIED FORCE.

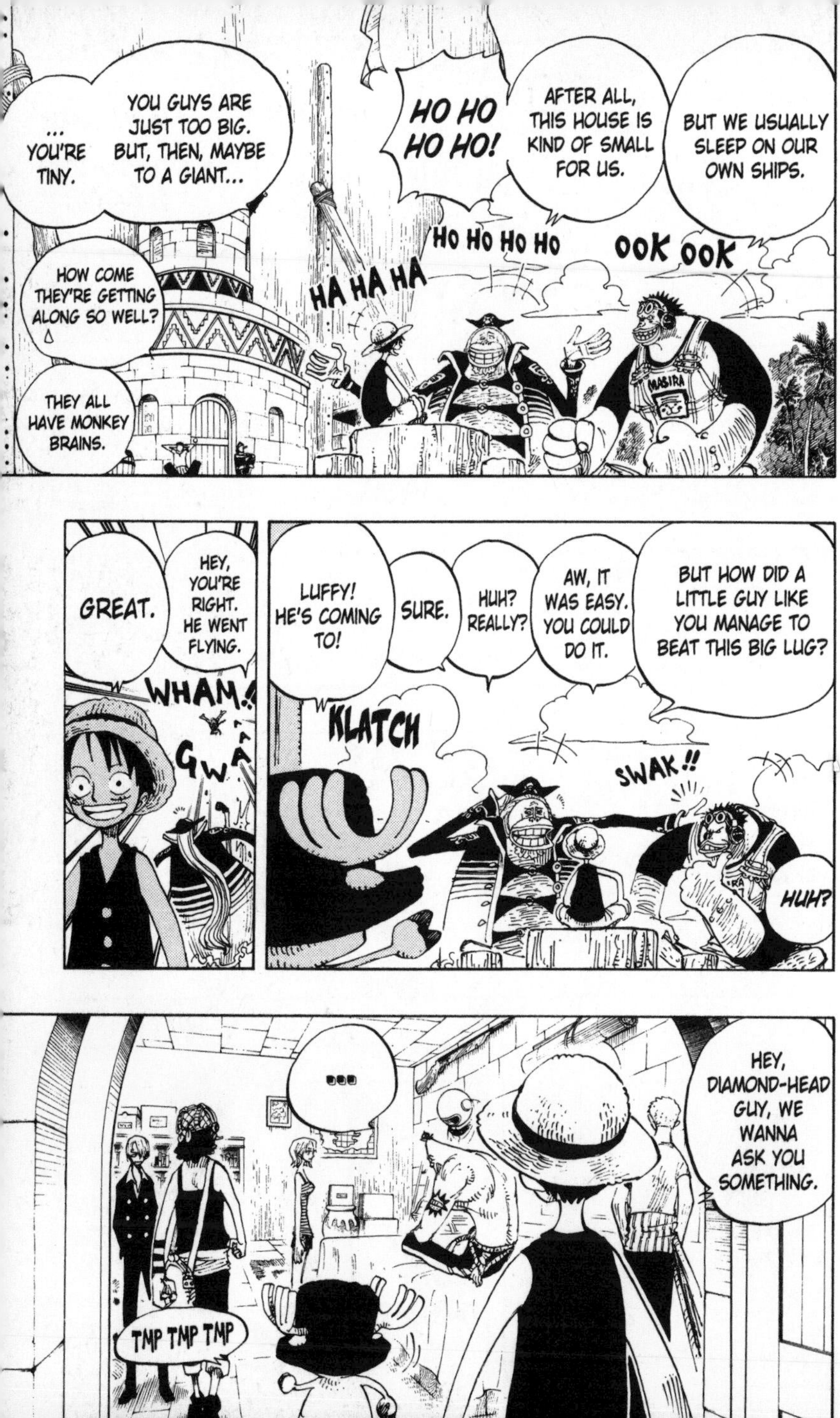
BUT WE USUALLY SLEEP ON OUR OWN SHIPS.
AFTER ALL, THIS HOUSE IS KIND OF SMALL FOR US.
HO HO HO HO!
YOU GUYS ARE JUST TOO BIG. BUT, THEN, MAYBE TO A GIANT...
... YOU'RE TINY.
OOK OOK
HO HO HO HO
HA HA HA
HOW COME THEY'RE GETTING ALONG SO WELL?
THEY ALL HAVE MONKEY BRAINS.
BUT HOW DID A LITTLE GUY LIKE YOU MANAGE TO BEAT THIS BIG LUG?
AW, IT WAS EASY. YOU COULD DO IT.
HUH? REALLY?
SURE.
LUFFY! HE'S COMING TO!
KLATCH
SWAK!!
HUH?
HEY, YOU'RE RIGHT. HE WENT FLYING.
GREAT.
WHAM!!
HEY, DIAMOND-HEAD GUY, WE WANNA ASK YOU SOMETHING.
...
TMP TMP TMP

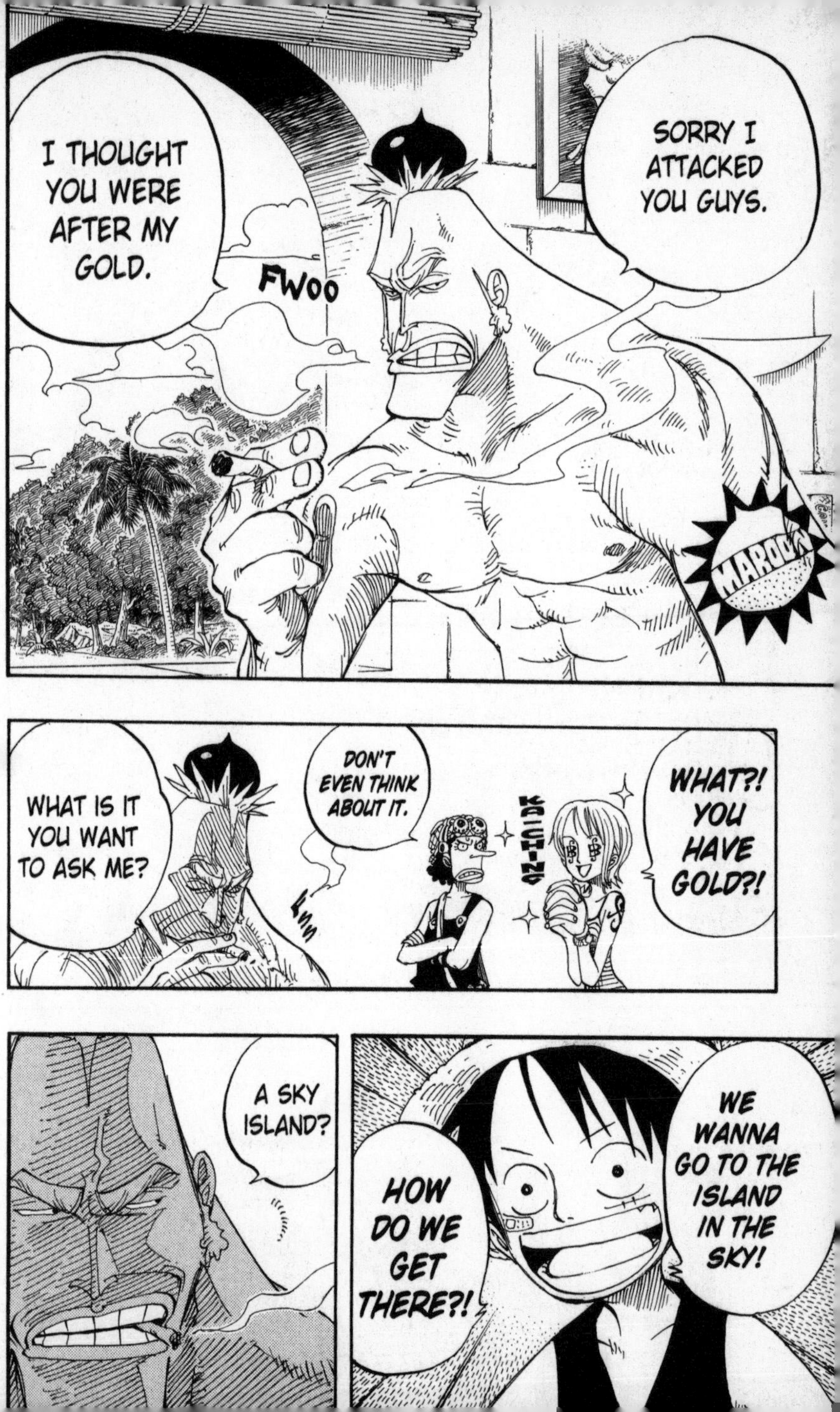
SORRY I ATTACKED YOU GUYS.
I THOUGHT YOU WERE AFTER MY GOLD.
FWOO
WHAT?! YOU HAVE GOLD?!
KA-CHING
DON'T EVEN THINK ABOUT IT.
WHAT IS IT YOU WANT TO ASK ME?
WE WANNA GO TO THE ISLAND IN THE SKY!
HOW DO WE GET THERE?!
A SKY ISLAND?

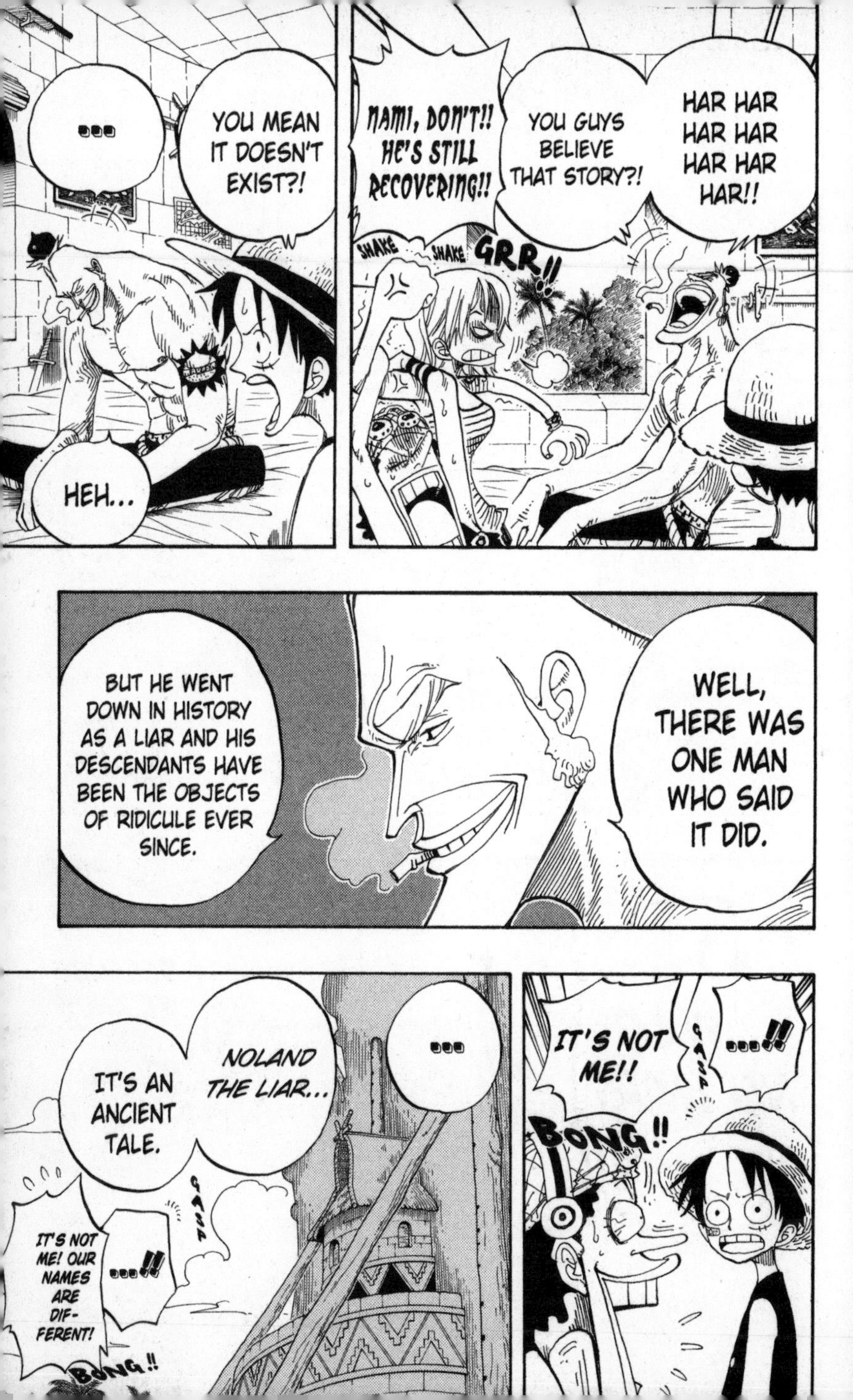
HAR HAR HAR HAR HAR HAR HAR!!
YOU GUYS BELIEVE THAT STORY?!
NAMI, DON'T!! HE'S STILL RECOVERING!!
SHAKE SHAKE
GRR!!
YOU MEAN IT DOESN'T EXIST?!
...
HEH...
WELL, THERE WAS ONE MAN WHO SAID IT DID.
BUT HE WENT DOWN IN HISTORY AS A LIAR AND HIS DESCENDANTS HAVE BEEN THE OBJECTS OF RIDICULE EVER SINCE.
...!!
IT'S NOT ME!!
BONG!!
...
NOLAND THE LIAR...
IT'S AN ANCIENT TALE.
...!!
IT'S NOT ME! OUR NAMES ARE DIF-FERENT!
BONG!!

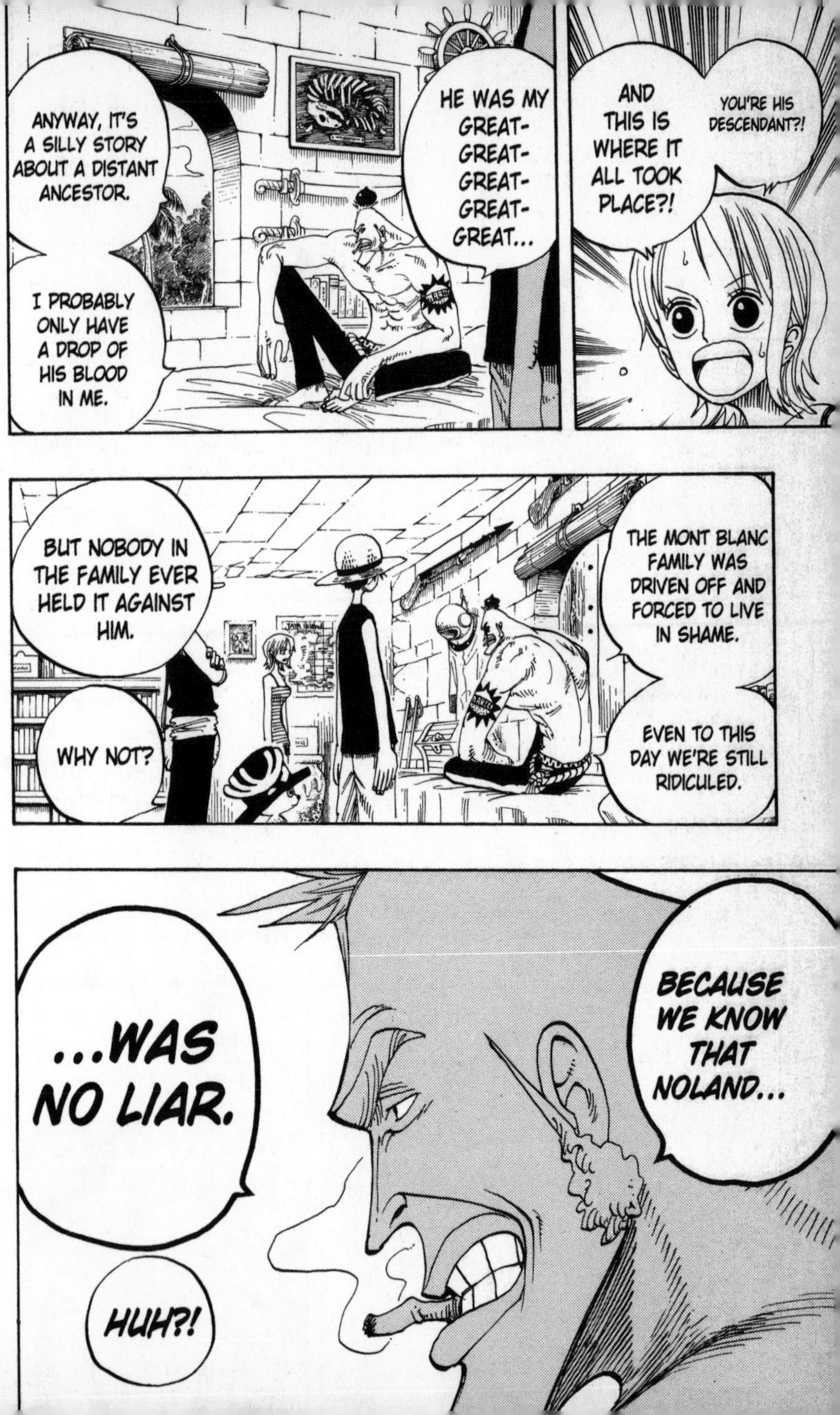
YOU'RE HIS DESCENDANT?!
AND THIS IS WHERE IT ALL TOOK PLACE?!
HE WAS MY GREAT-GREAT-GREAT-GREAT-GREAT...
ANYWAY, IT'S A SILLY STORY ABOUT A DISTANT ANCESTOR.
I PROBABLY ONLY HAVE A DROP OF HIS BLOOD IN ME.
THE MONT BLANC FAMILY WAS DRIVEN OFF AND FORCED TO LIVE IN SHAME.
EVEN TO THIS DAY WE'RE STILL RIDICULED.
BUT NOBODY IN THE FAMILY EVER HELD IT AGAINST HIM.
WHY NOT?
BECAUSE WE KNOW THAT NOLAND...
...WAS NO LIAR.
HUH?!

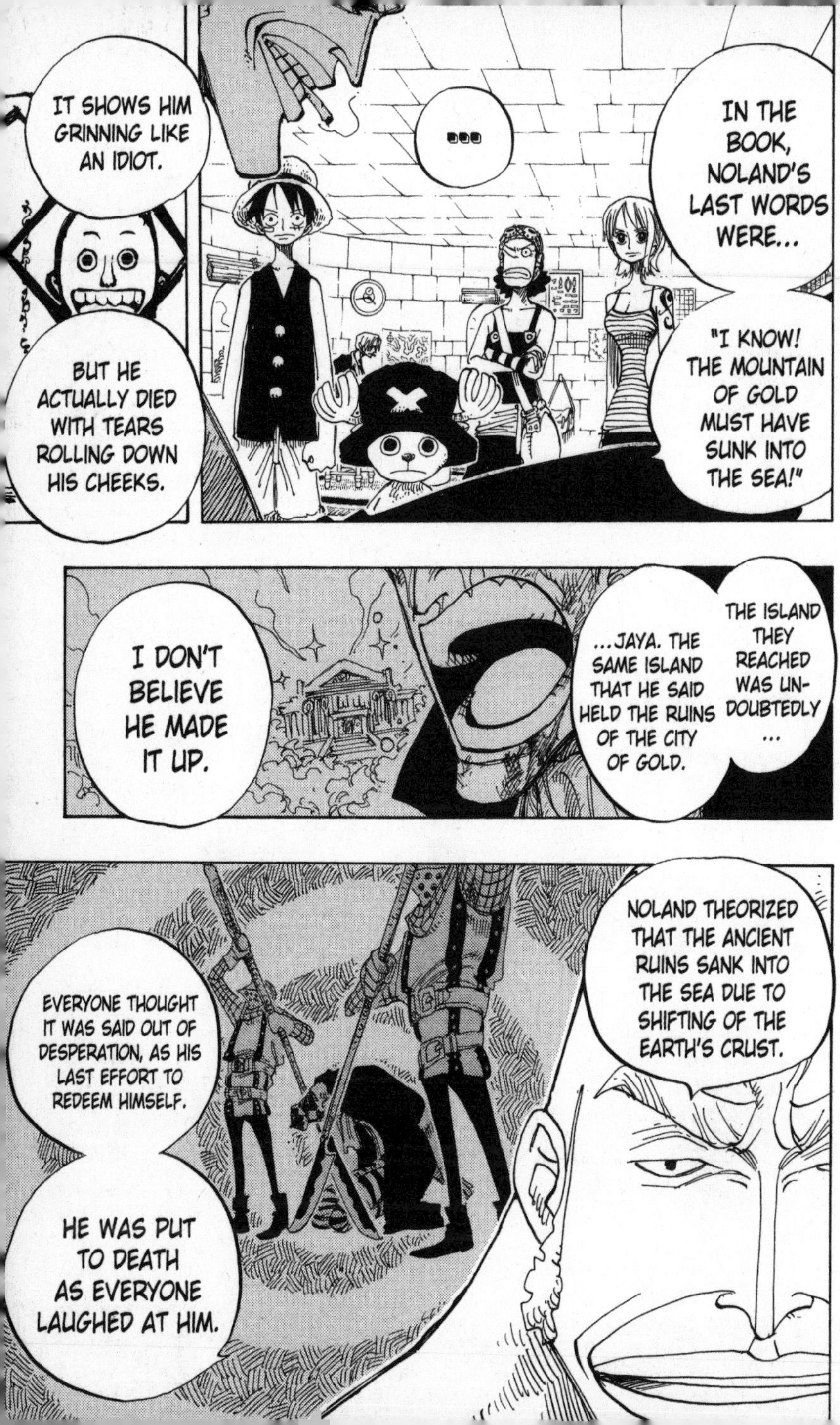
IN THE BOOK, NOLAND'S LAST WORDS WERE...
"I KNOW! THE MOUNTAIN OF GOLD MUST HAVE SUNK INTO THE SEA!"
...
IT SHOWS HIM GRINNING LIKE AN IDIOT.
BUT HE ACTUALLY DIED WITH TEARS ROLLING DOWN HIS CHEEKS.
THE ISLAND THEY REACHED WAS UN-DOUBTEDLY ...
...JAYA. THE SAME ISLAND THAT HE SAID HELD THE RUINS OF THE CITY OF GOLD.
I DON'T BELIEVE HE MADE IT UP.
NOLAND THEORIZED THAT THE ANCIENT RUINS SANK INTO THE SEA DUE TO SHIFTING OF THE EARTH'S CRUST.
EVERYONE THOUGHT IT WAS SAID OUT OF DESPERATION, AS HIS LAST EFFORT TO REDEEM HIMSELF.
HE WAS PUT TO DEATH AS EVERYONE LAUGHED AT HIM.

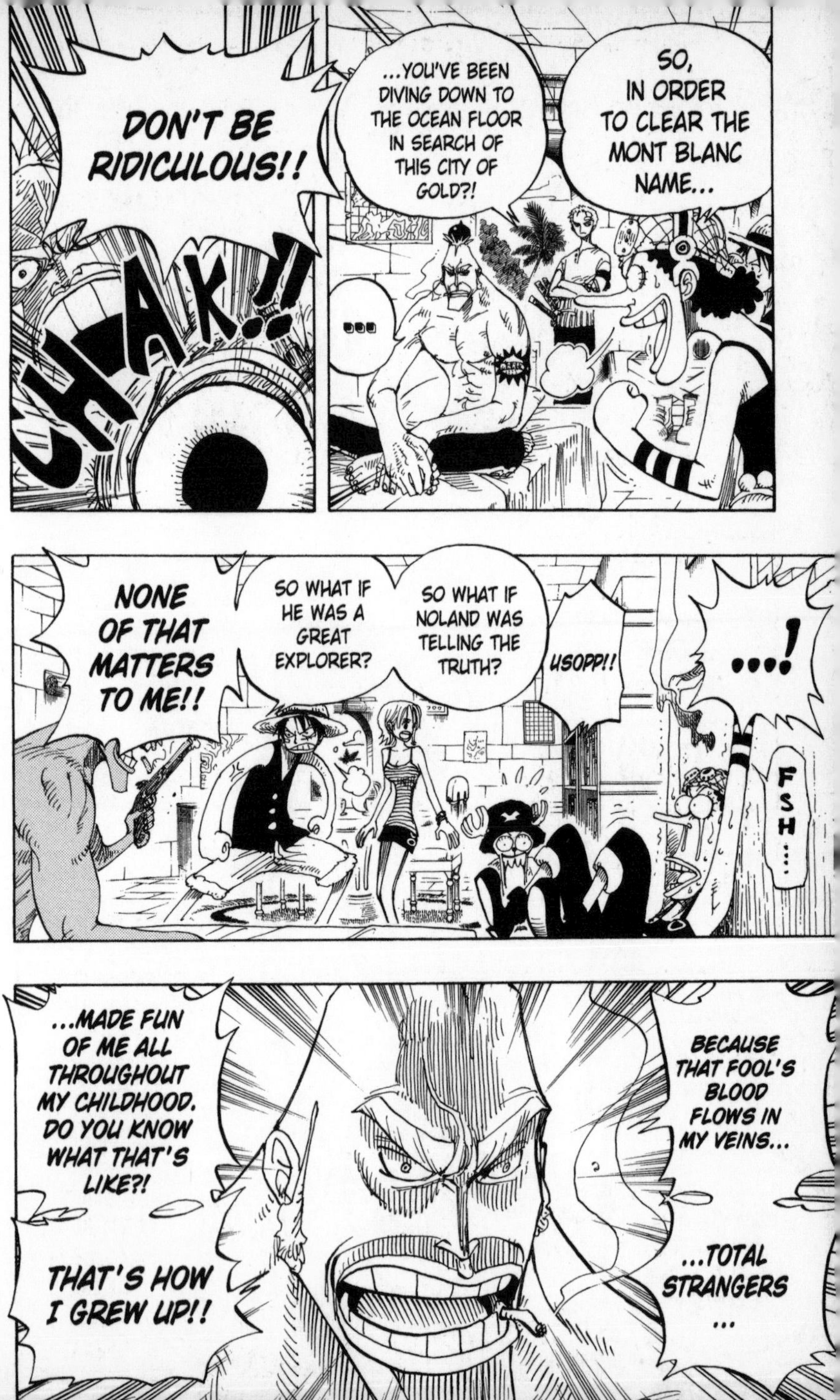
SO, IN ORDER TO CLEAR THE MONT BLANC NAME...
...YOU'VE BEEN DIVING DOWN TO THE OCEAN FLOOR IN SEARCH OF THIS CITY OF GOLD?!
...
DON'T BE RIDICULOUS!!
CHAK!!
...!
FSH...
USOPP!!
SO WHAT IF NOLAND WAS TELLING THE TRUTH?
SO WHAT IF HE WAS A GREAT EXPLORER?
NONE OF THAT MATTERS TO ME!!
BECAUSE THAT FOOL'S BLOOD FLOWS IN MY VEINS...
...TOTAL STRANGERS...
...MADE FUN OF ME ALL THROUGHOUT MY CHILDHOOD. DO YOU KNOW WHAT THAT'S LIKE?!
THAT'S HOW I GREW UP!!

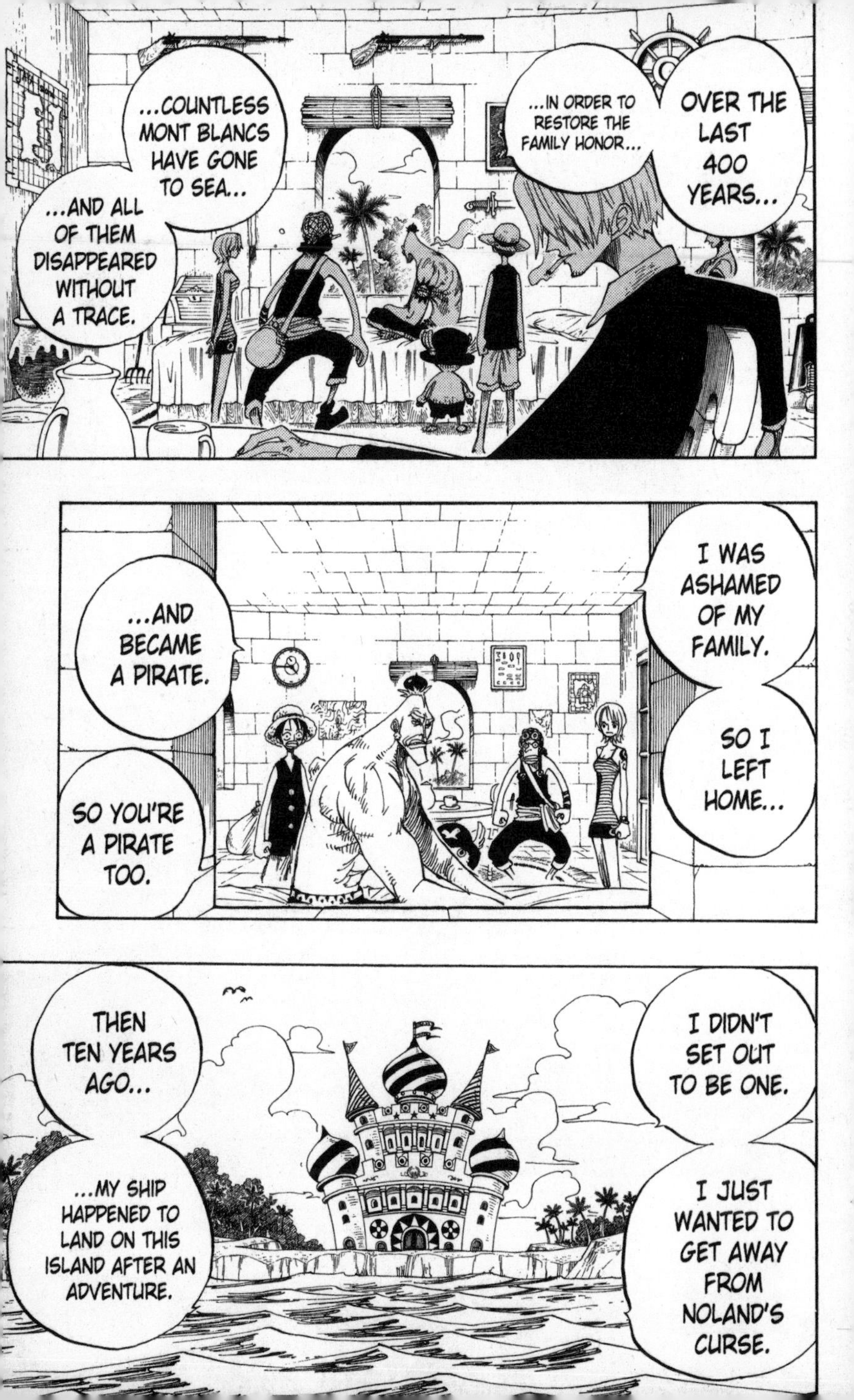
OVER THE LAST 400 YEARS...
...IN ORDER TO RESTORE THE FAMILY HONOR...
...COUNTLESS MONT BLANCS HAVE GONE TO SEA...
...AND ALL OF THEM DISAPPEARED WITHOUT A TRACE.
I WAS ASHAMED OF MY FAMILY.
SO I LEFT HOME...
...AND BECAME A PIRATE.
SO YOU'RE A PIRATE TOO.
I DIDN'T SET OUT TO BE ONE.
I JUST WANTED TO GET AWAY FROM NOLAND'S CURSE.
THEN TEN YEARS AGO...
...MY SHIP HAPPENED TO LAND ON THIS ISLAND AFTER AN ADVENTURE.

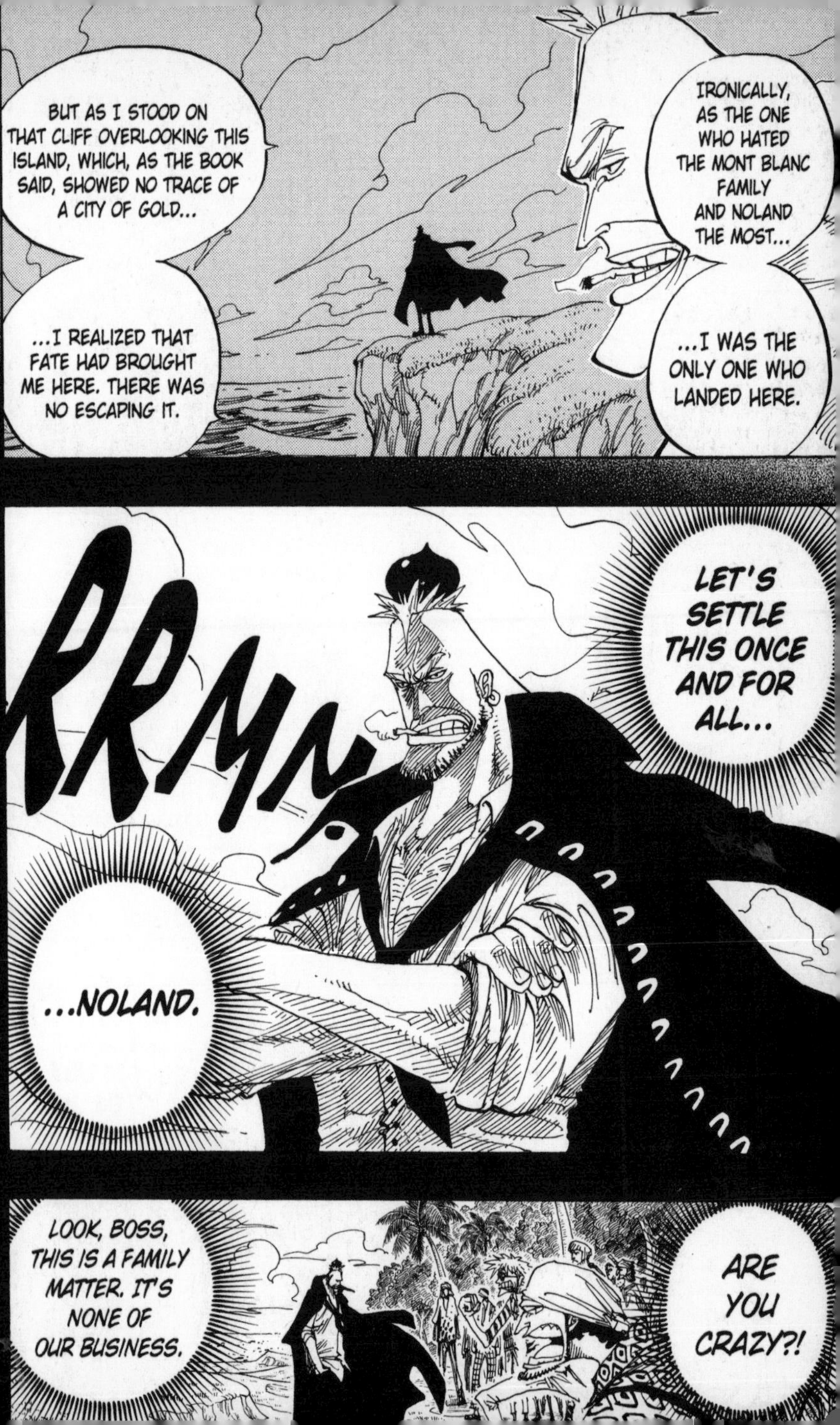
IRONICALLY, AS THE ONE WHO HATED THE MONT BLANC FAMILY AND NOLAND THE MOST...
...I WAS THE ONLY ONE WHO LANDED HERE.
BUT AS I STOOD ON THAT CLIFF OVERLOOKING THIS ISLAND, WHICH, AS THE BOOK SAID, SHOWED NO TRACE OF A CITY OF GOLD...
...I REALIZED THAT FATE HAD BROUGHT ME HERE. THERE WAS NO ESCAPING IT.
LET'S SETTLE THIS ONCE AND FOR ALL...
RRMN
...NOLAND.
ARE YOU CRAZY?!
LOOK, BOSS, THIS IS A FAMILY MATTER. IT'S NONE OF OUR BUSINESS.

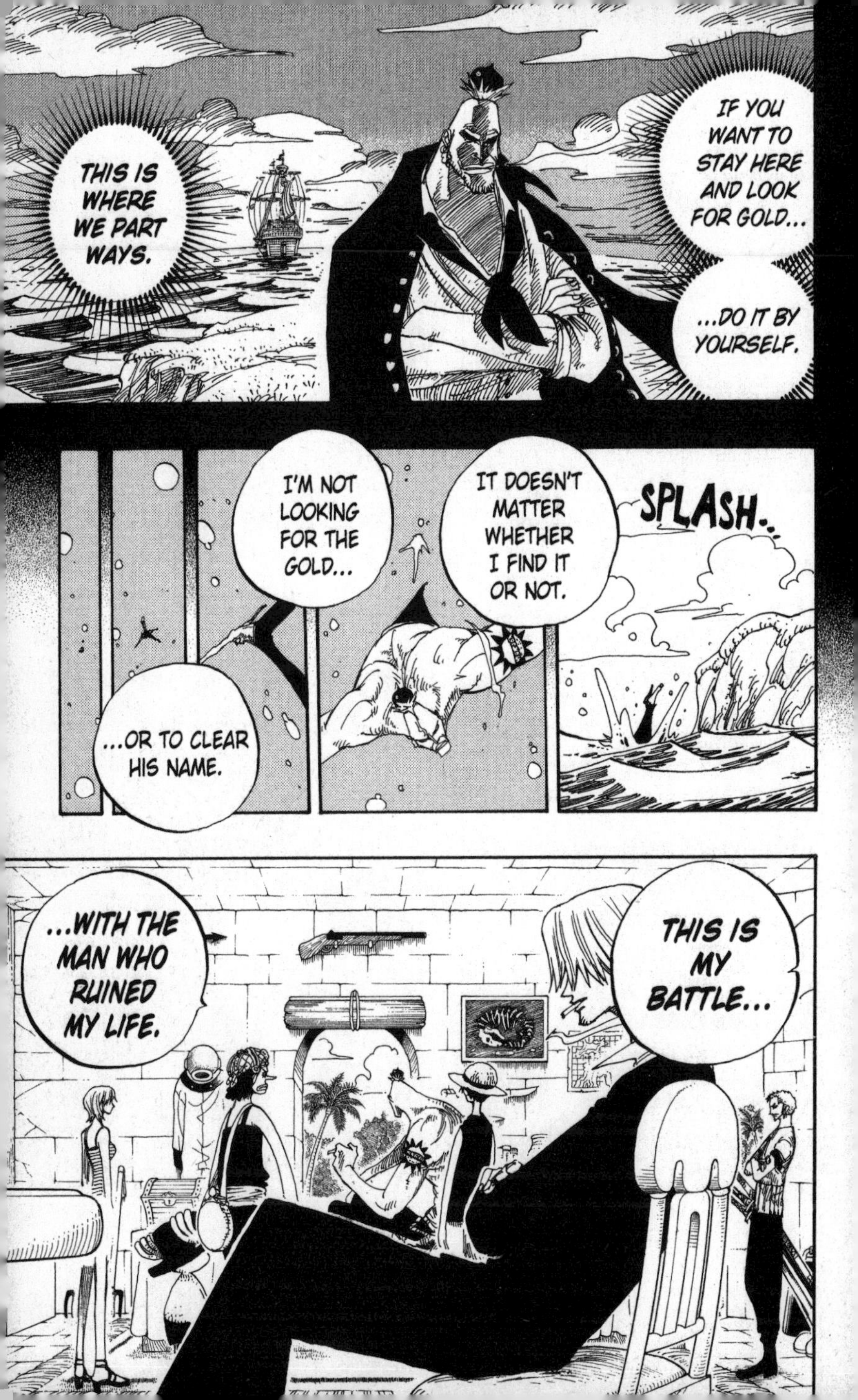

IF YOU WANT TO STAY HERE AND LOOK FOR GOLD...
...DO IT BY YOURSELF.
THIS IS WHERE WE PART WAYS.
SPLASH...
IT DOESN'T MATTER WHETHER I FIND IT OR NOT.
I'M NOT LOOKING FOR THE GOLD...
...OR TO CLEAR HIS NAME.
THIS IS MY BATTLE...
...WITH THE MAN WHO RUINED MY LIFE.

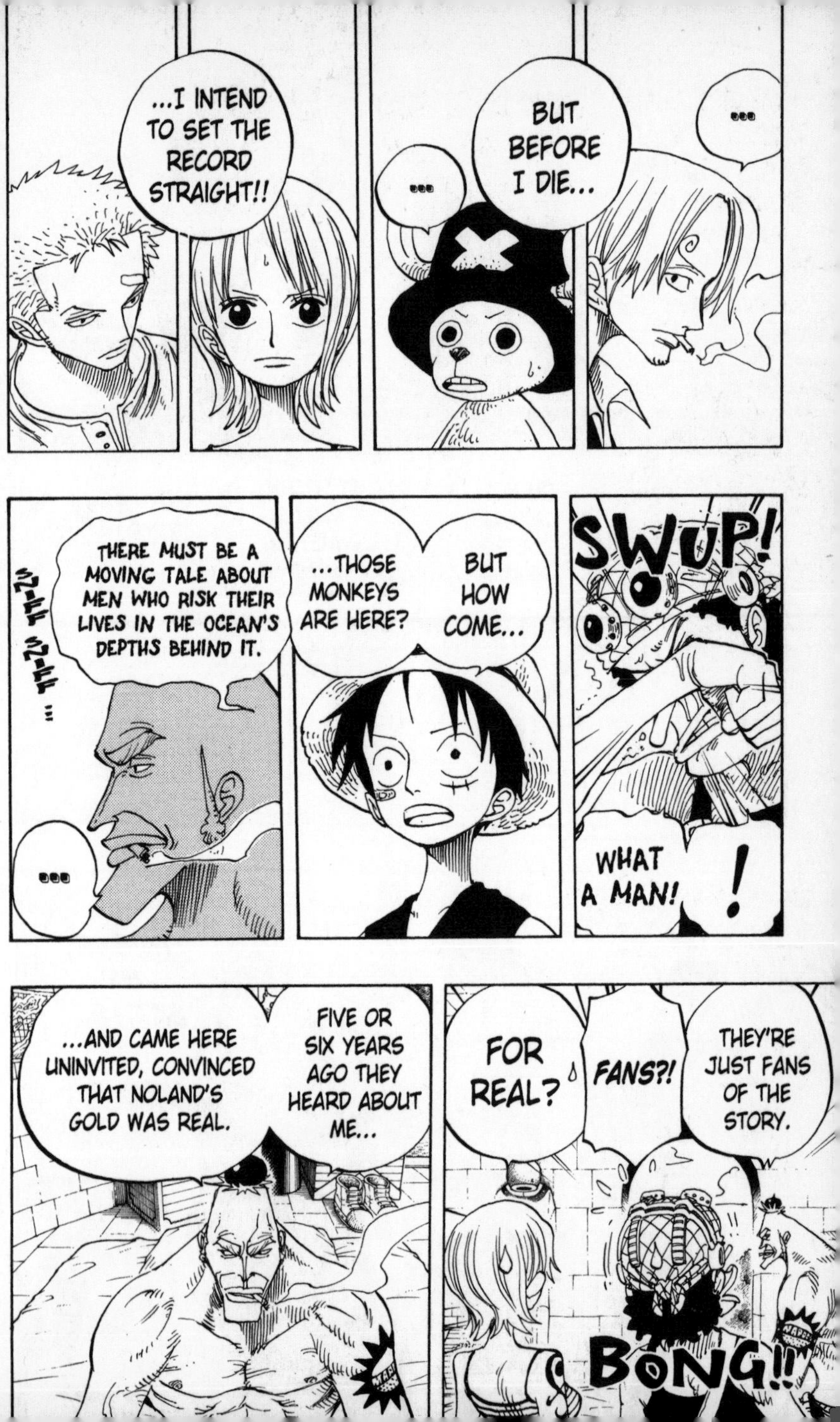
...
BUT BEFORE I DIE...
...
...I INTEND TO SET THE RECORD STRAIGHT!!
SWUP!
WHAT A MAN!
!
BUT HOW COME...
...THOSE MONKEYS ARE HERE?
THERE MUST BE A MOVING TALE ABOUT MEN WHO RISK THEIR LIVES IN THE OCEAN'S DEPTHS BEHIND IT.
SNIFF SNIFF
...
THEY'RE JUST FANS OF THE STORY.
FANS?!
FOR REAL?
BONG!!
FIVE OR SIX YEARS AGO THEY HEARD ABOUT ME...
...AND CAME HERE UNINVITED, CONVINCED THAT NOLAND'S GOLD WAS REAL.

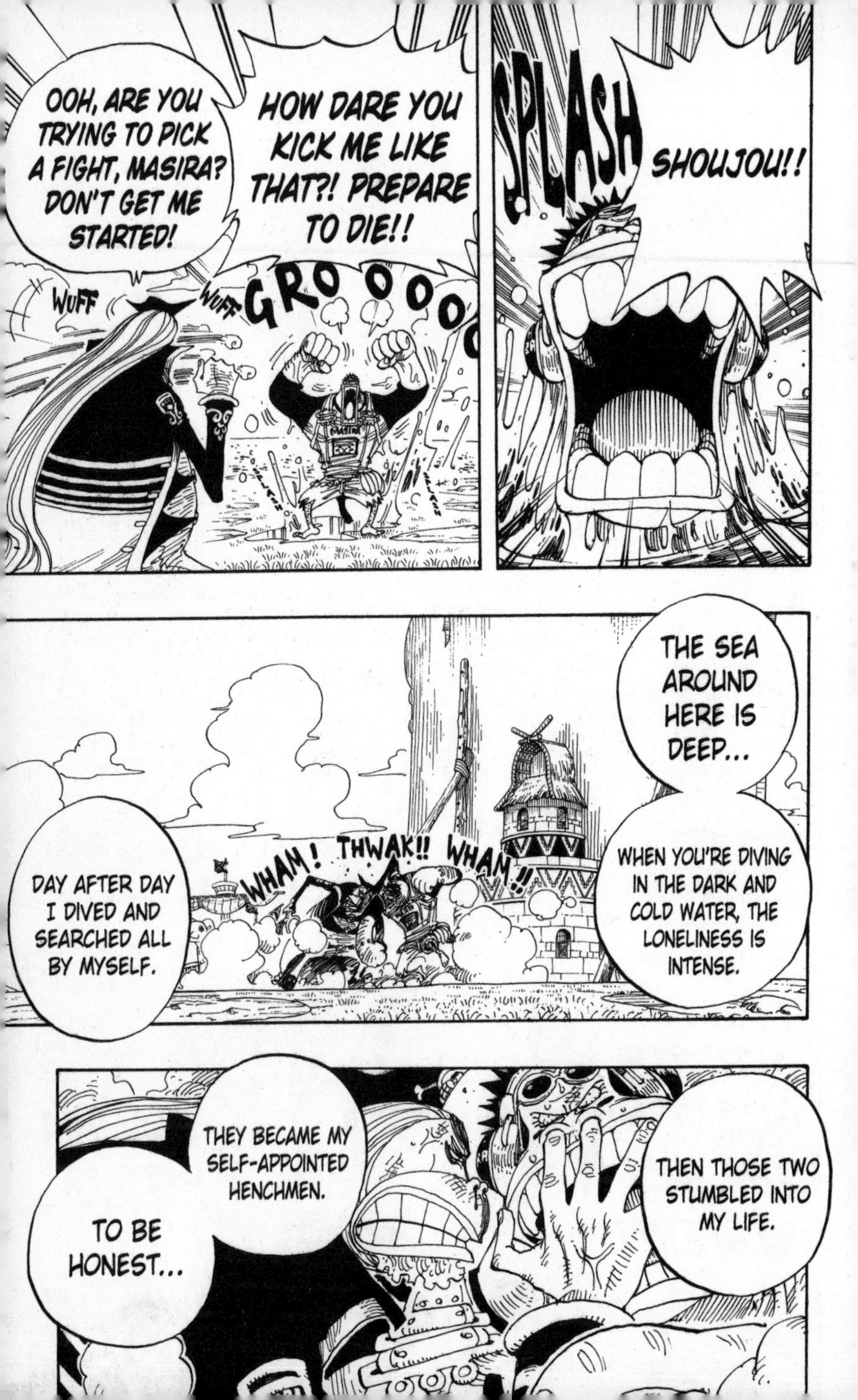
SPLASH
SHOUJOU!!
HOW DARE YOU KICK ME LIKE THAT?! PREPARE TO DIE!!
OOH, ARE YOU TRYING TO PICK A FIGHT, MASIRA? DON'T GET ME STARTED!
WUFF
GRO OOOO
WUFF
THE SEA AROUND HERE IS DEEP...
WHEN YOU'RE DIVING IN THE DARK AND COLD WATER, THE LONELINESS IS INTENSE.
WHAM! THWAK!! WHAM!!
DAY AFTER DAY I DIVED AND SEARCHED ALL BY MYSELF.
THEN THOSE TWO STUMBLED INTO MY LIFE.
THEY BECAME MY SELF-APPOINTED HENCHMEN.
TO BE HONEST...

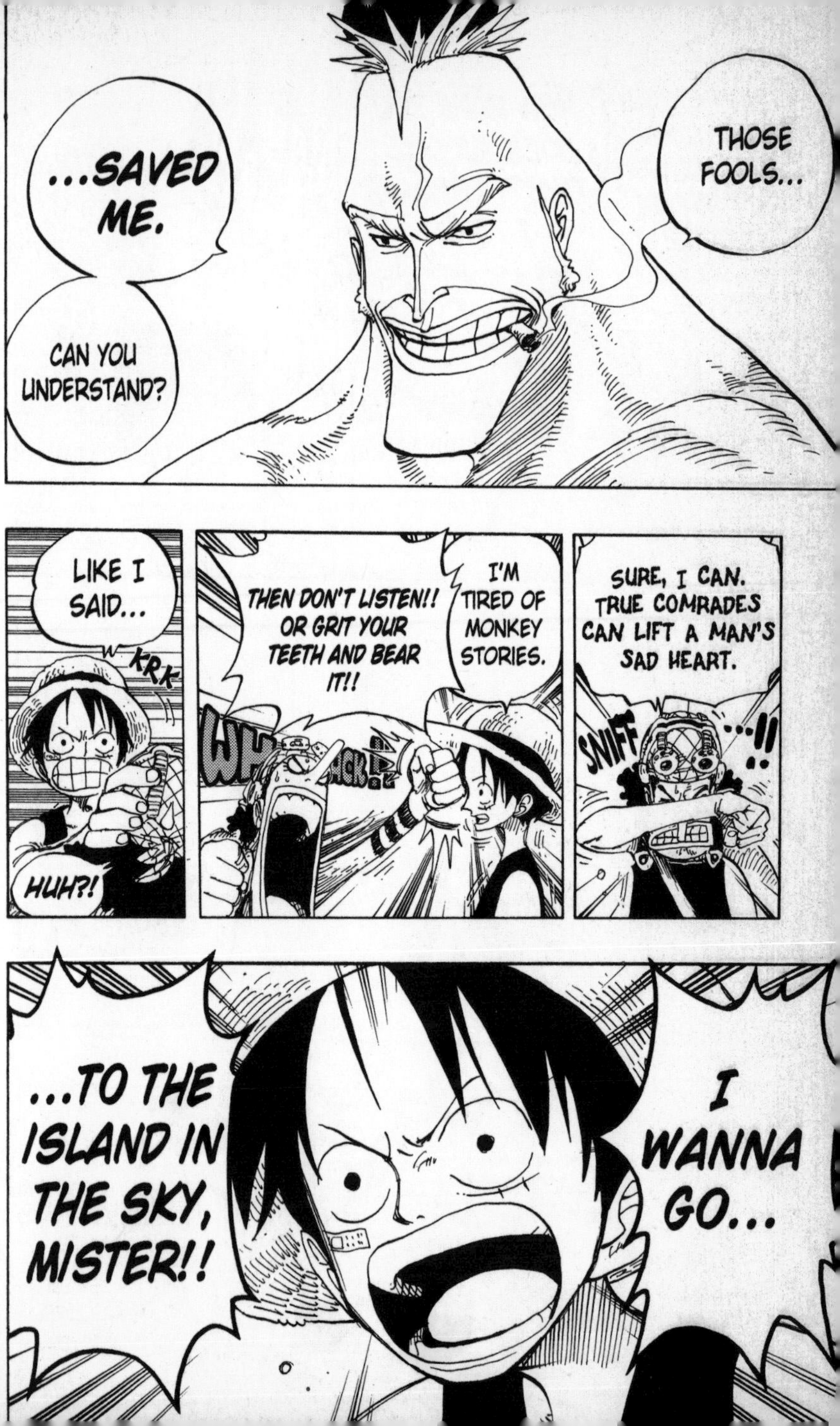
THOSE FOOLS...
...SAVED ME.
CAN YOU UNDERSTAND?
SURE, I CAN. TRUE COMRADES CAN LIFT A MAN'S SAD HEART.
SNIFF
...!!
I'M TIRED OF MONKEY STORIES.
THEN DON'T LISTEN!! OR GRIT YOUR TEETH AND BEAR IT!!
LIKE I SAID...
KRK
HUH?!
I WANNA GO...
...TO THE ISLAND IN THE SKY, MISTER!!

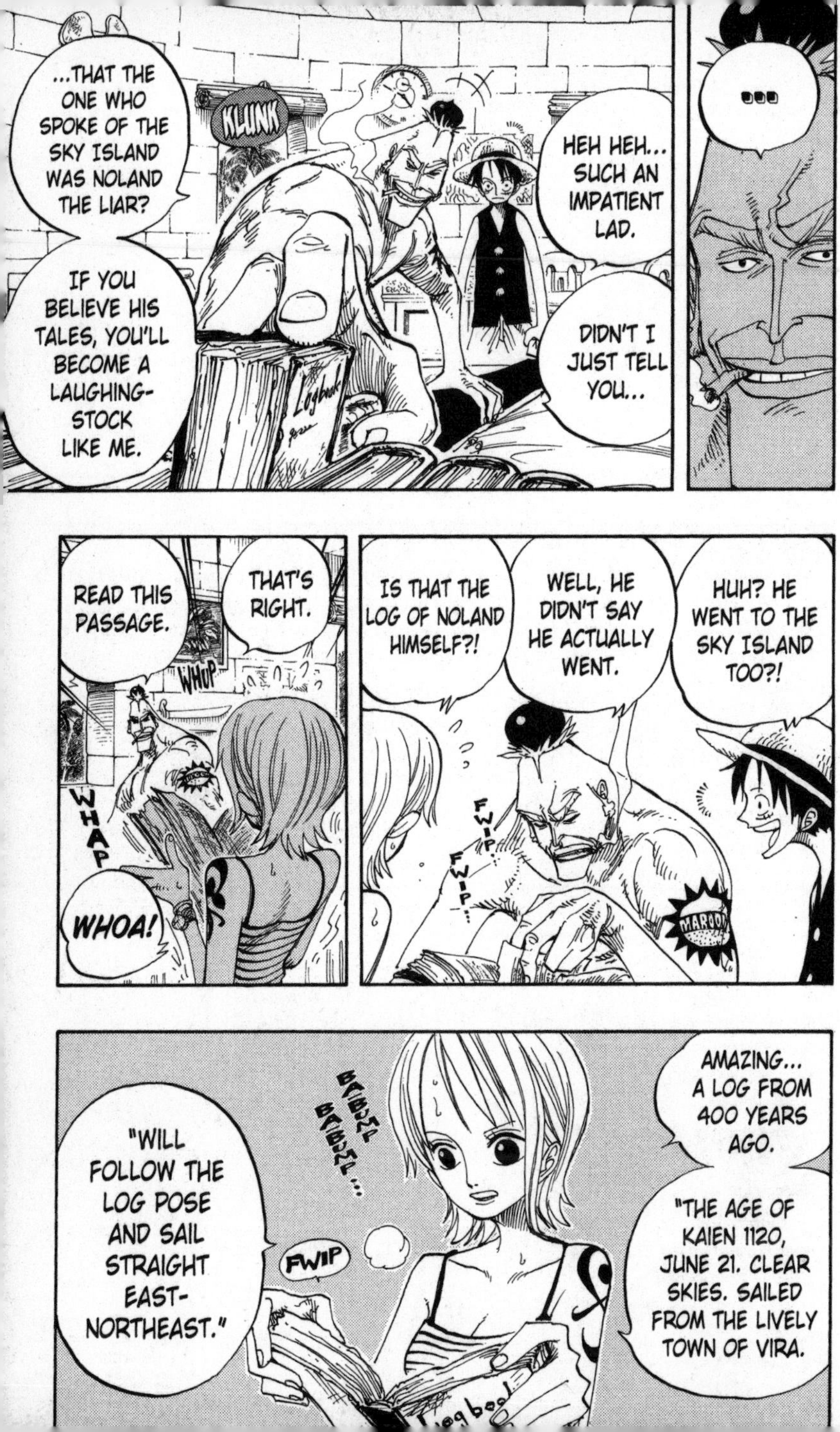
...
HEH HEH... SUCH AN IMPATIENT LAD.
DIDN'T I JUST TELL YOU...
KLUNK
...THAT THE ONE WHO SPOKE OF THE SKY ISLAND WAS NOLAND THE LIAR?
IF YOU BELIEVE HIS TALES, YOU'LL BECOME A LAUGHING-STOCK LIKE ME.
Logbook
HUH? HE WENT TO THE SKY ISLAND TOO?!
WELL, HE DIDN'T SAY HE ACTUALLY WENT.
IS THAT THE LOG OF NOLAND HIMSELF?!
FWIP...
FWIP...
MAROON
THAT'S RIGHT.
READ THIS PASSAGE.
WHUP
WHAP
WHOA!
AMAZING... A LOG FROM 400 YEARS AGO.
"THE AGE OF KAIEN 1120, JUNE 21. CLEAR SKIES. SAILED FROM THE LIVELY TOWN OF VIRA.
"WILL FOLLOW THE LOG POSE AND SAIL STRAIGHT EAST-NORTHEAST."
BABUMP BABUMP...
FWIP

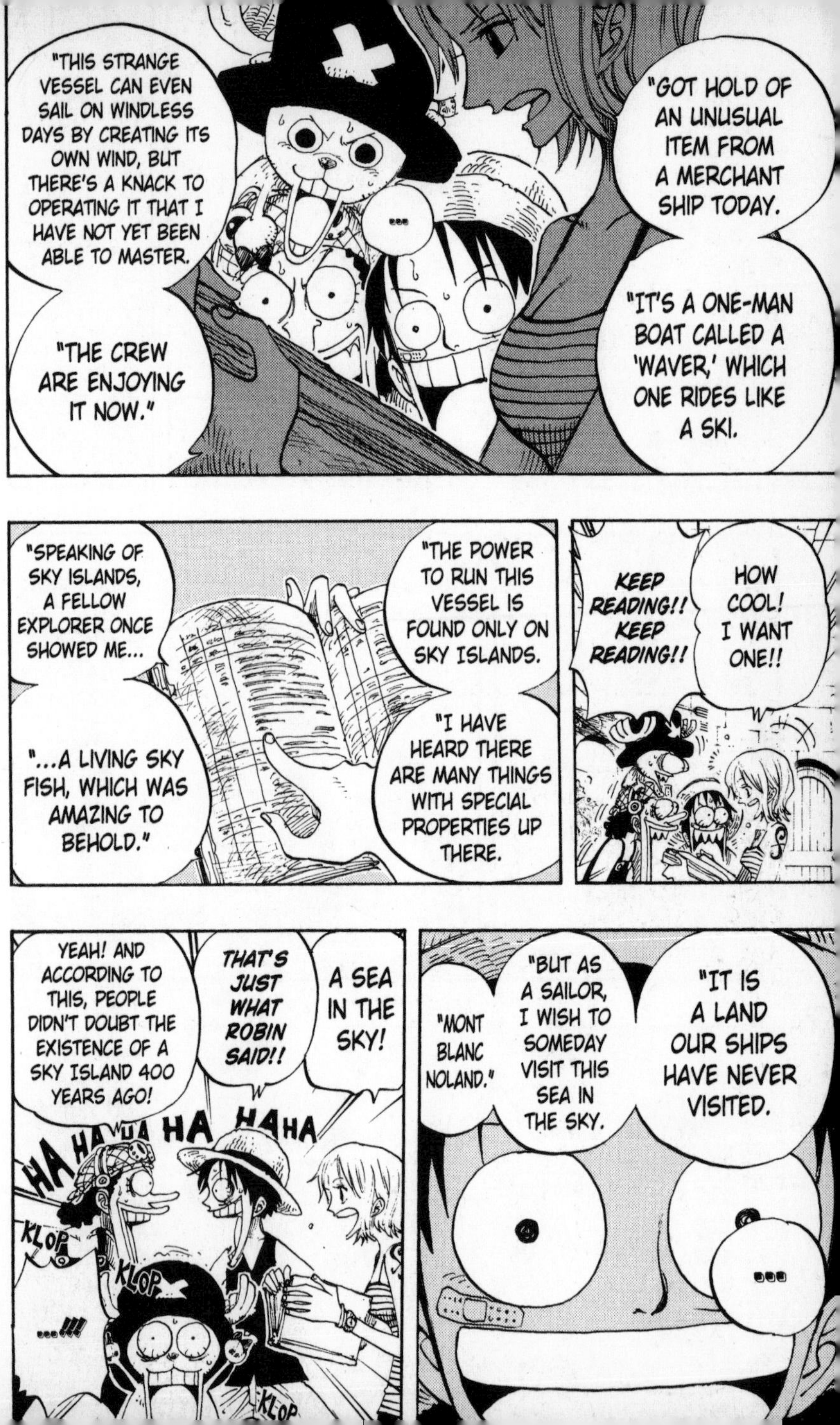
"GOT HOLD OF AN UNUSUAL ITEM FROM A MERCHANT SHIP TODAY.
"IT'S A ONE-MAN BOAT CALLED A 'WAVER,' WHICH ONE RIDES LIKE A SKI.
...
"THIS STRANGE VESSEL CAN EVEN SAIL ON WINDLESS DAYS BY CREATING ITS OWN WIND, BUT THERE'S A KNACK TO OPERATING IT THAT I HAVE NOT YET BEEN ABLE TO MASTER.
"THE CREW ARE ENJOYING IT NOW."
HOW COOL! I WANT ONE!!
KEEP READING!! KEEP READING!!
"THE POWER TO RUN THIS VESSEL IS FOUND ONLY ON SKY ISLANDS.
"I HAVE HEARD THERE ARE MANY THINGS WITH SPECIAL PROPERTIES UP THERE.
"SPEAKING OF SKY ISLANDS, A FELLOW EXPLORER ONCE SHOWED ME...
"...A LIVING SKY FISH, WHICH WAS AMAZING TO BEHOLD."
"IT IS A LAND OUR SHIPS HAVE NEVER VISITED.
"BUT AS A SAILOR, I WISH TO SOMEDAY VISIT THIS SEA IN THE SKY.
"MONT BLANC NOLAND."
...
A SEA IN THE SKY!
THAT'S JUST WHAT ROBIN SAID!!
YEAH! AND ACCORDING TO THIS, PEOPLE DIDN'T DOUBT THE EXISTENCE OF A SKY ISLAND 400 YEARS AGO!
HA HA WUA HA HA HAHA
KLOP
KLOP
...!!!
KLOP

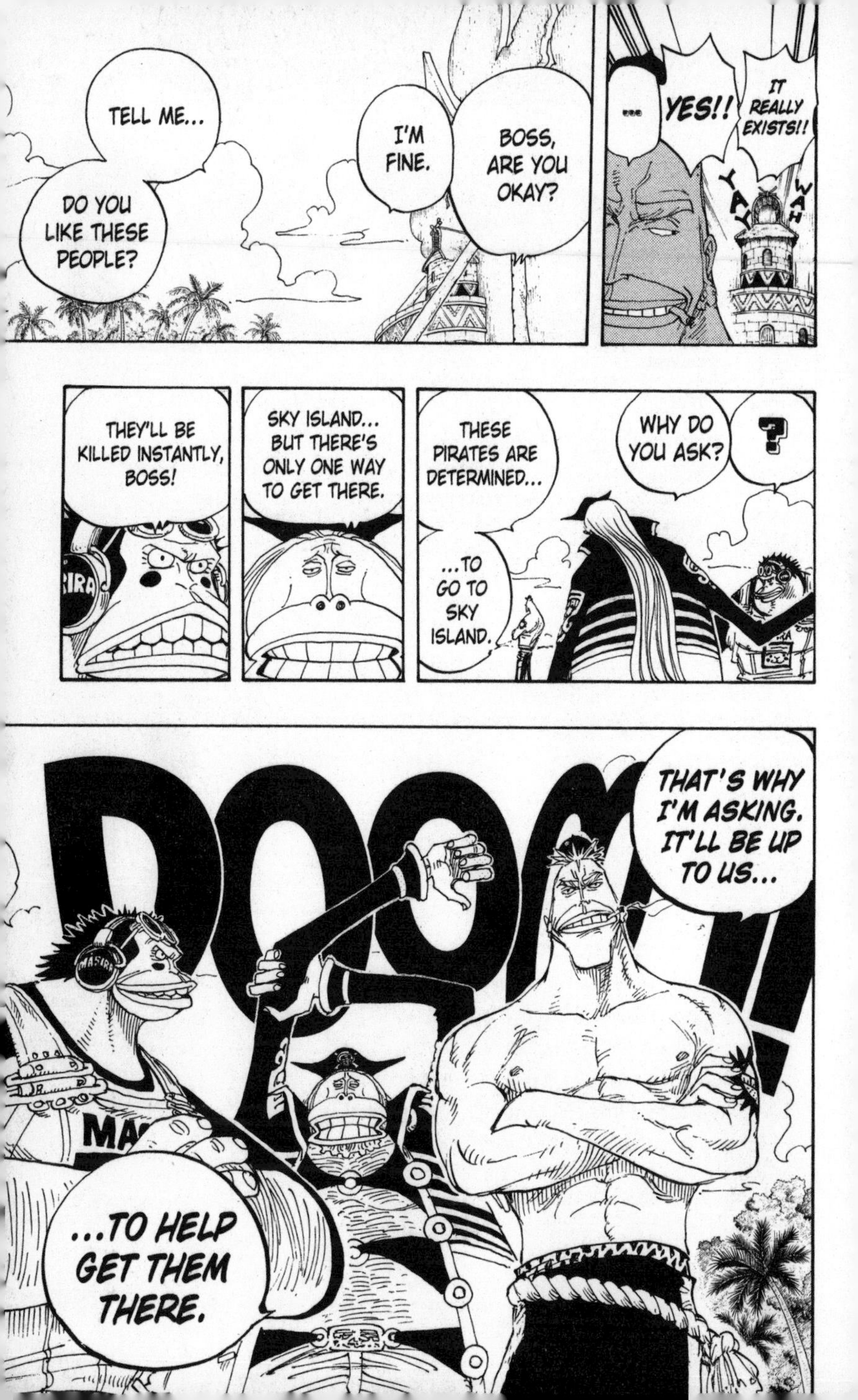
...
YES!!
IT REALLY EXISTS!!
YAY
WAH
BOSS, ARE YOU OKAY?
I'M FINE.
TELL ME...
DO YOU LIKE THESE PEOPLE?
?
WHY DO YOU ASK?
THESE PIRATES ARE DETERMINED...
...TO GO TO SKY ISLAND.
SKY ISLAND... BUT THERE'S ONLY ONE WAY TO GET THERE.
THEY'LL BE KILLED INSTANTLY, BOSS!
THAT'S WHY I'M ASKING. IT'LL BE UP TO US...
...TO HELP GET THEM THERE.

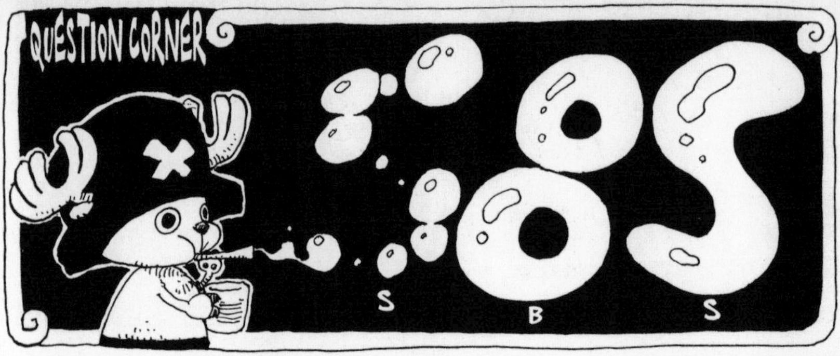
QUESTION CORNER
S
B
S

Reader: How are you, Mr. Oda? You must really love summer since you like to be naked. ♡

Oda: Yes, yes, I love to walk around in the nude. In the summer, I soak in the tub then go outside naked! I get a lot of looks from the girls' softball team as they jog along the riverbank! "Yay! It's summer!" I call out.

**Are you crazy?! I'd get arrested!!**

Q: I have a question, Oda Sensei! I understand that long ago in Britain, noblemen were addressed as "sir." Is that where you got the "sir" in Sir Crocodile?

A: Sir. (Sure.)

Q: On page 184 of volume 24, Usopp is making repairs to the ship, and he hits his middle finger with the hammer. So why is his index finger swollen in the next panel?!

--Orange Natchan

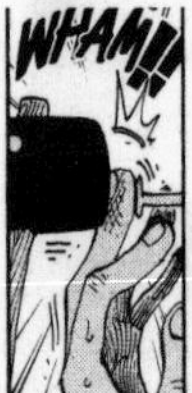
WHAM!!

A: That's the balloon principle. For example, if you have a long balloon and you squeeze it at one end, the other end suddenly gets bigger. Similarly, when Usopp hit his middle finger (bam!) his index finger swelled up. Get it?

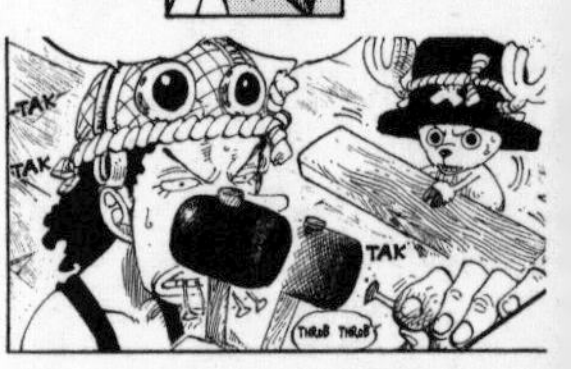
TAK
TAK
TAK
THROB THROB

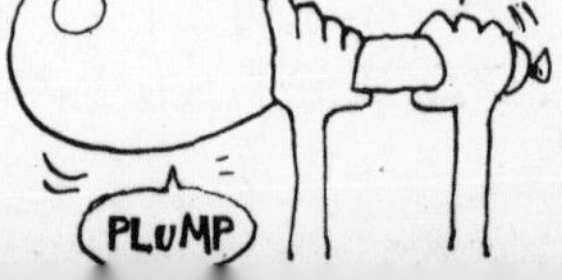
SQUEEZE
PLUMP

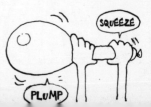

# Chapter 229:
# LET'S EAT

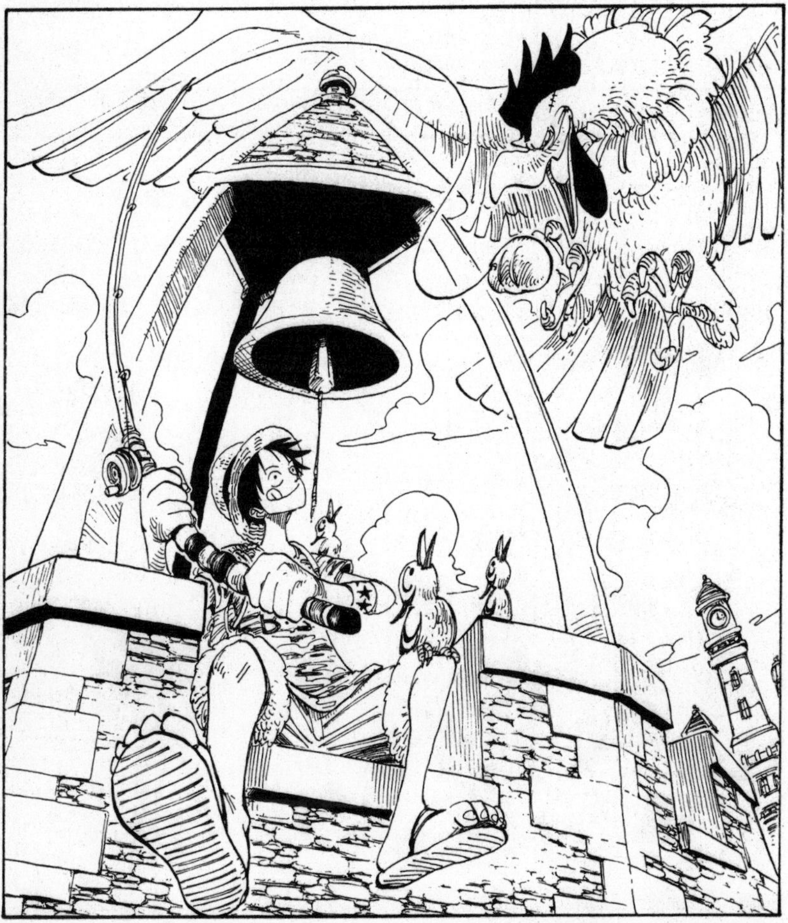

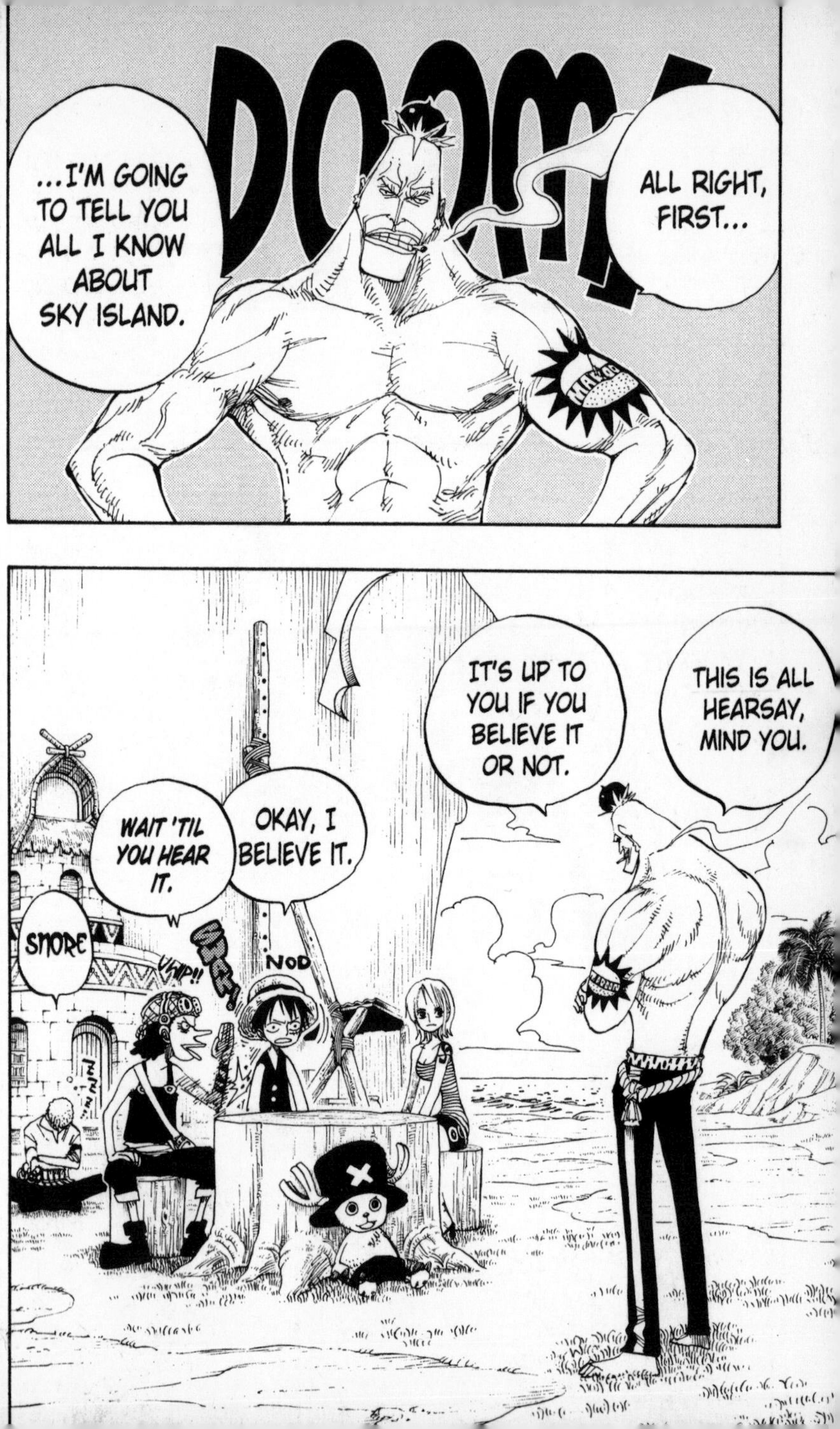
ALL RIGHT, FIRST...
DOOM
...I'M GOING TO TELL YOU ALL I KNOW ABOUT SKY ISLAND.
THIS IS ALL HEARSAY, MIND YOU.
IT'S UP TO YOU IF YOU BELIEVE IT OR NOT.
OKAY, I BELIEVE IT.
NOD
WAIT 'TIL YOU HEAR IT.
SNORE

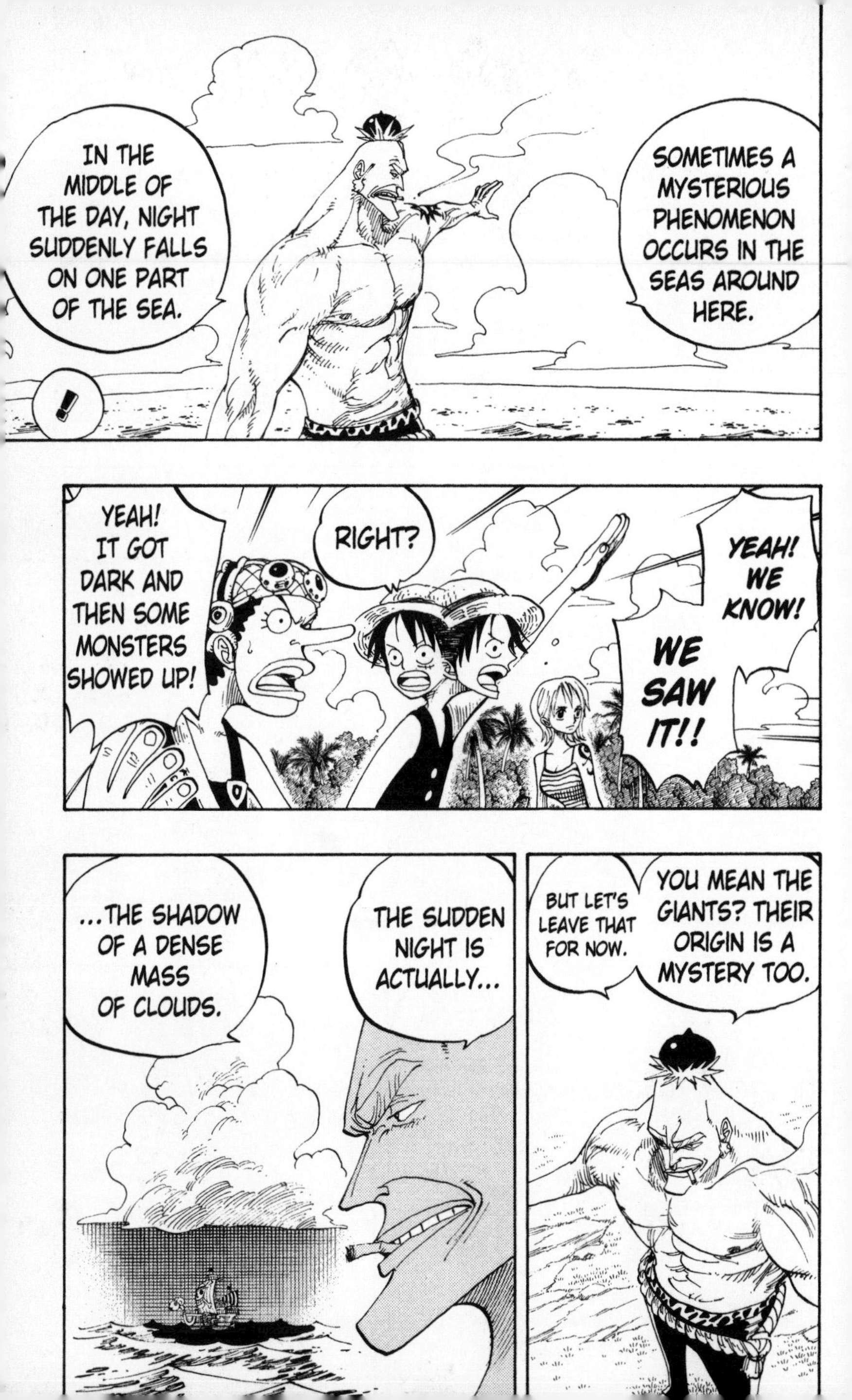
SOMETIMES A MYSTERIOUS PHENOMENON OCCURS IN THE SEAS AROUND HERE.
IN THE MIDDLE OF THE DAY, NIGHT SUDDENLY FALLS ON ONE PART OF THE SEA.
!
YEAH! WE KNOW!
WE SAW IT!!
RIGHT?
YEAH! IT GOT DARK AND THEN SOME MONSTERS SHOWED UP!
YOU MEAN THE GIANTS? THEIR ORIGIN IS A MYSTERY TOO.
BUT LET'S LEAVE THAT FOR NOW.
THE SUDDEN NIGHT IS ACTUALLY...
...THE SHADOW OF A DENSE MASS OF CLOUDS.

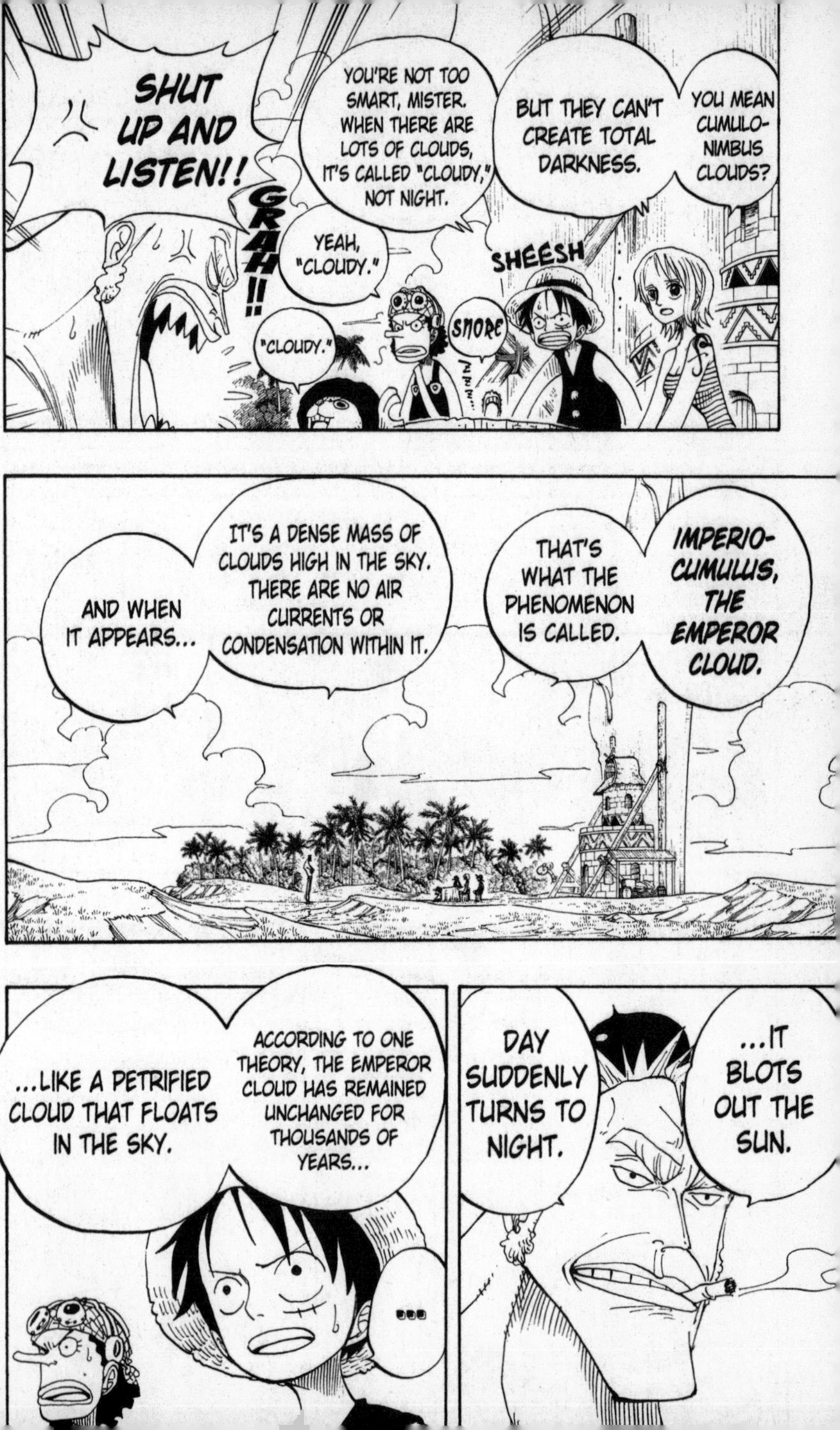
YOU MEAN CUMULO-NIMBUS CLOUDS?
BUT THEY CAN'T CREATE TOTAL DARKNESS.
YOU'RE NOT TOO SMART, MISTER. WHEN THERE ARE LOTS OF CLOUDS, IT'S CALLED "CLOUDY," NOT NIGHT.
SHEESH
SHUT UP AND LISTEN!!
GRAH!!
YEAH, "CLOUDY."
SNORE
"CLOUDY."
IMPERIO-CUMULUS, THE EMPEROR CLOUD.
THAT'S WHAT THE PHENOMENON IS CALLED.
IT'S A DENSE MASS OF CLOUDS HIGH IN THE SKY. THERE ARE NO AIR CURRENTS OR CONDENSATION WITHIN IT.
AND WHEN IT APPEARS...
...IT BLOTS OUT THE SUN.
DAY SUDDENLY TURNS TO NIGHT.
ACCORDING TO ONE THEORY, THE EMPEROR CLOUD HAS REMAINED UNCHANGED FOR THOUSANDS OF YEARS...
...LIKE A PETRIFIED CLOUD THAT FLOATS IN THE SKY.
...

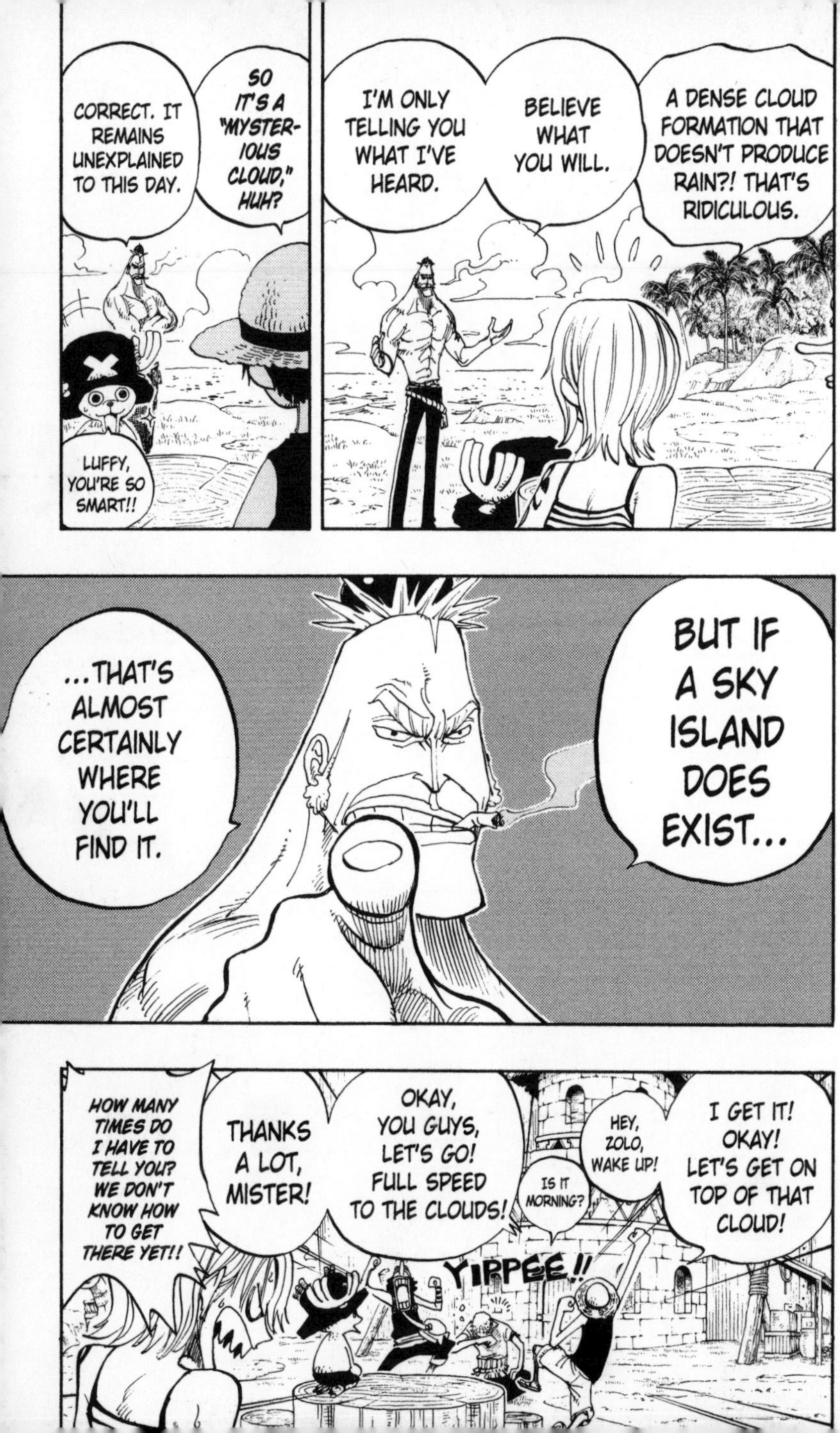
A DENSE CLOUD FORMATION THAT DOESN'T PRODUCE RAIN?! THAT'S RIDICULOUS.
BELIEVE WHAT YOU WILL.
I'M ONLY TELLING YOU WHAT I'VE HEARD.
SO IT'S A "MYSTERIOUS CLOUD," HUH?
CORRECT. IT REMAINS UNEXPLAINED TO THIS DAY.
LUFFY, YOU'RE SO SMART!!
BUT IF A SKY ISLAND DOES EXIST...
...THAT'S ALMOST CERTAINLY WHERE YOU'LL FIND IT.
I GET IT! OKAY! LET'S GET ON TOP OF THAT CLOUD!
HEY, ZOLO, WAKE UP!
IS IT MORNING?
OKAY, YOU GUYS, LET'S GO! FULL SPEED TO THE CLOUDS!
YIPPEE!!
THANKS A LOT, MISTER!
HOW MANY TIMES DO I HAVE TO TELL YOU? WE DON'T KNOW HOW TO GET THERE YET!!

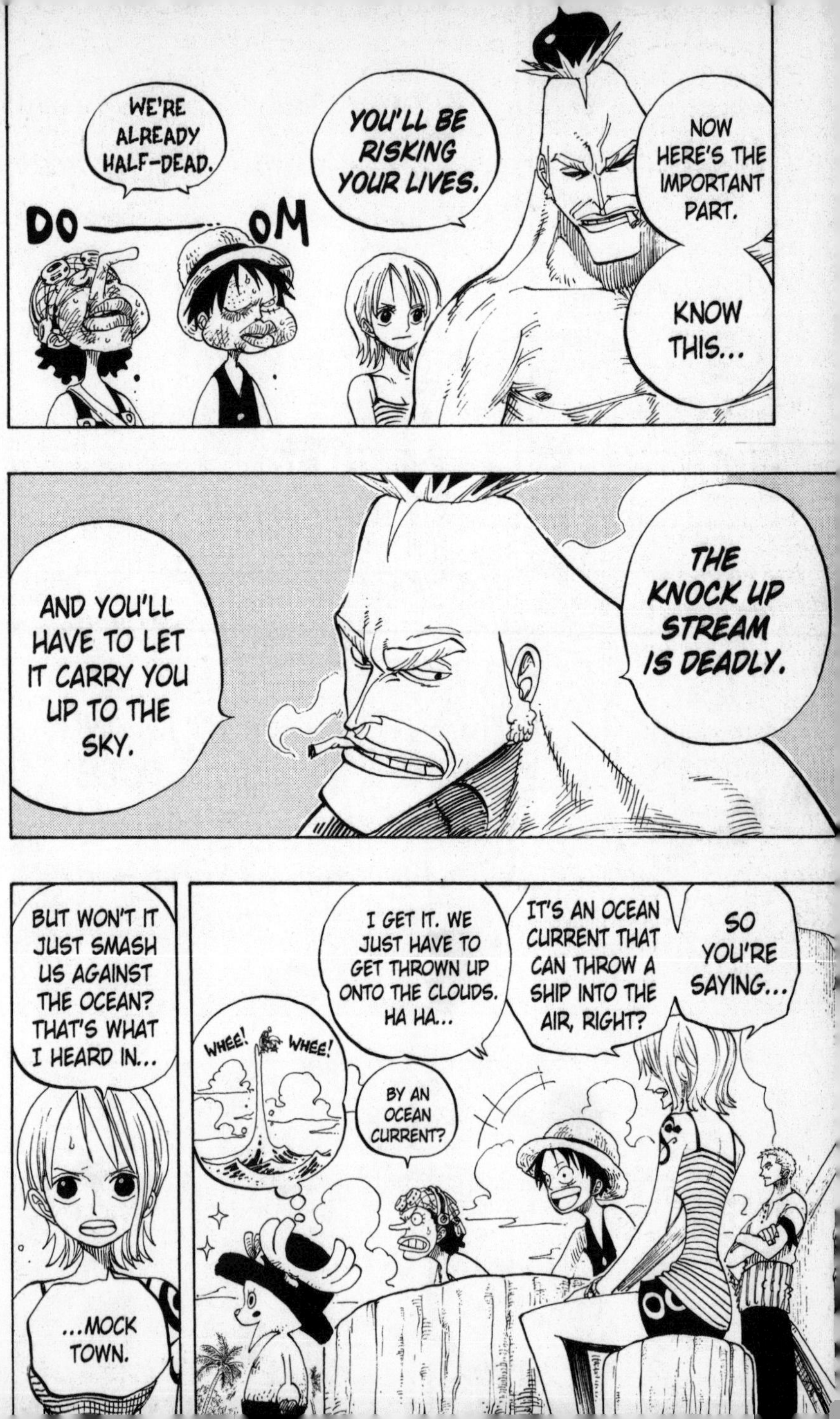
NOW HERE'S THE IMPORTANT PART.
KNOW THIS...
YOU'LL BE RISKING YOUR LIVES.
DO———OM
WE'RE ALREADY HALF-DEAD.
THE KNOCK UP STREAM IS DEADLY.
AND YOU'LL HAVE TO LET IT CARRY YOU UP TO THE SKY.
SO YOU'RE SAYING...
IT'S AN OCEAN CURRENT THAT CAN THROW A SHIP INTO THE AIR, RIGHT?
I GET IT. WE JUST HAVE TO GET THROWN UP ONTO THE CLOUDS. HA HA...
BY AN OCEAN CURRENT?
WHEE! WHEE!
BUT WON'T IT JUST SMASH US AGAINST THE OCEAN? THAT'S WHAT I HEARD IN...
...MOCK TOWN.

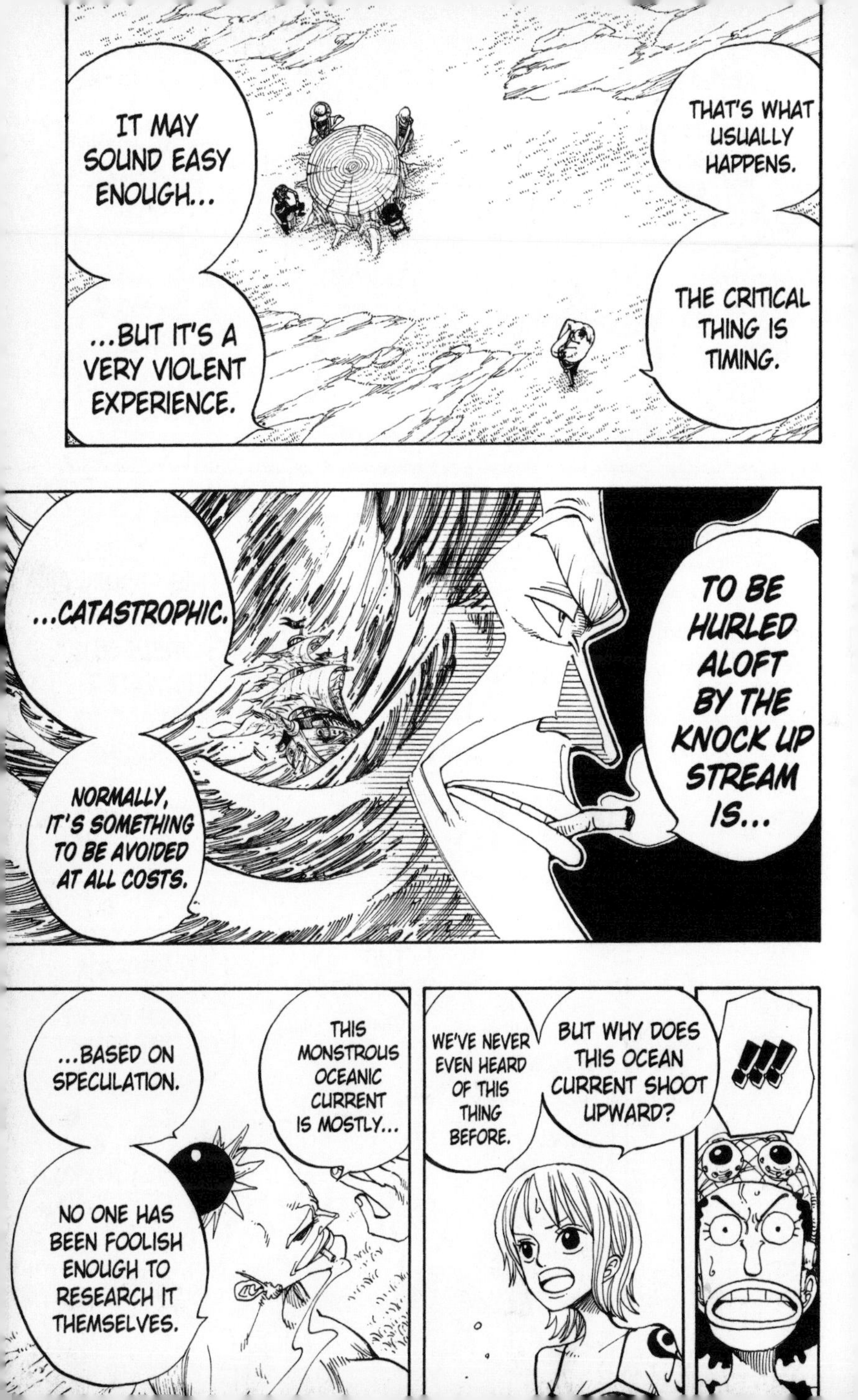
THAT'S WHAT USUALLY HAPPENS.
THE CRITICAL THING IS TIMING.
IT MAY SOUND EASY ENOUGH...
...BUT IT'S A VERY VIOLENT EXPERIENCE.
TO BE HURLED ALOFT BY THE KNOCK UP STREAM IS...
...CATASTROPHIC.
NORMALLY, IT'S SOMETHING TO BE AVOIDED AT ALL COSTS.
!!!
BUT WHY DOES THIS OCEAN CURRENT SHOOT UPWARD?
WE'VE NEVER EVEN HEARD OF THIS THING BEFORE.
THIS MONSTROUS OCEANIC CURRENT IS MOSTLY...
...BASED ON SPECULATION.
NO ONE HAS BEEN FOOLISH ENOUGH TO RESEARCH IT THEMSELVES.

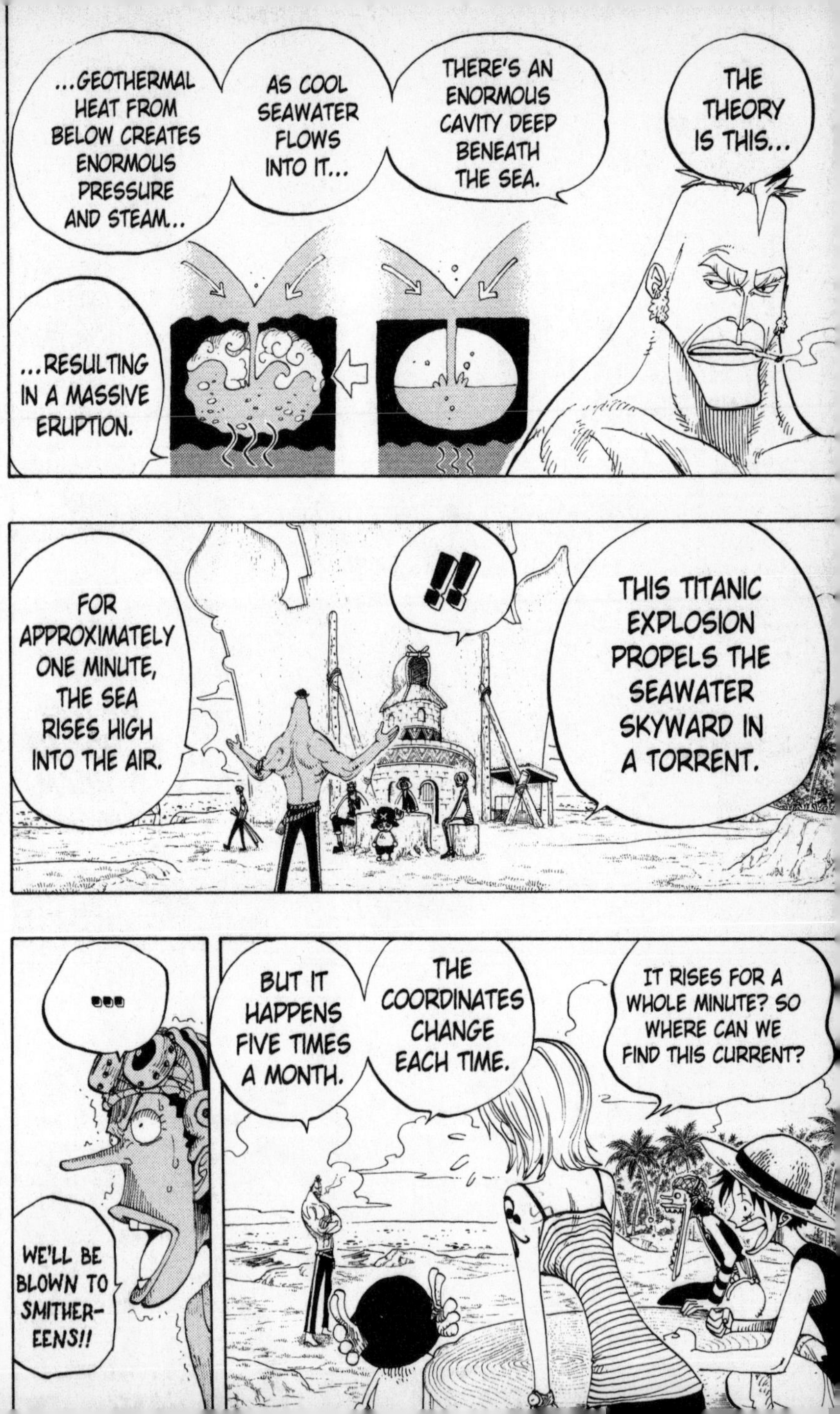
THE THEORY IS THIS...
THERE'S AN ENORMOUS CAVITY DEEP BENEATH THE SEA.
AS COOL SEAWATER FLOWS INTO IT...
...GEOTHERMAL HEAT FROM BELOW CREATES ENORMOUS PRESSURE AND STEAM...
...RESULTING IN A MASSIVE ERUPTION.
THIS TITANIC EXPLOSION PROPELS THE SEAWATER SKYWARD IN A TORRENT.
!!
FOR APPROXIMATELY ONE MINUTE, THE SEA RISES HIGH INTO THE AIR.
IT RISES FOR A WHOLE MINUTE? SO WHERE CAN WE FIND THIS CURRENT?
THE COORDINATES CHANGE EACH TIME.
BUT IT HAPPENS FIVE TIMES A MONTH.
...
WE'LL BE BLOWN TO SMITHER-EENS!!

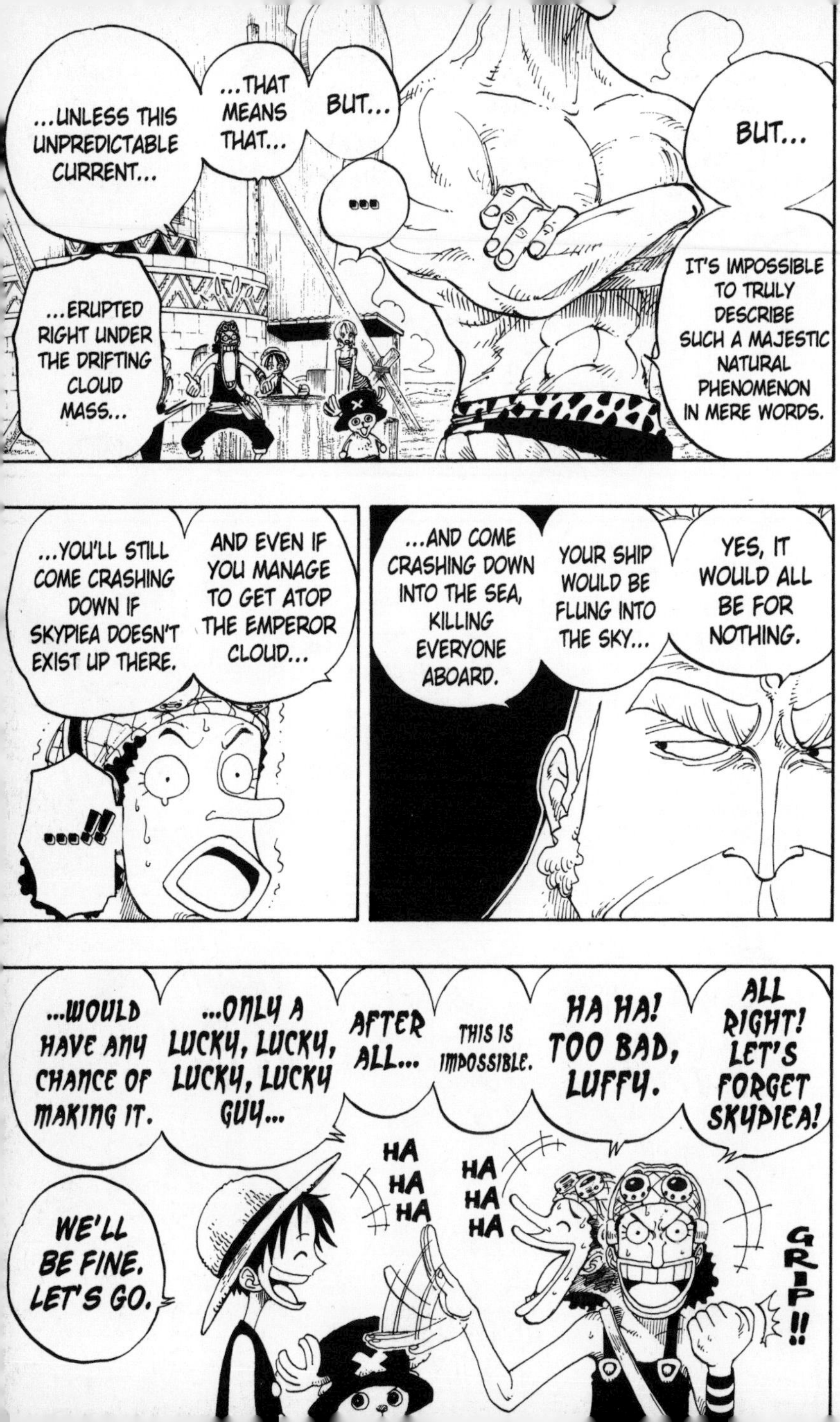
BUT...
IT'S IMPOSSIBLE TO TRULY DESCRIBE SUCH A MAJESTIC NATURAL PHENOMENON IN MERE WORDS.
BUT...
...THAT MEANS THAT...
...UNLESS THIS UNPREDICTABLE CURRENT...
...
...ERUPTED RIGHT UNDER THE DRIFTING CLOUD MASS...
YES, IT WOULD ALL BE FOR NOTHING.
YOUR SHIP WOULD BE FLUNG INTO THE SKY...
...AND COME CRASHING DOWN INTO THE SEA, KILLING EVERYONE ABOARD.
AND EVEN IF YOU MANAGE TO GET ATOP THE EMPEROR CLOUD...
...YOU'LL STILL COME CRASHING DOWN IF SKYPIEA DOESN'T EXIST UP THERE.
...!!
ALL RIGHT! LET'S FORGET SKYPIEA!
GRIP!!
HA HA! TOO BAD, LUFFY.
THIS IS IMPOSSIBLE.
AFTER ALL...
...ONLY A LUCKY, LUCKY, LUCKY, LUCKY GUY...
...WOULD HAVE ANY CHANCE OF MAKING IT.
HA HA HA
HA HA HA
WE'LL BE FINE. LET'S GO.

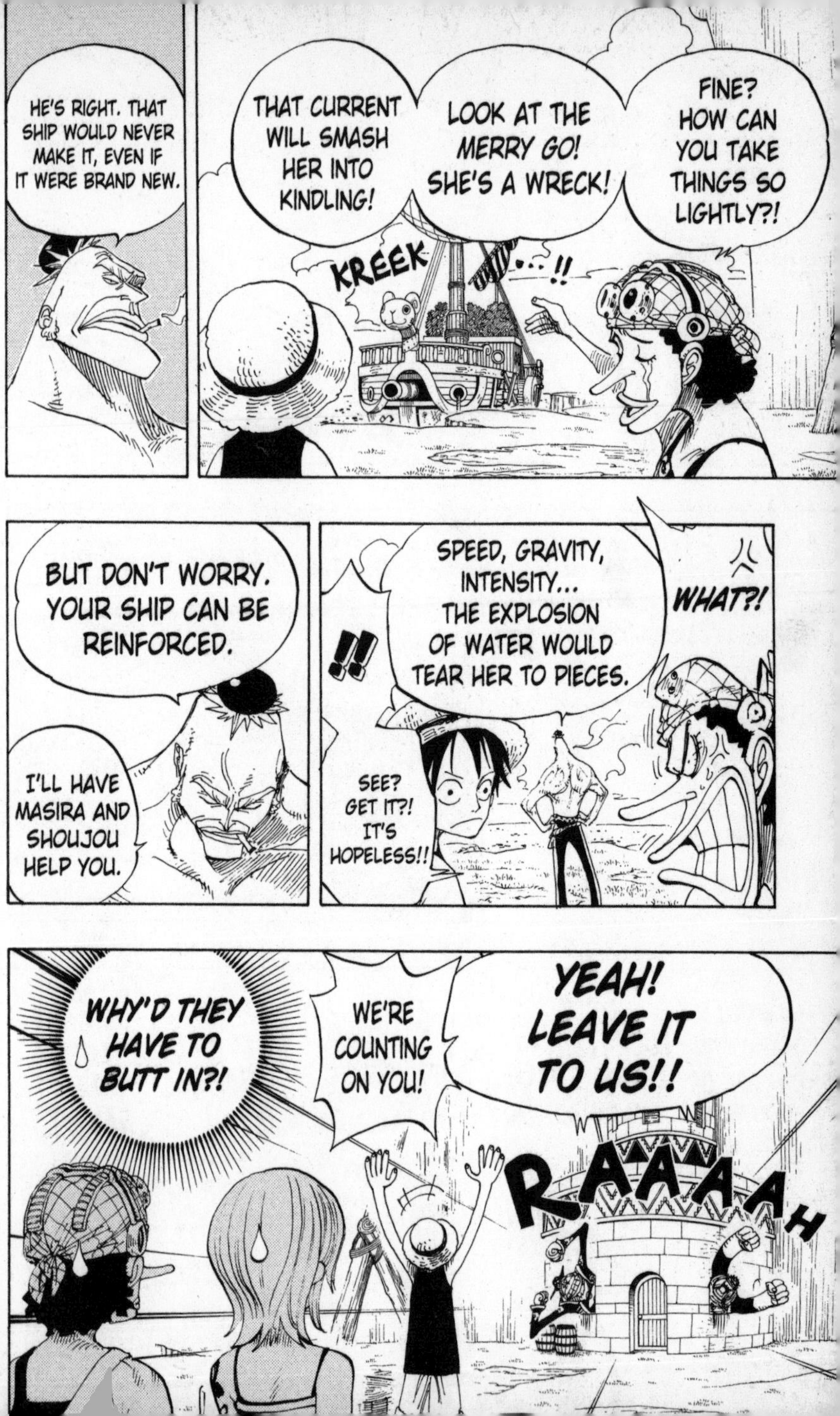
FINE? HOW CAN YOU TAKE THINGS SO LIGHTLY?!
LOOK AT THE MERRY GO! SHE'S A WRECK!
THAT CURRENT WILL SMASH HER INTO KINDLING!
KREEK
...!!
HE'S RIGHT. THAT SHIP WOULD NEVER MAKE IT, EVEN IF IT WERE BRAND NEW.
WHAT?!
SPEED, GRAVITY, INTENSITY... THE EXPLOSION OF WATER WOULD TEAR HER TO PIECES.
!!
SEE? GET IT?! IT'S HOPELESS!!
BUT DON'T WORRY. YOUR SHIP CAN BE REINFORCED.
I'LL HAVE MASIRA AND SHOUJOU HELP YOU.
YEAH! LEAVE IT TO US!!
WE'RE COUNTING ON YOU!
WHY'D THEY HAVE TO BUTT IN?!
RAAAAH

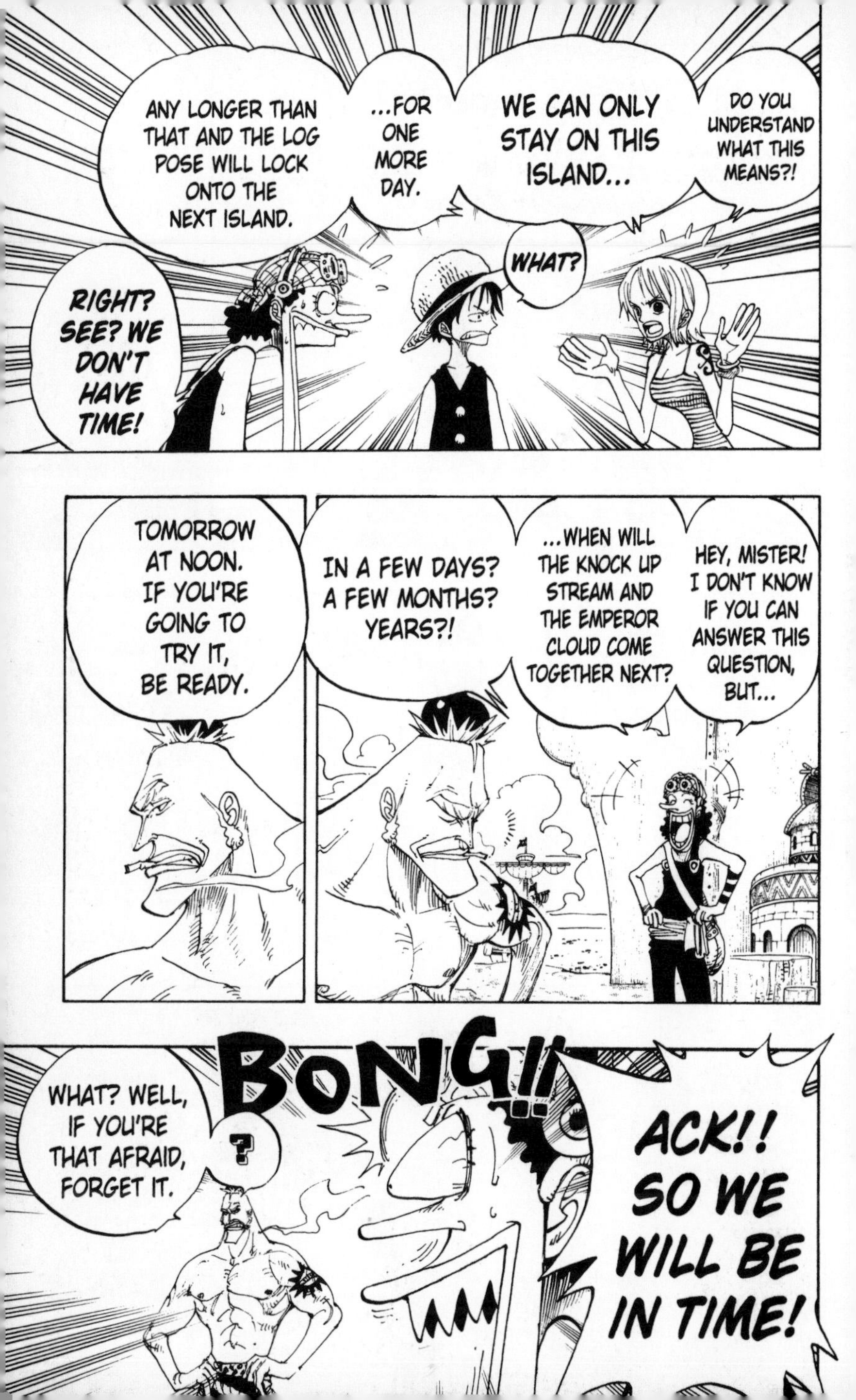
DO YOU UNDERSTAND WHAT THIS MEANS?!
WE CAN ONLY STAY ON THIS ISLAND...
...FOR ONE MORE DAY.
ANY LONGER THAN THAT AND THE LOG POSE WILL LOCK ONTO THE NEXT ISLAND.
WHAT?
RIGHT? SEE? WE DON'T HAVE TIME!
HEY, MISTER! I DON'T KNOW IF YOU CAN ANSWER THIS QUESTION, BUT...
...WHEN WILL THE KNOCK UP STREAM AND THE EMPEROR CLOUD COME TOGETHER NEXT?
IN A FEW DAYS? A FEW MONTHS? YEARS?!
TOMORROW AT NOON. IF YOU'RE GOING TO TRY IT, BE READY.
ACK!! SO WE WILL BE IN TIME!
BONG!!
?
WHAT? WELL, IF YOU'RE THAT AFRAID, FORGET IT.

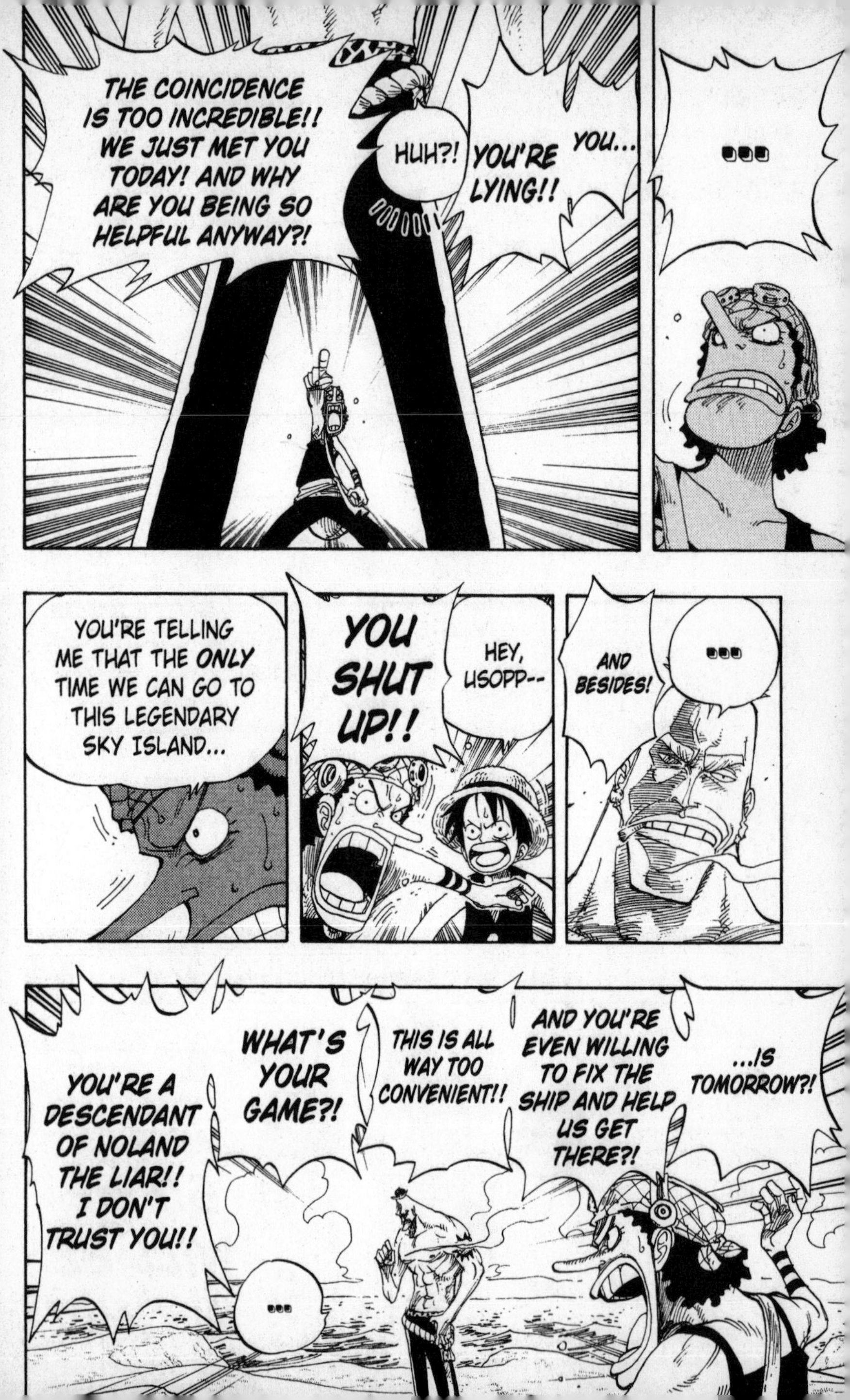
...
YOU...
YOU'RE LYING!!
HUH?!
THE COINCIDENCE IS TOO INCREDIBLE!! WE JUST MET YOU TODAY! AND WHY ARE YOU BEING SO HELPFUL ANYWAY?!
...
AND BESIDES!
HEY, USOPP--
YOU SHUT UP!!
YOU'RE TELLING ME THAT THE ONLY TIME WE CAN GO TO THIS LEGENDARY SKY ISLAND...
...IS TOMORROW?!
AND YOU'RE EVEN WILLING TO FIX THE SHIP AND HELP US GET THERE?!
THIS IS ALL WAY TOO CONVENIENT!!
WHAT'S YOUR GAME?!
YOU'RE A DESCENDANT OF NOLAND THE LIAR!! I DON'T TRUST YOU!!
...

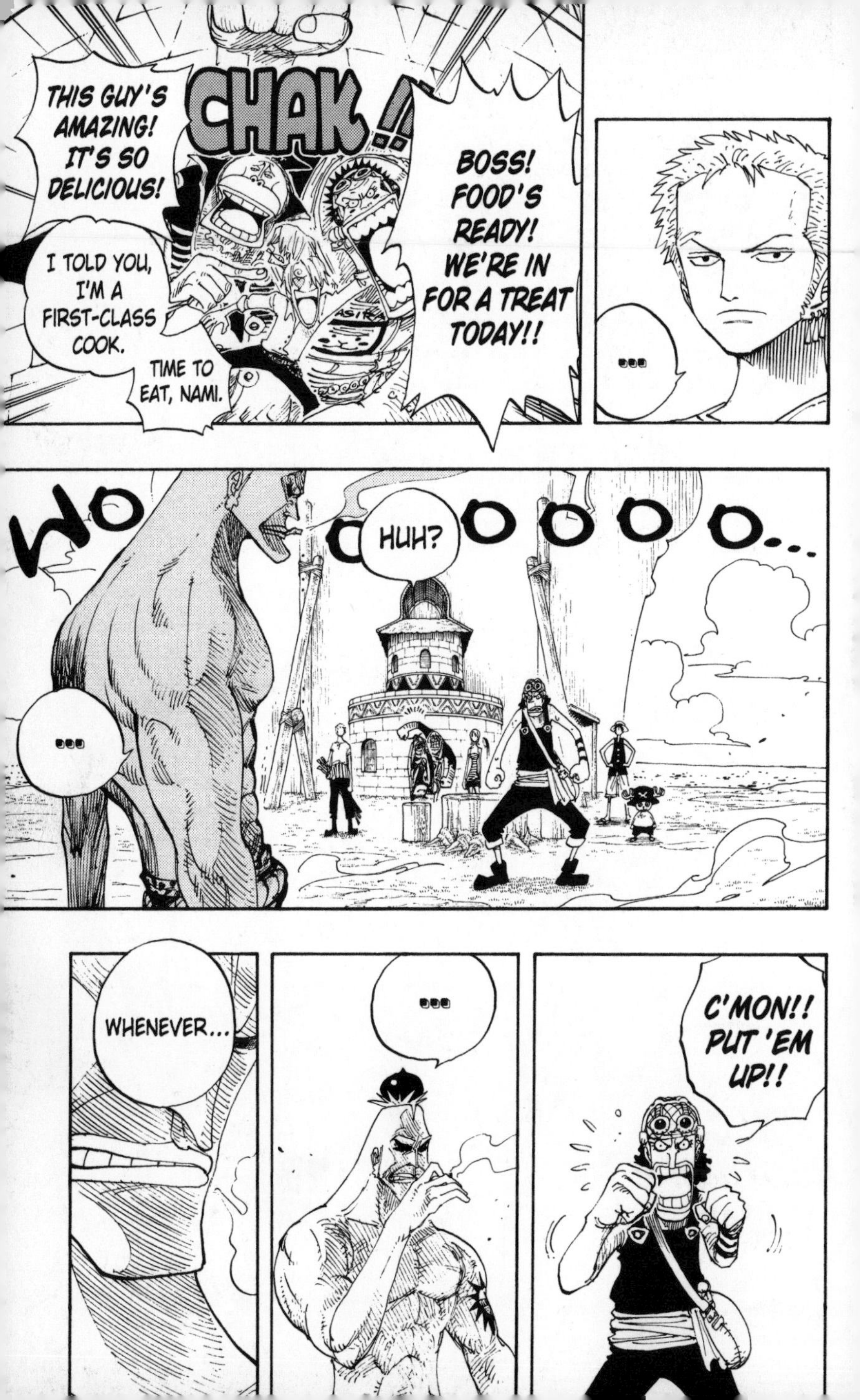
...
BOSS! FOOD'S READY! WE'RE IN FOR A TREAT TODAY!!
CHAK!!
THIS GUY'S AMAZING! IT'S SO DELICIOUS!
I TOLD YOU, I'M A FIRST-CLASS COOK.
TIME TO EAT, NAMI.
WOOOOOO...
HUH?
...
C'MON!! PUT 'EM UP!!
...
WHENEVER...

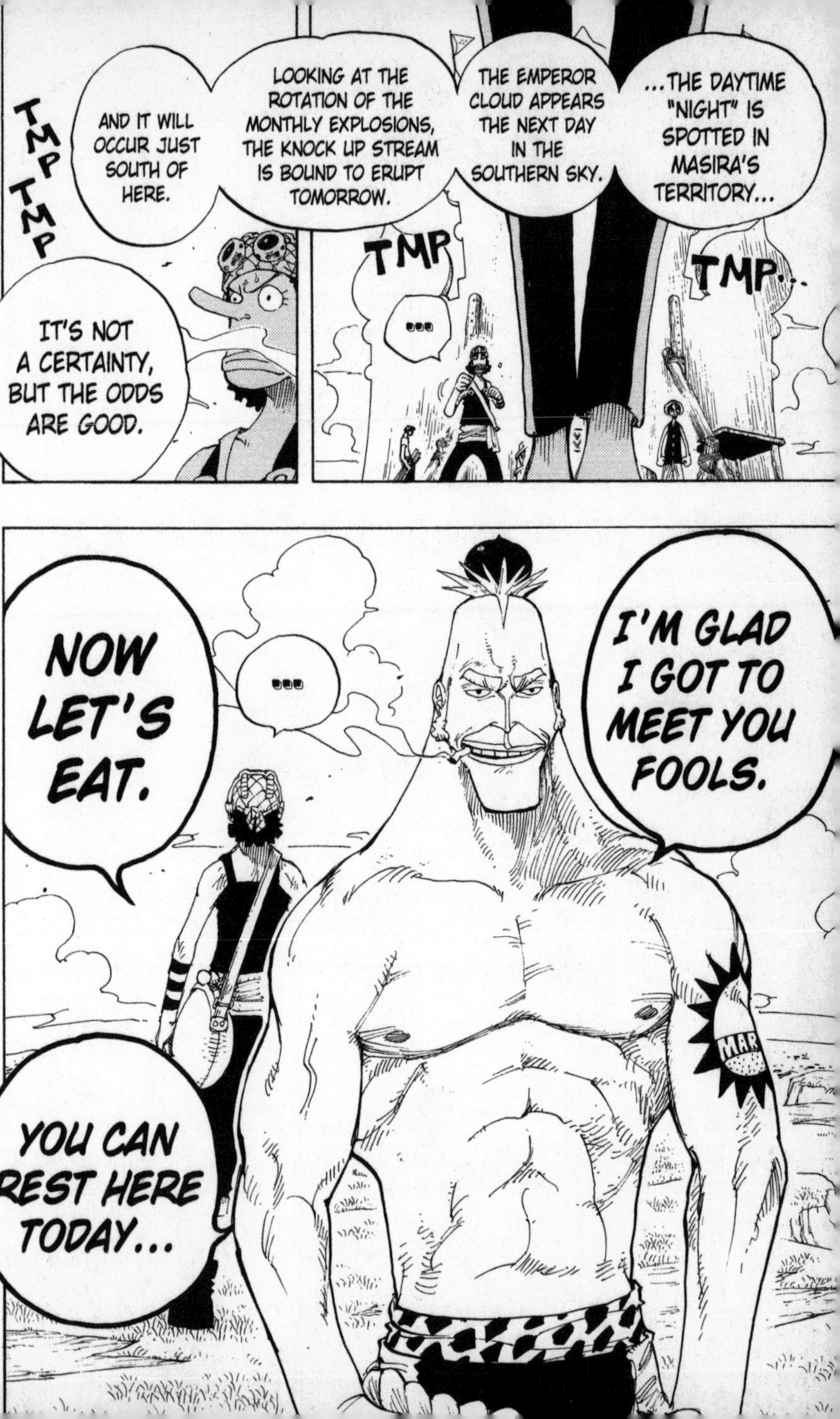
...THE DAYTIME "NIGHT" IS SPOTTED IN MASIRA'S TERRITORY...
THE EMPEROR CLOUD APPEARS THE NEXT DAY IN THE SOUTHERN SKY.
LOOKING AT THE ROTATION OF THE MONTHLY EXPLOSIONS, THE KNOCK UP STREAM IS BOUND TO ERUPT TOMORROW.
AND IT WILL OCCUR JUST SOUTH OF HERE.
TMP...
...
TMP
TMP TMP
IT'S NOT A CERTAINTY, BUT THE ODDS ARE GOOD.
I'M GLAD I GOT TO MEET YOU FOOLS.
...
NOW LET'S EAT.
YOU CAN REST HERE TODAY...
MAR

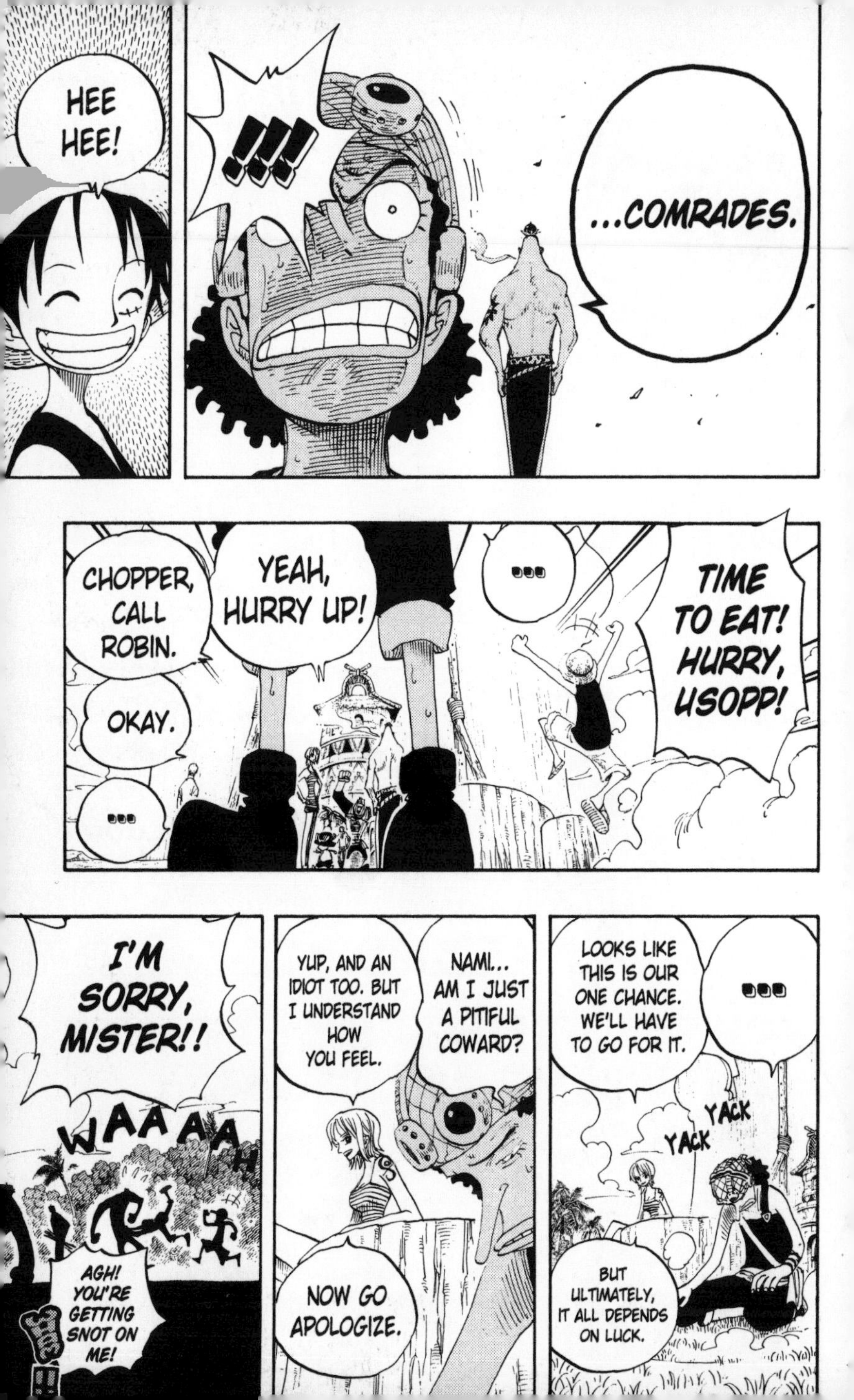

...COMRADES.
!!!
HEE HEE!
TIME TO EAT! HURRY, USOPP!
...
YEAH, HURRY UP!
CHOPPER, CALL ROBIN.
OKAY.
...
...
LOOKS LIKE THIS IS OUR ONE CHANCE. WE'LL HAVE TO GO FOR IT.
YACK
YACK
BUT ULTIMATELY, IT ALL DEPENDS ON LUCK.
NAMI... AM I JUST A PITIFUL COWARD?
YUP, AND AN IDIOT TOO. BUT I UNDERSTAND HOW YOU FEEL.
NOW GO APOLOGIZE.
I'M SORRY, MISTER!!
WAAAAAH
AGH! YOU'RE GETTING SNOT ON ME!

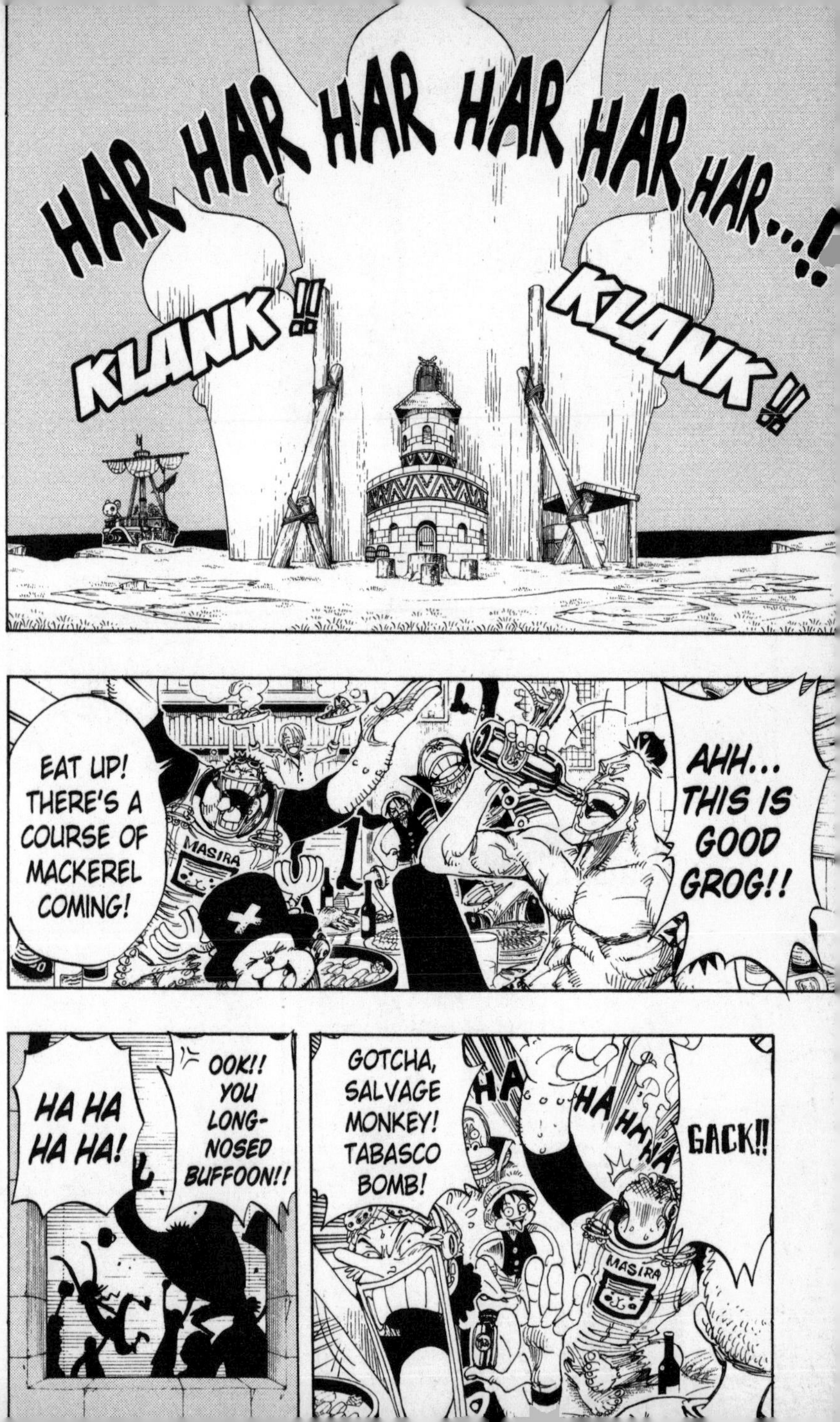
HAR HAR HAR HAR HAR HAR...!
KLANK!!
KLANK!!
AHH... THIS IS GOOD GROG!!
EAT UP! THERE'S A COURSE OF MACKEREL COMING!
MASIRA
GACK!!
HA HA HAHA
HA
GOTCHA, SALVAGE MONKEY! TABASCO BOMB!
MASIRA
OOK!! YOU LONG-NOSED BUFFOON!!
HA HA HA HA!

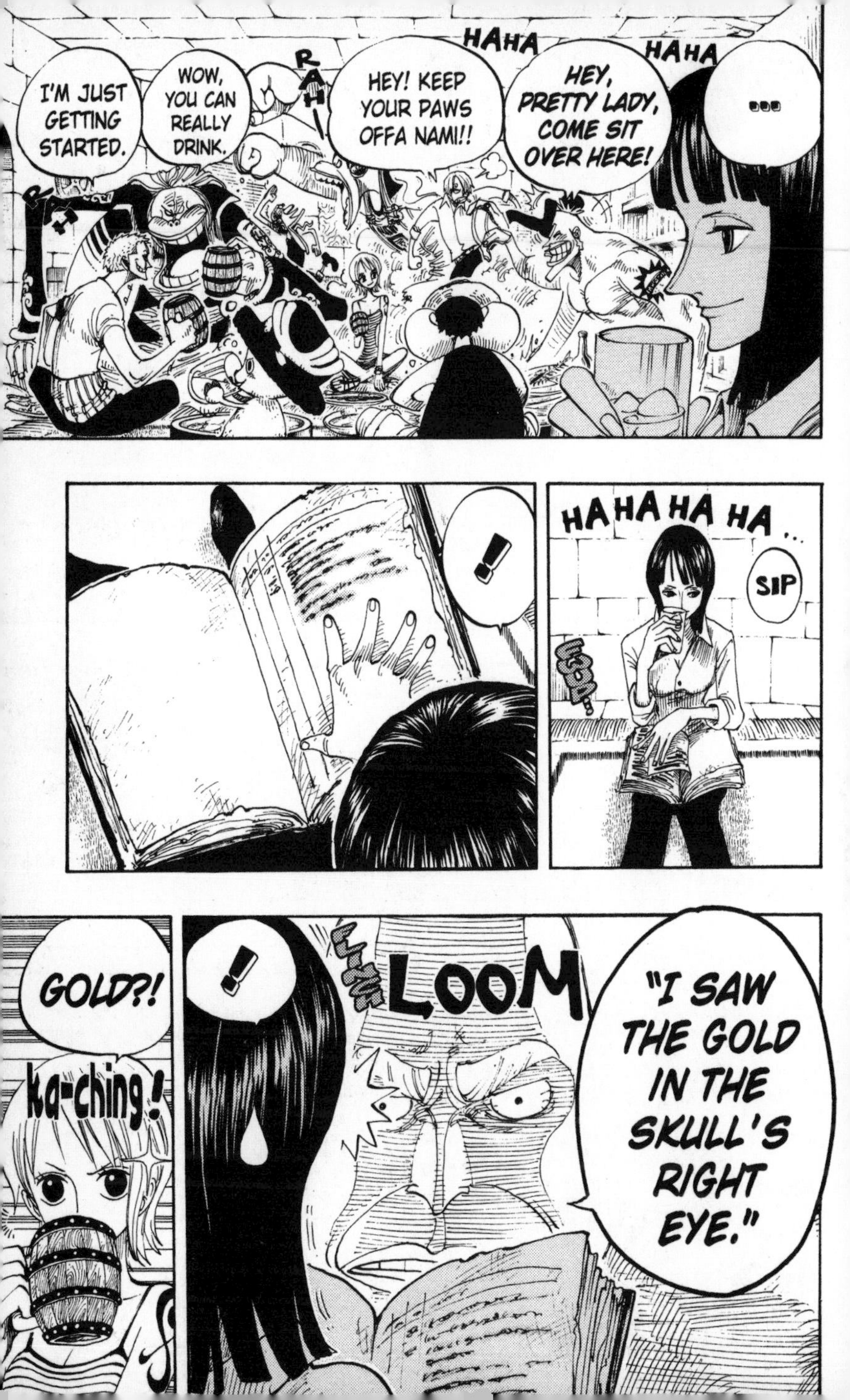
...
HAHA
HEY, PRETTY LADY, COME SIT OVER HERE!
HAHA
HEY! KEEP YOUR PAWS OFFA NAMI!!
RAH!
WOW, YOU CAN REALLY DRINK.
I'M JUST GETTING STARTED.
HAHAHA HA HA...
SIP
!
"I SAW THE GOLD IN THE SKULL'S RIGHT EYE."
LOOM
!
GOLD?!
ka-ching!

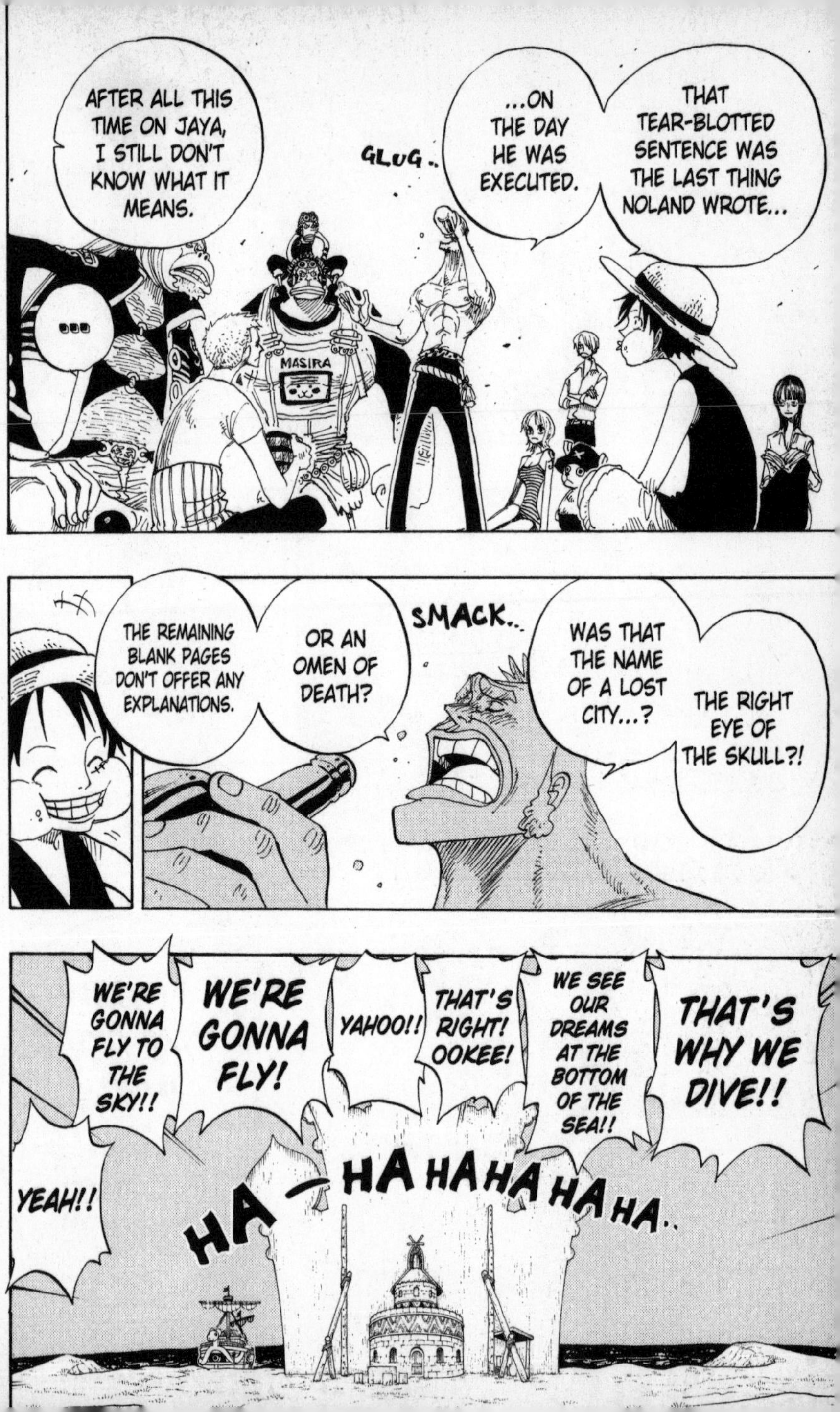
THAT TEAR-BLOTTED SENTENCE WAS THE LAST THING NOLAND WROTE...
...ON THE DAY HE WAS EXECUTED.
GLUG..
AFTER ALL THIS TIME ON JAYA, I STILL DON'T KNOW WHAT IT MEANS.
...
THE RIGHT EYE OF THE SKULL?!
WAS THAT THE NAME OF A LOST CITY...?
SMACK..
OR AN OMEN OF DEATH?
THE REMAINING BLANK PAGES DON'T OFFER ANY EXPLANATIONS.
THAT'S WHY WE DIVE!!
WE SEE OUR DREAMS AT THE BOTTOM OF THE SEA!!
THAT'S RIGHT! OOKEE!
YAHOO!!
WE'RE GONNA FLY!
WE'RE GONNA FLY TO THE SKY!!
YEAH!!
HA—HA HA HA HA HA HA HA..

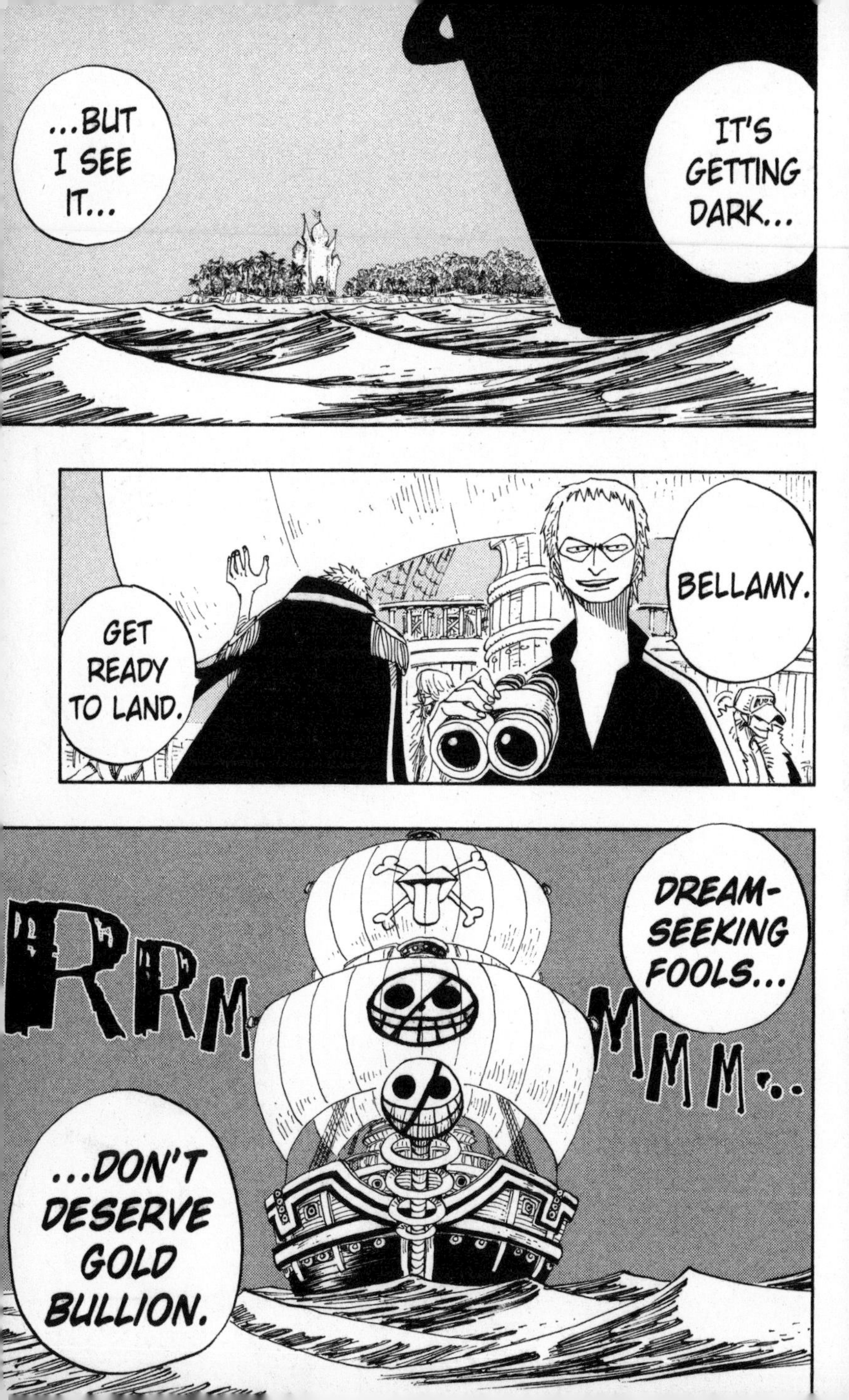
IT'S GETTING DARK...
...BUT I SEE IT...
BELLAMY.
GET READY TO LAND.
DREAM-SEEKING FOOLS...
RRRMMMMM...
...DON'T DESERVE GOLD BULLION.

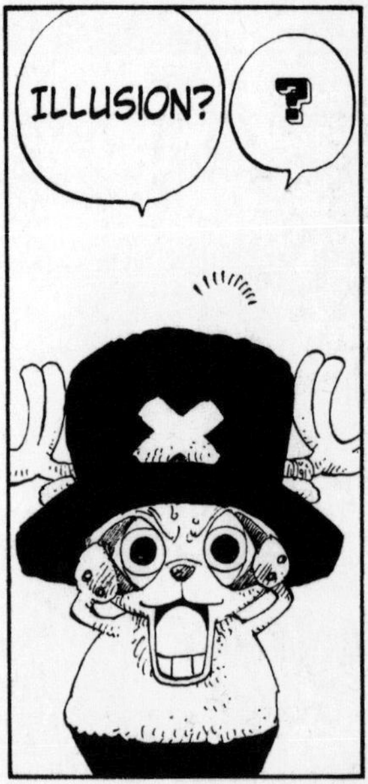
ILLUSION?
?

# Chapter 230:
# PURSUE THE SOUTH BIRD!

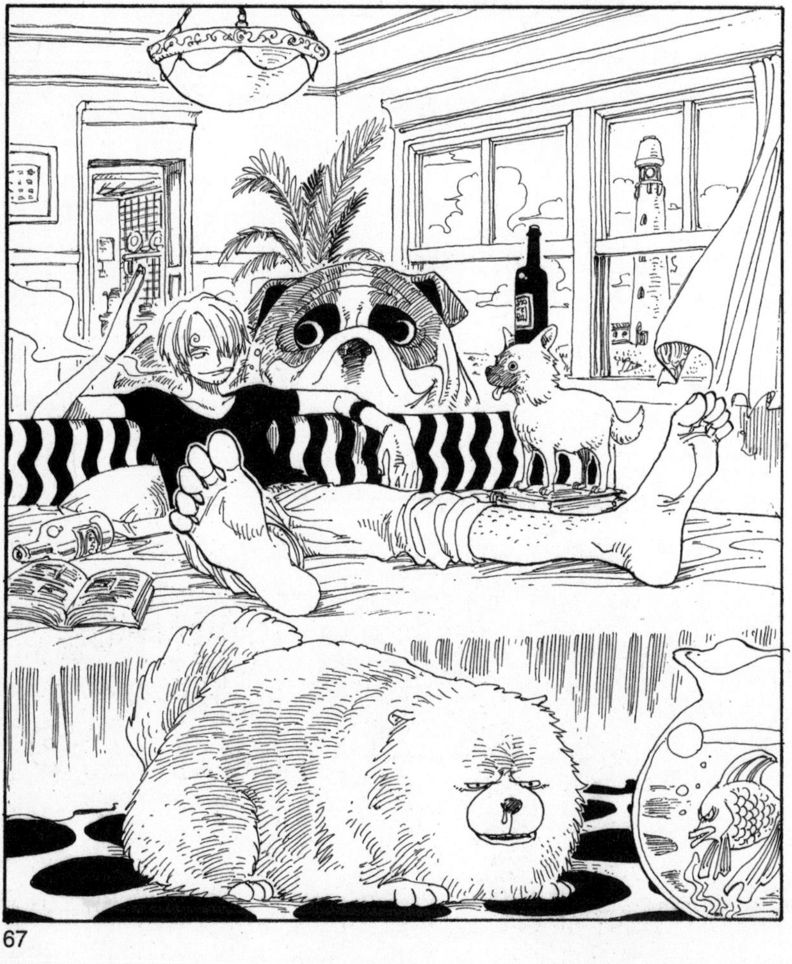

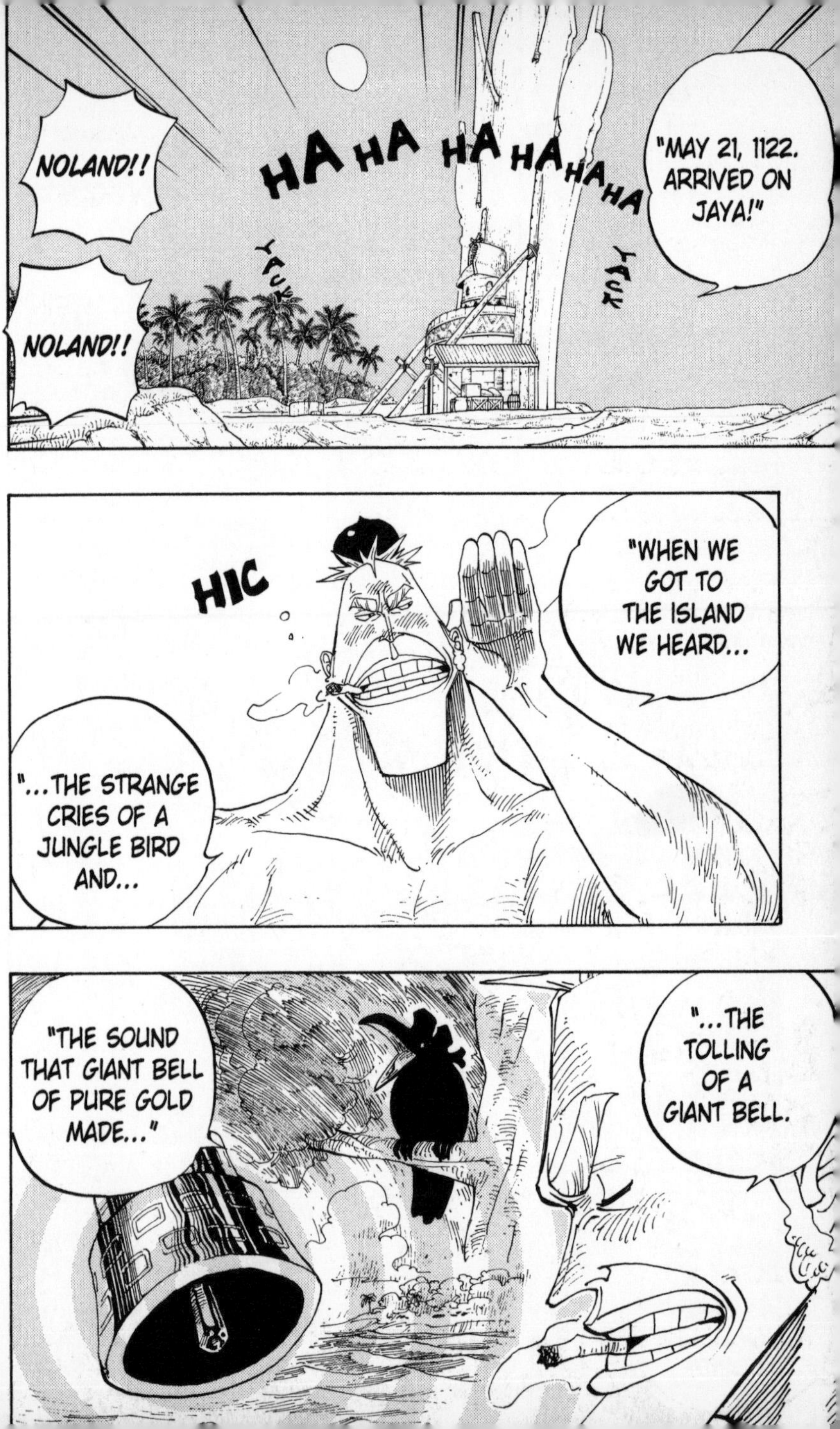
"MAY 21, 1122. ARRIVED ON JAYA!"
YAUK
HA HA HA HA HA HA HA HA
YAUK
NOLAND!!
NOLAND!!
"WHEN WE GOT TO THE ISLAND WE HEARD...
HIC
"...THE STRANGE CRIES OF A JUNGLE BIRD AND...
"...THE TOLLING OF A GIANT BELL.
"THE SOUND THAT GIANT BELL OF PURE GOLD MADE..."

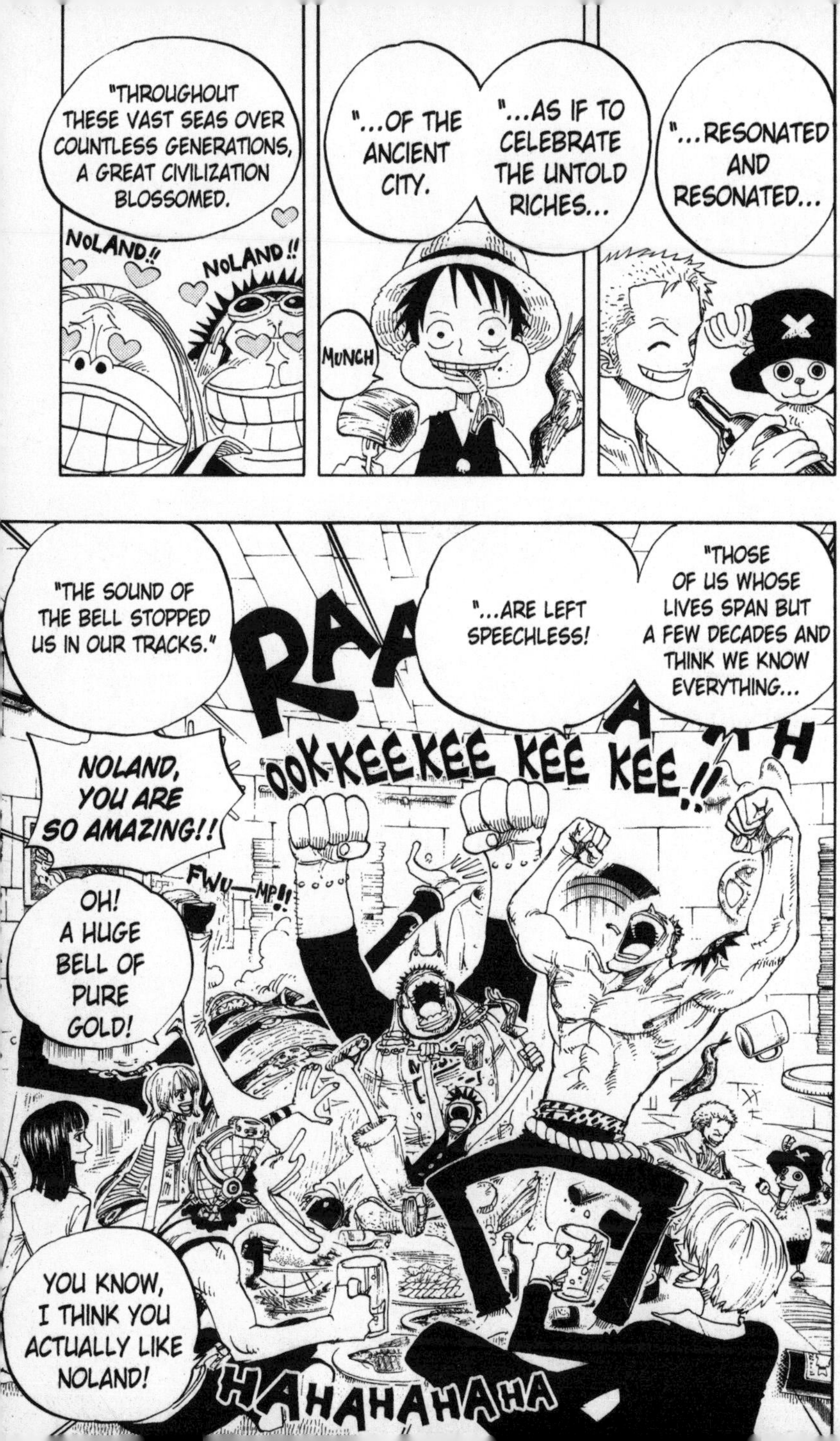
"...RESONATED AND RESONATED...
"...AS IF TO CELEBRATE THE UNTOLD RICHES...
"...OF THE ANCIENT CITY.
MUNCH
"THROUGHOUT THESE VAST SEAS OVER COUNTLESS GENERATIONS, A GREAT CIVILIZATION BLOSSOMED.
NOLAND!!
NOLAND!!
"THOSE OF US WHOSE LIVES SPAN BUT A FEW DECADES AND THINK WE KNOW EVERYTHING...
"...ARE LEFT SPEECHLESS!
"THE SOUND OF THE BELL STOPPED US IN OUR TRACKS."
RAAAH
OOKKEEKEE KEE KEE!!
NOLAND, YOU ARE SO AMAZING!!
FWU—MP!!
OH! A HUGE BELL OF PURE GOLD!
YOU KNOW, I THINK YOU ACTUALLY LIKE NOLAND!
HAHAHAHAHAHA

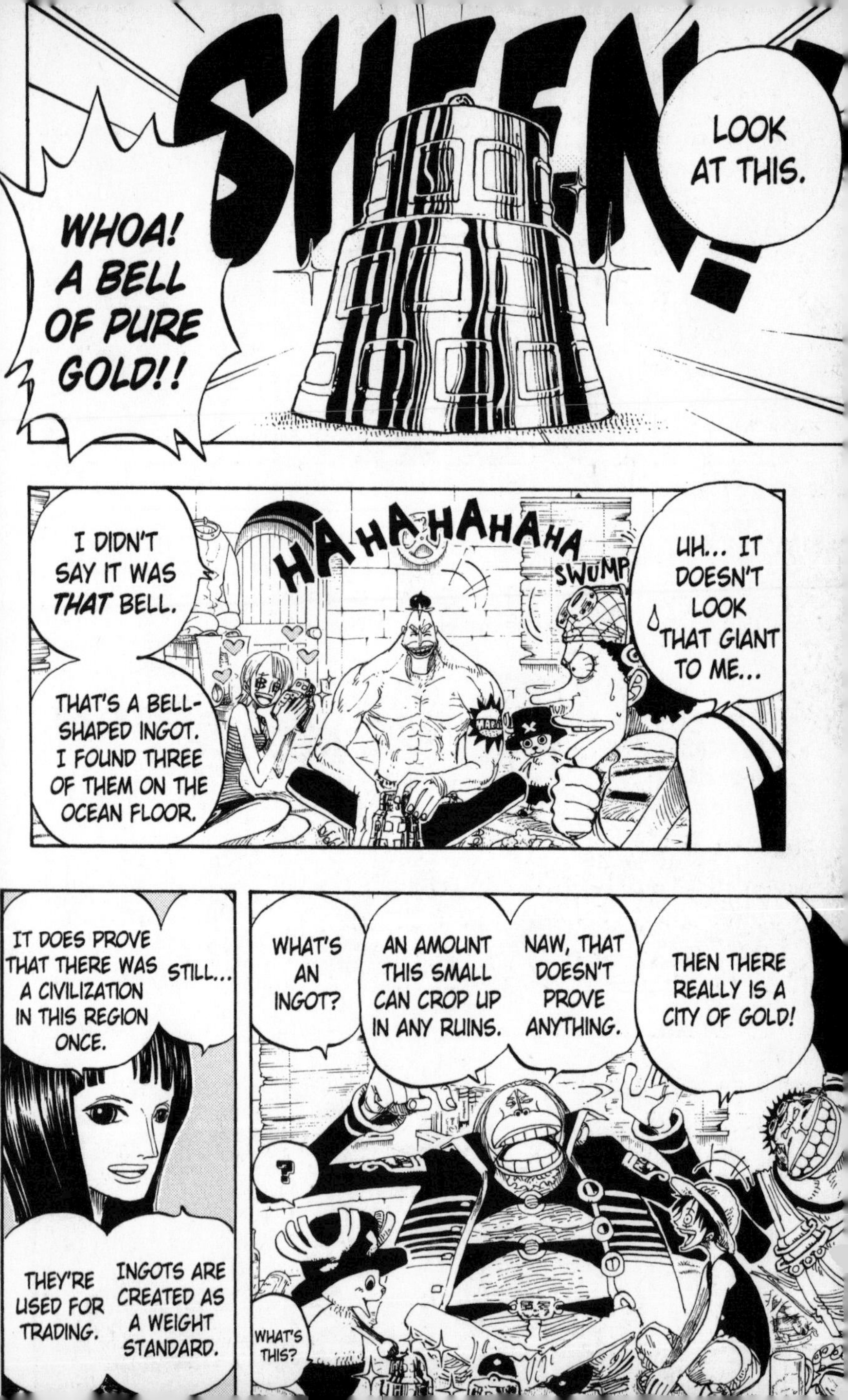
SHEEN!
LOOK AT THIS.
WHOA! A BELL OF PURE GOLD!!
UH... IT DOESN'T LOOK THAT GIANT TO ME...
SWUMP
HAHAHAHAHAHA
I DIDN'T SAY IT WAS *THAT* BELL.
THAT'S A BELL-SHAPED INGOT. I FOUND THREE OF THEM ON THE OCEAN FLOOR.
THEN THERE REALLY IS A CITY OF GOLD!
NAW, THAT DOESN'T PROVE ANYTHING.
AN AMOUNT THIS SMALL CAN CROP UP IN ANY RUINS.
WHAT'S AN INGOT?
WHAT'S THIS?
STILL...
IT DOES PROVE THAT THERE WAS A CIVILIZATION IN THIS REGION ONCE.
INGOTS ARE CREATED AS A WEIGHT STANDARD.
THEY'RE USED FOR TRADING.

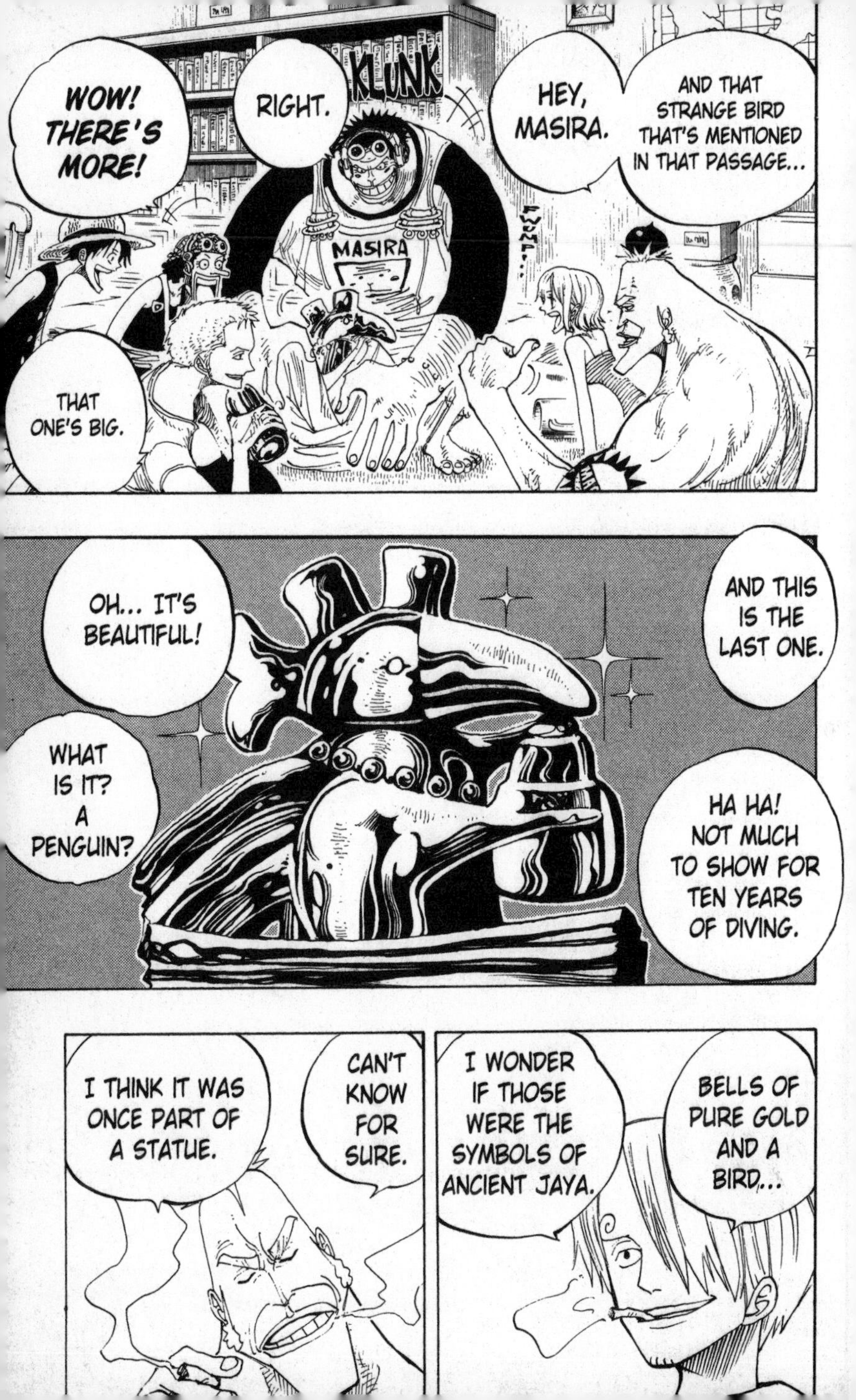
AND THAT STRANGE BIRD THAT'S MENTIONED IN THAT PASSAGE...
HEY, MASIRA.
KLUNK
RIGHT.
FWUMP!!
WOW! THERE'S MORE!
THAT ONE'S BIG.
AND THIS IS THE LAST ONE.
OH... IT'S BEAUTIFUL!
HA HA! NOT MUCH TO SHOW FOR TEN YEARS OF DIVING.
WHAT IS IT? A PENGUIN?
BELLS OF PURE GOLD AND A BIRD...
I WONDER IF THOSE WERE THE SYMBOLS OF ANCIENT JAYA.
CAN'T KNOW FOR SURE.
I THINK IT WAS ONCE PART OF A STATUE.

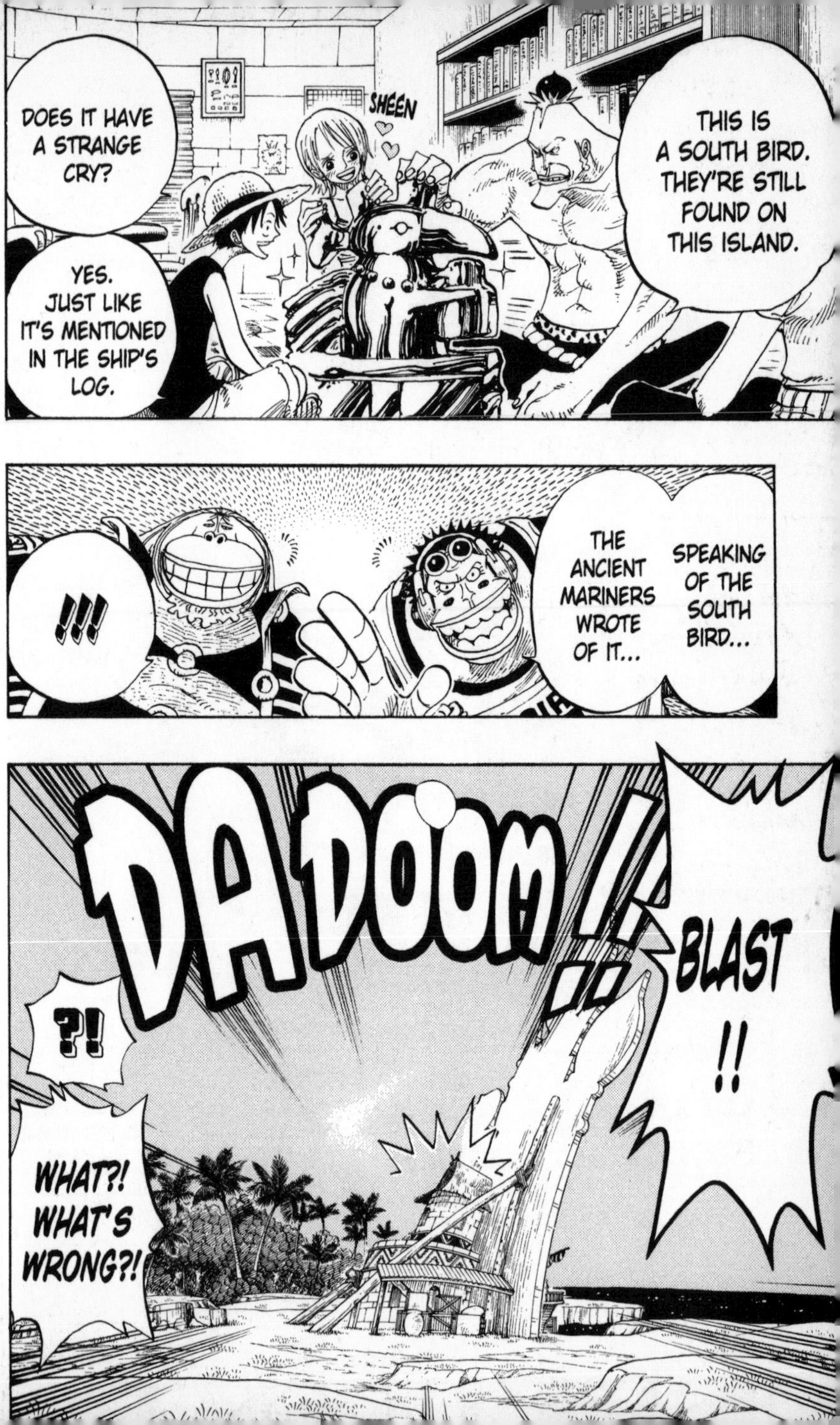
THIS IS A SOUTH BIRD. THEY'RE STILL FOUND ON THIS ISLAND.
SHEEN
DOES IT HAVE A STRANGE CRY?
YES. JUST LIKE IT'S MENTIONED IN THE SHIP'S LOG.
SPEAKING OF THE SOUTH BIRD...
THE ANCIENT MARINERS WROTE OF IT...
!!!
BLAST!!
DADOOM!!
?!
WHAT?! WHAT'S WRONG?!

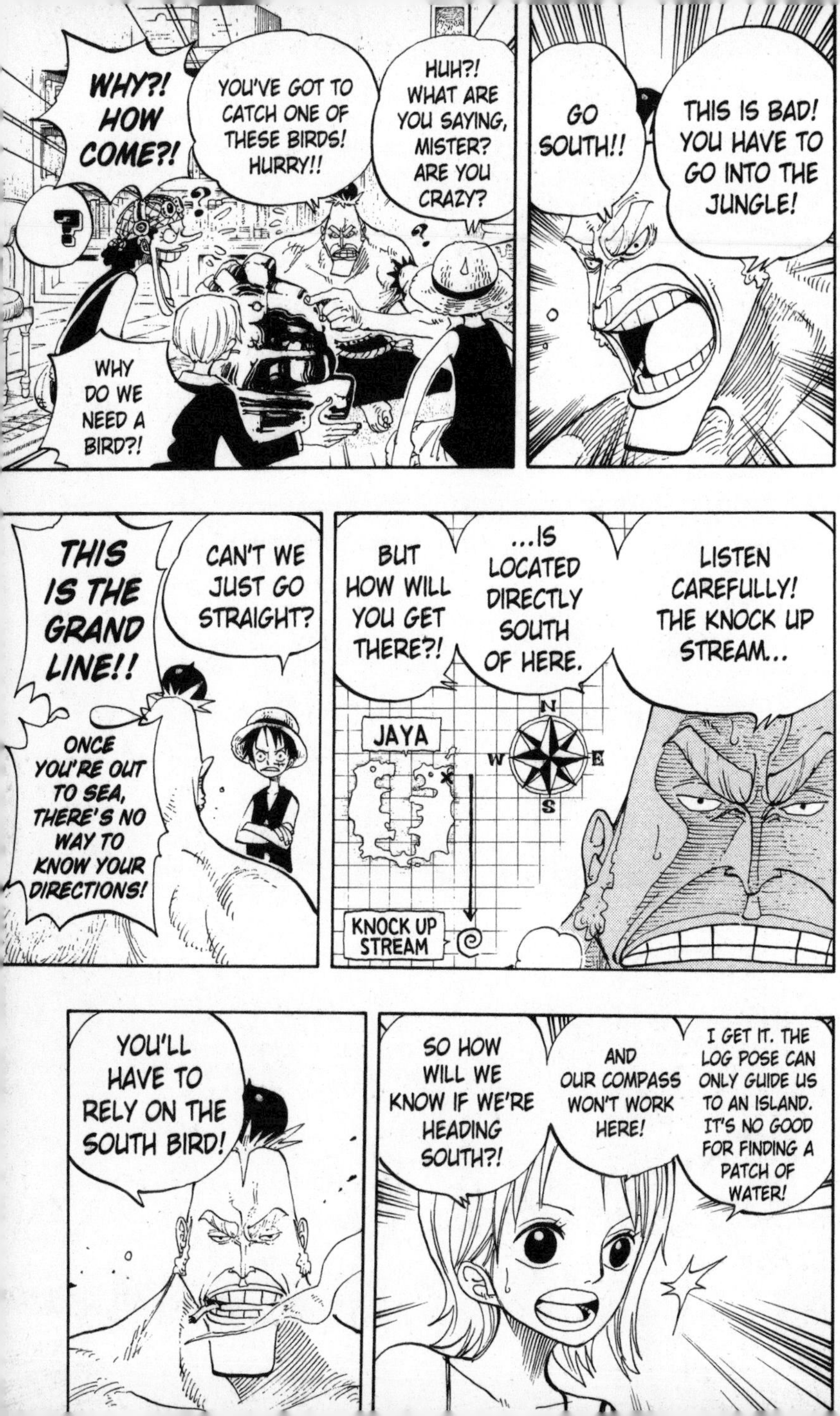
THIS IS BAD! YOU HAVE TO GO INTO THE JUNGLE!
GO SOUTH!!
HUH?! WHAT ARE YOU SAYING, MISTER? ARE YOU CRAZY?
YOU'VE GOT TO CATCH ONE OF THESE BIRDS! HURRY!!
WHY?! HOW COME?!
?
WHY DO WE NEED A BIRD?!
LISTEN CAREFULLY! THE KNOCK UP STREAM...
...IS LOCATED DIRECTLY SOUTH OF HERE.
BUT HOW WILL YOU GET THERE?!
N
W
E
S
JAYA
KNOCK UP STREAM
CAN'T WE JUST GO STRAIGHT?
THIS IS THE GRAND LINE!!
ONCE YOU'RE OUT TO SEA, THERE'S NO WAY TO KNOW YOUR DIRECTIONS!
I GET IT. THE LOG POSE CAN ONLY GUIDE US TO AN ISLAND. IT'S NO GOOD FOR FINDING A PATCH OF WATER!
AND OUR COMPASS WON'T WORK HERE!
SO HOW WILL WE KNOW IF WE'RE HEADING SOUTH?!
YOU'LL HAVE TO RELY ON THE SOUTH BIRD!

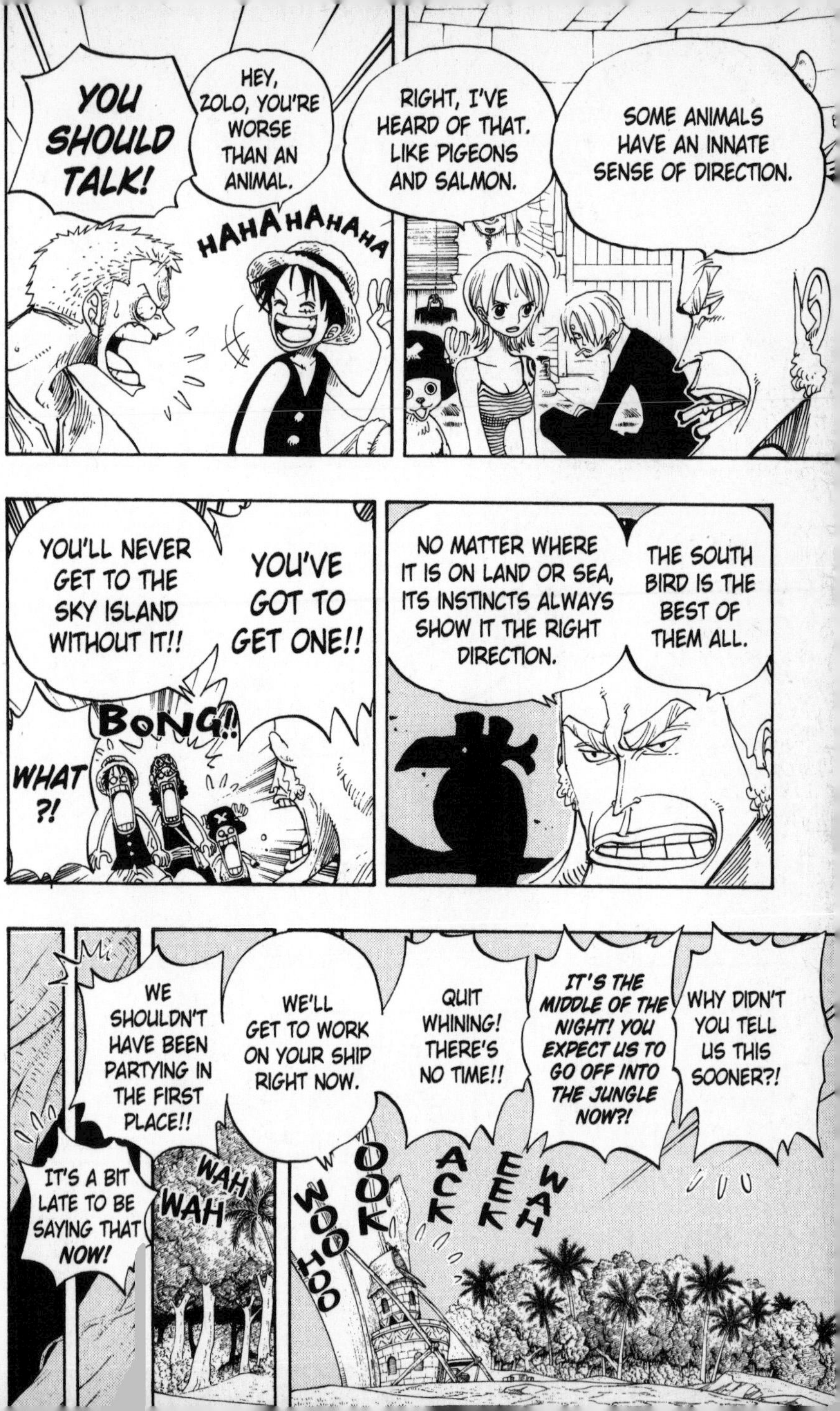
SOME ANIMALS HAVE AN INNATE SENSE OF DIRECTION.
RIGHT, I'VE HEARD OF THAT. LIKE PIGEONS AND SALMON.
HEY, ZOLO, YOU'RE WORSE THAN AN ANIMAL.
HAHAHAHAHAHA
YOU SHOULD TALK!
THE SOUTH BIRD IS THE BEST OF THEM ALL.
NO MATTER WHERE IT IS ON LAND OR SEA, ITS INSTINCTS ALWAYS SHOW IT THE RIGHT DIRECTION.
YOU'VE GOT TO GET ONE!!
YOU'LL NEVER GET TO THE SKY ISLAND WITHOUT IT!!
BONG!!
WHAT?!
WHY DIDN'T YOU TELL US THIS SOONER?!
IT'S THE MIDDLE OF THE NIGHT! YOU EXPECT US TO GO OFF INTO THE JUNGLE NOW?!
QUIT WHINING! THERE'S NO TIME!!
WE'LL GET TO WORK ON YOUR SHIP RIGHT NOW.
WE SHOULDN'T HAVE BEEN PARTYING IN THE FIRST PLACE!!
WAH
EEK
ACK
OOK
WOOHOO
WAH WAH
IT'S A BIT LATE TO BE SAYING THAT NOW!

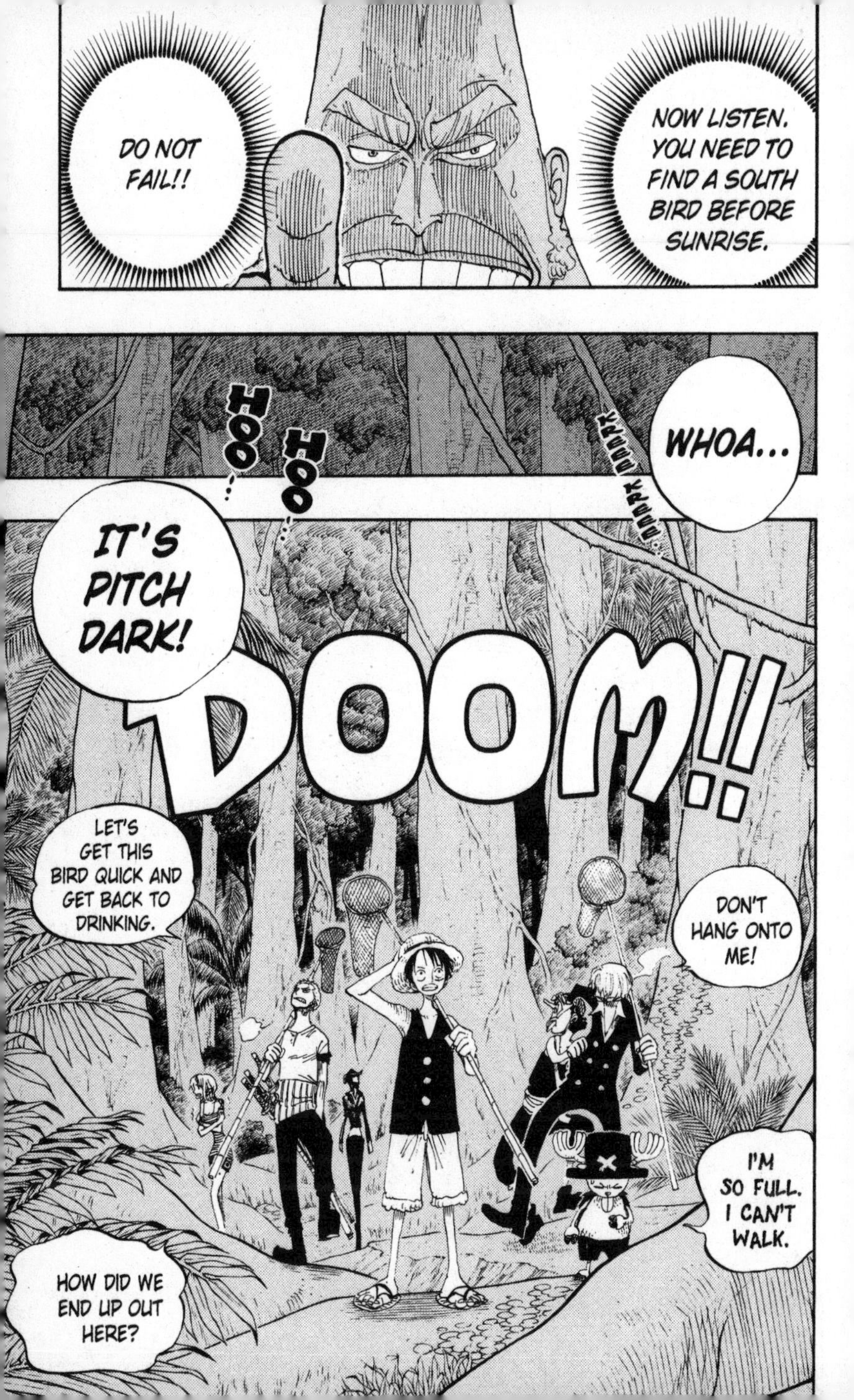
NOW LISTEN. YOU NEED TO FIND A SOUTH BIRD BEFORE SUNRISE.
DO NOT FAIL!!
WHOA...
KREEEE KREEE...
HOO... HOO...
IT'S PITCH DARK!
DOOM!!
DON'T HANG ONTO ME!
I'M SO FULL. I CAN'T WALK.
LET'S GET THIS BIRD QUICK AND GET BACK TO DRINKING.
HOW DID WE END UP OUT HERE?

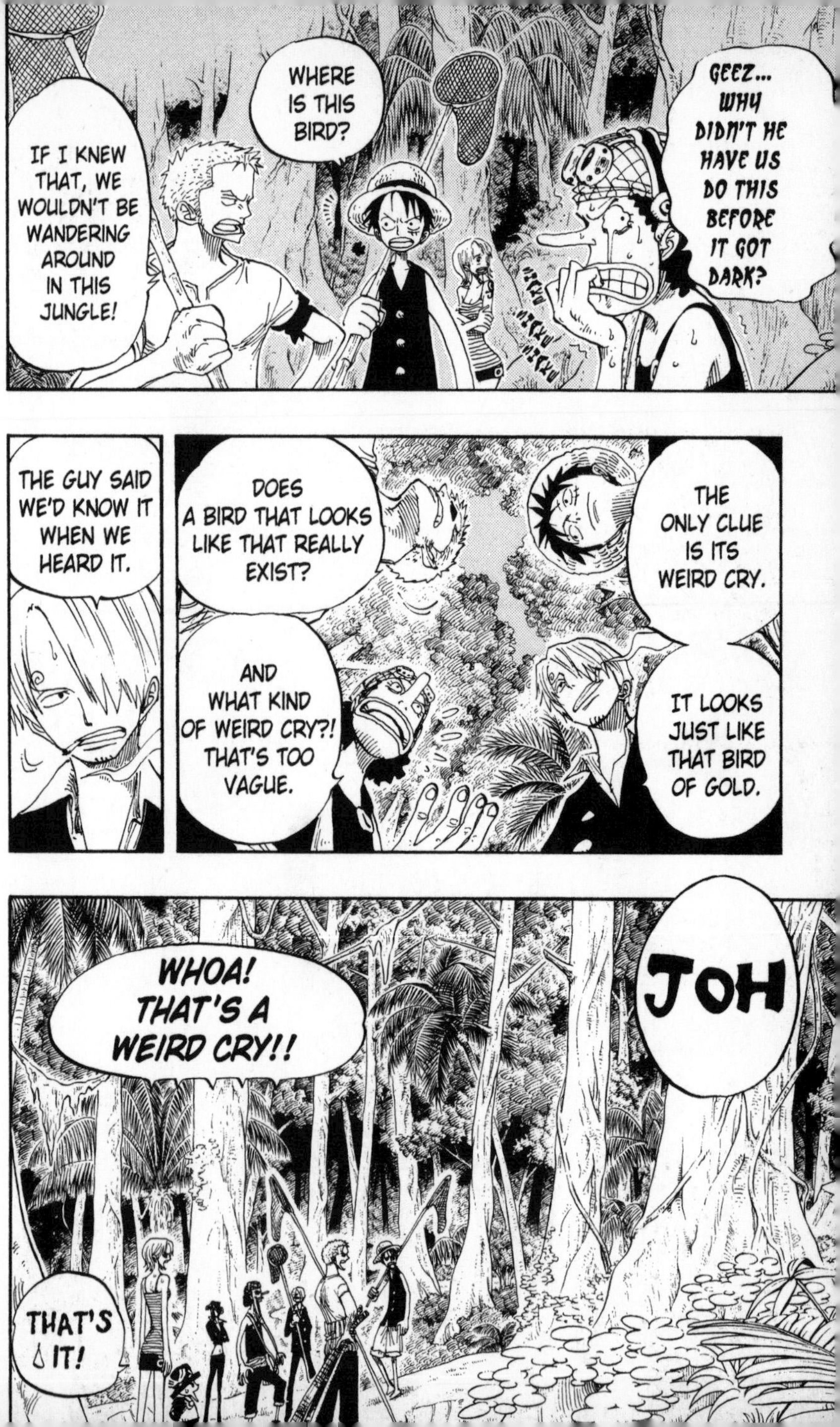
GEEZ... WHY DIDN'T HE HAVE US DO THIS BEFORE IT GOT DARK?
WHERE IS THIS BIRD?
IF I KNEW THAT, WE WOULDN'T BE WANDERING AROUND IN THIS JUNGLE!
THE ONLY CLUE IS ITS WEIRD CRY.
DOES A BIRD THAT LOOKS LIKE THAT REALLY EXIST?
IT LOOKS JUST LIKE THAT BIRD OF GOLD.
AND WHAT KIND OF WEIRD CRY?! THAT'S TOO VAGUE.
THE GUY SAID WE'D KNOW IT WHEN WE HEARD IT.
JOH
WHOA! THAT'S A WEIRD CRY!!
THAT'S IT!

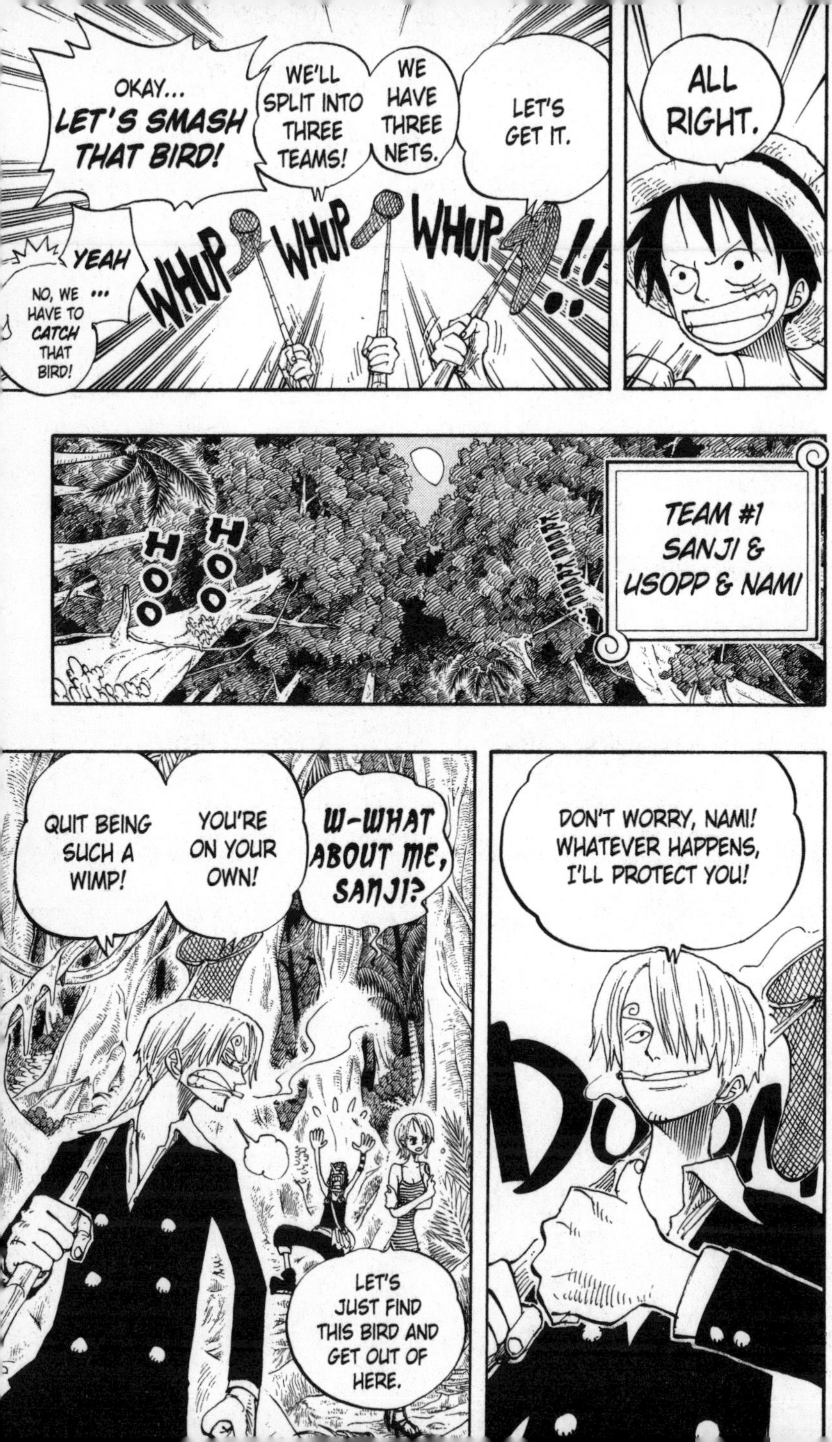
ALL RIGHT.
LET'S GET IT.
WE HAVE THREE NETS.
WE'LL SPLIT INTO THREE TEAMS!
OKAY... LET'S SMASH THAT BIRD!
!!
WHUP
WHUP
WHUP
YEAH
NO, WE... HAVE TO CATCH THAT BIRD!
TEAM #1
SANJI & USOPP & NAMI
HOO
HOO
DON'T WORRY, NAMI! WHATEVER HAPPENS, I'LL PROTECT YOU!
W-WHAT ABOUT ME, SANJI?
YOU'RE ON YOUR OWN!
QUIT BEING SUCH A WIMP!
LET'S JUST FIND THIS BIRD AND GET OUT OF HERE.

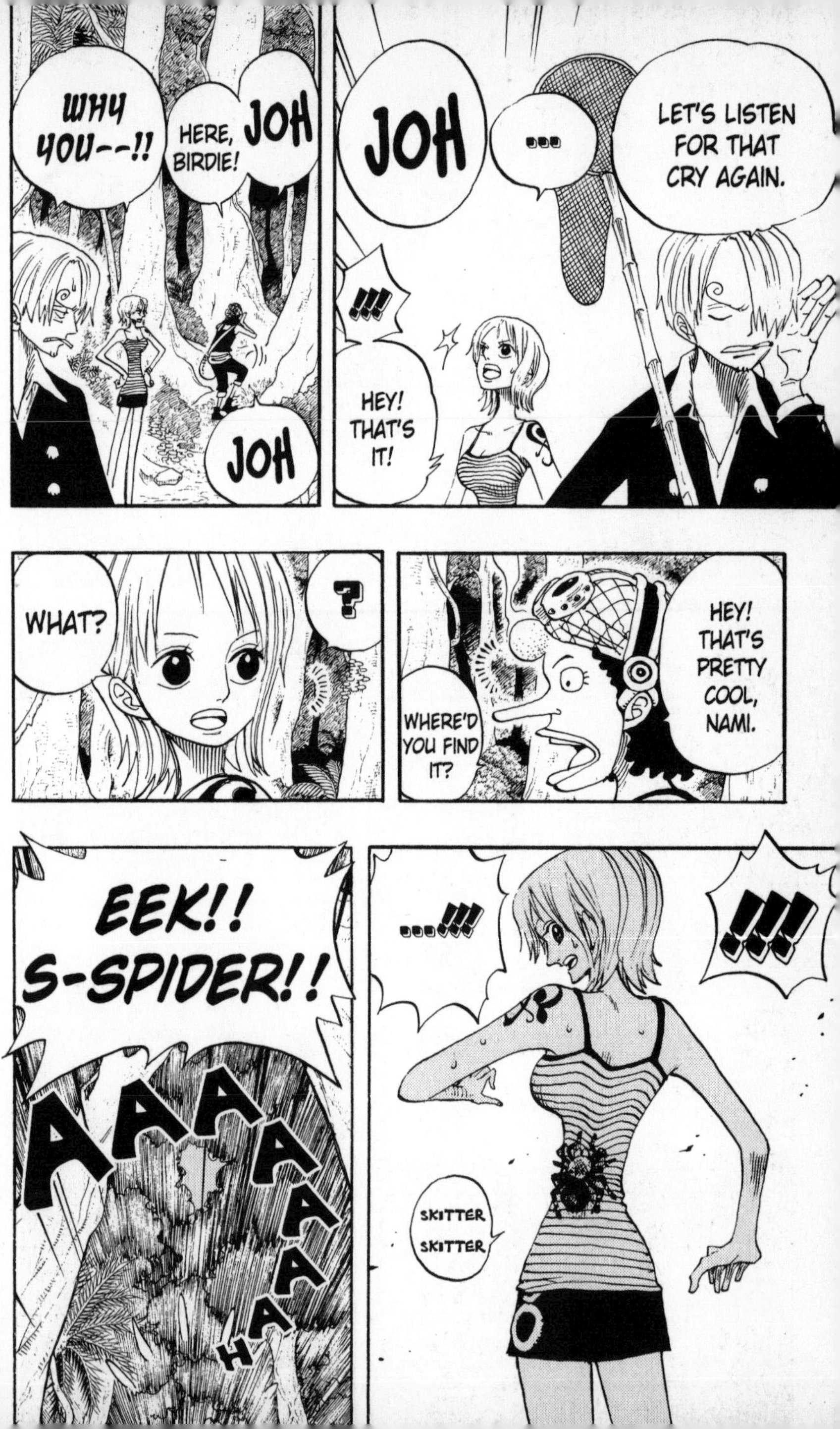
LET'S LISTEN FOR THAT CRY AGAIN.
...
JOH
!!!
HEY! THAT'S IT!
JOH
HERE, BIRDIE!
WHY YOU--!!
JOH
HEY! THAT'S PRETTY COOL, NAMI.
WHERE'D YOU FIND IT?
?
WHAT?
!!!
...!!!
SKITTER SKITTER
EEK!! S-SPIDER!!
AAAAAAAAH

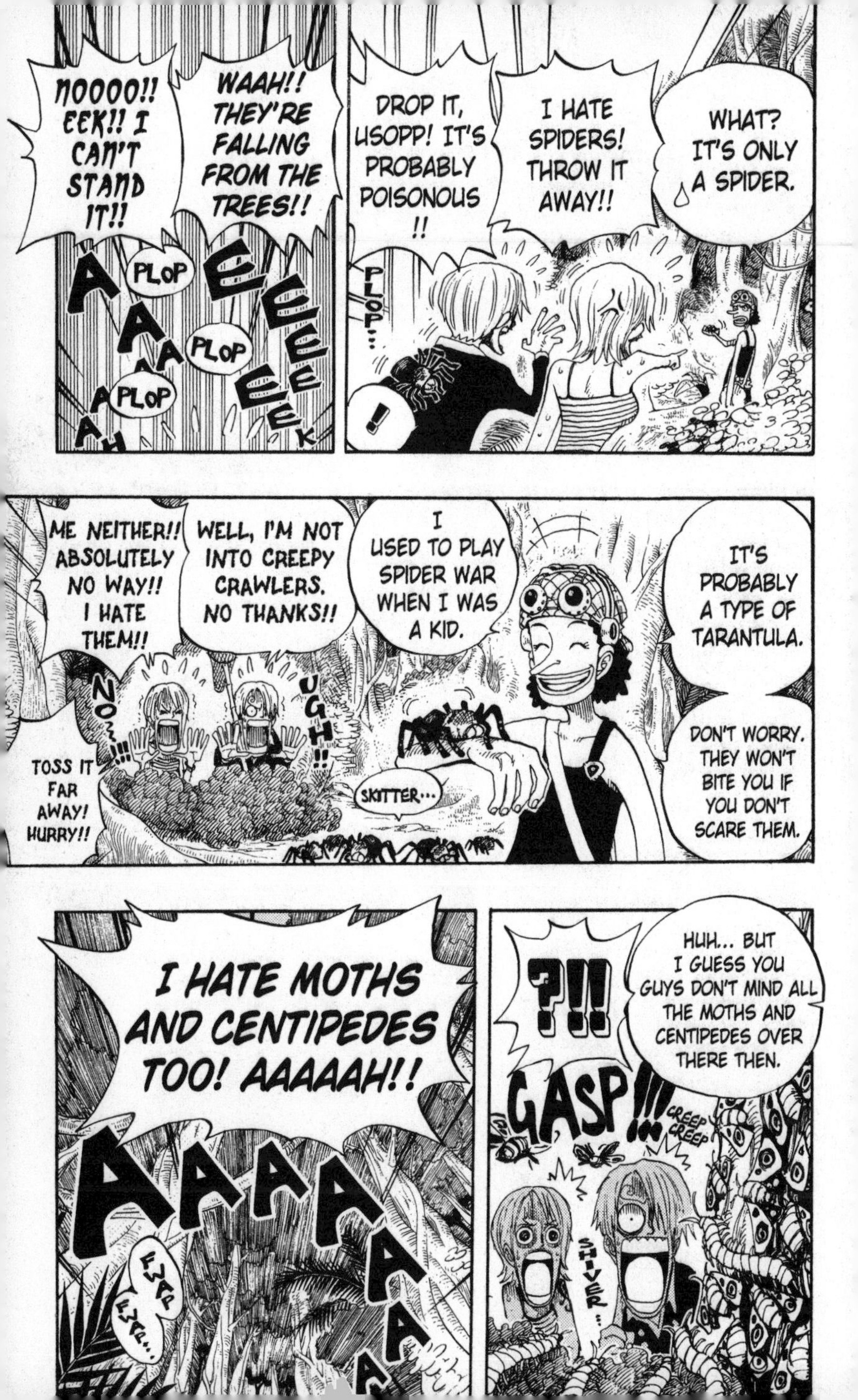
WHAT? IT'S ONLY A SPIDER.
I HATE SPIDERS! THROW IT AWAY!!
DROP IT, USOPP! IT'S PROBABLY POISONOUS!!
PLOP...
!
WAAH!! THEY'RE FALLING FROM THE TREES!!
NOOOO!! EEK!! I CAN'T STAND IT!!
EEEEEEEK
PLOP
PLOP
AAAAAH
PLOP
IT'S PROBABLY A TYPE OF TARANTULA.
DON'T WORRY. THEY WON'T BITE YOU IF YOU DON'T SCARE THEM.
I USED TO PLAY SPIDER WAR WHEN I WAS A KID.
SKITTER...
WELL, I'M NOT INTO CREEPY CRAWLERS. NO THANKS!!
UGH!!
ME NEITHER!! ABSOLUTELY NO WAY!! I HATE THEM!!
NO!!
TOSS IT FAR AWAY! HURRY!!
HUH... BUT I GUESS YOU GUYS DON'T MIND ALL THE MOTHS AND CENTIPEDES OVER THERE THEN.
?!!
GASP!!!
CREEP CREEP
SHIVER...
I HATE MOTHS AND CENTIPEDES TOO! AAAAAH!!
AAAAAAA
FWAP
FWAP...

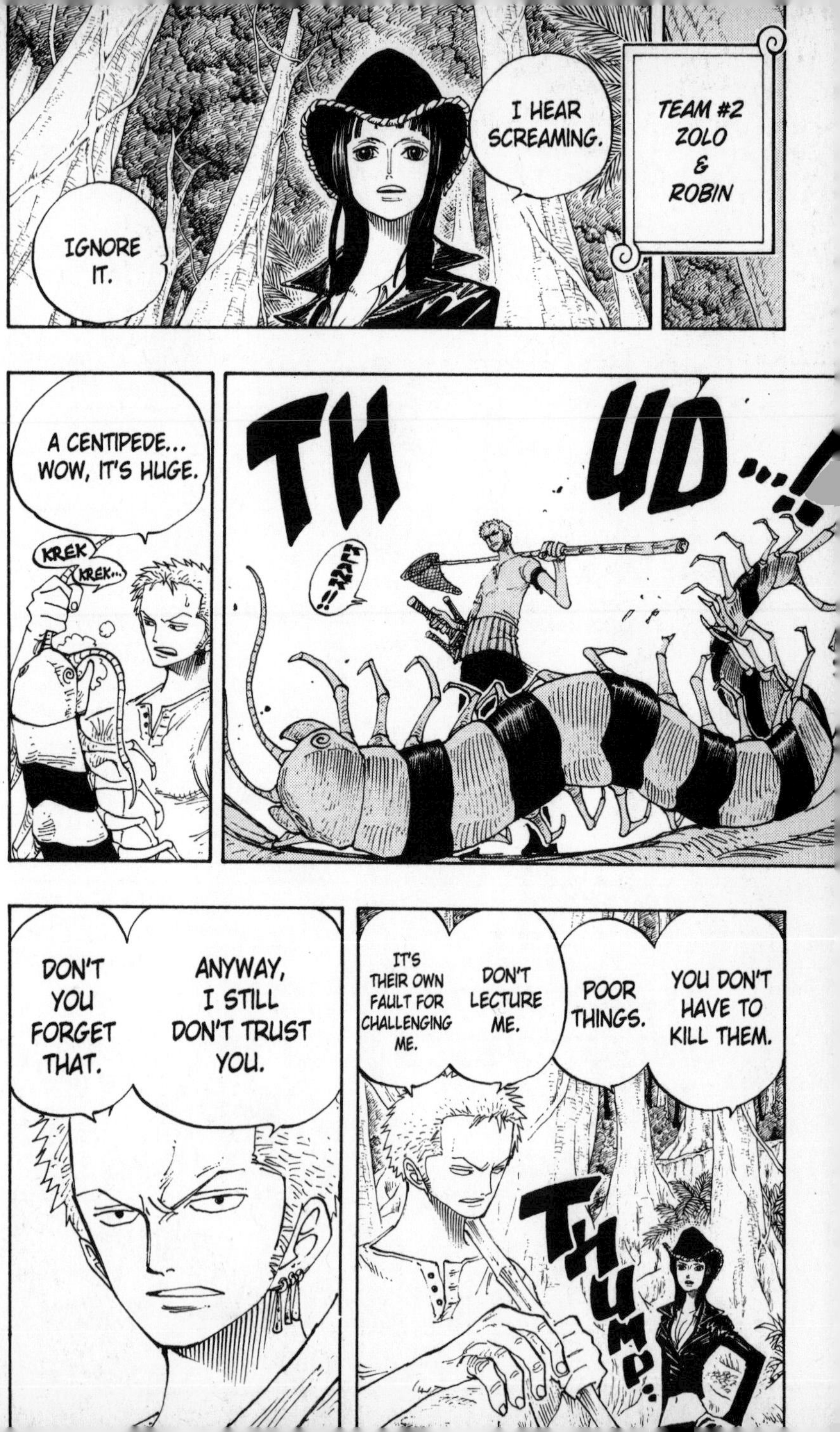
TEAM #2 ZOLO & ROBIN
I HEAR SCREAMING.
IGNORE IT.
THUD...!!
KLANK!!
A CENTIPEDE... WOW, IT'S HUGE.
KREK
KREK...
YOU DON'T HAVE TO KILL THEM.
POOR THINGS.
DON'T LECTURE ME.
IT'S THEIR OWN FAULT FOR CHALLENGING ME.
THUMP...
ANYWAY, I STILL DON'T TRUST YOU.
DON'T YOU FORGET THAT.

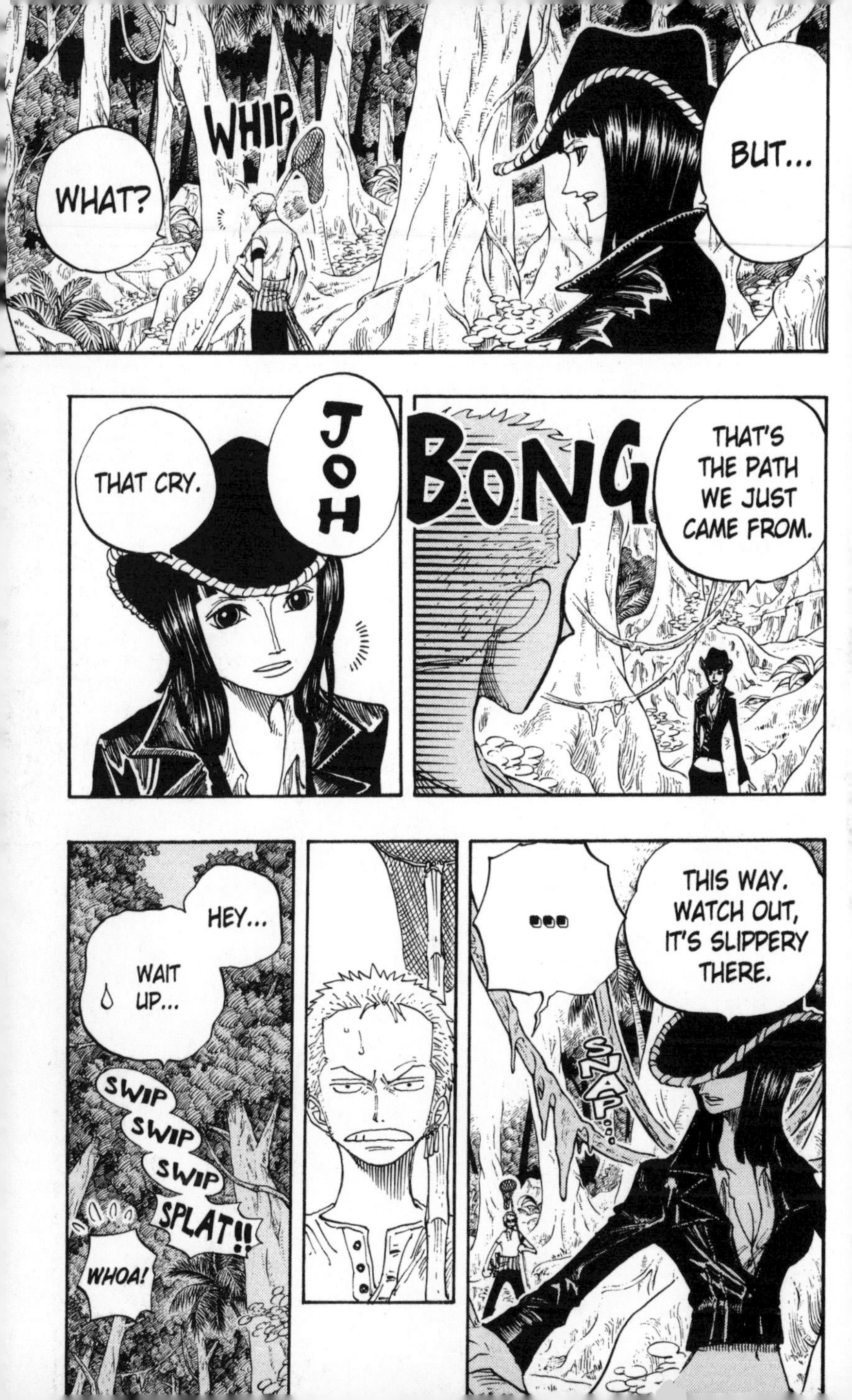
BUT...
WHIP
WHAT?
THAT'S THE PATH WE JUST CAME FROM.
BONG
JOH
THAT CRY.
THIS WAY. WATCH OUT, IT'S SLIPPERY THERE.
...
SNAP...
HEY...
WAIT UP...
SWIP
SWIP
SWIP
SPLAT!!
WHOA!

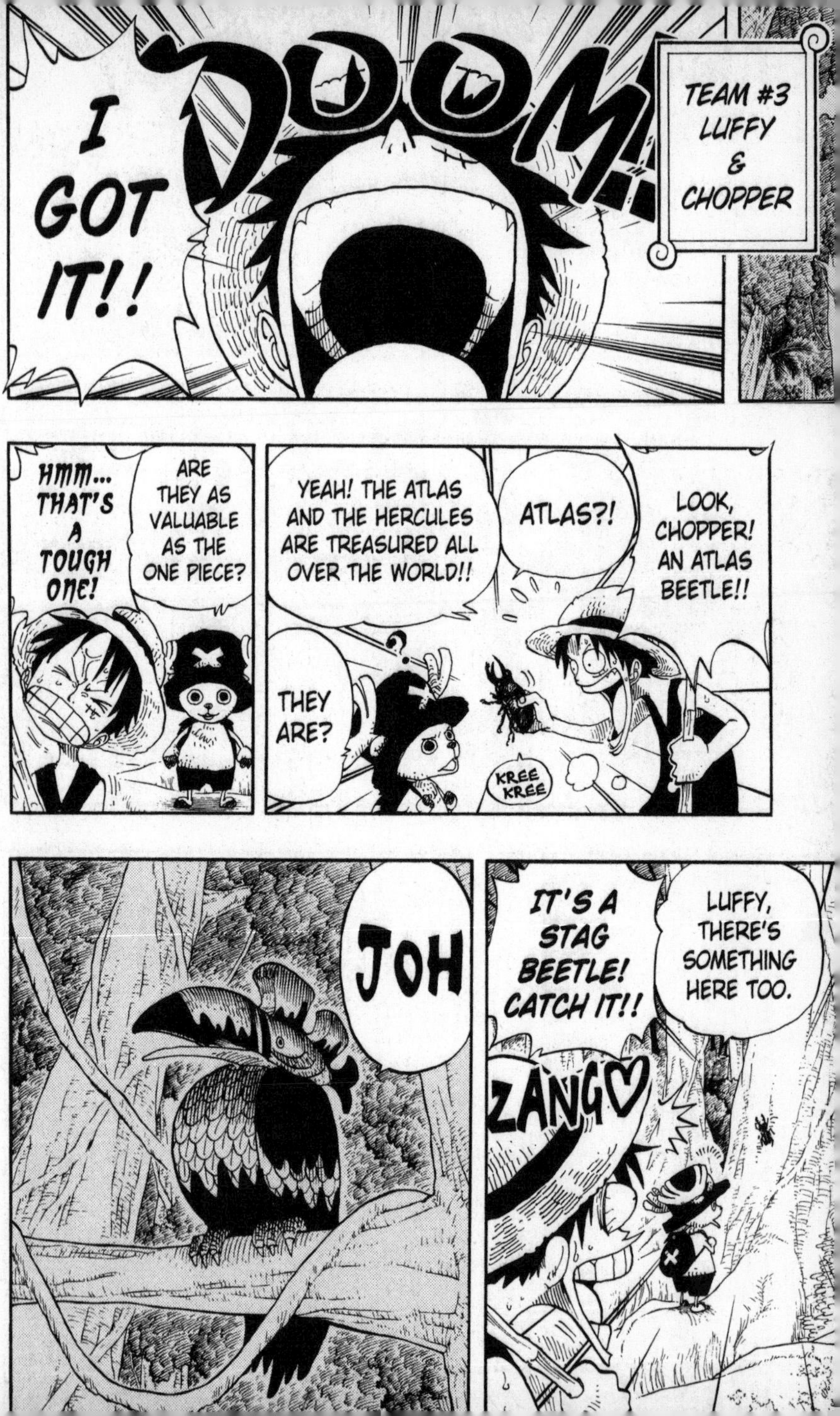
TEAM #3 LUFFY & CHOPPER
DOOM!!
I GOT IT!!
LOOK, CHOPPER! AN ATLAS BEETLE!!
ATLAS?!
YEAH! THE ATLAS AND THE HERCULES ARE TREASURED ALL OVER THE WORLD!!
THEY ARE?
KREE KREE
ARE THEY AS VALUABLE AS THE ONE PIECE?
HMM... THAT'S A TOUGH ONE!
LUFFY, THERE'S SOMETHING HERE TOO.
IT'S A STAG BEETLE! CATCH IT!!
ZANG♡
JOH

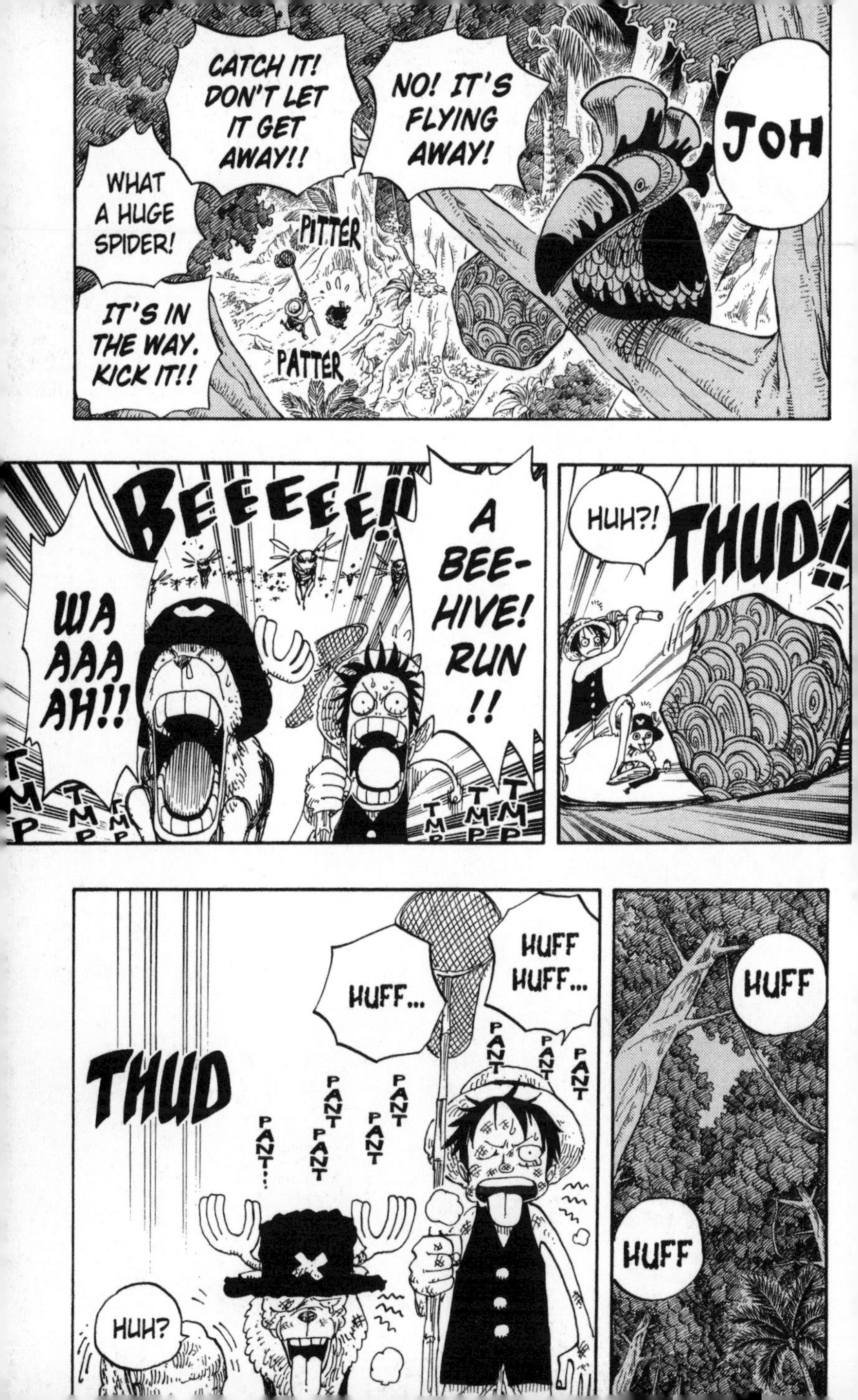
JOH
NO! IT'S FLYING AWAY!
CATCH IT! DON'T LET IT GET AWAY!!
WHAT A HUGE SPIDER!
PITTER
IT'S IN THE WAY. KICK IT!!
PATTER
HUH?!
THUD!!
A BEE-HIVE! RUN!!
BEEEEEE!!
TMP TMP TMP
WAAAAAH!!
TMP TMP TMP
HUFF
HUFF
HUFF HUFF...
HUFF...
PANT PANT PANT
PANT PANT PANT PANT...
THUD
HUH?

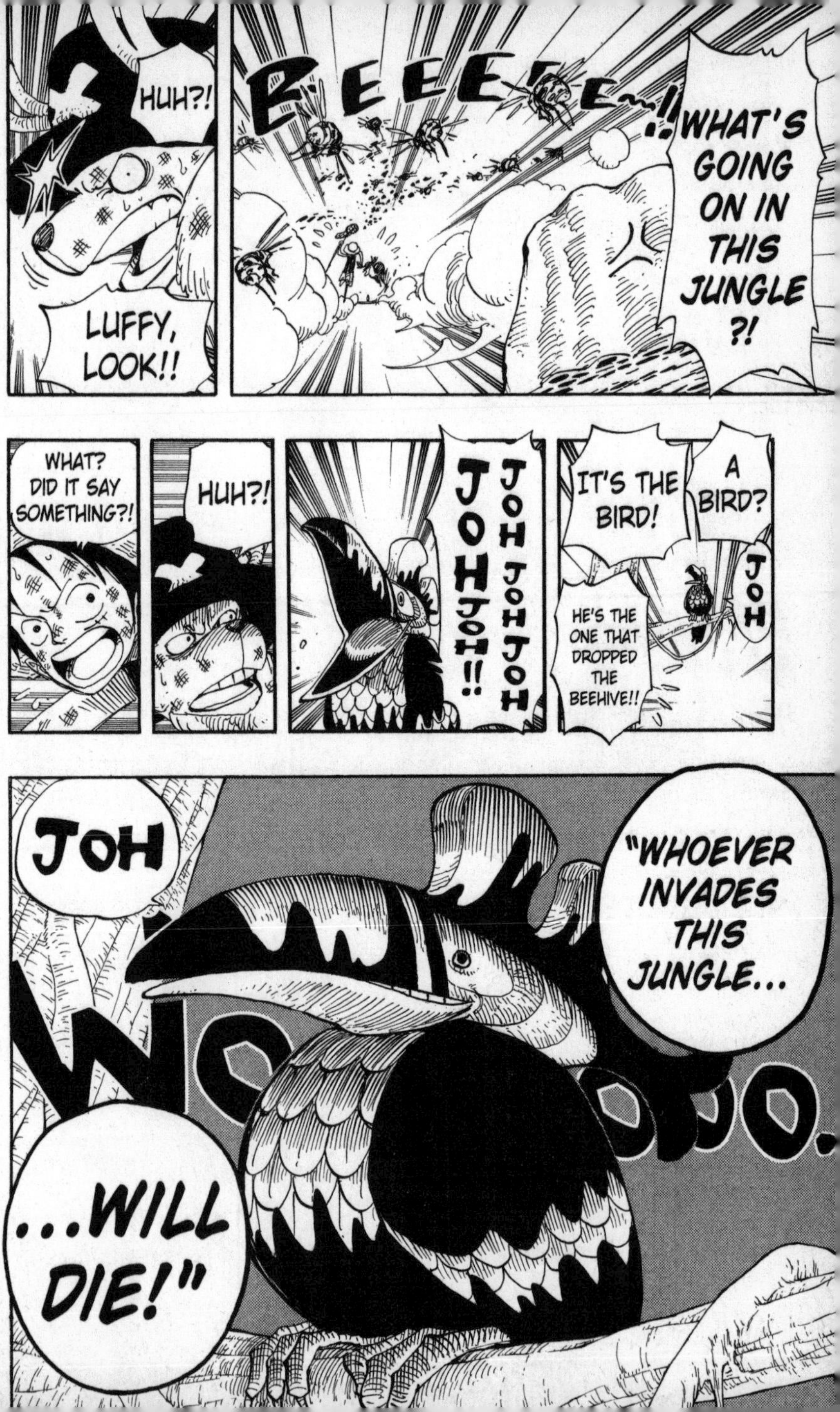
BEEEEE~!!
WHAT'S GOING ON IN THIS JUNGLE ?!
HUH?!
LUFFY, LOOK!!
A BIRD?
IT'S THE BIRD!
JOH
HE'S THE ONE THAT DROPPED THE BEEHIVE!!
JOH JOH JOH
JOH JOH!!
HUH?!
WHAT? DID IT SAY SOMETHING?!
"WHOEVER INVADES THIS JUNGLE...
JOH
...WILL DIE!"

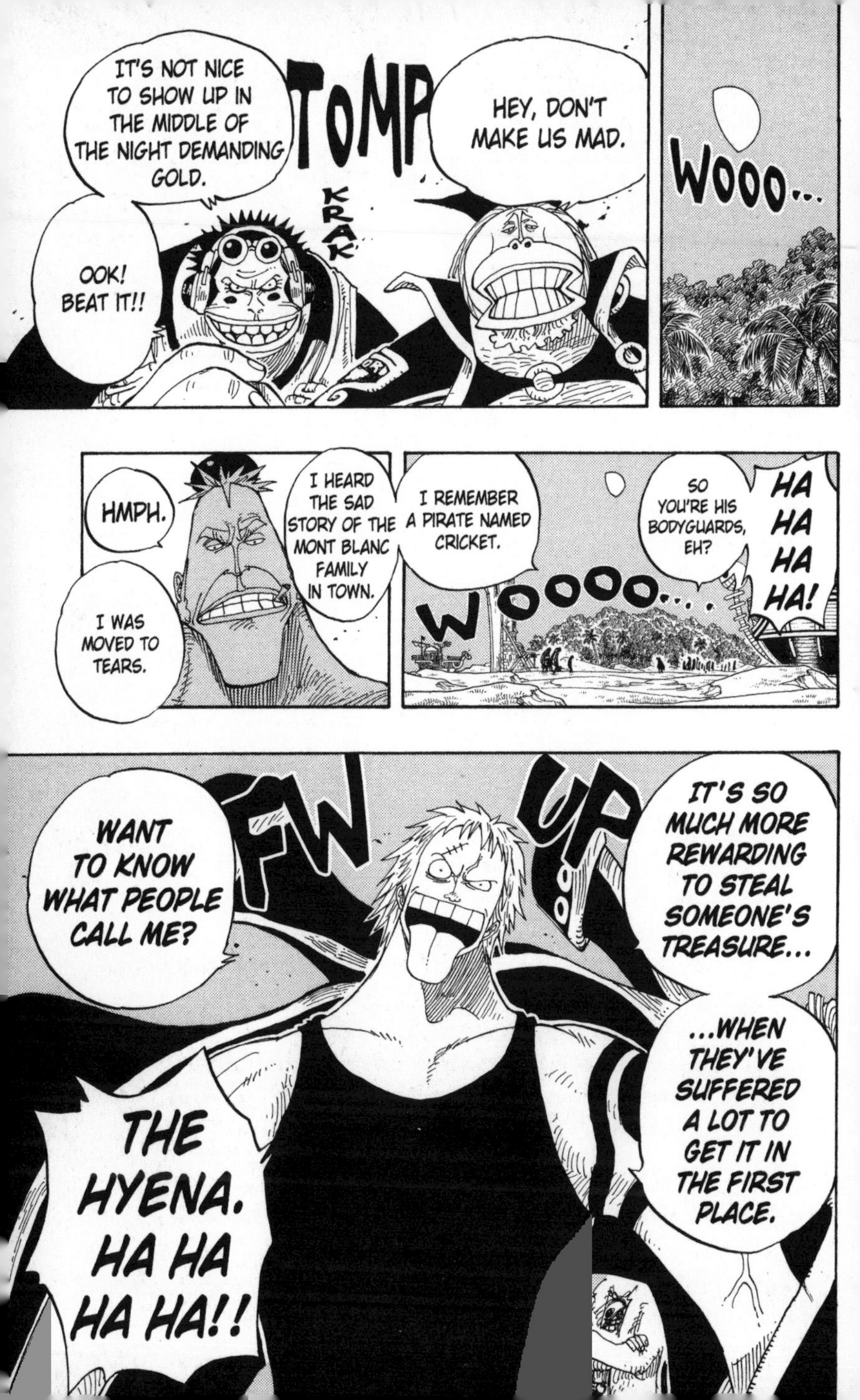
WOOO...
HEY, DON'T MAKE US MAD.
TOMP
IT'S NOT NICE TO SHOW UP IN THE MIDDLE OF THE NIGHT DEMANDING GOLD.
KRAK
OOK! BEAT IT!!
HA HA HA HA!
SO YOU'RE HIS BODYGUARDS, EH?
I REMEMBER A PIRATE NAMED CRICKET.
WOOOO...
I HEARD THE SAD STORY OF THE MONT BLANC FAMILY IN TOWN.
HMPH.
I WAS MOVED TO TEARS.
IT'S SO MUCH MORE REWARDING TO STEAL SOMEONE'S TREASURE...
FW
UP
WANT TO KNOW WHAT PEOPLE CALL ME?
...WHEN THEY'VE SUFFERED A LOT TO GET IT IN THE FIRST PLACE.
THE HYENA. HA HA HA HA!!

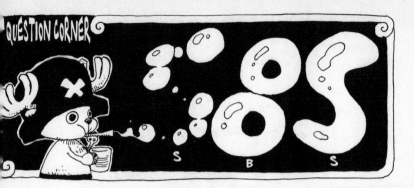

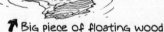

**QUESTION CORNER**

Reader: Uh, hello (x2), pleased to meet you, Oda Sensei! Nami uses the Tornado Tempo feature of her Climate Baton a lot. But what does tempo mean? Please tell me!

--Traveler (15 years old)

Oda: Tempo means weather in Italian. Tempo. I like the way it sounds.

Q: Mr. 3 has Devil Fruit powers, so how come in volume 19, page 185, panel 3, he's floating on the water?

A: I got a lot of inquiries about this one. There were lots of guesses, too. However, you're all wrong. There's a good reason for this. There just happened to be a big piece of floating wood under Mr. 3's body.

↗ Big piece of floating wood

Mr. 3 was floating on top of it. Anyway, on average, the bouyancy of a human is about three splays. A sumo wrestlers is about five splays. But that huge piece of wood was especially magnificent and had a record bouyancy of 13 splays. That's according to Floatus Stretchington.

Q: Hello, Oda Sensei. I'll come right to the point. Did you get the name "Bellamy the Hyena" from the English pirate Samuel "Black Sam" Bellamy?

A: That's right. Bellamy was a notorious, and very talkative, pirate. But maybe he was more like a lion than a hyena because he loved an audience.

# Chapter 231: BELLAMY THE HYENA

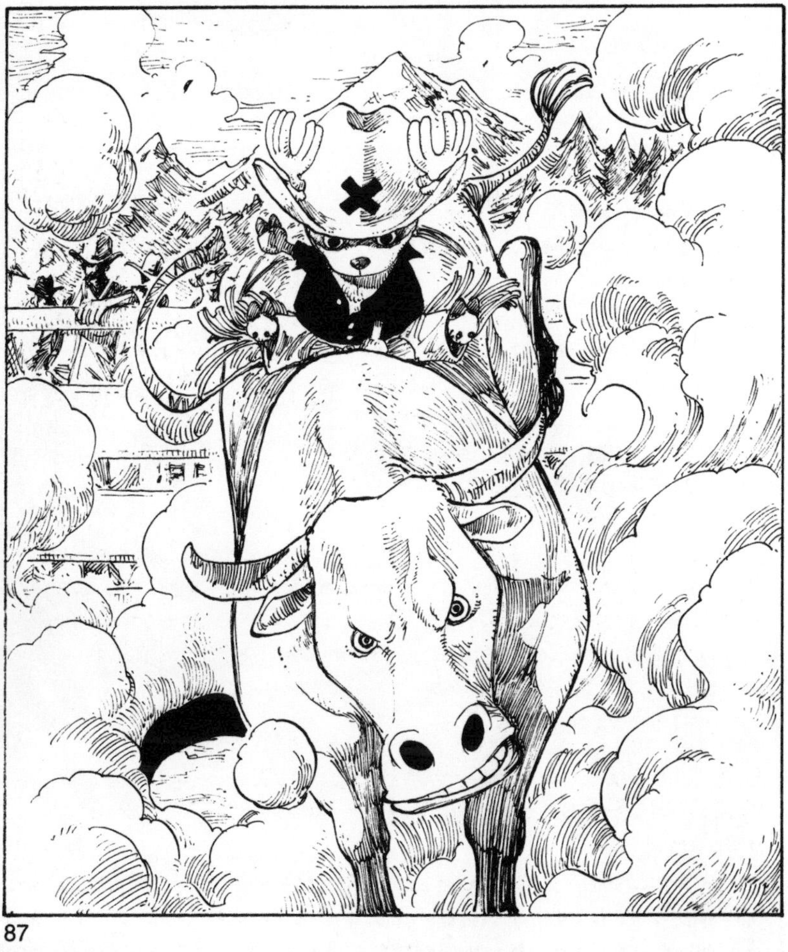

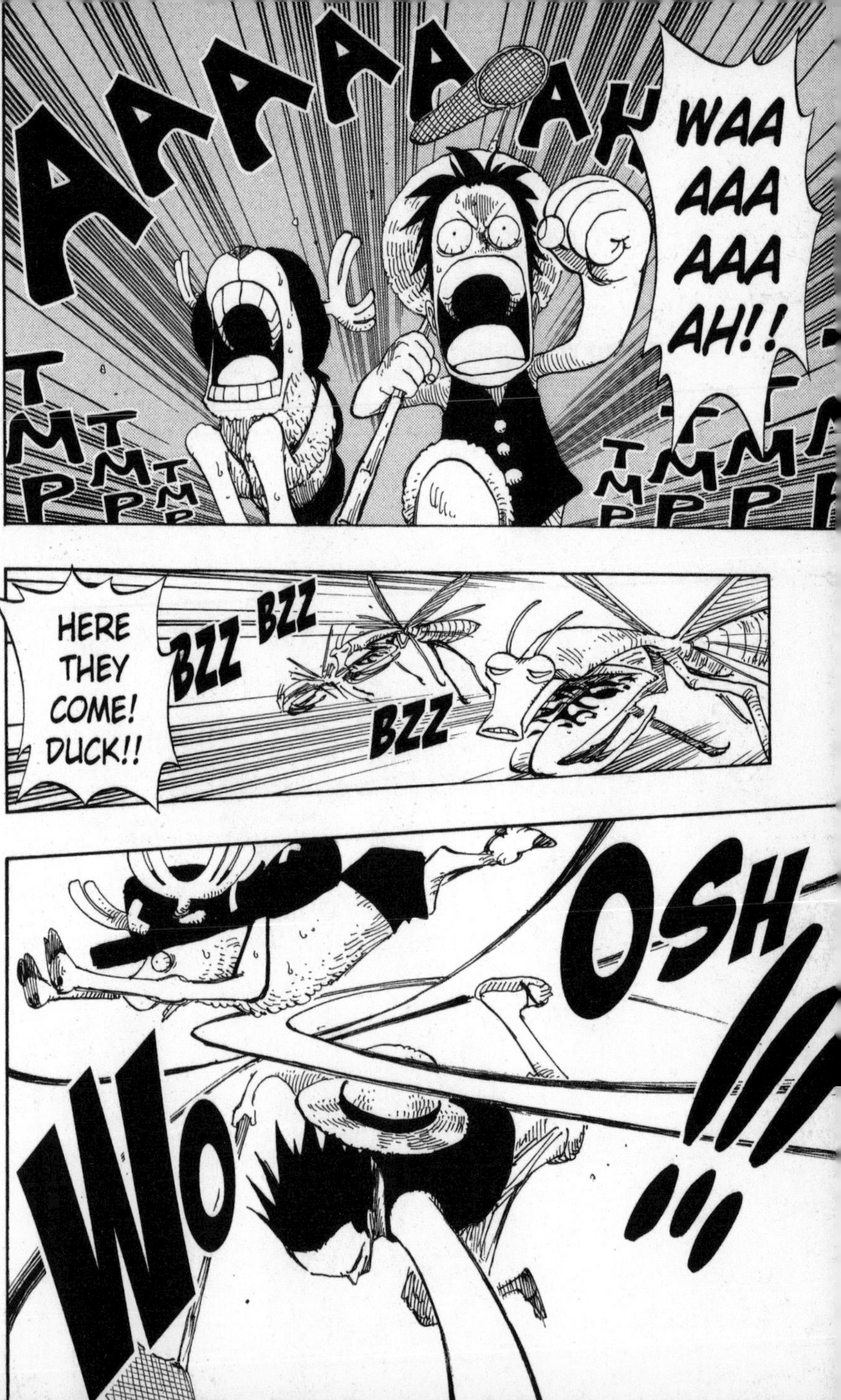
WAA AAA AAA AH!!
AAAAAAH
TMP TMP TMP
TMP TMP TMP TMP
HERE THEY COME! DUCK!!
BZZ BZZ
BZZ
WOOSH!!!

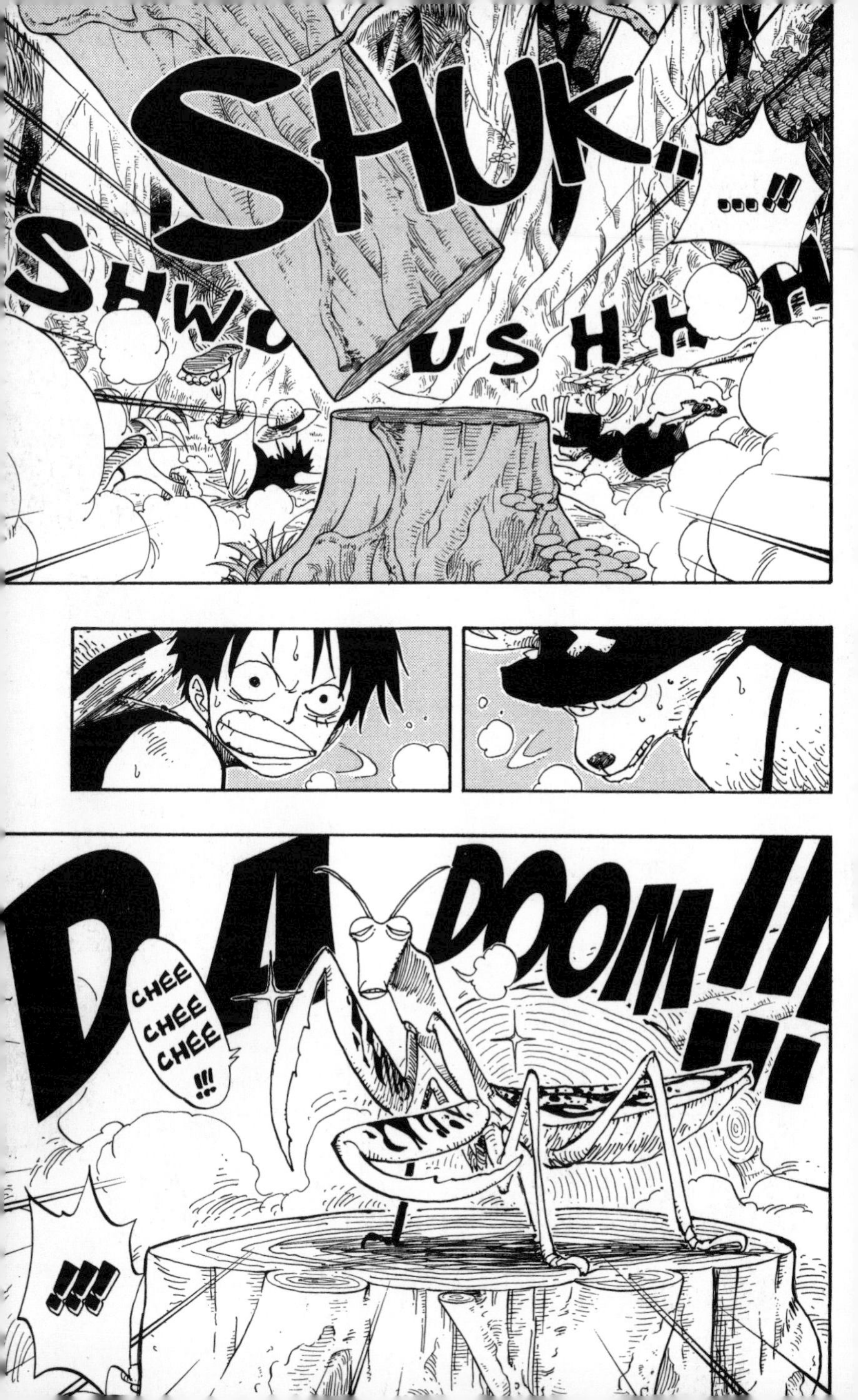
SHUK...!!
SHWOOSHHH
DA DOOM!!!!
CHEE CHEE CHEE !!!
!!!!

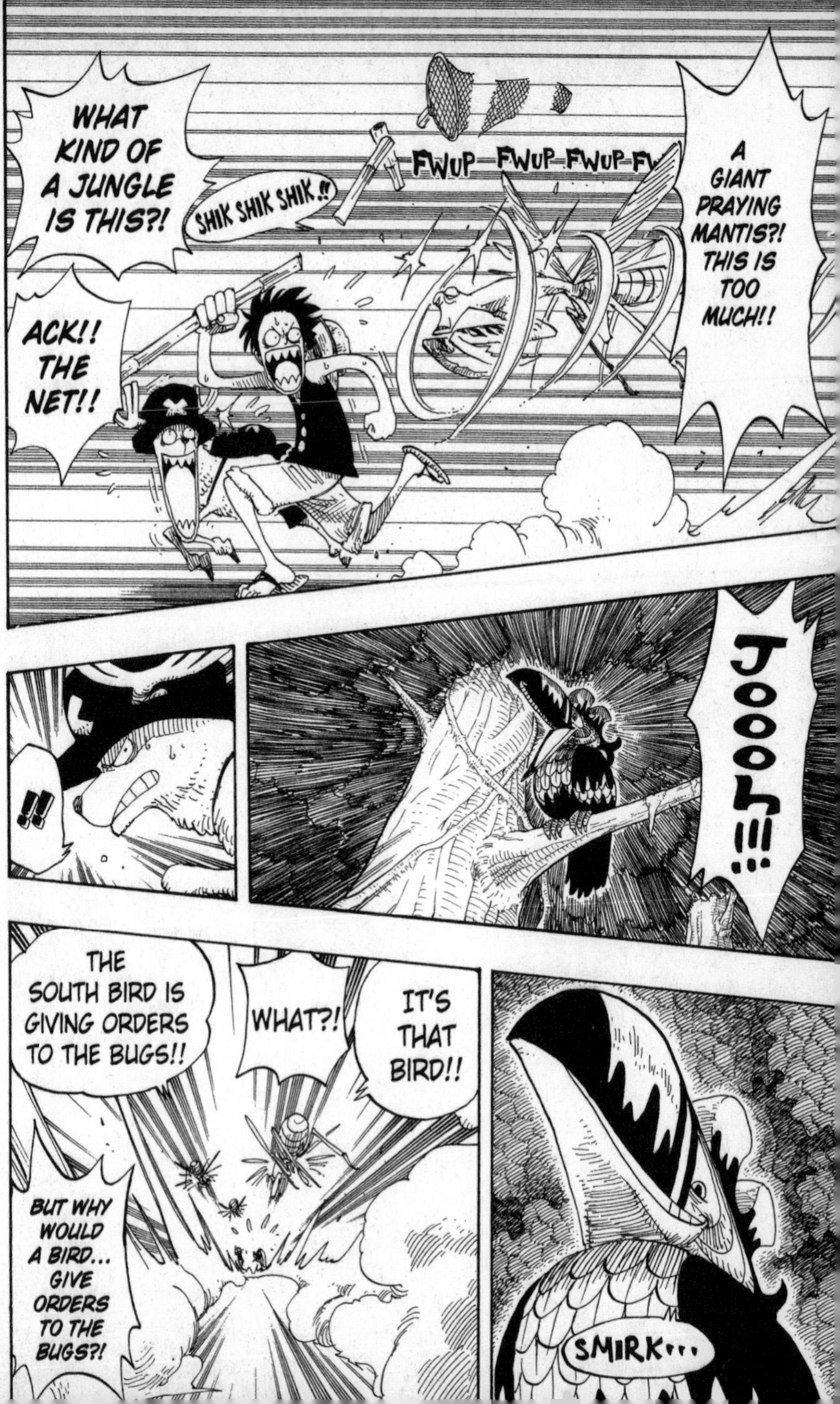
A GIANT PRAYING MANTIS?! THIS IS TOO MUCH!!
FWUP FWUP FWUP FW
SHIK SHIK SHIK!!
WHAT KIND OF A JUNGLE IS THIS?!
ACK!! THE NET!!
JOOOH!!!
!!
SMIRK...
IT'S THAT BIRD!!
WHAT?!
THE SOUTH BIRD IS GIVING ORDERS TO THE BUGS!!
BUT WHY WOULD A BIRD... GIVE ORDERS TO THE BUGS?!

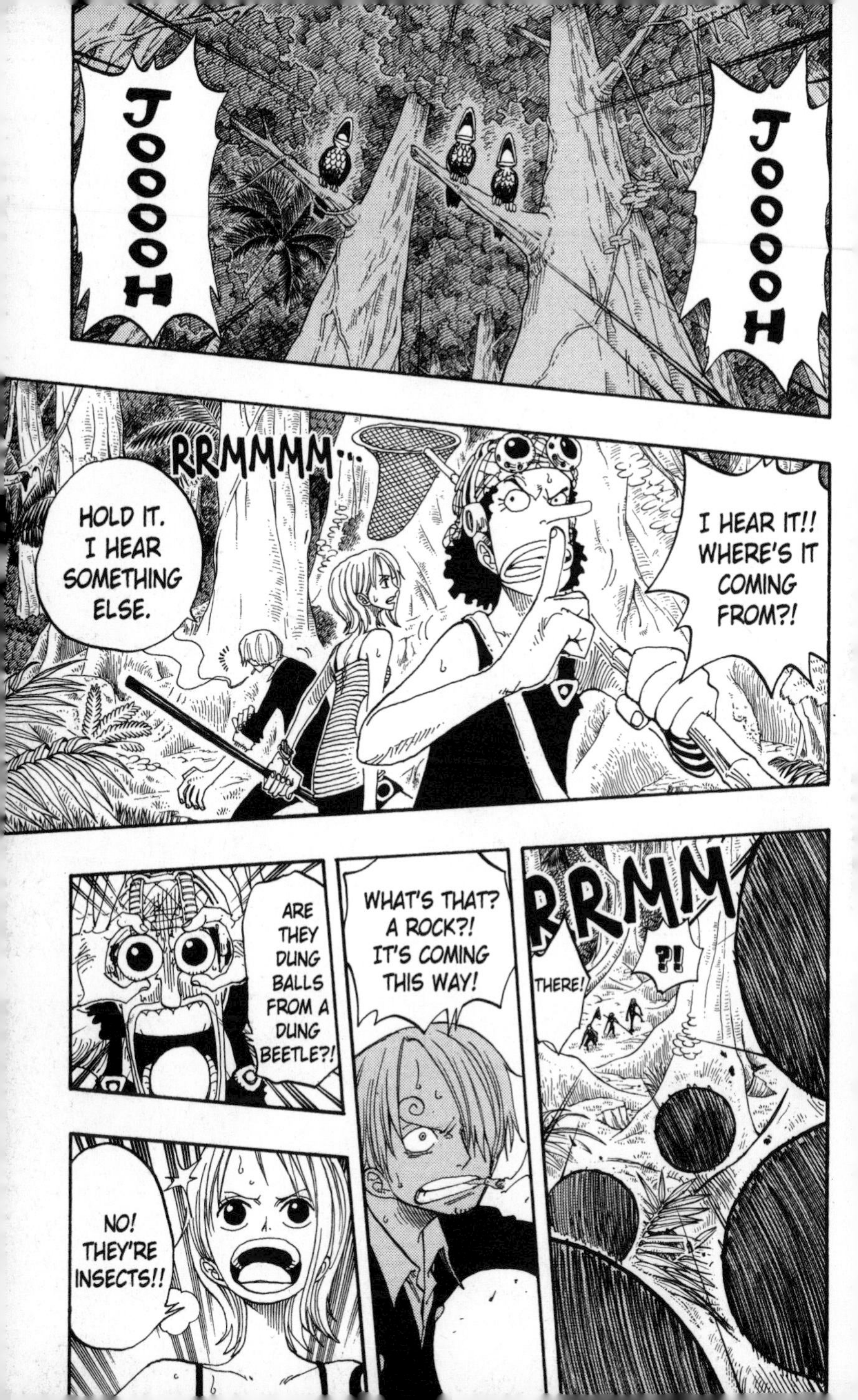
JOOOOOH
JOOOOOH
I HEAR IT!! WHERE'S IT COMING FROM?!
RRMMMM...
HOLD IT. I HEAR SOMETHING ELSE.
RRMM
?!
THERE!
WHAT'S THAT? A ROCK?! IT'S COMING THIS WAY!
ARE THEY DUNG BALLS FROM A DUNG BEETLE?!
NO! THEY'RE INSECTS!!

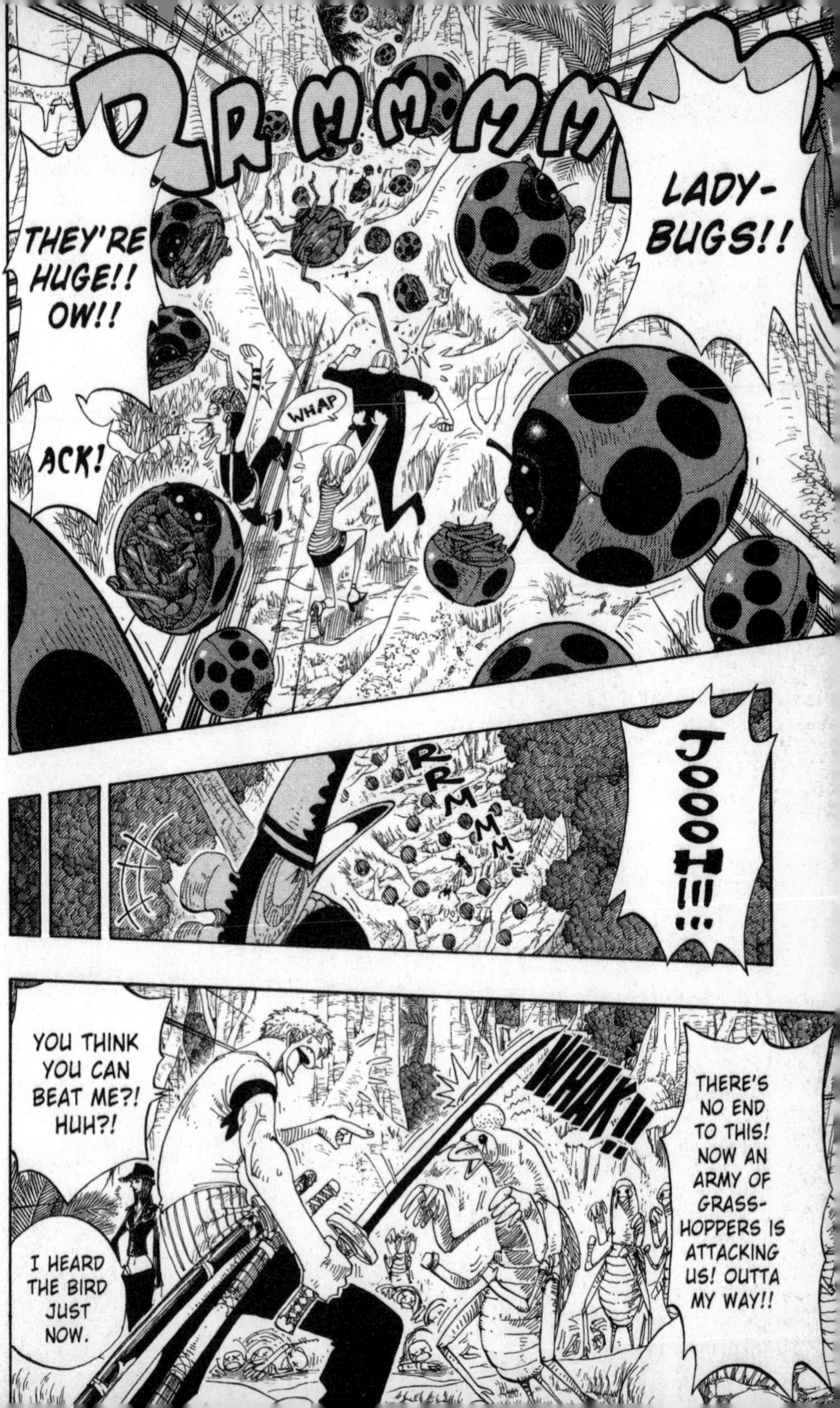
DRMMMM
LADY-BUGS!!
THEY'RE HUGE!! OW!!
WHAP
ACK!
JOOOOH!!!!
RRMMM
THERE'S NO END TO THIS! NOW AN ARMY OF GRASS-HOPPERS IS ATTACKING US! OUTTA MY WAY!!
WHAK!!
YOU THINK YOU CAN BEAT ME?! HUH?!
I HEARD THE BIRD JUST NOW.

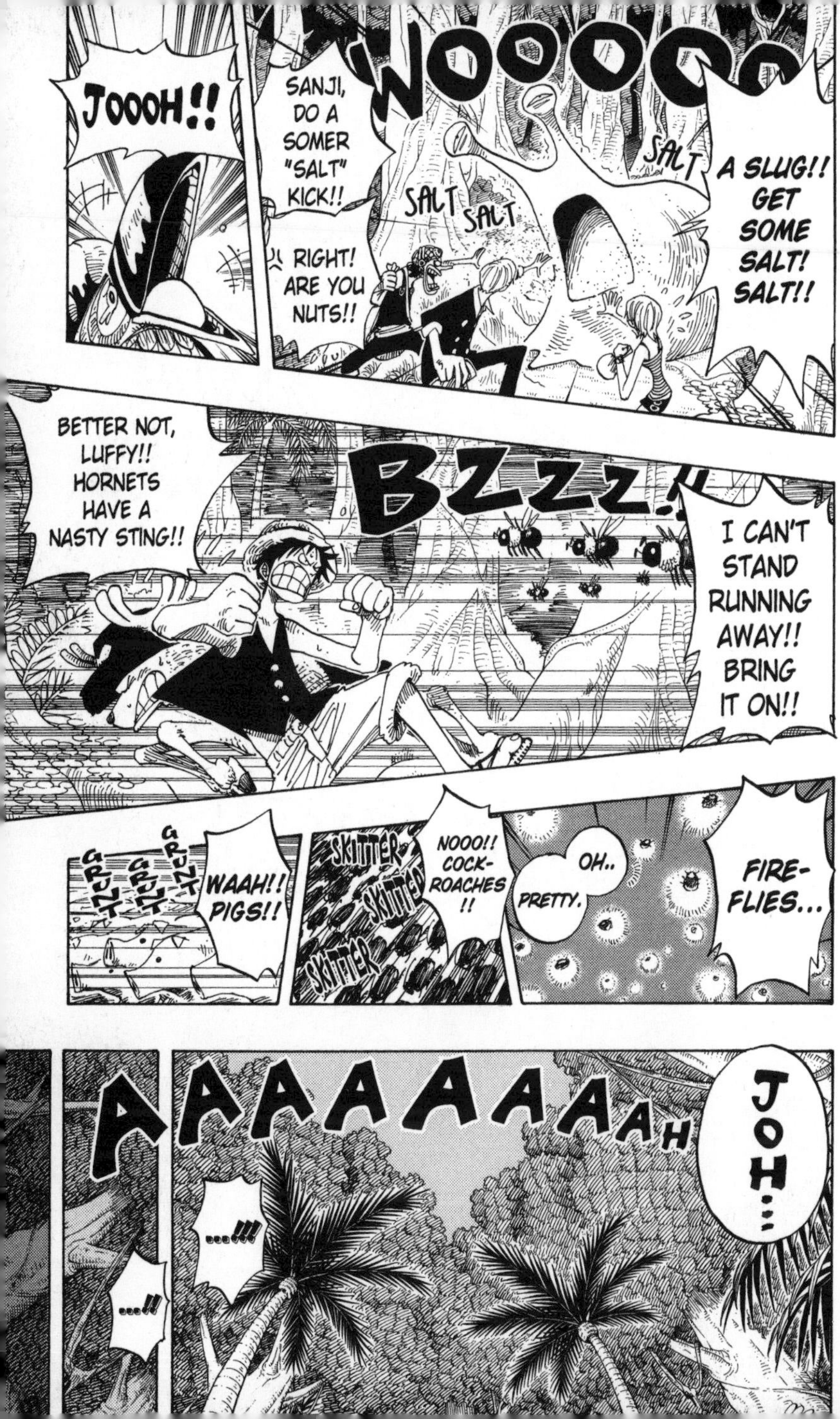
WOOOOO
SALT
A SLUG!! GET SOME SALT! SALT!!
SANJI, DO A SOMER "SALT" KICK!!
SALT SALT
RIGHT! ARE YOU NUTS!!
JOOOH!!
BZZZZ!!
I CAN'T STAND RUNNING AWAY!! BRING IT ON!!
BETTER NOT, LUFFY!! HORNETS HAVE A NASTY STING!!
FIRE-FLIES...
OH.. PRETTY.
NOOO!! COCK-ROACHES!!
SKITTER
SKITTER
SKITTER
WAAH!! PIGS!!
GRUNT
GRUNT
GRUNT
JOH!!
AAAAAAAH
...!!!
...!!

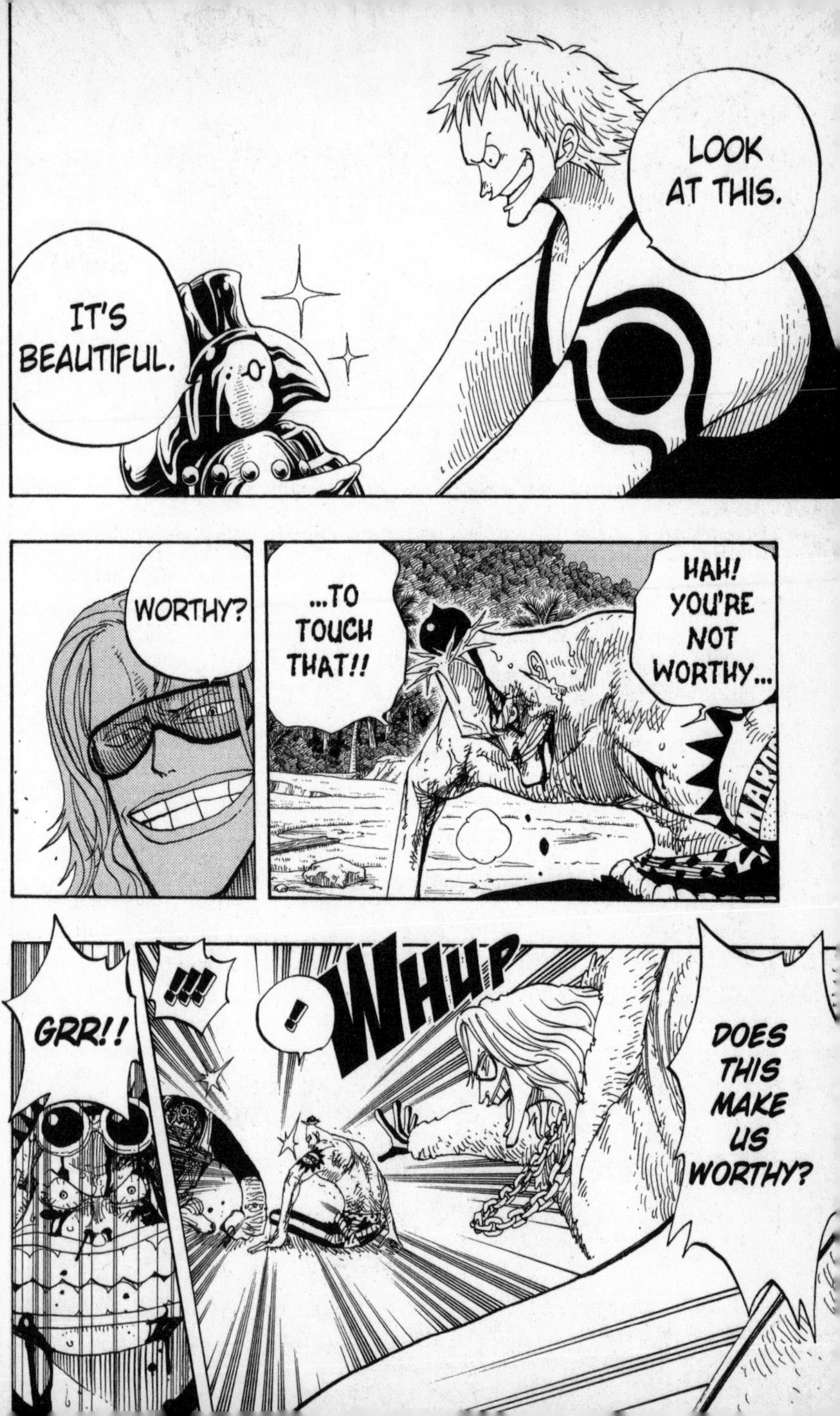
LOOK AT THIS.
IT'S BEAUTIFUL.
HAH! YOU'RE NOT WORTHY...
...TO TOUCH THAT!!
WORTHY?
DOES THIS MAKE US WORTHY?
WHUP
!
!!!
GRR!!

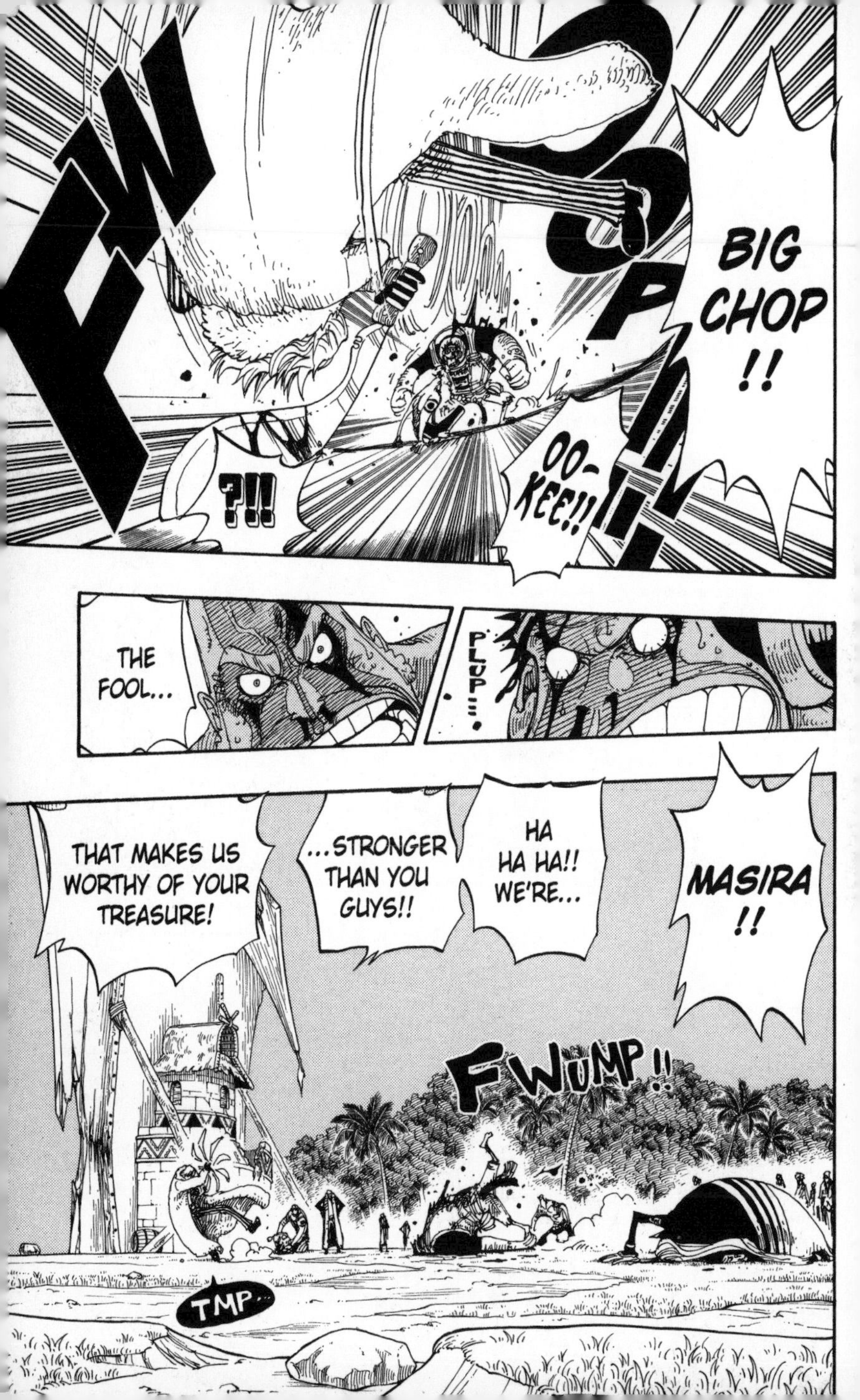
BIG CHOP !!
OO-KEE!!
?!!
PLUP...
THE FOOL...
MASIRA !!
HA HA HA!! WE'RE...
...STRONGER THAN YOU GUYS!!
THAT MAKES US WORTHY OF YOUR TREASURE!
FWUMP!!
TMP...

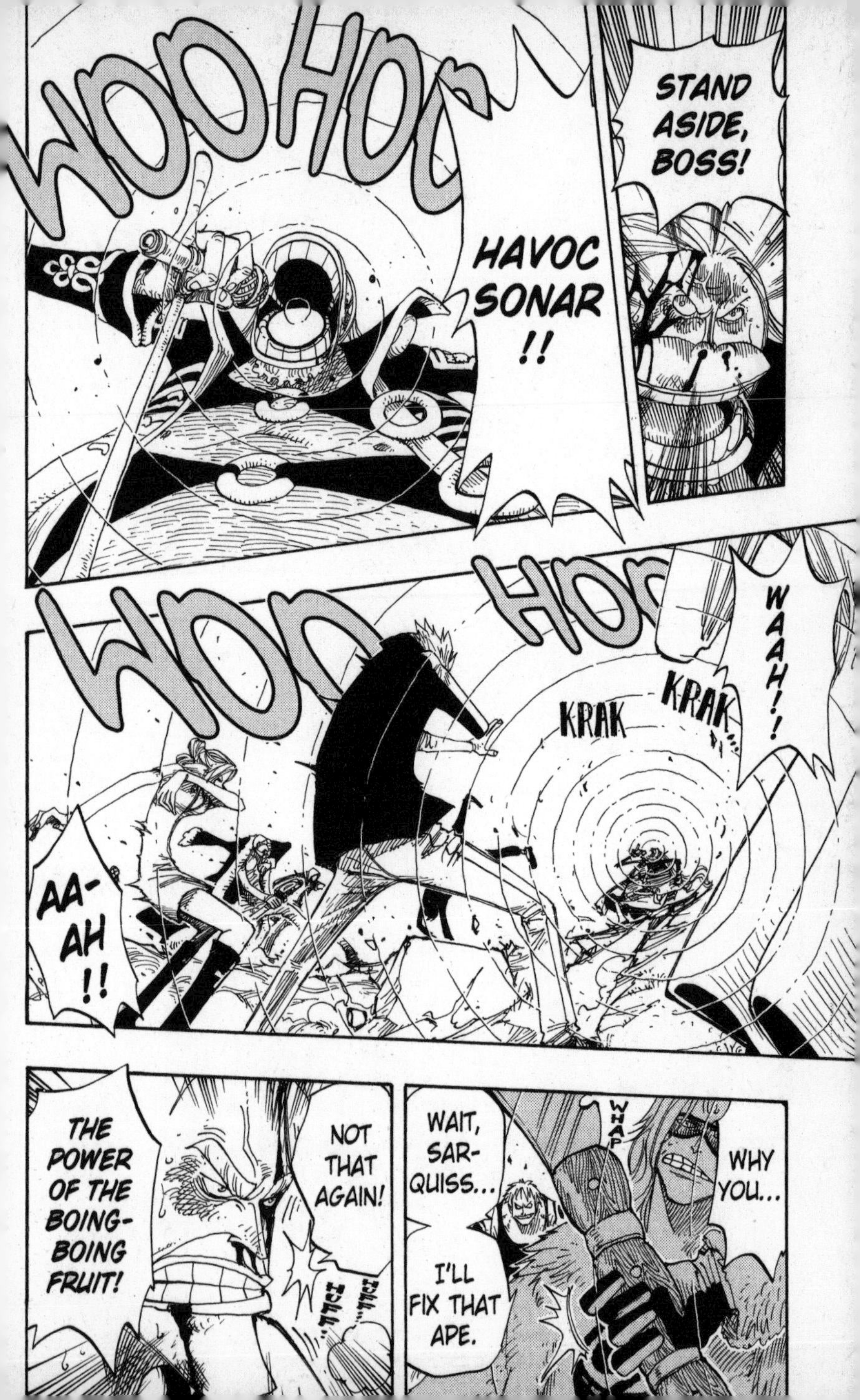
STAND ASIDE, BOSS!
HAVOC SONAR!!
WOOHOO
WAAAH!!
KRAK
KRAK
WOOHOO
AA-AH!!
WHY YOU...
WHAP
WAIT, SAR-QUISS...
I'LL FIX THAT APE.
NOT THAT AGAIN!
THE POWER OF THE BOING-BOING FRUIT!
HUFF...
HUFF...

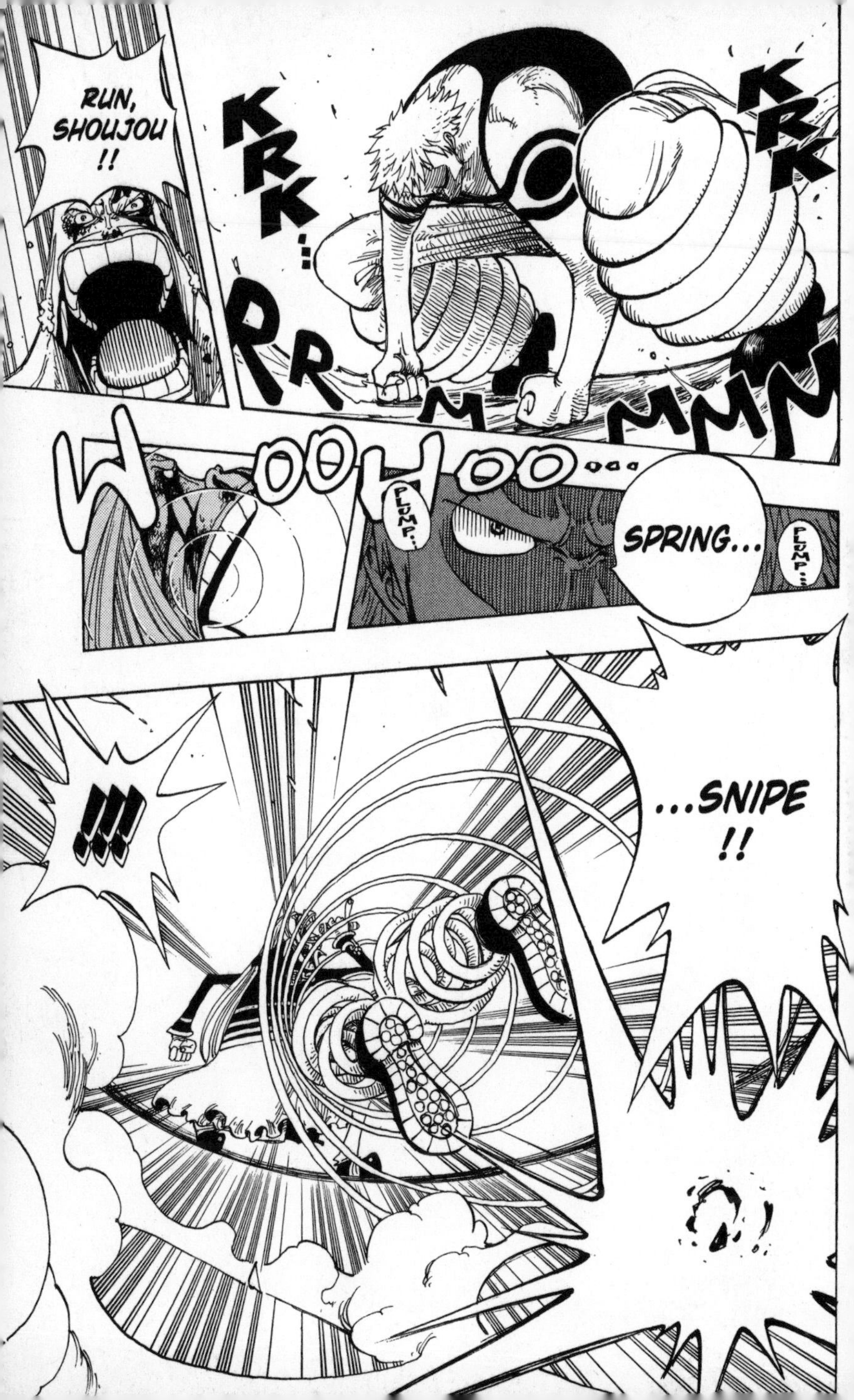

KRK
KRK..
RRRMMMMMM
RUN, SHOUJOU!!
PLUMP...
SPRING...
PLUMP...
WOOHOO...
...SNIPE!!
!!!

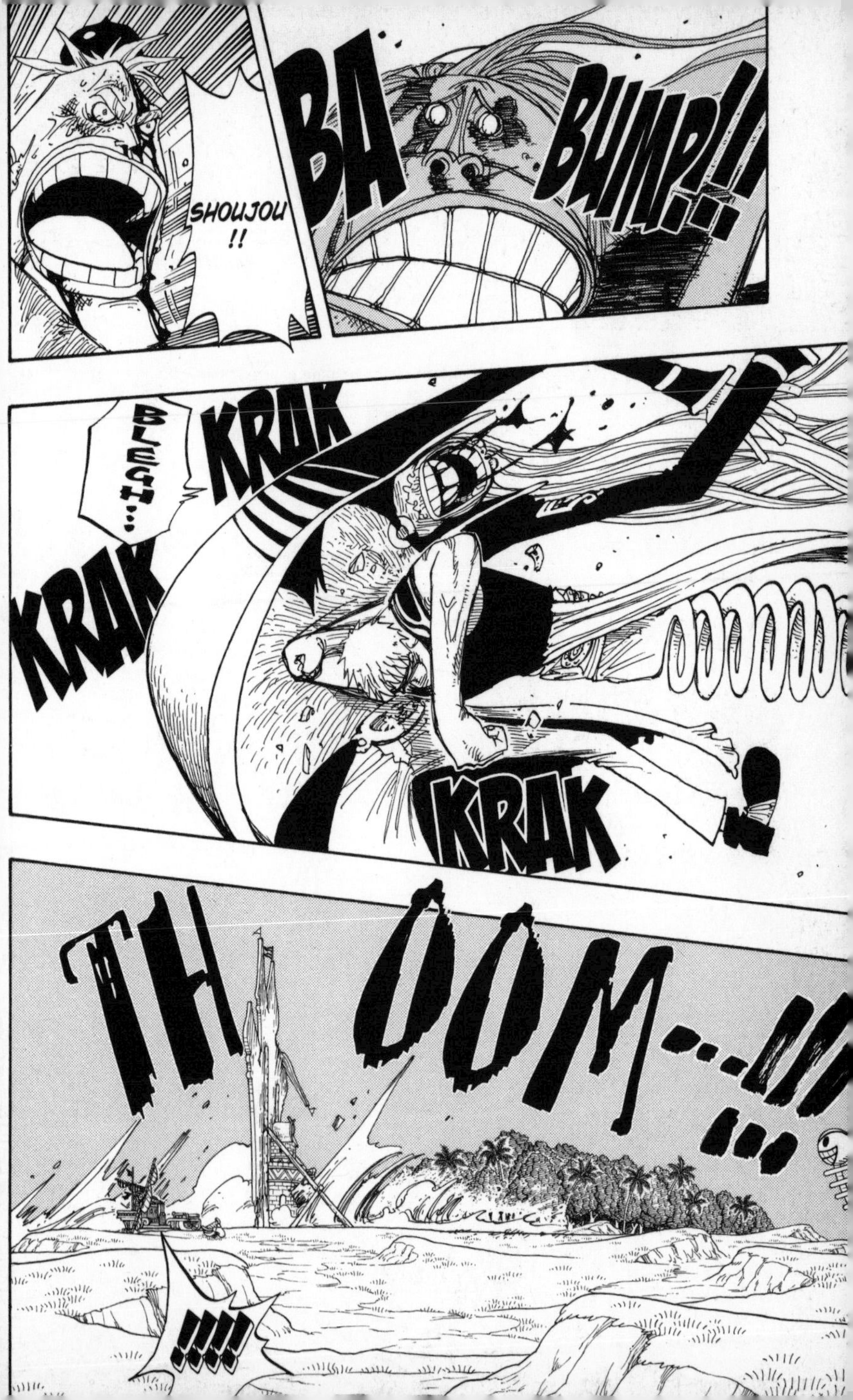
BA BUMP!!
SHOUJOU !!
KRAK
BLEGH...
KRAK
KRAK
THOOOM...!!!
!!!!

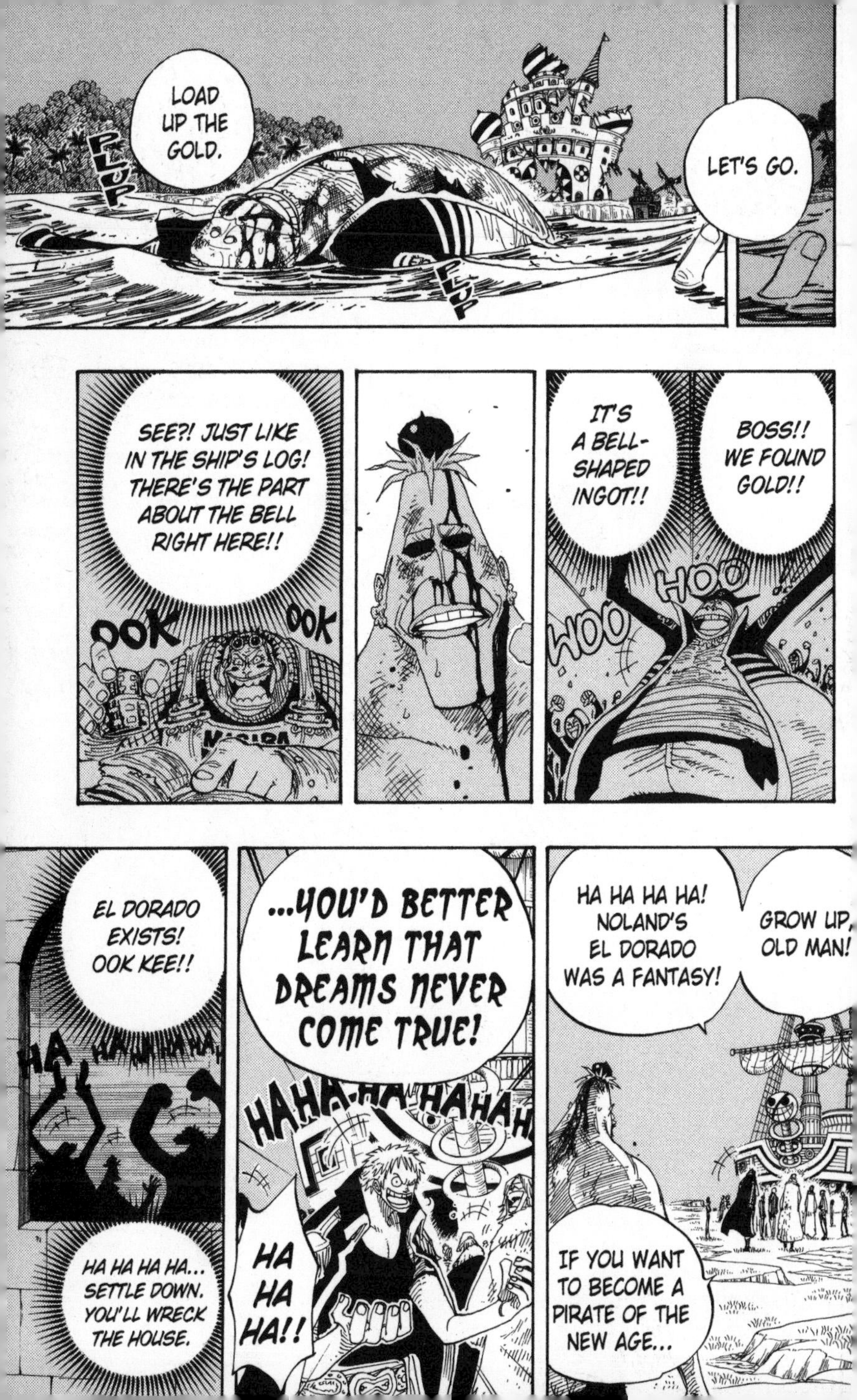
LET'S GO.
LOAD UP THE GOLD.
PLUP
PLUP
BOSS!! WE FOUND GOLD!!
IT'S A BELL-SHAPED INGOT!!
HOO
WOO
SEE?! JUST LIKE IN THE SHIP'S LOG! THERE'S THE PART ABOUT THE BELL RIGHT HERE!!
OOK
OOK
GROW UP, OLD MAN!
HA HA HA HA! NOLAND'S EL DORADO WAS A FANTASY!
IF YOU WANT TO BECOME A PIRATE OF THE NEW AGE...
...YOU'D BETTER LEARN THAT DREAMS NEVER COME TRUE!
HAHA-HA-HAHAH
HA HA HA!!
EL DORADO EXISTS! OOK KEE!!
HA
HA HA... SETTLE DOWN. YOU'LL WRECK THE HOUSE.

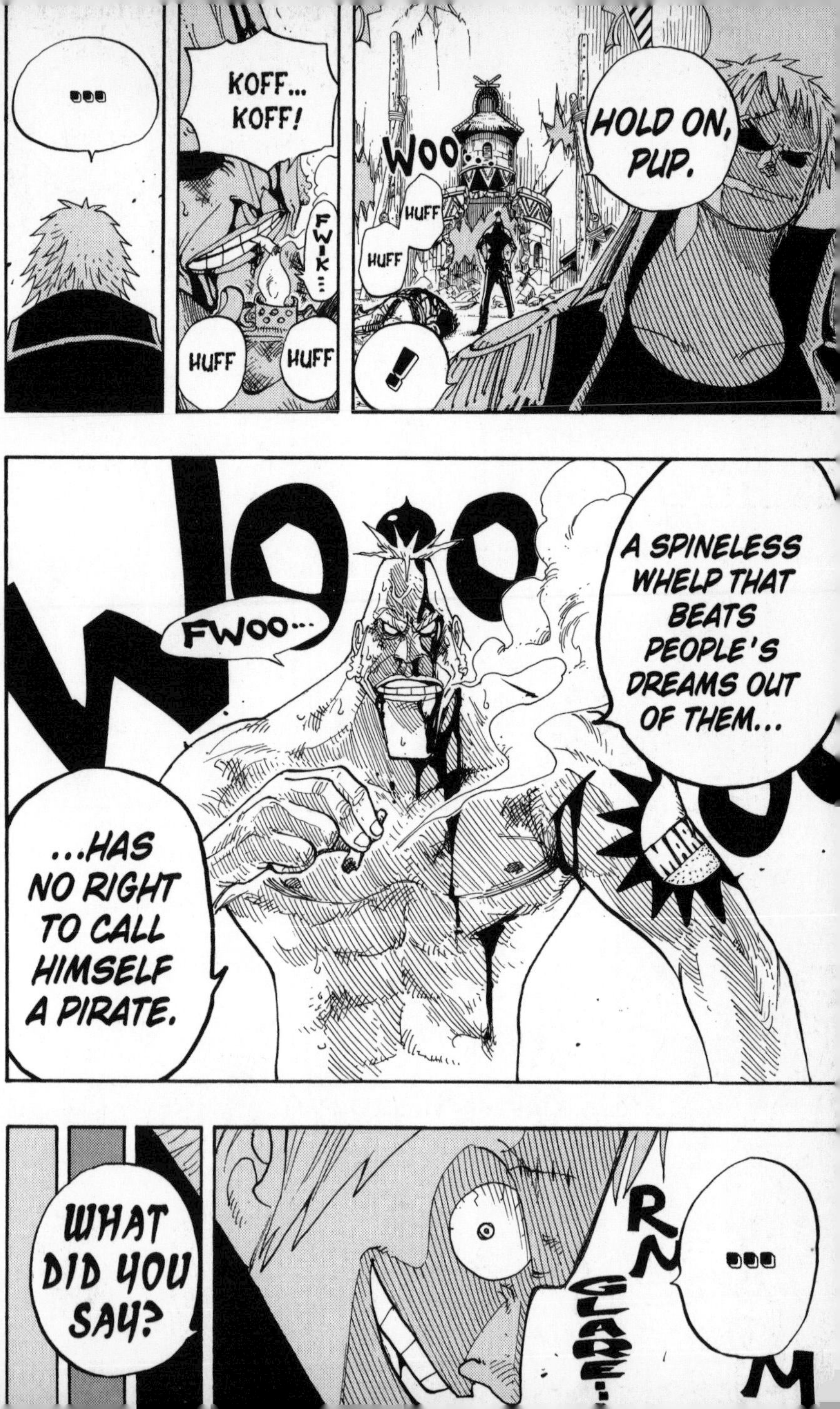
HOLD ON, PUP.
WOO
HUFF
HUFF
!
KOFF... KOFF!
FWIK...
HUFF
HUFF
...
A SPINELESS WHELP THAT BEATS PEOPLE'S DREAMS OUT OF THEM...
FWOO...
...HAS NO RIGHT TO CALL HIMSELF A PIRATE.
RN
...
GLARE!
M
WHAT DID YOU SAY?

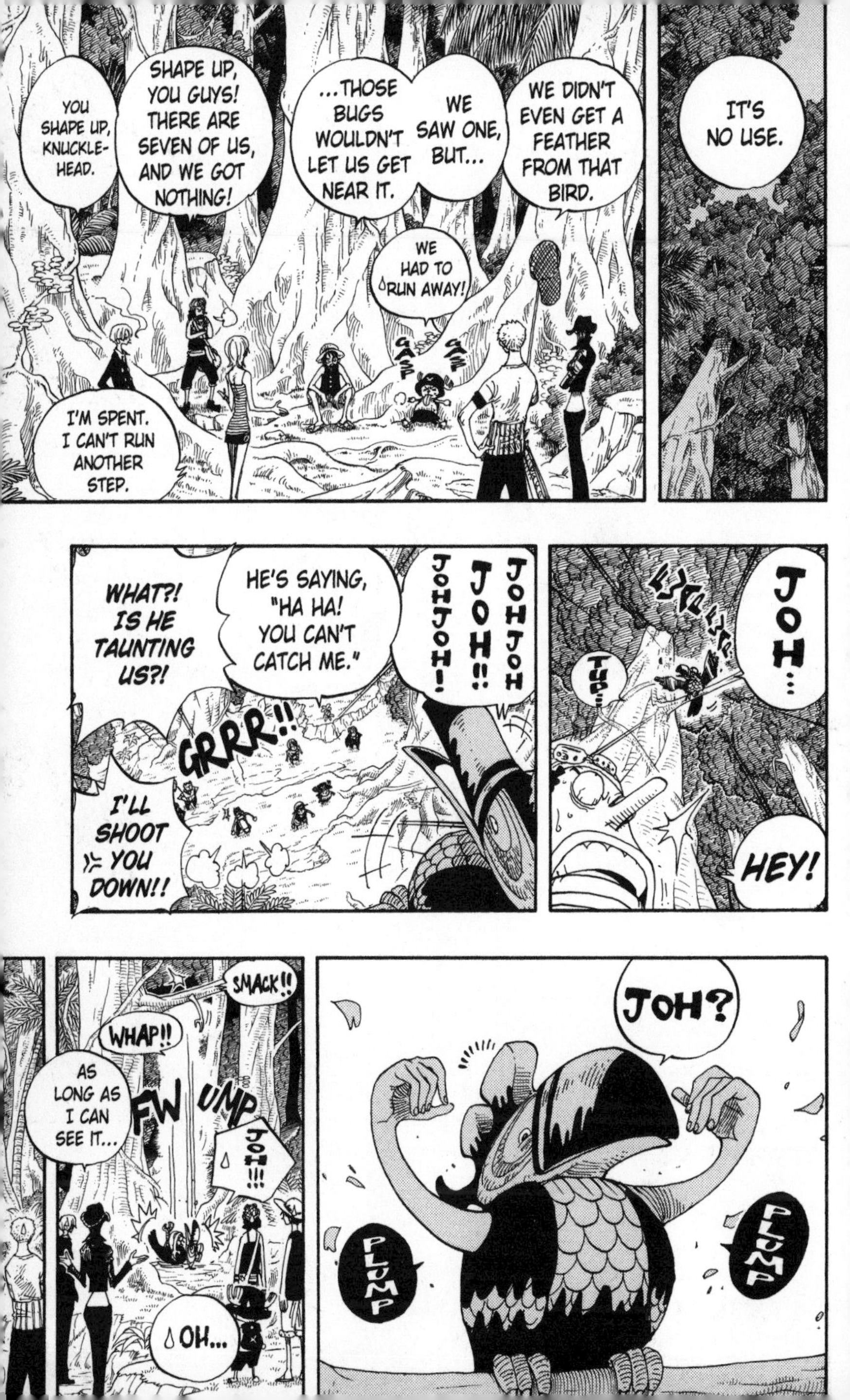
IT'S NO USE.
WE DIDN'T EVEN GET A FEATHER FROM THAT BIRD.
WE SAW ONE, BUT...
...THOSE BUGS WOULDN'T LET US GET NEAR IT.
SHAPE UP, YOU GUYS! THERE ARE SEVEN OF US, AND WE GOT NOTHING!
YOU SHAPE UP, KNUCKLE-HEAD.
WE HAD TO RUN AWAY!
GASP
GASP
I'M SPENT. I CAN'T RUN ANOTHER STEP.
JOH...
TUP...
HEY!
JOHJOH
JOH!!
JOHJOH!
HE'S SAYING, "HA HA! YOU CAN'T CATCH ME."
WHAT?! IS HE TAUNTING US?!
GRRR!!
I'LL SHOOT YOU DOWN!!
JOH?
PLUMP
PLUMP
SMACK!!
JOH!!!
FWUMP
WHAP!!
AS LONG AS I CAN SEE IT...
OH...

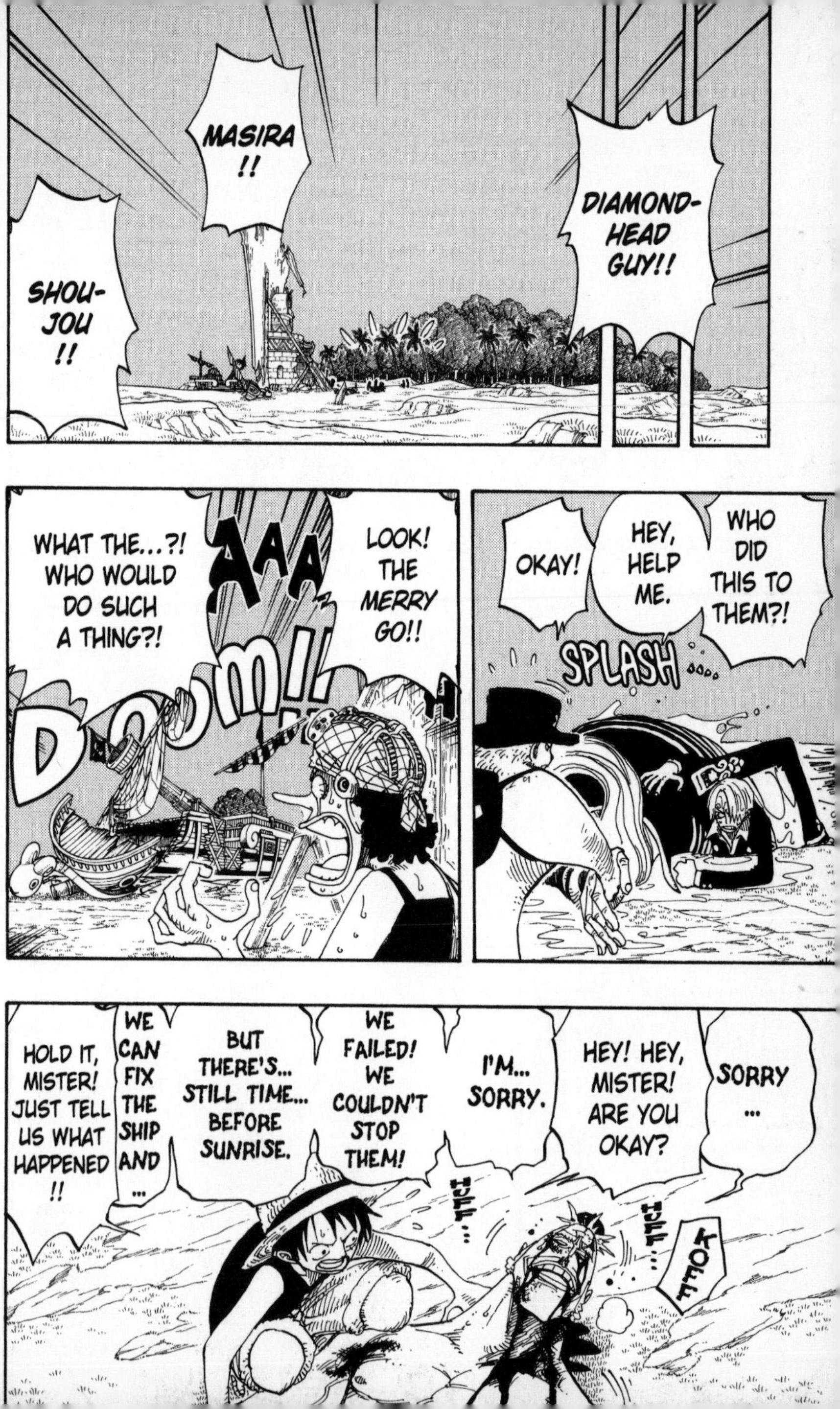
DIAMOND-HEAD GUY!!
MASIRA !!
SHOU-JOU !!
WHO DID THIS TO THEM?!
HEY, HELP ME.
OKAY!
SPLASH
LOOK! THE MERRY GO!!
AAA
DOOM!!
WHAT THE...?! WHO WOULD DO SUCH A THING?!
SORRY ...
HEY! HEY, MISTER! ARE YOU OKAY?
KOFF
HUFF...
HUFF...
I'M... SORRY.
WE FAILED! WE COULDN'T STOP THEM!
BUT THERE'S... STILL TIME... BEFORE SUNRISE.
WE CAN FIX THE SHIP AND ...
HOLD IT, MISTER! JUST TELL US WHAT HAPPENED !!

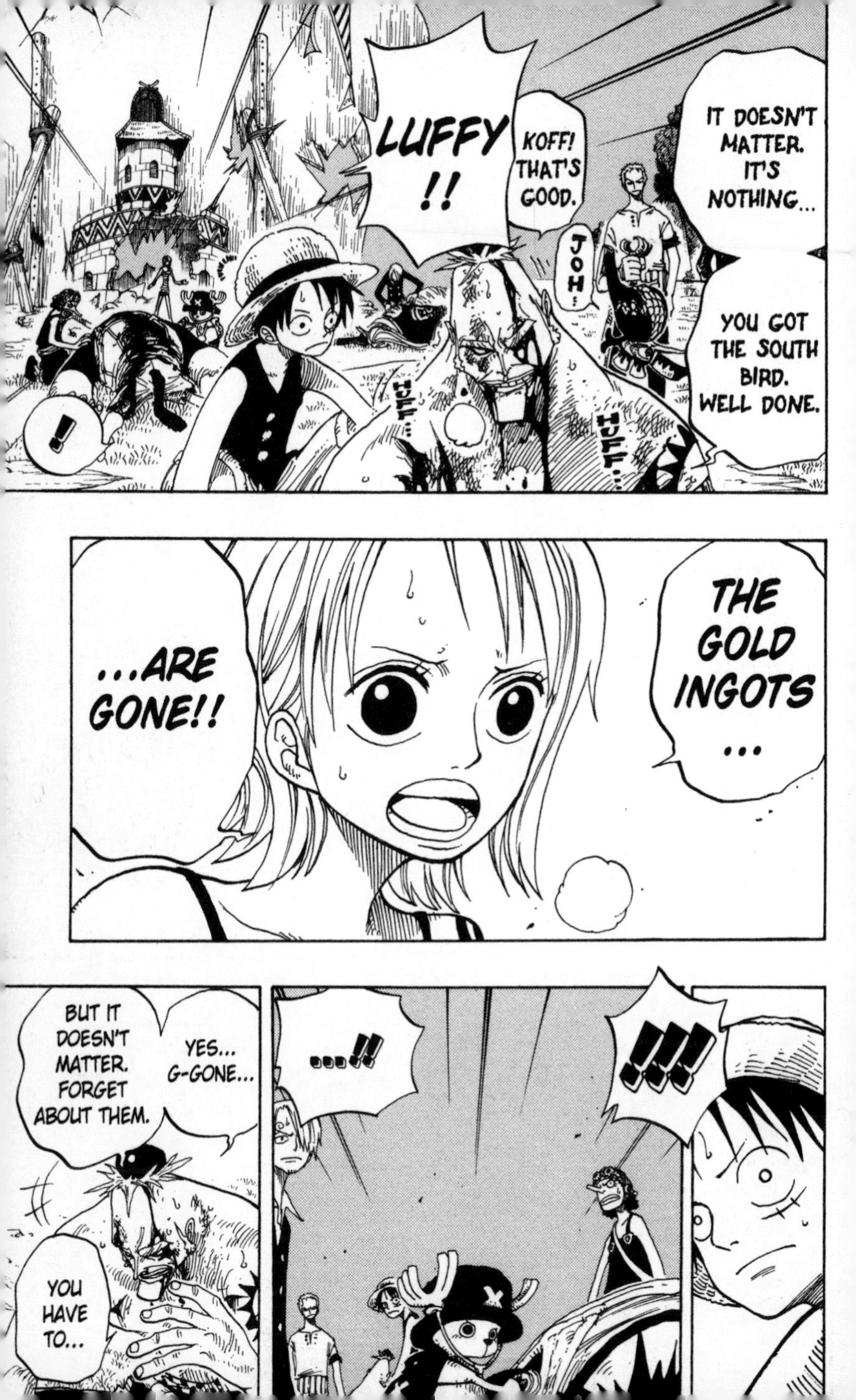
IT DOESN'T MATTER. IT'S NOTHING...
YOU GOT THE SOUTH BIRD. WELL DONE.
JOH...
KOFF! THAT'S GOOD.
LUFFY !!
HUFF...
HUFF...
!
THE GOLD INGOTS ...
...ARE GONE!!
!!!
...!!
YES... G-GONE...
BUT IT DOESN'T MATTER. FORGET ABOUT THEM.
YOU HAVE TO...

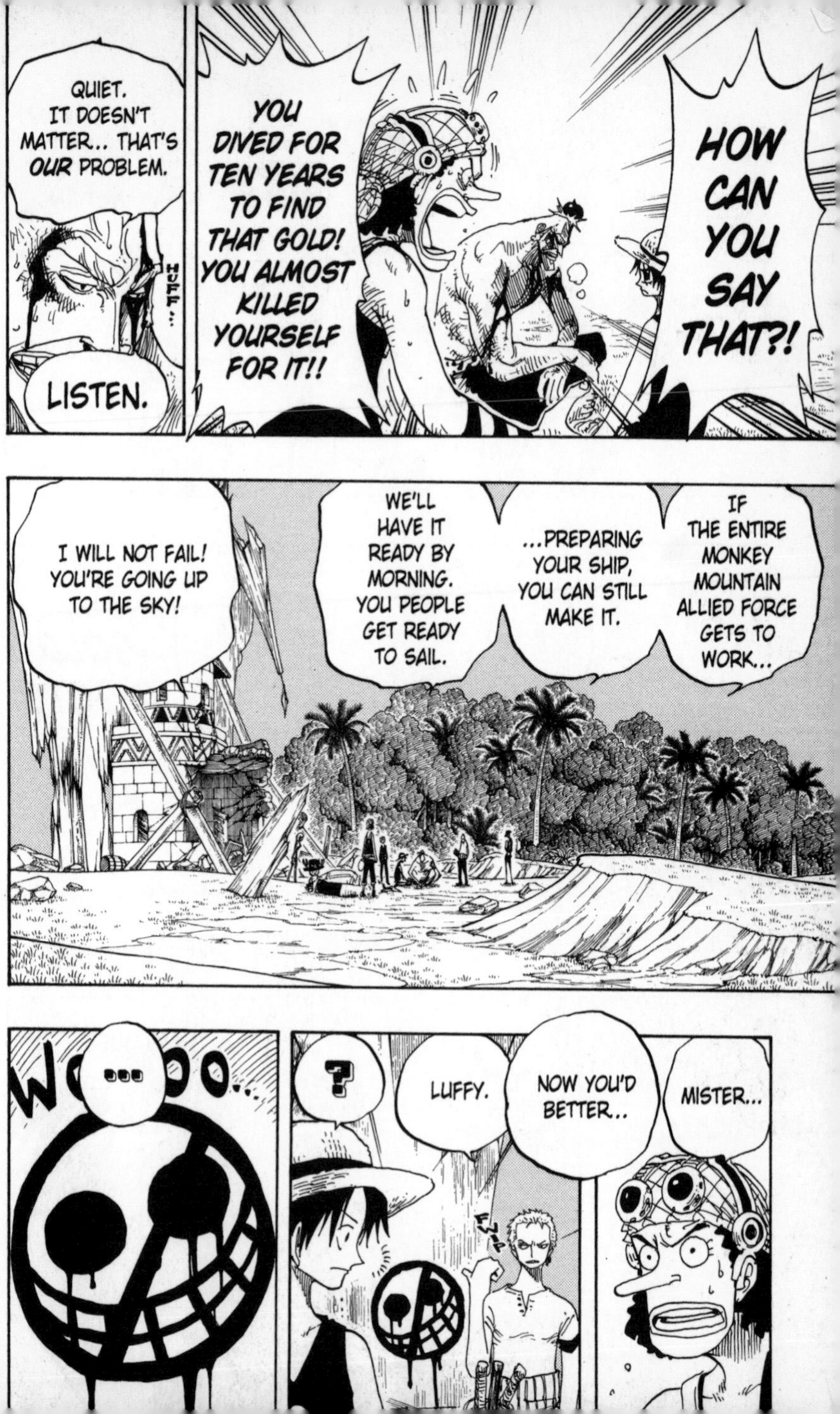
HOW CAN YOU SAY THAT?!
YOU DIVED FOR TEN YEARS TO FIND THAT GOLD! YOU ALMOST KILLED YOURSELF FOR IT!!
QUIET. IT DOESN'T MATTER... THAT'S OUR PROBLEM.
HUFF...
LISTEN.
IF THE ENTIRE MONKEY MOUNTAIN ALLIED FORCE GETS TO WORK...
...PREPARING YOUR SHIP, YOU CAN STILL MAKE IT.
WE'LL HAVE IT READY BY MORNING. YOU PEOPLE GET READY TO SAIL.
I WILL NOT FAIL! YOU'RE GOING UP TO THE SKY!
MISTER...
NOW YOU'D BETTER..
LUFFY.
?
FWIP
...

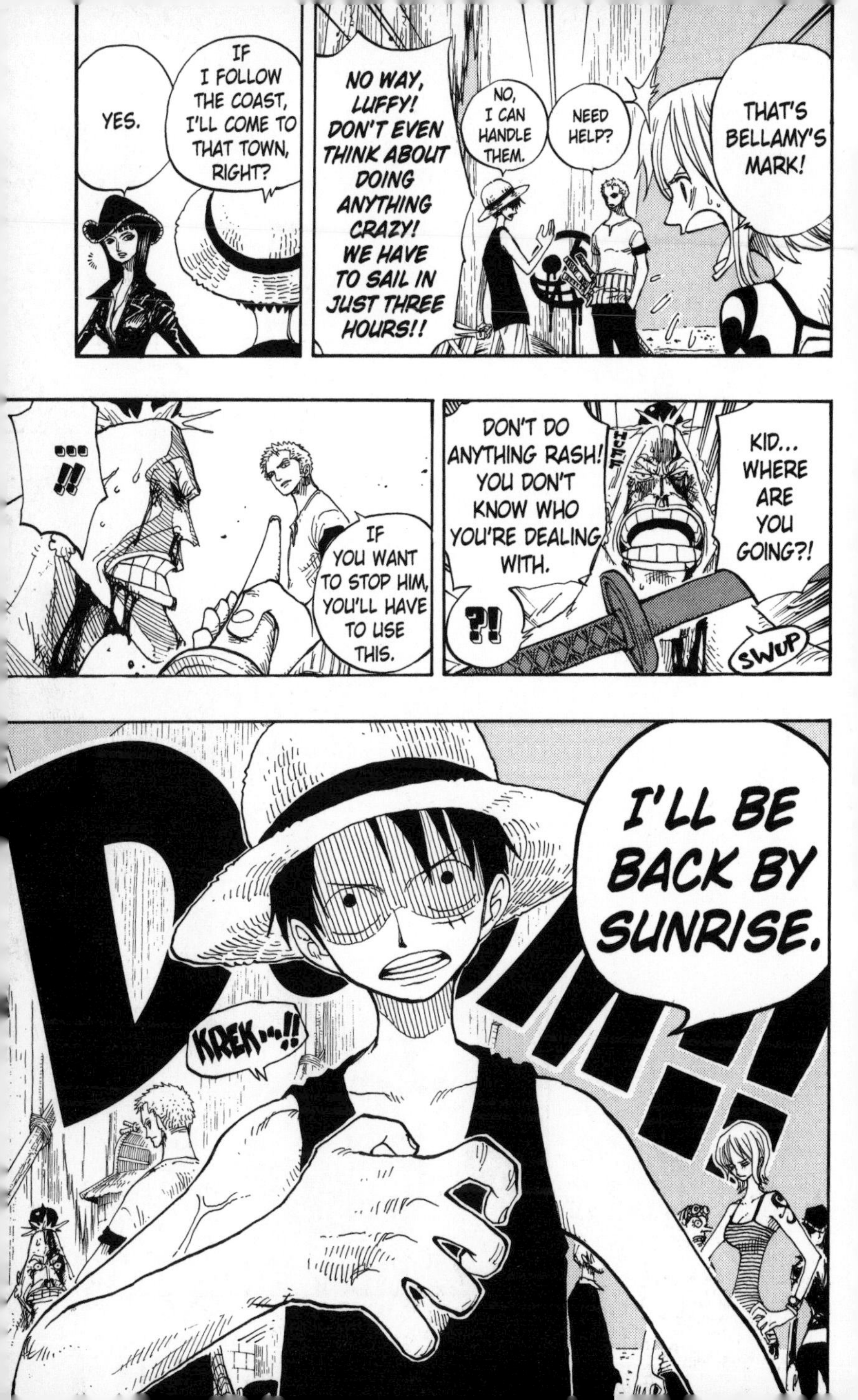
THAT'S BELLAMY'S MARK!
NEED HELP?
NO, I CAN HANDLE THEM.
NO WAY, LUFFY! DON'T EVEN THINK ABOUT DOING ANYTHING CRAZY! WE HAVE TO SAIL IN JUST THREE HOURS!!
IF I FOLLOW THE COAST, I'LL COME TO THAT TOWN, RIGHT?
YES.
KID... WHERE ARE YOU GOING?!
HUFF
DON'T DO ANYTHING RASH! YOU DON'T KNOW WHO YOU'RE DEALING WITH.
?!
SWUP
IF YOU WANT TO STOP HIM, YOU'LL HAVE TO USE THIS.
...!!
I'LL BE BACK BY SUNRISE.
KREK...!!

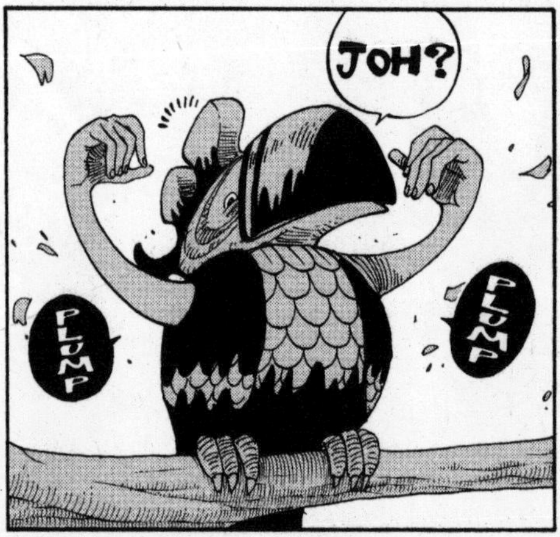
JOH?
PLUMP
PLUMP

# Chapter 232:
# THE 100 MILLION BERRY MAN

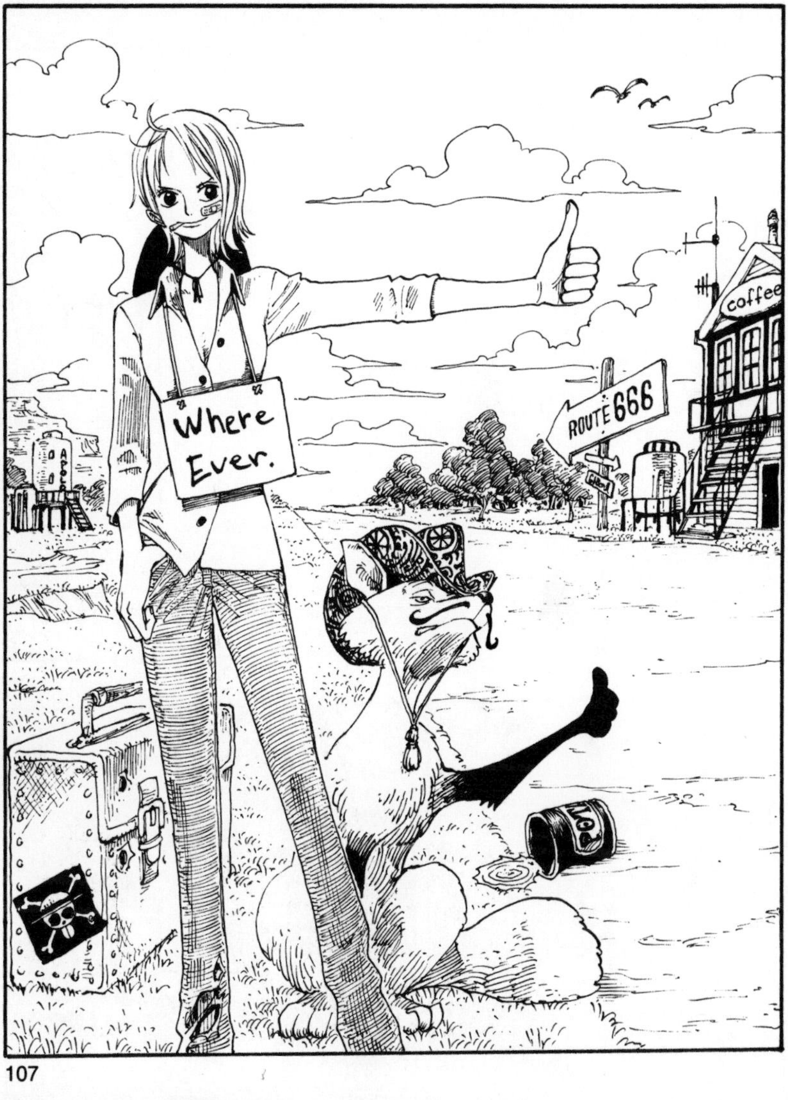
coffee
ROUTE 666
Where Ever.

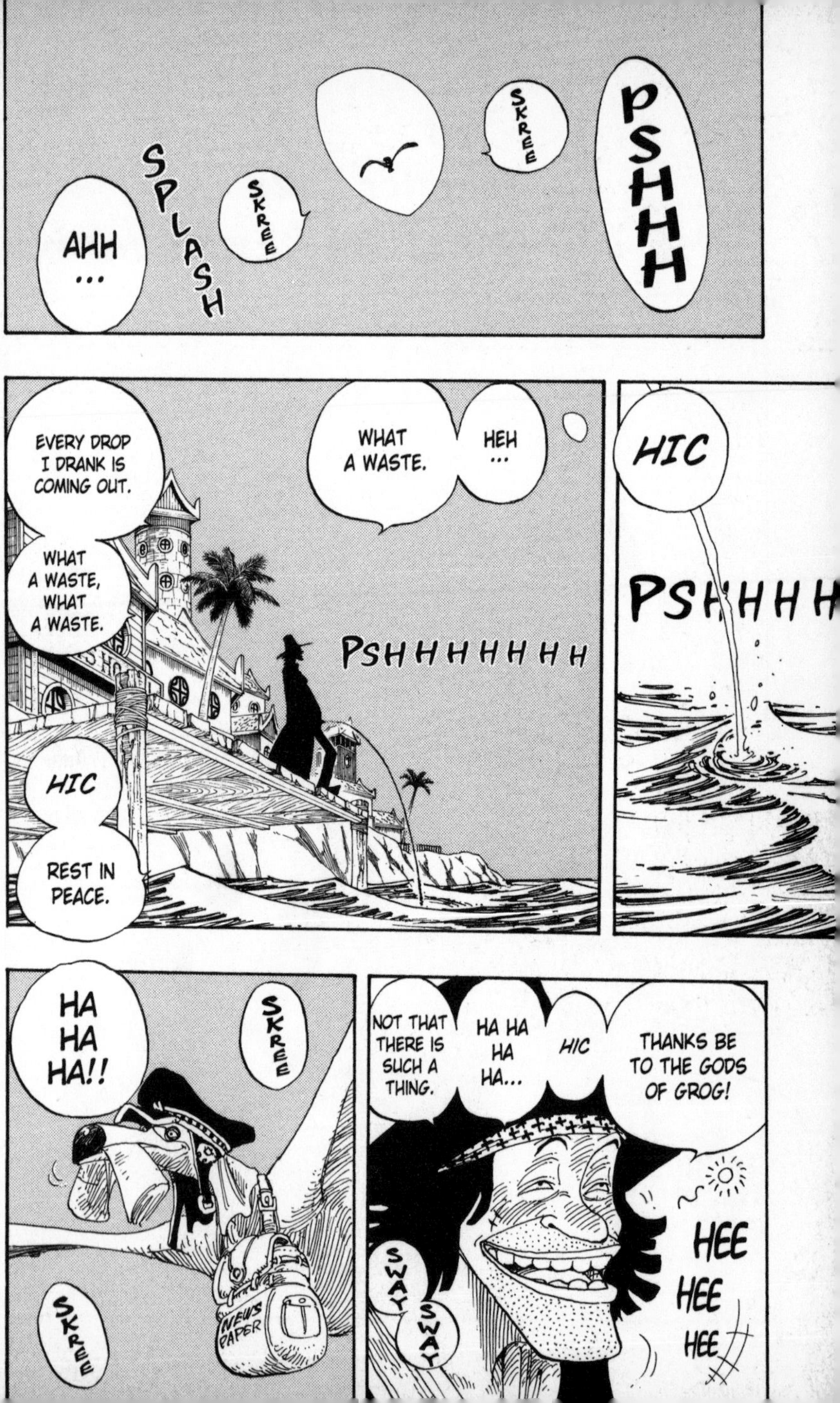
PSHHH
SKREE
SKREE
SPLASH
AHH...
HIC
PSHHHHH
HEH...
WHAT A WASTE.
EVERY DROP I DRANK IS COMING OUT.
WHAT A WASTE, WHAT A WASTE.
PSHHHHHHH
HIC
REST IN PEACE.
THANKS BE TO THE GODS OF GROG!
HIC
HA HA HA HA...
NOT THAT THERE IS SUCH A THING.
HEE HEE HEE
SWAY SWAY
SKREE
HA HA HA!!
SKREE
NEWS PAPER

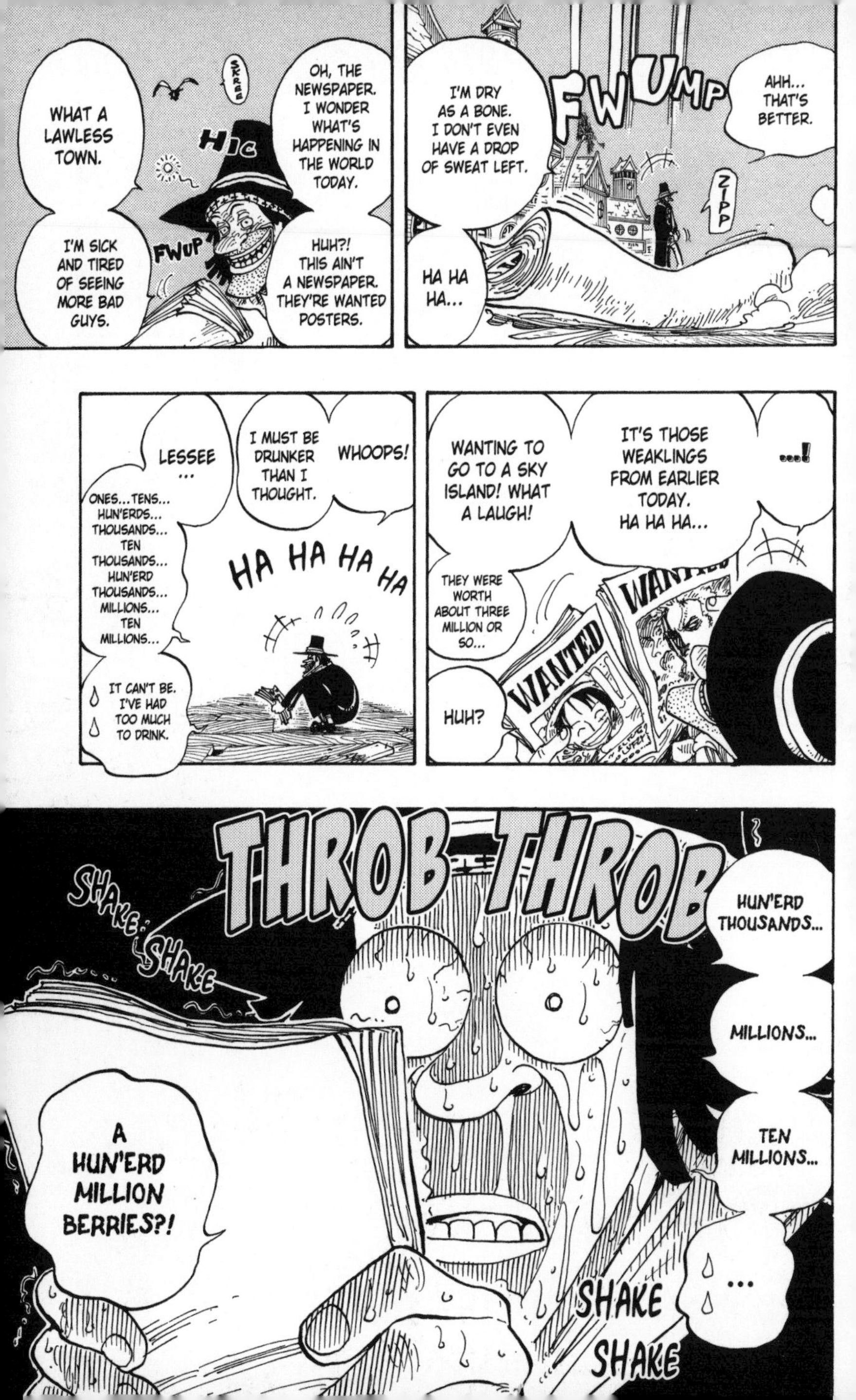
AHH... THAT'S BETTER.
FWUMP
ZIPP
I'M DRY AS A BONE. I DON'T EVEN HAVE A DROP OF SWEAT LEFT.
HA HA HA...
OH, THE NEWSPAPER. I WONDER WHAT'S HAPPENING IN THE WORLD TODAY.
SKREE
HIC
WHAT A LAWLESS TOWN.
HUH?! THIS AIN'T A NEWSPAPER. THEY'RE WANTED POSTERS.
FWUP
I'M SICK AND TIRED OF SEEING MORE BAD GUYS.
...!
IT'S THOSE WEAKLINGS FROM EARLIER TODAY. HA HA HA...
WANTING TO GO TO A SKY ISLAND! WHAT A LAUGH!
THEY WERE WORTH ABOUT THREE MILLION OR SO...
WANTED
WANTED
HUH?
WHOOPS!
I MUST BE DRUNKER THAN I THOUGHT.
LESSEE...
ONES...TENS... HUN'ERDS... THOUSANDS... TEN THOUSANDS... HUN'ERD THOUSANDS... MILLIONS... TEN MILLIONS...
HA HA HA HA
IT CAN'T BE. I'VE HAD TOO MUCH TO DRINK.
THROB THROB
HUN'ERD THOUSANDS...
MILLIONS...
TEN MILLIONS...
SHAKE SHAKE
A HUN'ERD MILLION BERRIES?!
...
SHAKE SHAKE

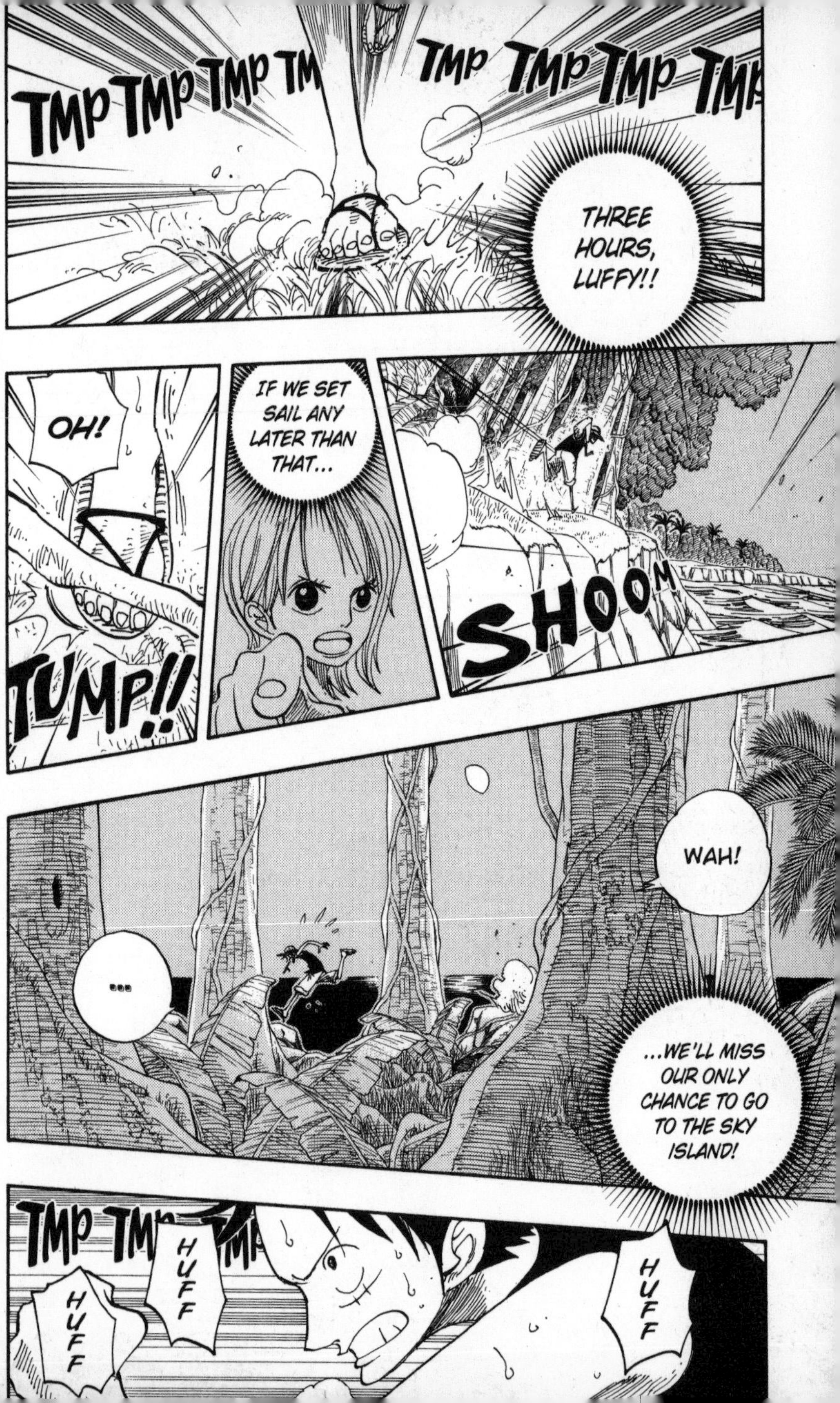
TMP TMP TMP TMP
THREE HOURS, LUFFY!!
TMP TMP TMP TM
SHOOM
IF WE SET SAIL ANY LATER THAN THAT...
OH!
TUMP!!
WAH!
...WE'LL MISS OUR ONLY CHANCE TO GO TO THE SKY ISLAND!
...
HUFF
HUFF
HUFF
TMP TMP TMP TMP

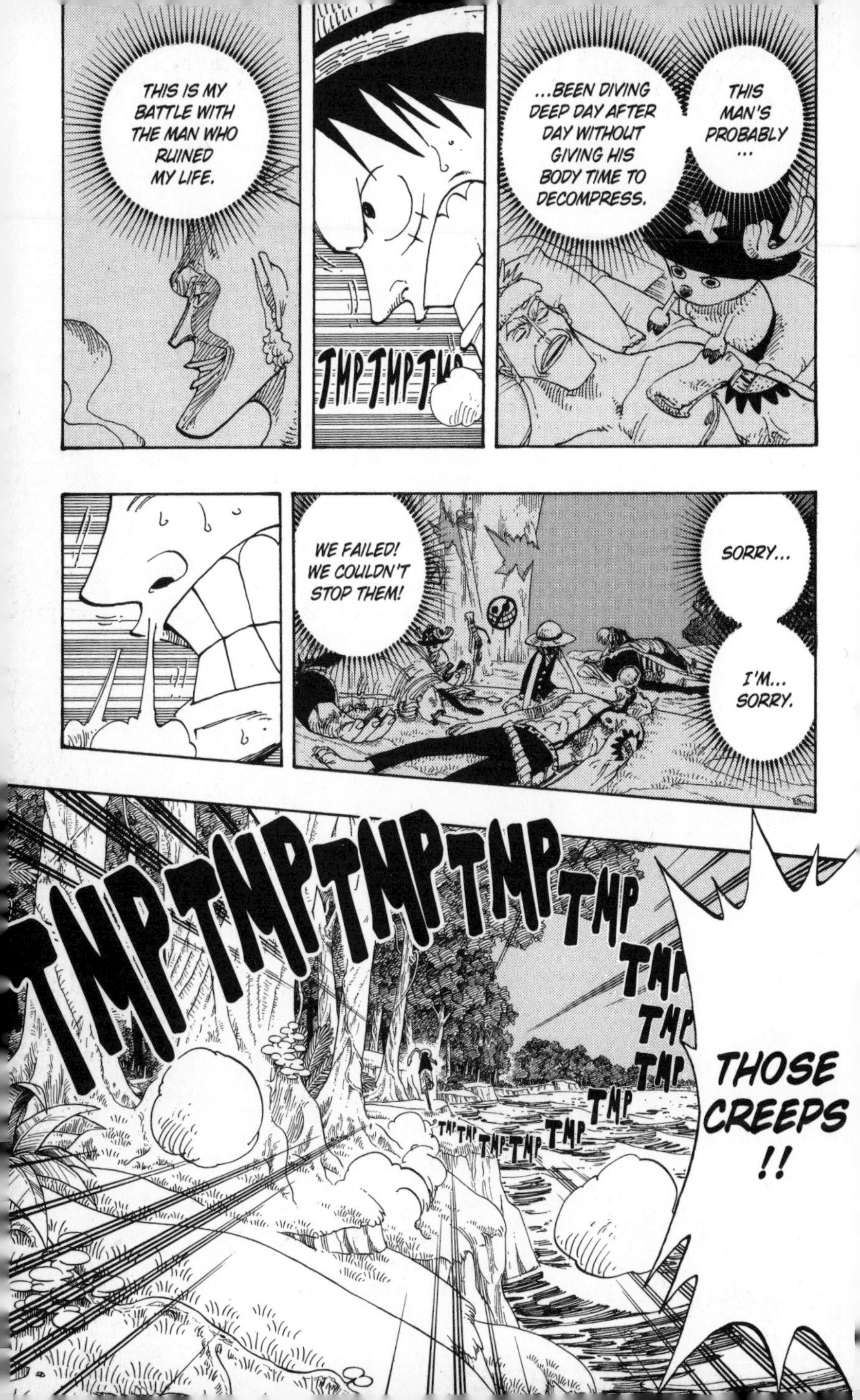
THIS MAN'S PROBABLY ...
...BEEN DIVING DEEP DAY AFTER DAY WITHOUT GIVING HIS BODY TIME TO DECOMPRESS.
TMP TMP TM
THIS IS MY BATTLE WITH THE MAN WHO RUINED MY LIFE.
SORRY...
I'M... SORRY.
WE FAILED! WE COULDN'T STOP THEM!
THOSE CREEPS !!
TMP TMP TMP TMP TMP TMP TMP TMP TMP TMP TMP
TMP TMP TMP TMP TMP

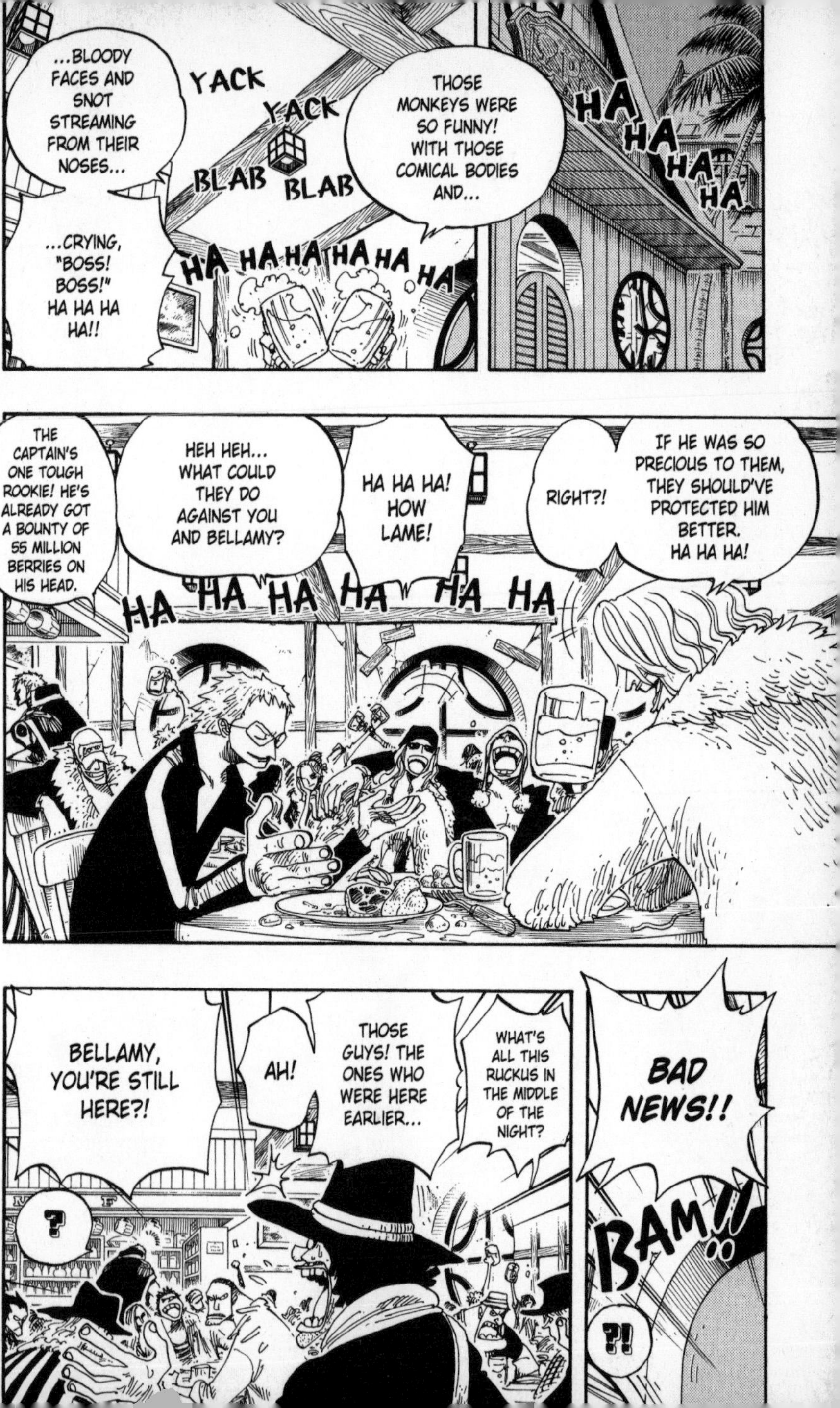
HA HA HA HA HA HA
THOSE MONKEYS WERE SO FUNNY! WITH THOSE COMICAL BODIES AND...
YACK YACK
BLAB BLAB
...BLOODY FACES AND SNOT STREAMING FROM THEIR NOSES...
...CRYING, "BOSS! BOSS!" HA HA HA HA!!
HA HA HA HA HA HA
IF HE WAS SO PRECIOUS TO THEM, THEY SHOULD'VE PROTECTED HIM BETTER. HA HA HA!
RIGHT?!
HA HA HA! HOW LAME!
HEH HEH... WHAT COULD THEY DO AGAINST YOU AND BELLAMY?
THE CAPTAIN'S ONE TOUGH ROOKIE! HE'S ALREADY GOT A BOUNTY OF 55 MILLION BERRIES ON HIS HEAD.
HA HA HA HA HA HA
BAD NEWS!!
BAM!!
?!
WHAT'S ALL THIS RUCKUS IN THE MIDDLE OF THE NIGHT?
THOSE GUYS! THE ONES WHO WERE HERE EARLIER...
AH!
BELLAMY, YOU'RE STILL HERE?!
?

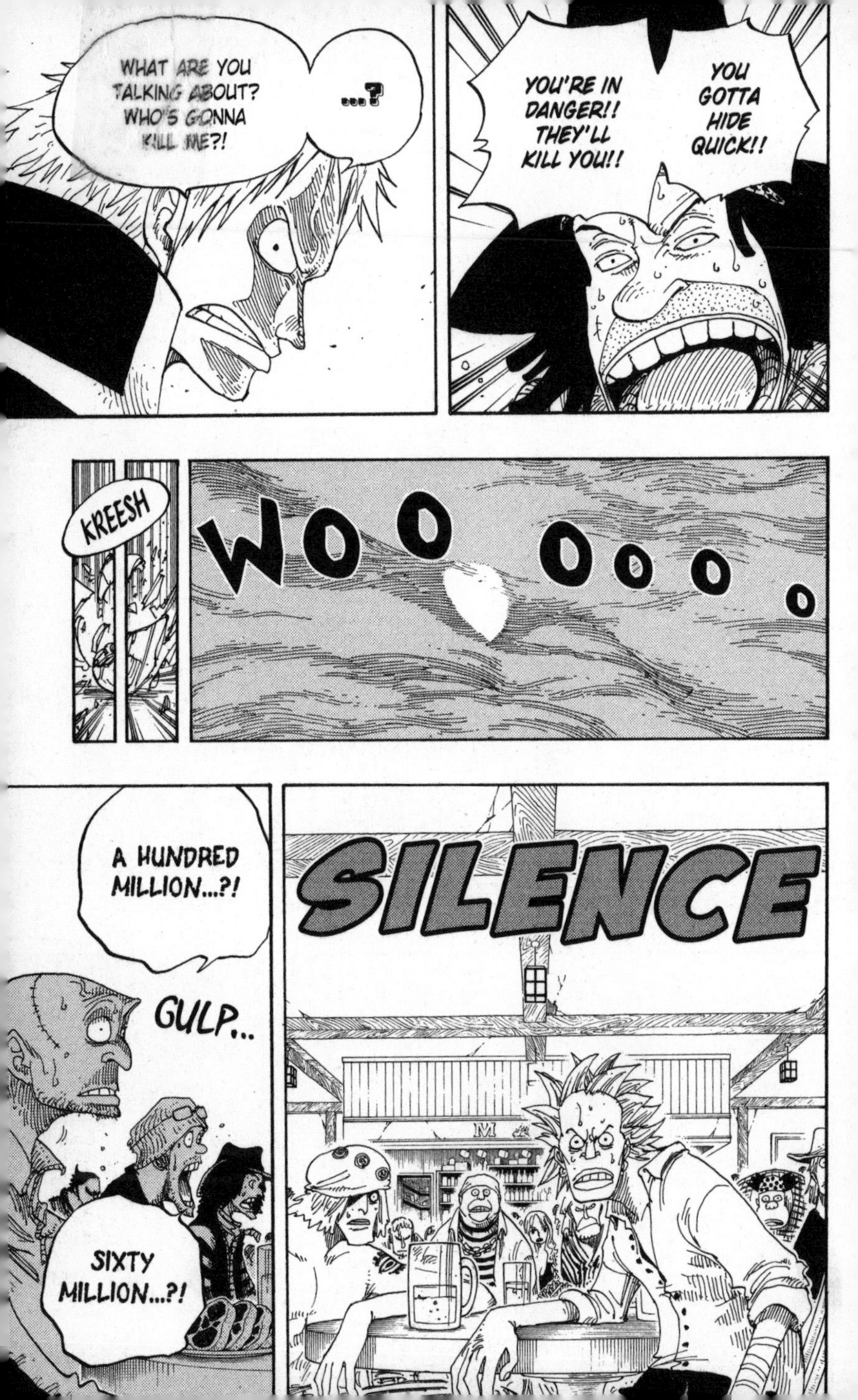
YOU'RE IN DANGER!! THEY'LL KILL YOU!!
YOU GOTTA HIDE QUICK!!
...?
WHAT ARE YOU TALKING ABOUT? WHO'S GONNA KILL ME?!
WOOOOOO
KREESH
SILENCE
A HUNDRED MILLION...?!
GULP...
SIXTY MILLION...?!

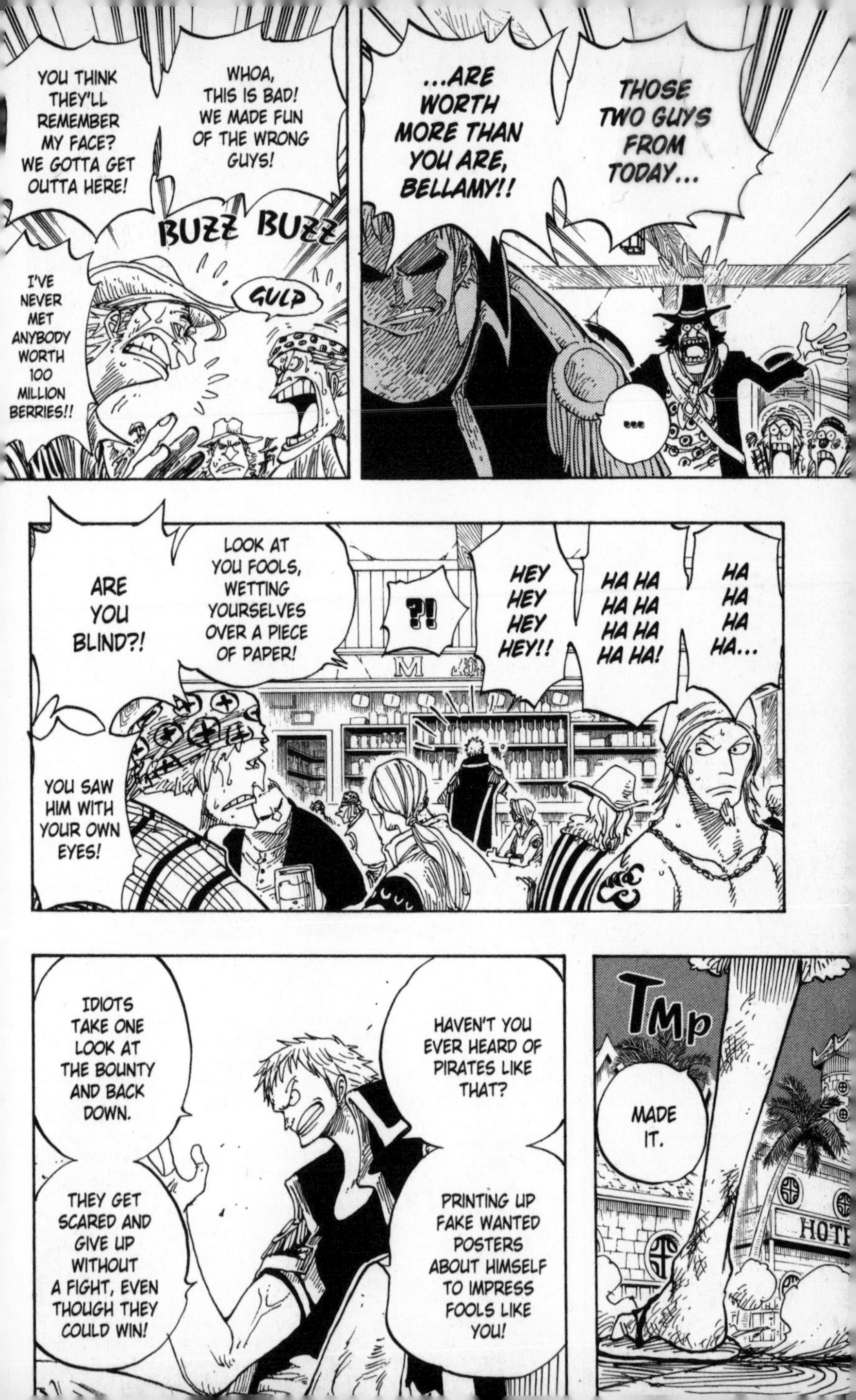
THOSE TWO GUYS FROM TODAY...
...ARE WORTH MORE THAN YOU ARE, BELLAMY!!
...
WHOA, THIS IS BAD! WE MADE FUN OF THE WRONG GUYS!
YOU THINK THEY'LL REMEMBER MY FACE? WE GOTTA GET OUTTA HERE!
BUZZ BUZZ
GULP
I'VE NEVER MET ANYBODY WORTH 100 MILLION BERRIES!!
HA HA HA HA...
HA HA HA HA HA HA HA HA!
HEY HEY HEY HEY!!
?!
LOOK AT YOU FOOLS, WETTING YOURSELVES OVER A PIECE OF PAPER!
ARE YOU BLIND?!
YOU SAW HIM WITH YOUR OWN EYES!
TMP
MADE IT.
HAVEN'T YOU EVER HEARD OF PIRATES LIKE THAT?
PRINTING UP FAKE WANTED POSTERS ABOUT HIMSELF TO IMPRESS FOOLS LIKE YOU!
IDIOTS TAKE ONE LOOK AT THE BOUNTY AND BACK DOWN.
THEY GET SCARED AND GIVE UP WITHOUT A FIGHT, EVEN THOUGH THEY COULD WIN!

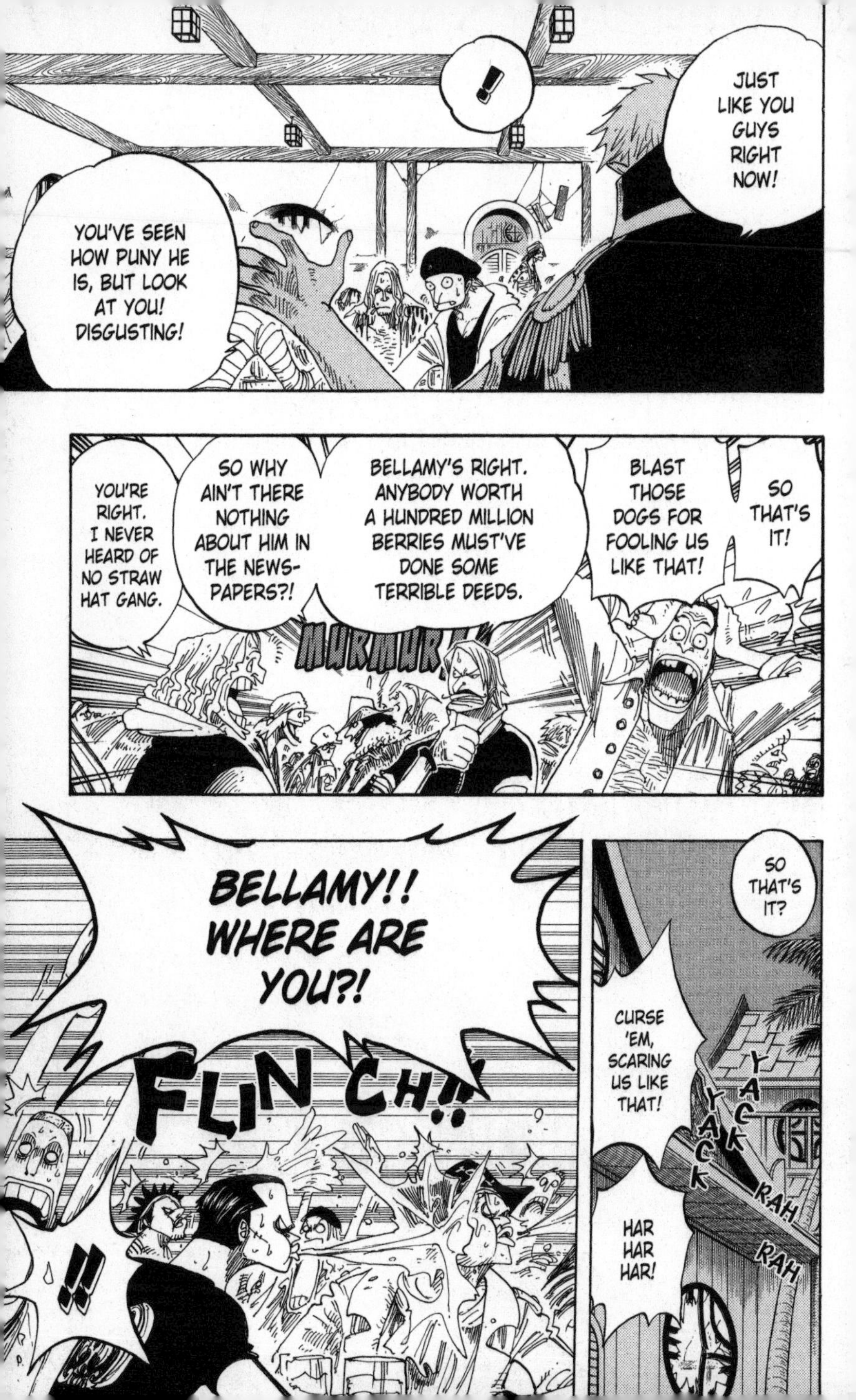
JUST LIKE YOU GUYS RIGHT NOW!
!
YOU'VE SEEN HOW PUNY HE IS, BUT LOOK AT YOU! DISGUSTING!
SO THAT'S IT!
BLAST THOSE DOGS FOR FOOLING US LIKE THAT!
BELLAMY'S RIGHT. ANYBODY WORTH A HUNDRED MILLION BERRIES MUST'VE DONE SOME TERRIBLE DEEDS.
SO WHY AIN'T THERE NOTHING ABOUT HIM IN THE NEWS-PAPERS?!
YOU'RE RIGHT. I NEVER HEARD OF NO STRAW HAT GANG.
MURMUR
SO THAT'S IT?
CURSE 'EM, SCARING US LIKE THAT!
YACK YACK
YACK
RAH
RAH
HAR HAR HAR!
BELLAMY!! WHERE ARE YOU?!
FLINCH!!
!!

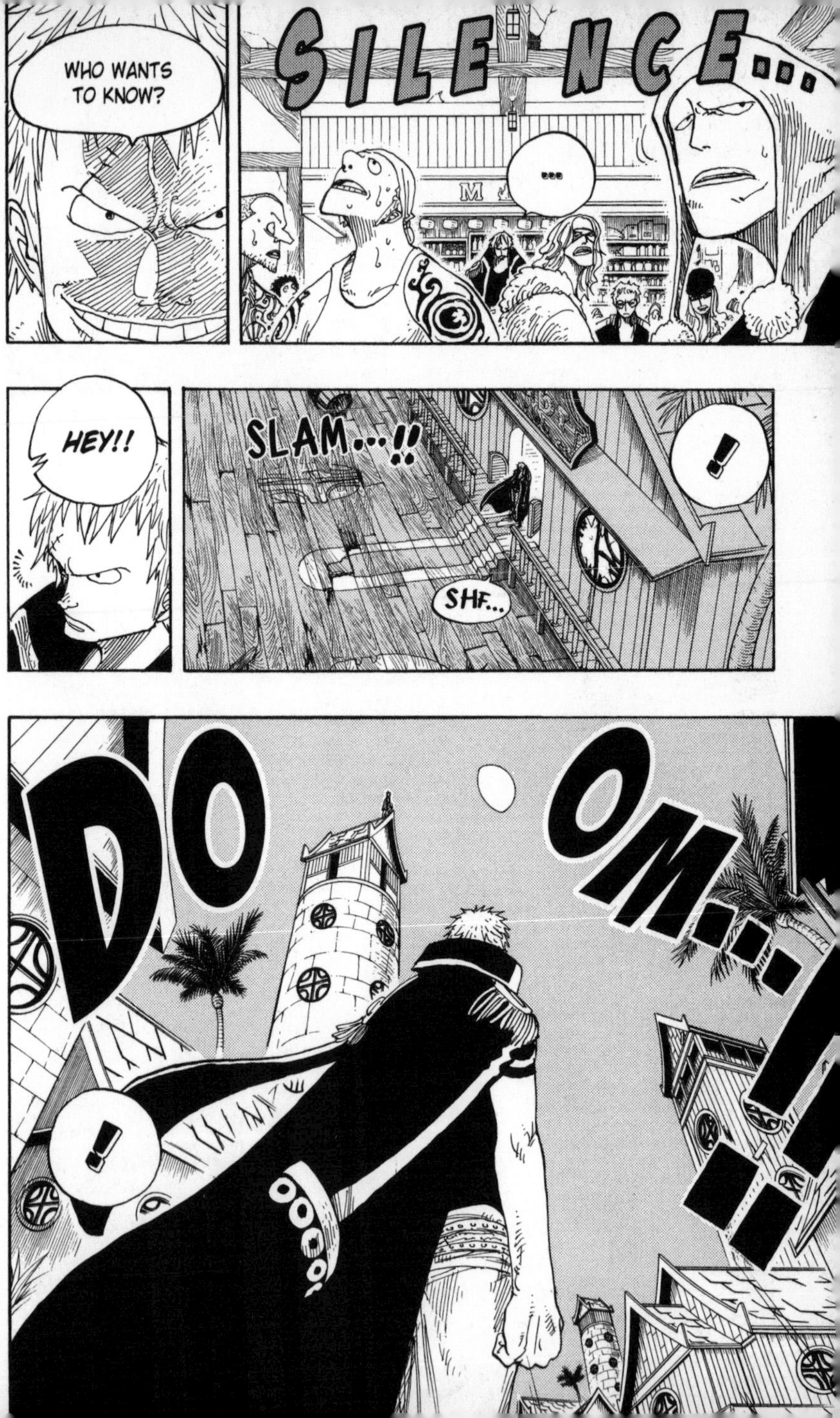
SILENCE...
...
WHO WANTS TO KNOW?
!
SLAM...!!
SHF...
HEY!!
DOOM...!!
!

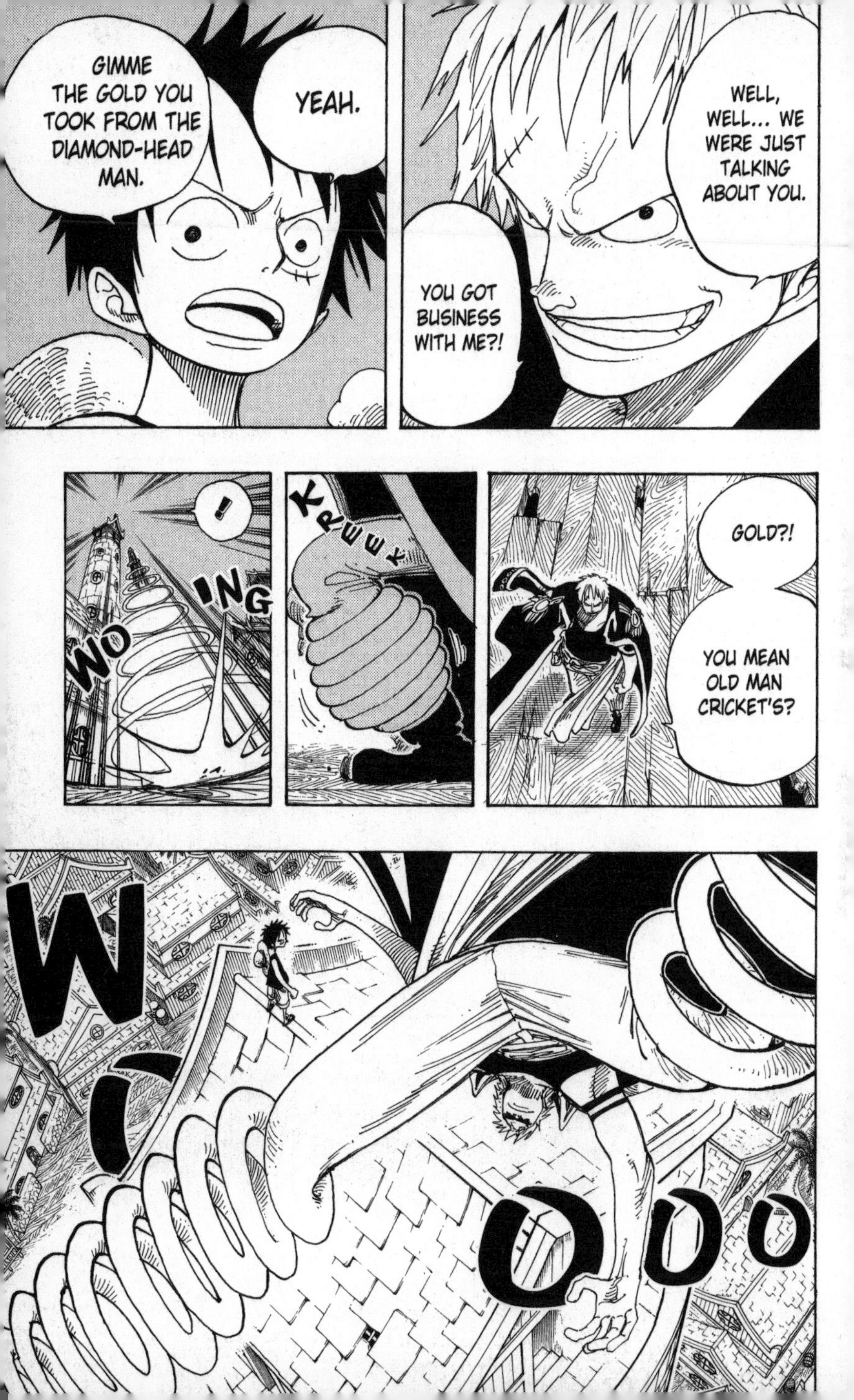
WELL, WELL... WE WERE JUST TALKING ABOUT YOU.
YOU GOT BUSINESS WITH ME?!
YEAH.
GIMME THE GOLD YOU TOOK FROM THE DIAMOND-HEAD MAN.
GOLD?!
YOU MEAN OLD MAN CRICKET'S?
KREEK
!
WOING
WOOOO

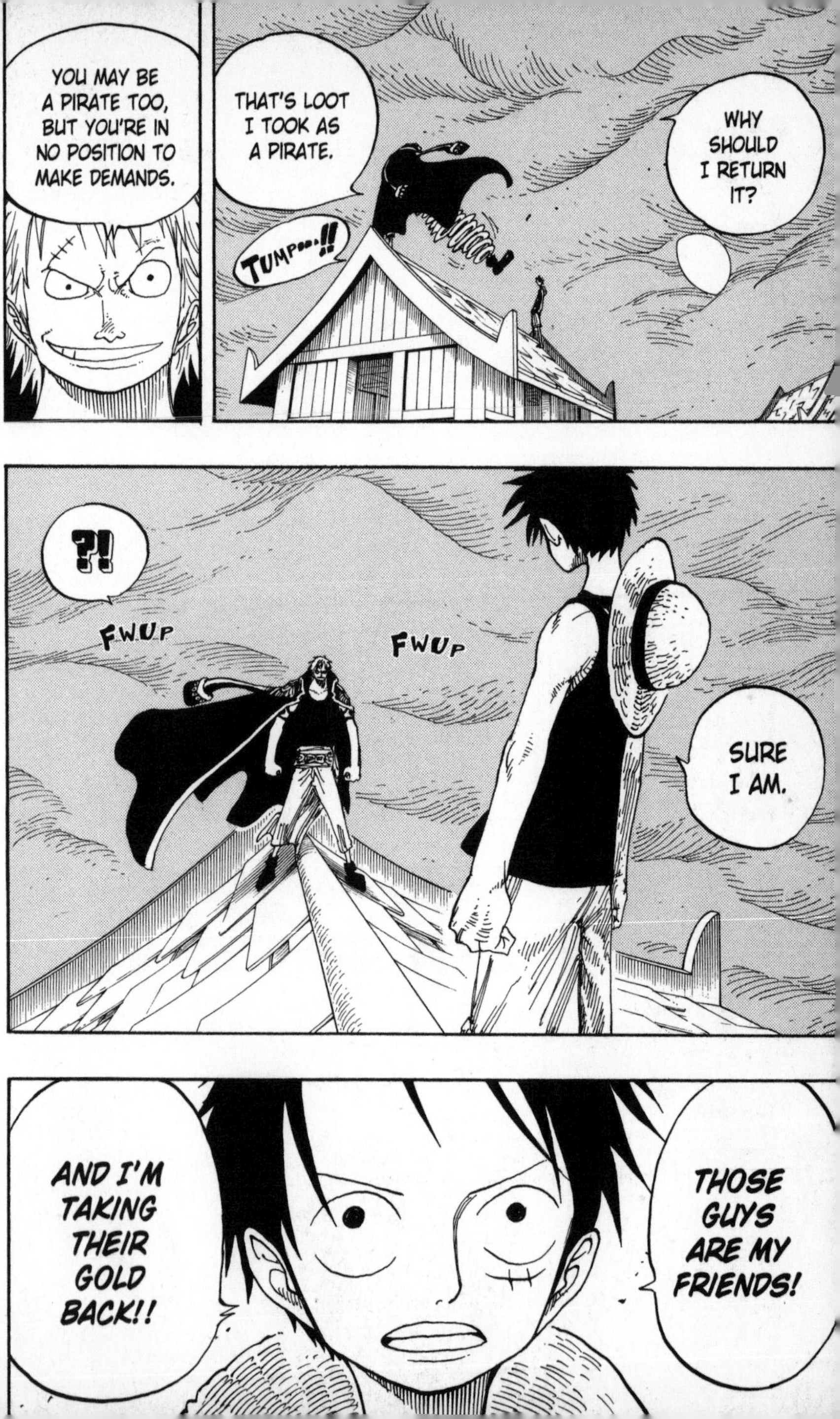
WHY SHOULD I RETURN IT?
THAT'S LOOT I TOOK AS A PIRATE.
TUMP!!
YOU MAY BE A PIRATE TOO, BUT YOU'RE IN NO POSITION TO MAKE DEMANDS.
?!
FWUP
FWUP
SURE I AM.
THOSE GUYS ARE MY FRIENDS!
AND I'M TAKING THEIR GOLD BACK!!

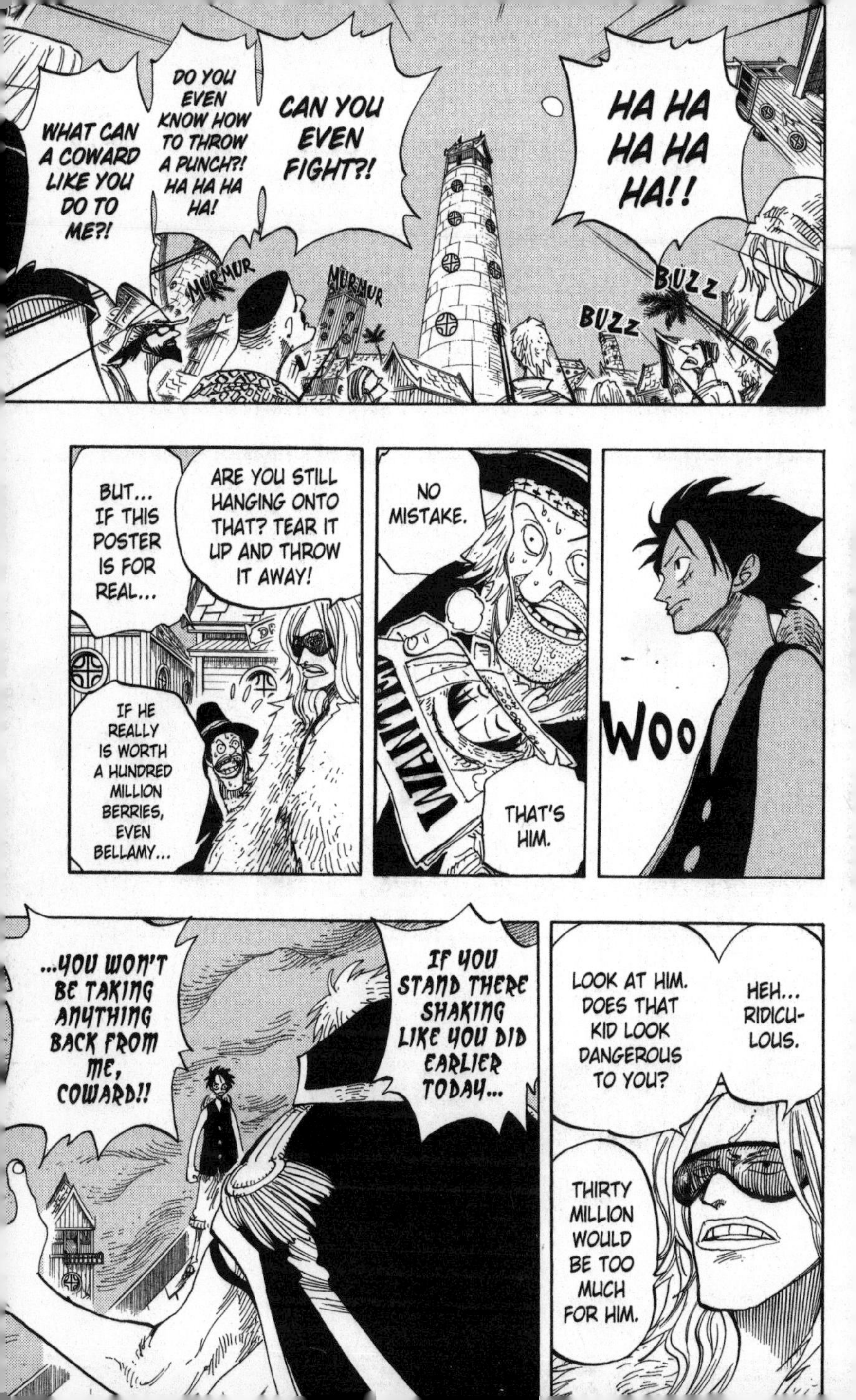
HA HA HA HA HA!!
CAN YOU EVEN FIGHT?!
DO YOU EVEN KNOW HOW TO THROW A PUNCH?! HA HA HA HA!
WHAT CAN A COWARD LIKE YOU DO TO ME?!
BUZZ
BUZZ
MURMUR
MURMUR
WOO
NO MISTAKE.
THAT'S HIM.
ARE YOU STILL HANGING ONTO THAT? TEAR IT UP AND THROW IT AWAY!
BUT... IF THIS POSTER IS FOR REAL...
IF HE REALLY IS WORTH A HUNDRED MILLION BERRIES, EVEN BELLAMY...
HEH... RIDICULOUS.
LOOK AT HIM. DOES THAT KID LOOK DANGEROUS TO YOU?
THIRTY MILLION WOULD BE TOO MUCH FOR HIM.
IF YOU STAND THERE SHAKING LIKE YOU DID EARLIER TODAY...
...YOU WON'T BE TAKING ANYTHING BACK FROM ME, COWARD!!

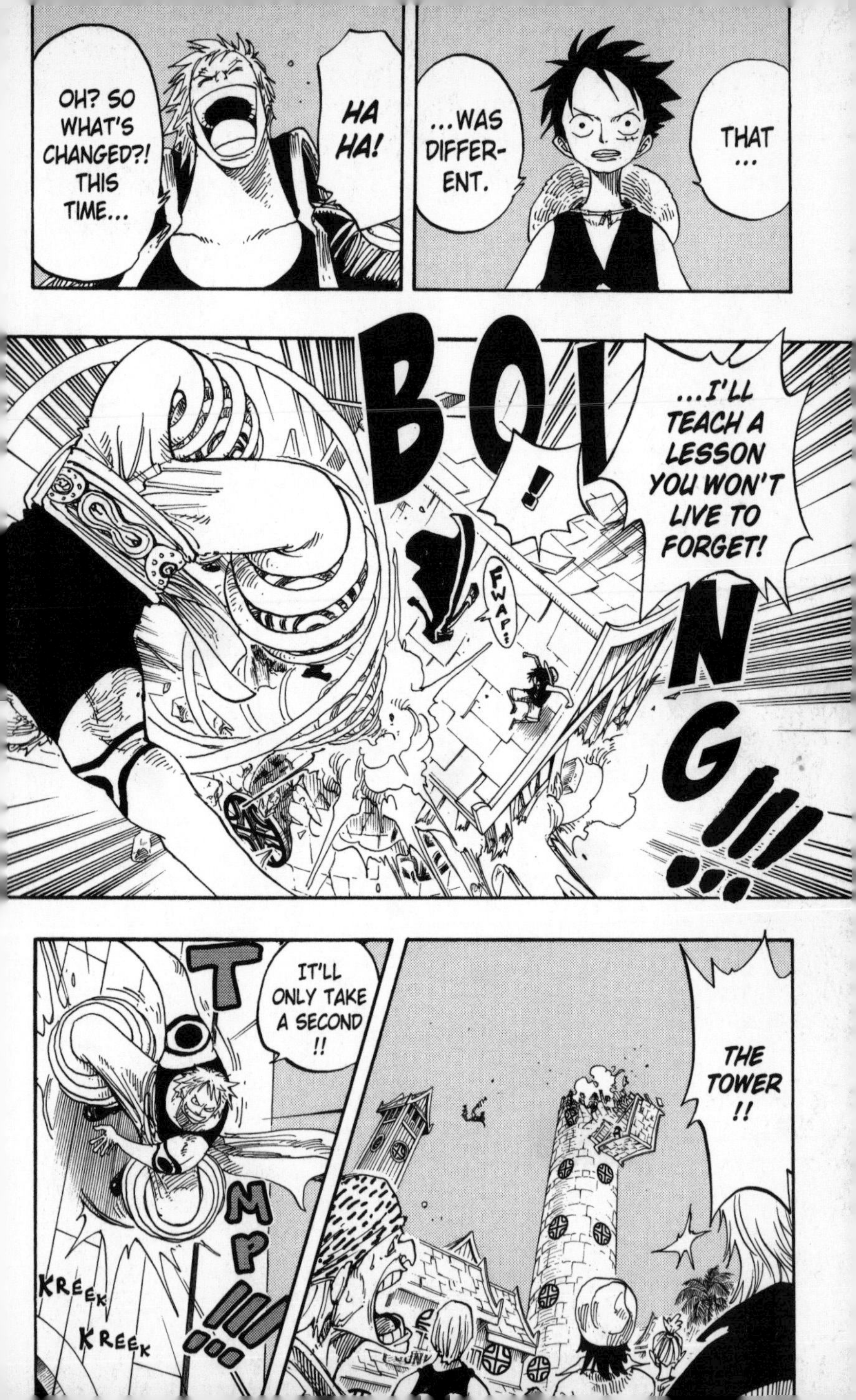
THAT ...
...WAS DIFFER-ENT.
HA HA!
OH? SO WHAT'S CHANGED?! THIS TIME...
...I'LL TEACH A LESSON YOU WON'T LIVE TO FORGET!
BOING!!!
FWAP!
THE TOWER !!
IT'LL ONLY TAKE A SECOND !!
TMP!!!
KREEK
KREEK

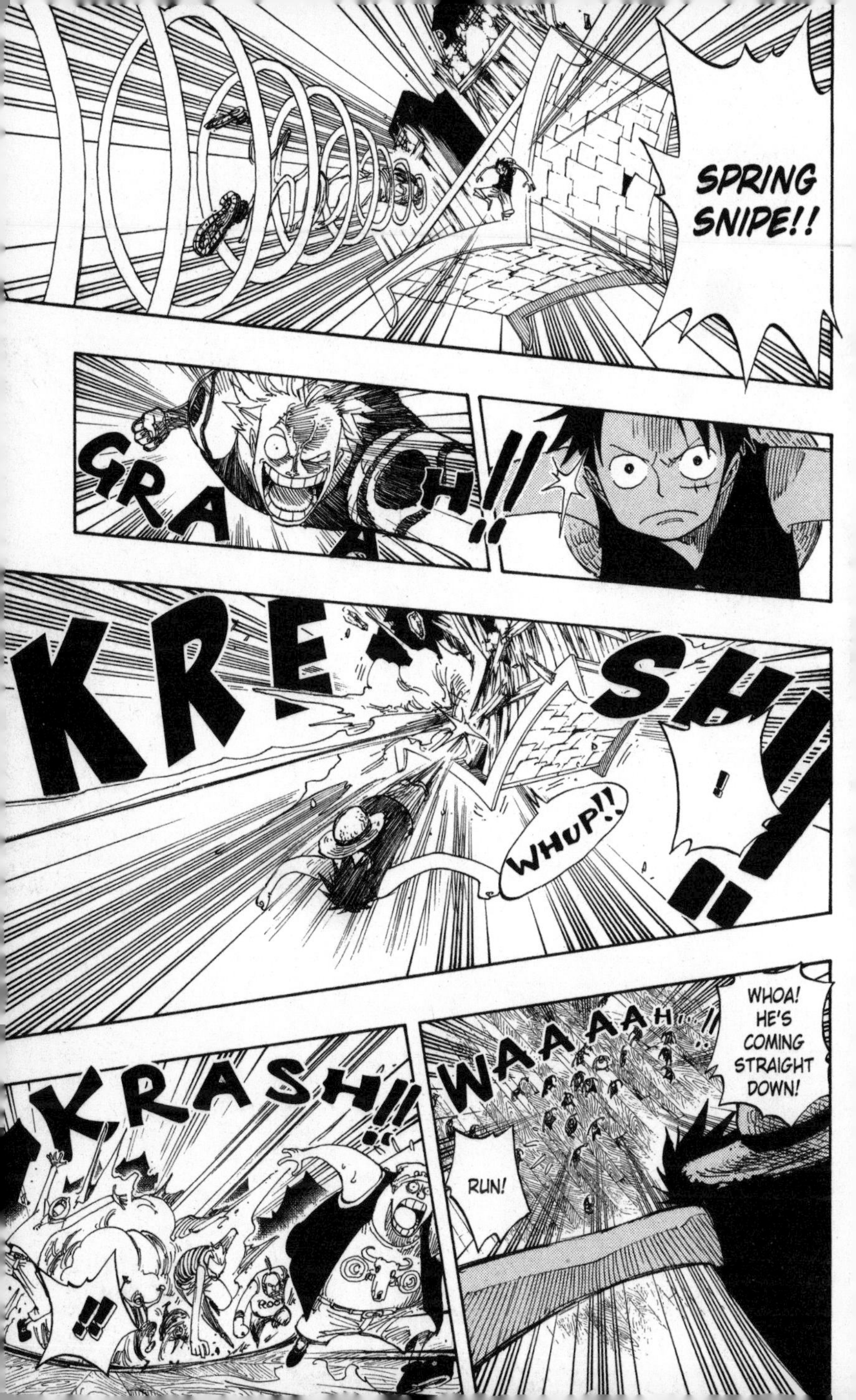
SPRING SNIPE!!
GRAAACH!!
KREESH!!
WHUP!!
!
WHOA! HE'S COMING STRAIGHT DOWN!
WAAAAAH...!!
RUN!
KRASH!!
!!

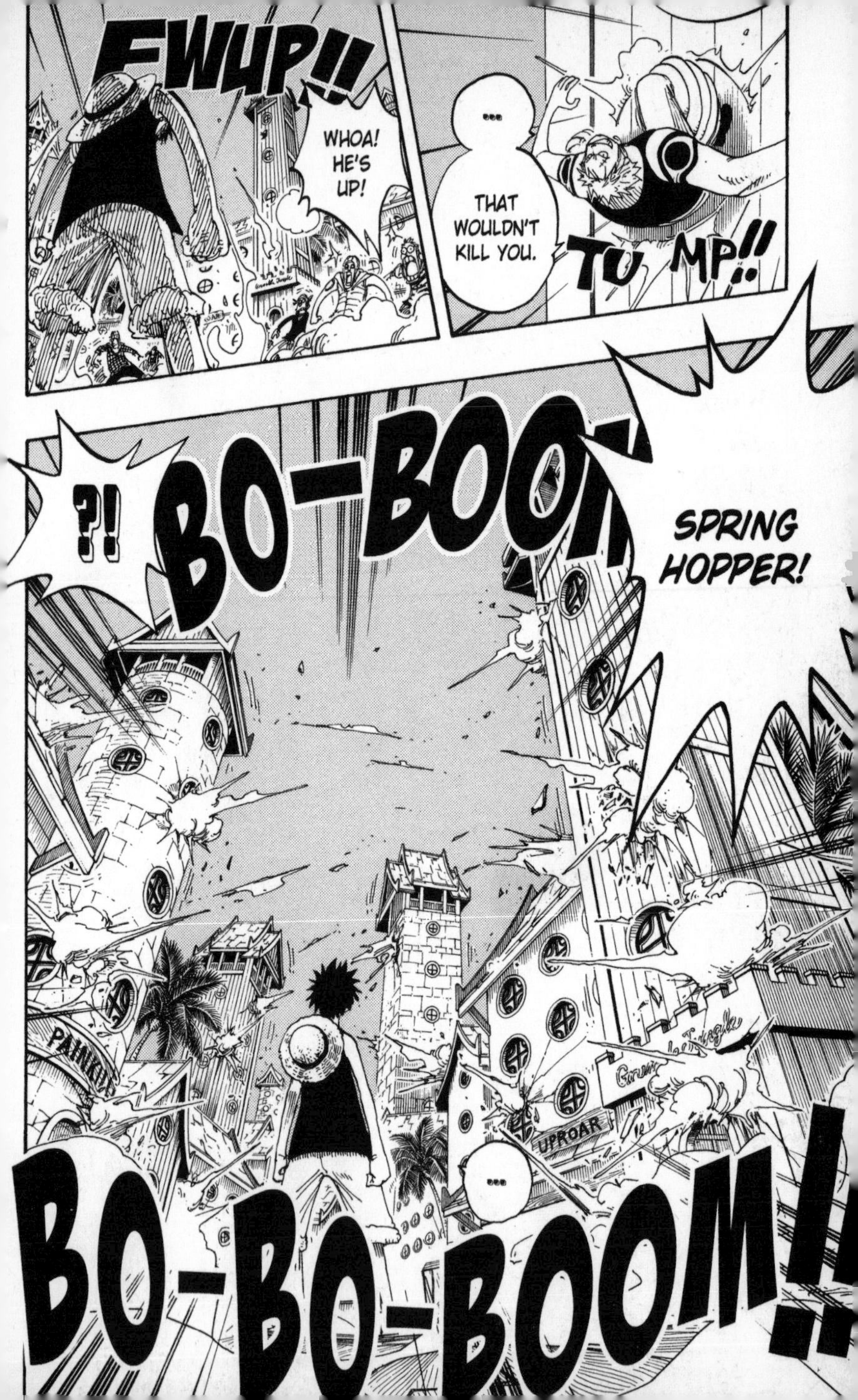

...
THAT WOULDN'T KILL YOU.
TU MP!!
FWUP!!
WHOA! HE'S UP!
SPRING HOPPER!
BO-BOOM
?!
UPROAR
...
BO-BO-BOOM!!

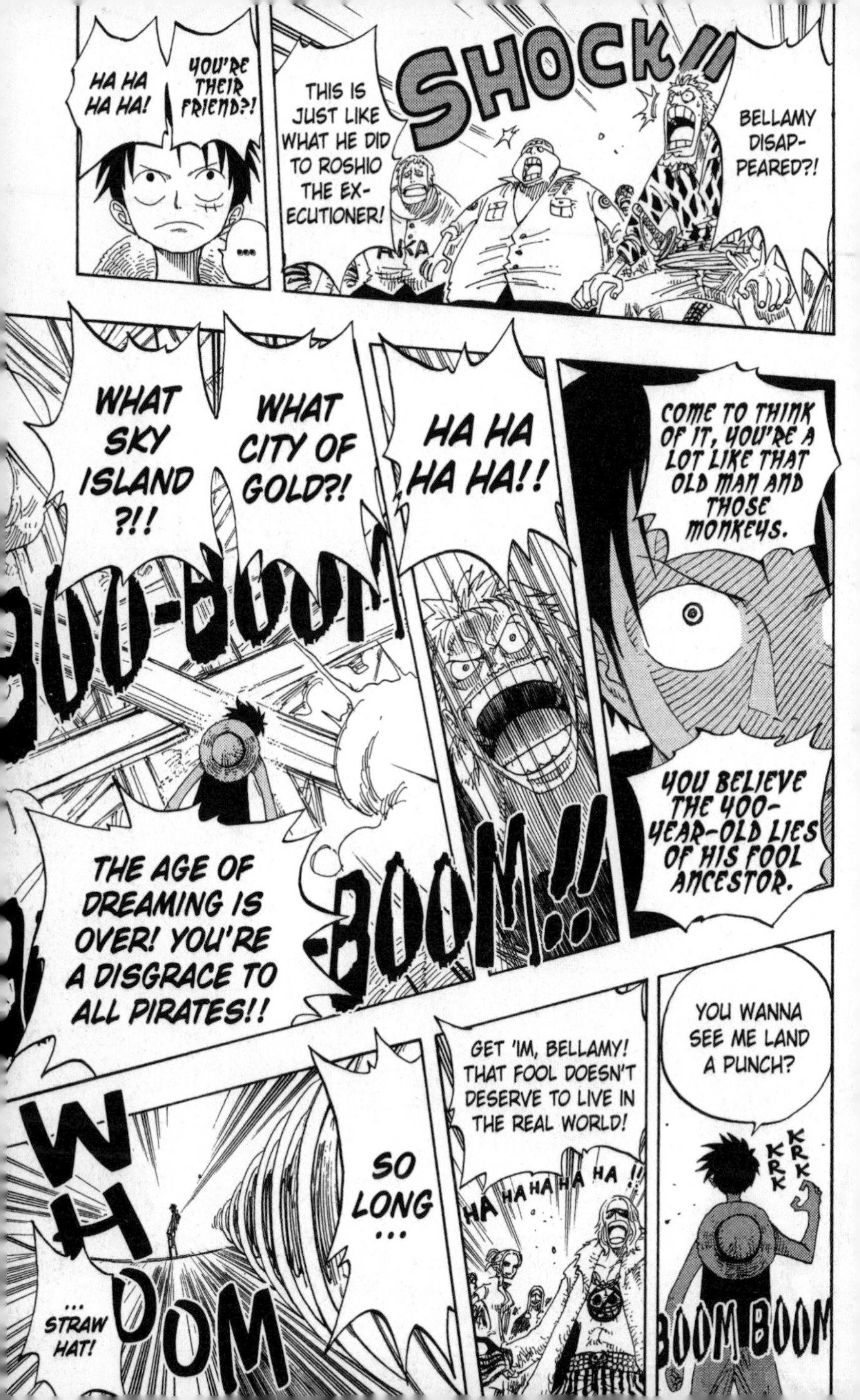
SHOCK!!
BELLAMY DISAP-PEARED?!
THIS IS JUST LIKE WHAT HE DID TO ROSHIO THE EX-ECUTIONER!
YOU'RE THEIR FRIEND?!
HA HA HA HA!
...
COME TO THINK OF IT, YOU'RE A LOT LIKE THAT OLD MAN AND THOSE MONKEYS.
YOU BELIEVE THE 400-YEAR-OLD LIES OF HIS FOOL ANCESTOR.
HA HA HA HA!!
BOOM!!
WHAT CITY OF GOLD?!
WHAT SKY ISLAND ?!!
THE AGE OF DREAMING IS OVER! YOU'RE A DISGRACE TO ALL PIRATES!!
YOU WANNA SEE ME LAND A PUNCH?
KRK KRK
BOOM BOOM
GET 'IM, BELLAMY! THAT FOOL DOESN'T DESERVE TO LIVE IN THE REAL WORLD!
HA HA HA HA HA HA!!
SO LONG ...
WHOOM
... STRAW HAT!

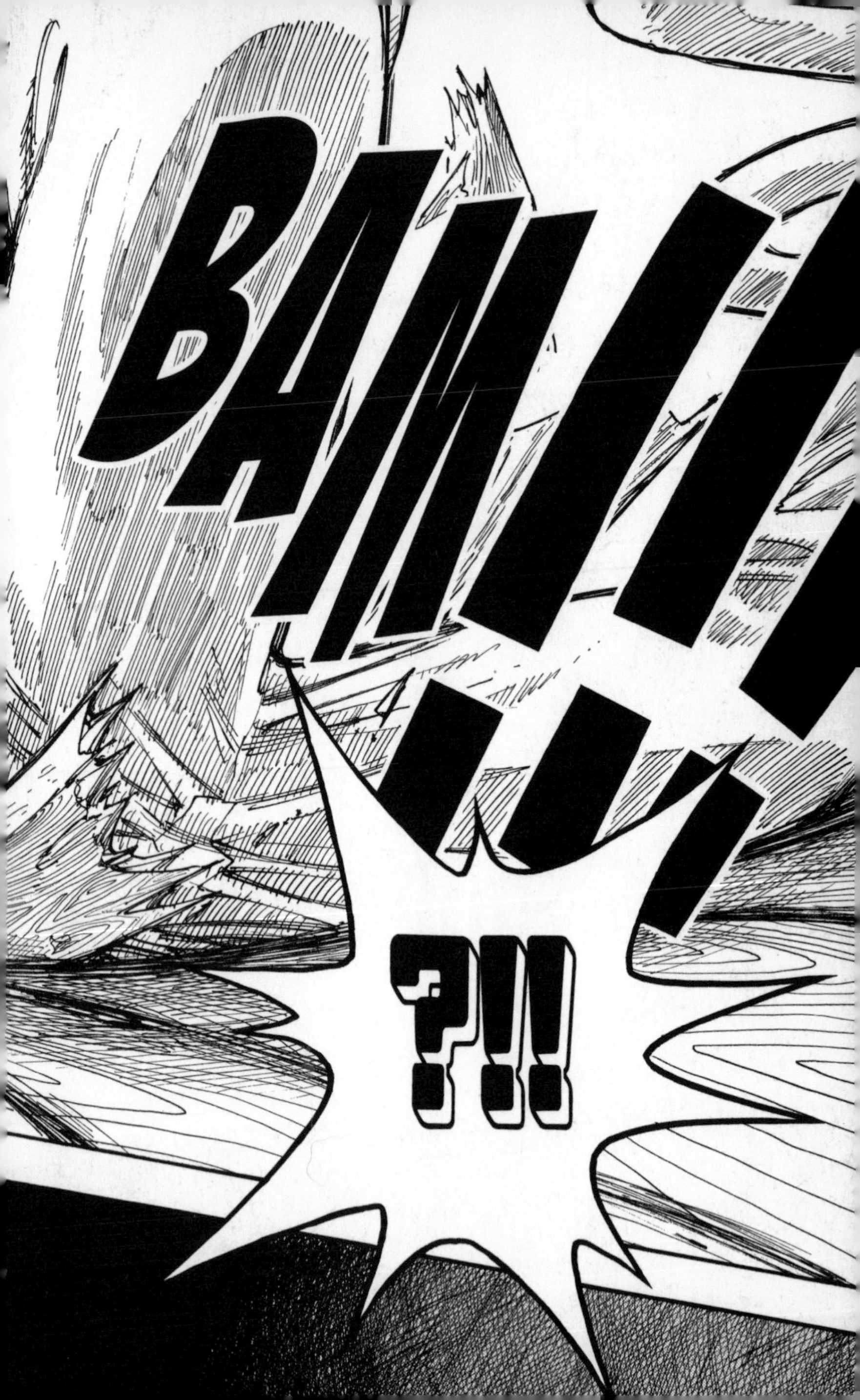
BAMMM
?!!

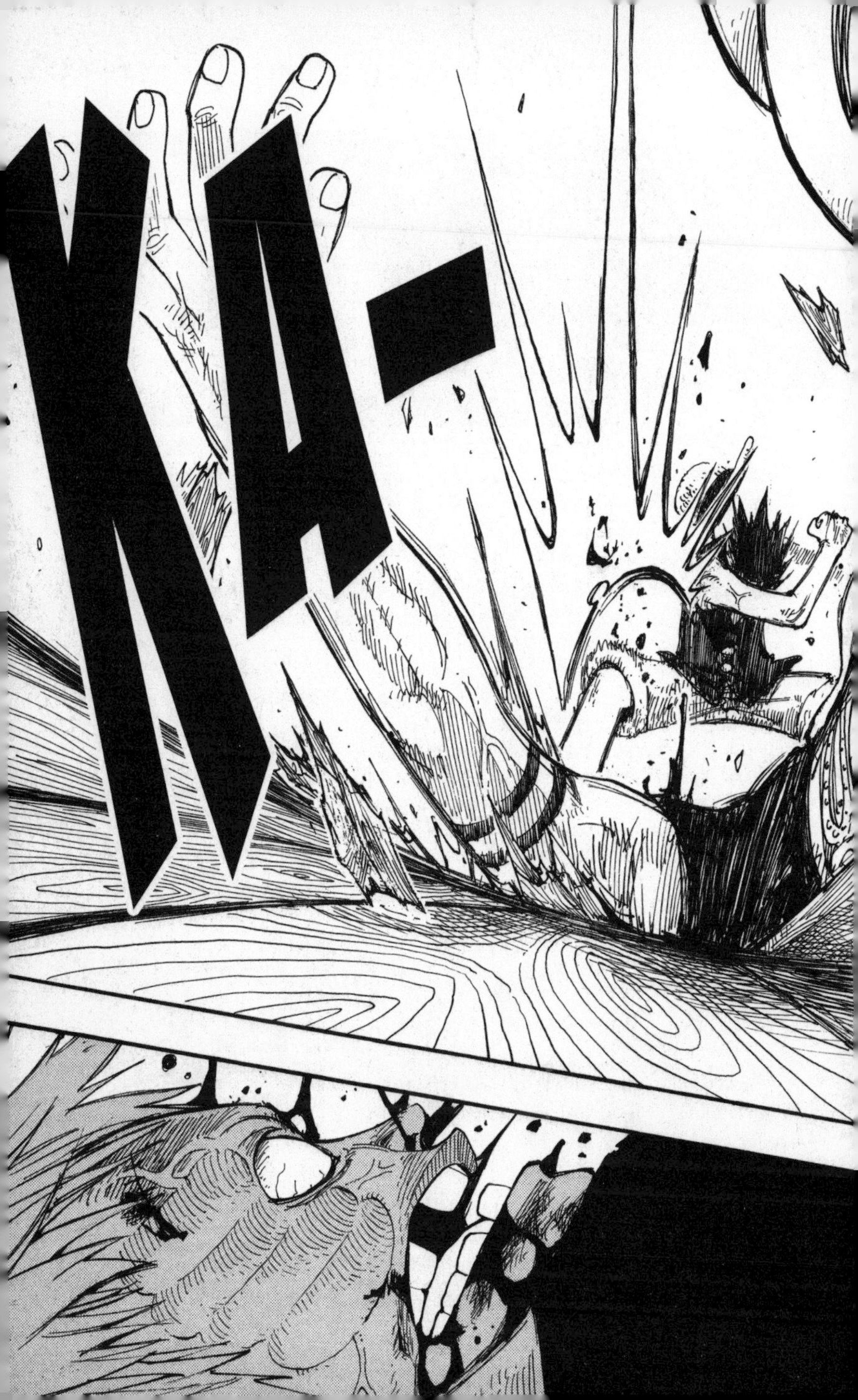
KA-

QUESTION CORNER
SBS

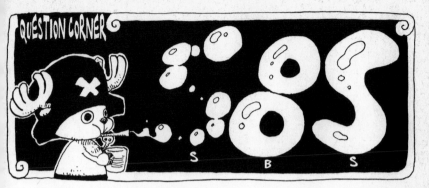

Q: I'll dispense with formalities. Why does Zolo wear his swords at his right hip? They're usually worn on the left.

--Sousou

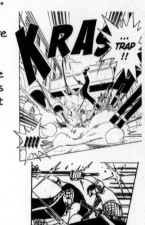

A: Well... Because if Zolo doesn't weigh down his right side, he leans to the left. (Casually.) Oh, so now here's a question from me. In volume 21, chapter 194, "Cutting Steel," you can see Zolo with his swords at his left hip, right? And on page 154, where are his scabbards? And is it true that hardly any of you readers noticed this obvious error? Yes, that's true. And is it also true that, though aware of the mistake, it was left untouched for the simple reason that there were too many panels to fix? Yes it is. Which inspires a haiku.

**Poor Oda Sensei**
**Is tired again today**
**Weather is so nice**

Thank you very much, Sensei.
Don't mention it.

...TRAP!!
KRASH!!
!!!!

Q: I have a serious question for you, Oda Sensei. Why is it that in the manga world people always understand whatever language is being spoken no matter where they go?

--Chobbi

A: Because manga is about people's dreams.

# Chapter 233:
# THE WORLD'S GREATEST POWER

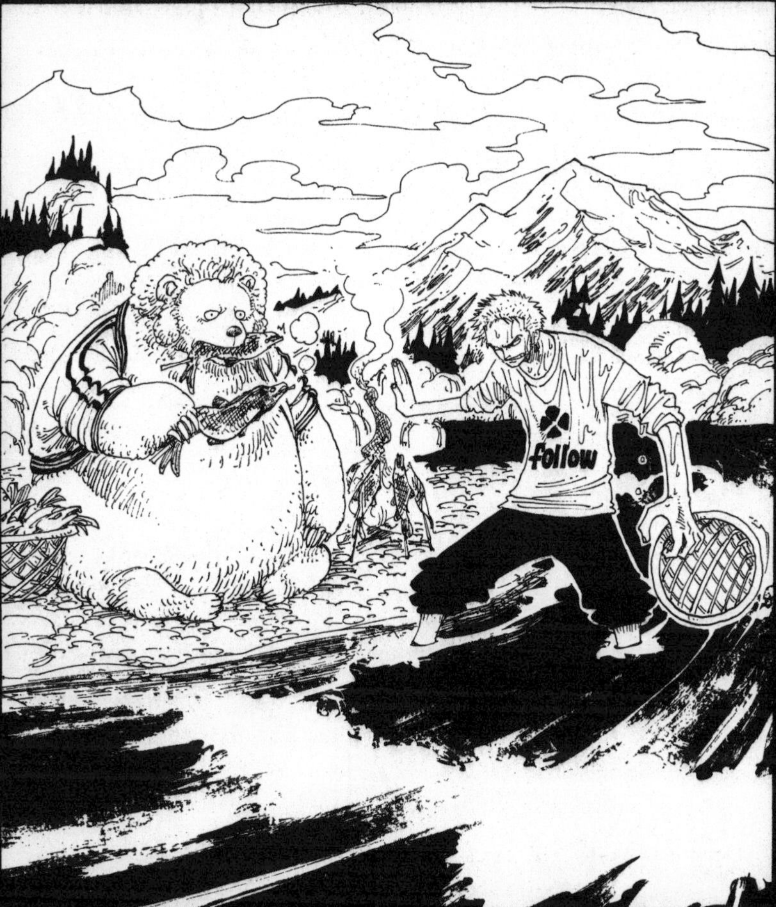
follow

WOOOO

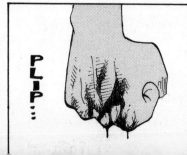

PLIP...

PLIP...

HUH?!

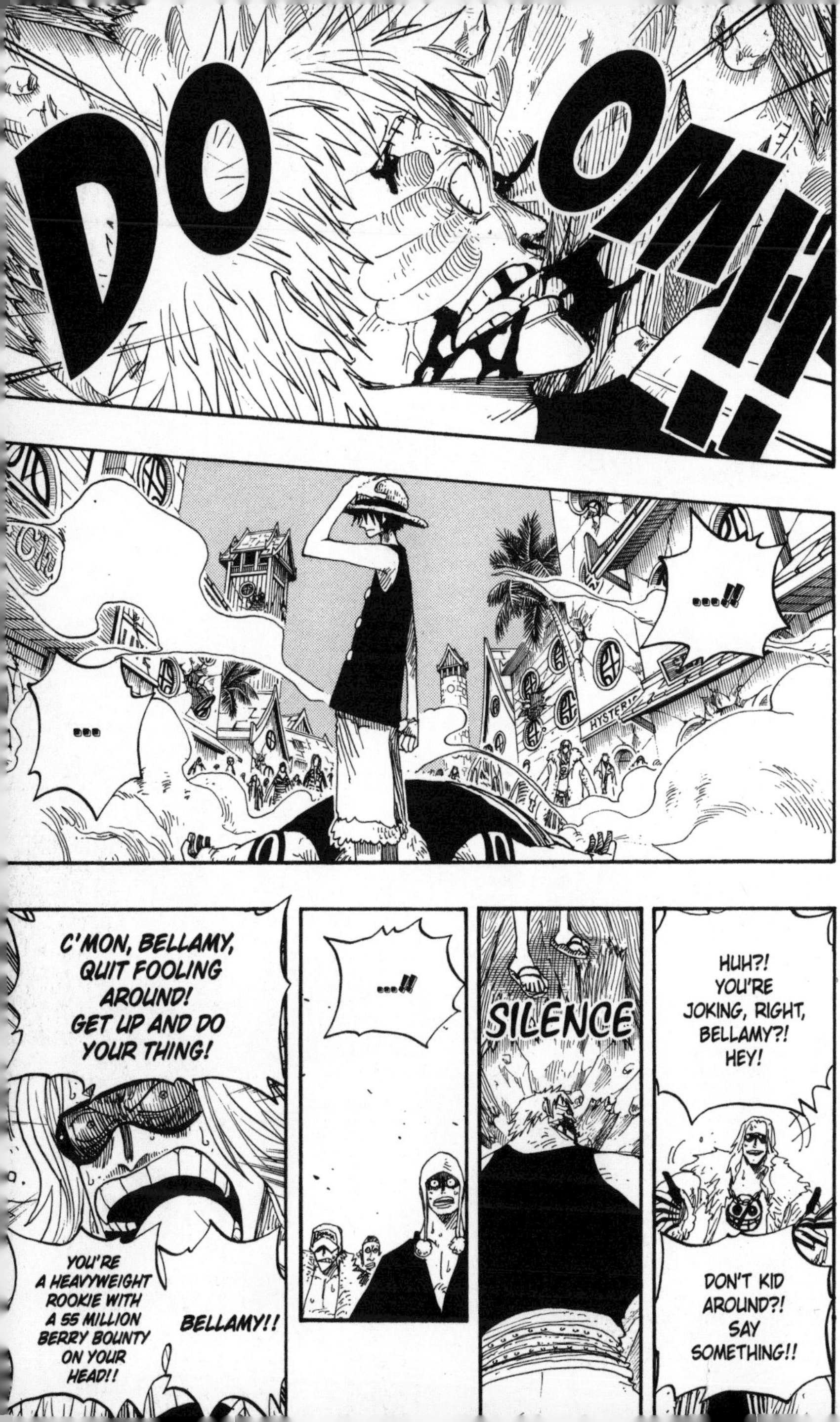
DOON!!!
...!!
...
HUH?! YOU'RE JOKING, RIGHT, BELLAMY?! HEY!
DON'T KID AROUND?! SAY SOMETHING!!
SILENCE
...!!
C'MON, BELLAMY, QUIT FOOLING AROUND! GET UP AND DO YOUR THING!
BELLAMY!!
YOU'RE A HEAVYWEIGHT ROOKIE WITH A 55 MILLION BERRY BOUNTY ON YOUR HEAD!!

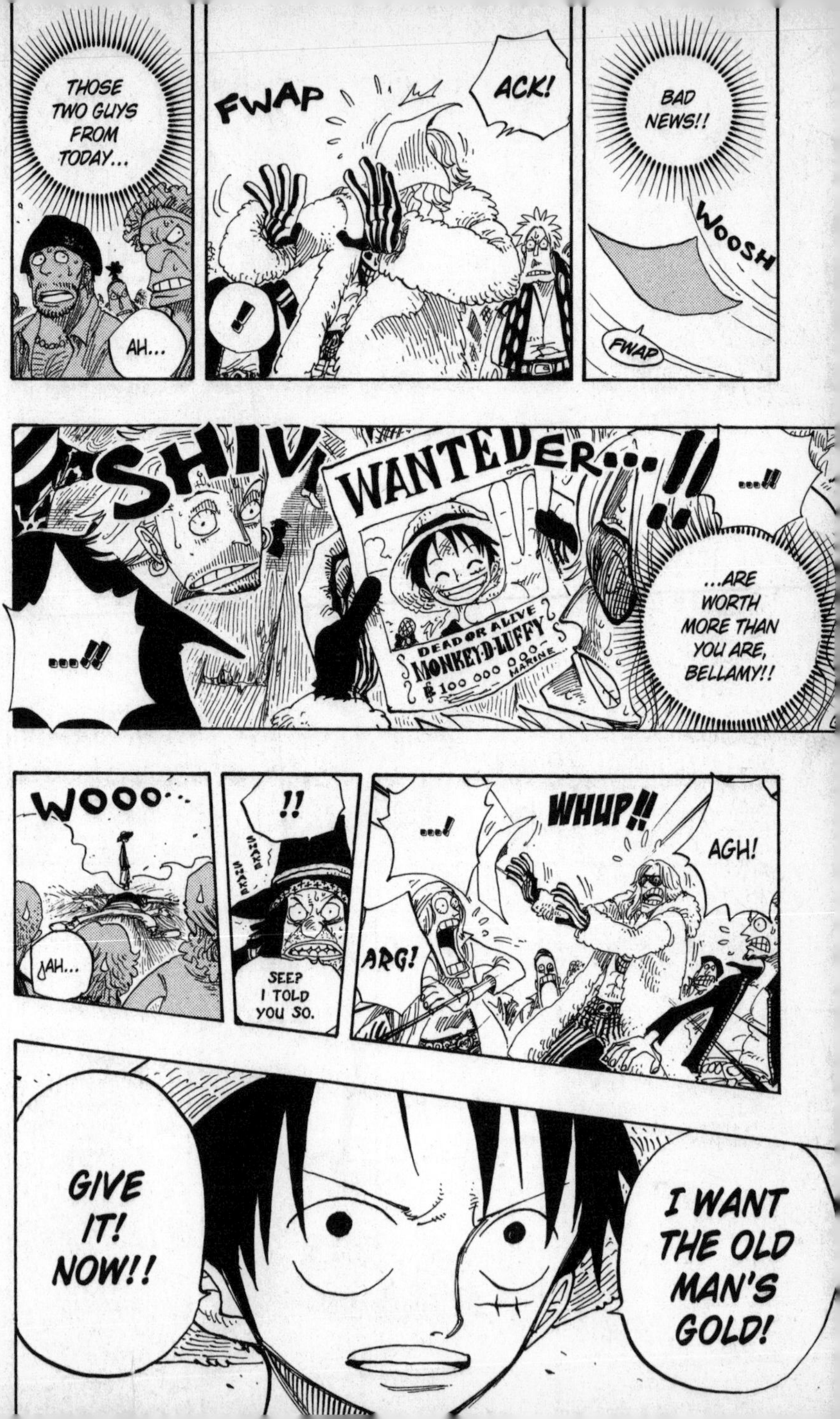
BAD NEWS!!
WOOSH
FWAP
ACK!
FWAP
!
THOSE TWO GUYS FROM TODAY...
AH...
...!!
...ARE WORTH MORE THAN YOU ARE, BELLAMY!!
WANTEDER...!!
DEAD OR ALIVE
MONKEY·D·LUFFY
฿100 000 000-
MARINE
SHIV
...!!
AGH!
WHUP!!
...!
ARG!
!!
SHAKE
SHAKE
SEE? I TOLD YOU SO.
WOOO...
AH...
I WANT THE OLD MAN'S GOLD!
GIVE IT! NOW!!

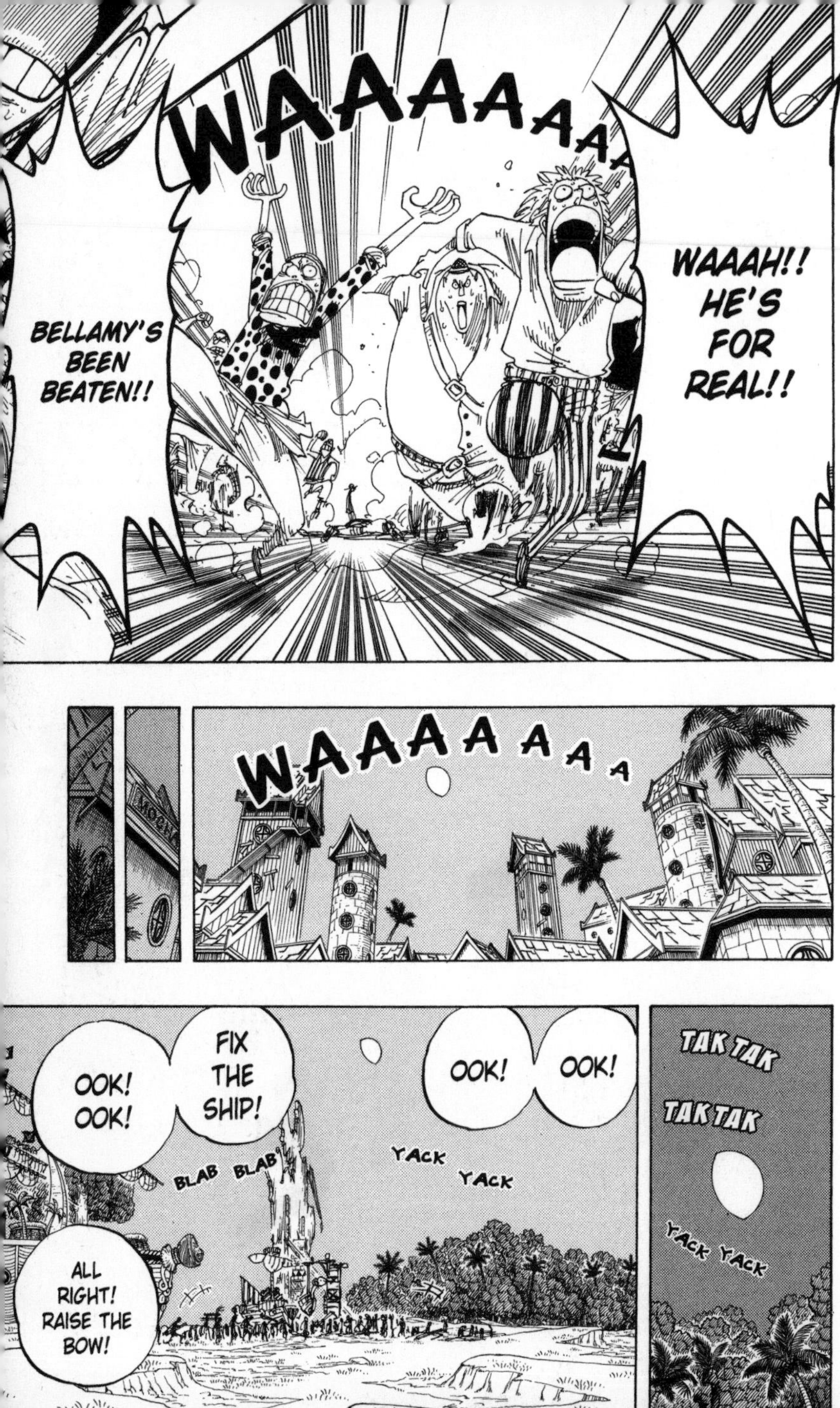
WAAAAAAAA
WAAAH!! HE'S FOR REAL!!
BELLAMY'S BEEN BEATEN!!
WAAAAAAAA
TAK TAK
TAK TAK
YACK YACK
OOK!
OOK!
YACK
YACK
FIX THE SHIP!
OOK! OOK!
BLAB BLAB
ALL RIGHT! RAISE THE BOW!

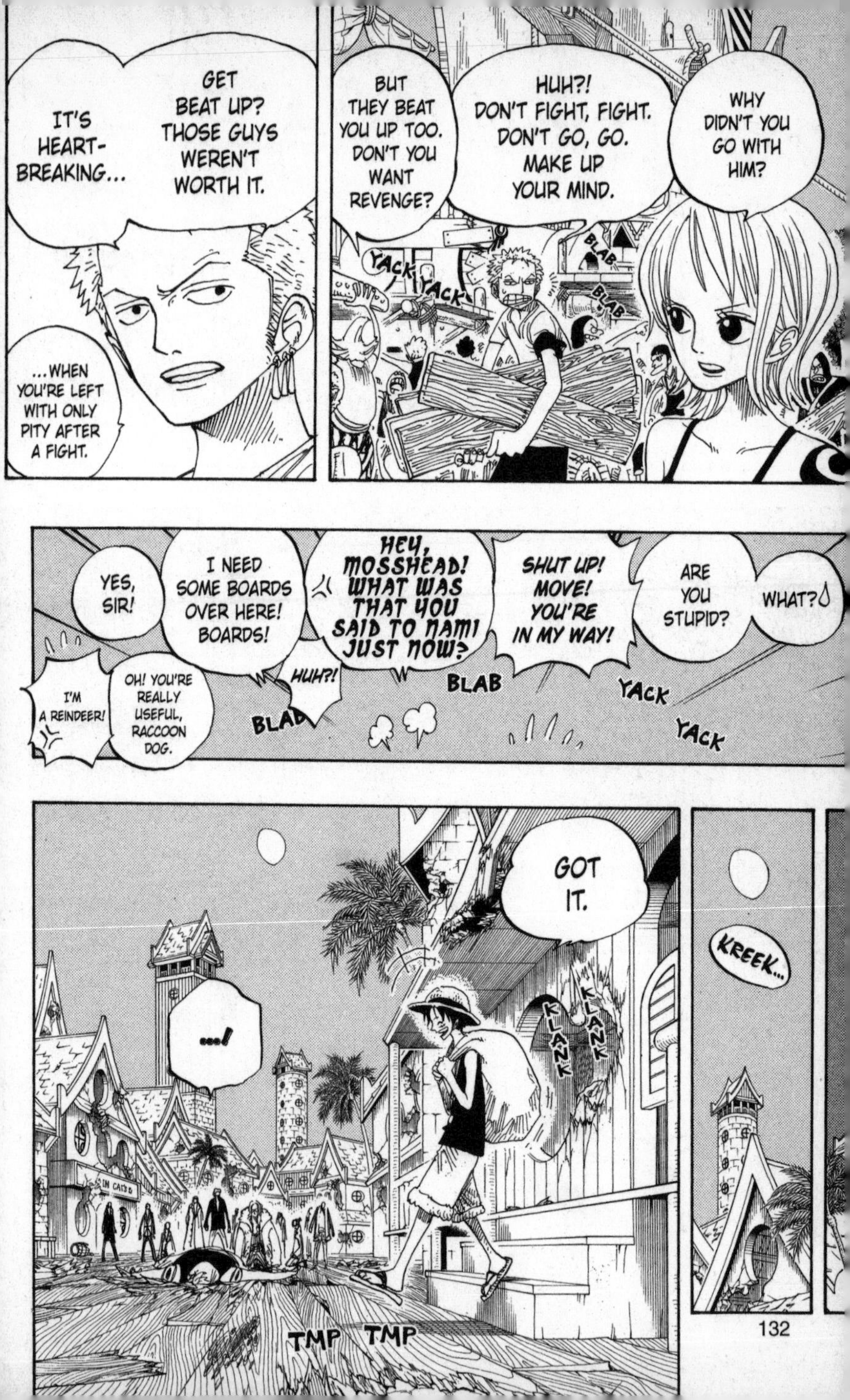
WHY DIDN'T YOU GO WITH HIM?
HUH?! DON'T FIGHT, FIGHT. DON'T GO, GO. MAKE UP YOUR MIND.
BUT THEY BEAT YOU UP TOO. DON'T YOU WANT REVENGE?
BLAB
BLAB
YACK
YACK
GET BEAT UP? THOSE GUYS WEREN'T WORTH IT.
IT'S HEART-BREAKING...
...WHEN YOU'RE LEFT WITH ONLY PITY AFTER A FIGHT.
WHAT?
ARE YOU STUPID?
SHUT UP! MOVE! YOU'RE IN MY WAY!
HEY, MOSSHEAD! WHAT WAS THAT YOU SAID TO NAMI JUST NOW?
I NEED SOME BOARDS OVER HERE! BOARDS!
YES, SIR!
YACK
YACK
BLAB
HUH?!
OH! YOU'RE REALLY USEFUL, RACCOON DOG.
I'M A REINDEER!
BLAB
KREEK...
GOT IT.
KLANK
KLANK
...!
TMP TMP

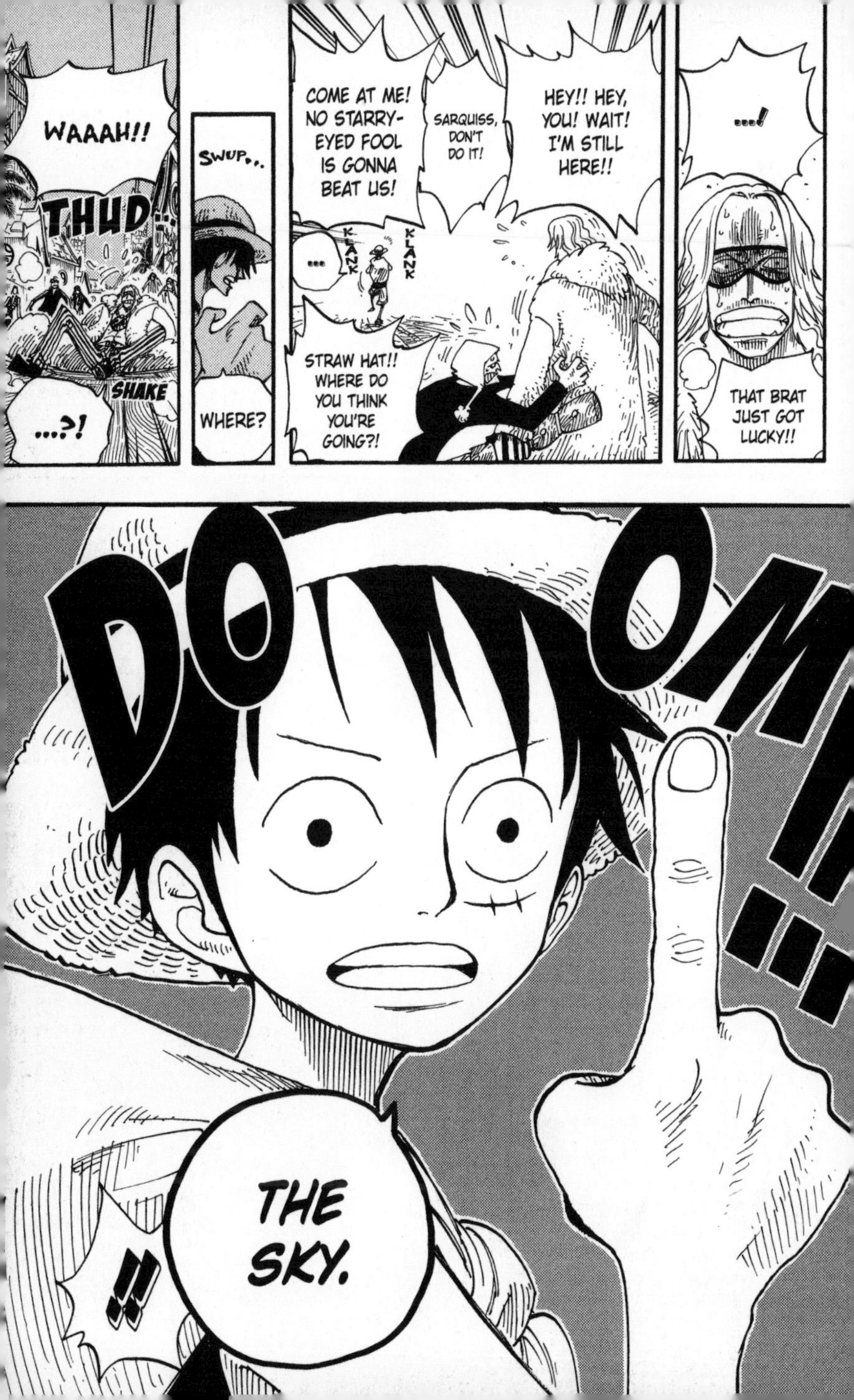
...!
THAT BRAT JUST GOT LUCKY!!
HEY!! HEY, YOU! WAIT! I'M STILL HERE!!
SARQUISS, DON'T DO IT!
COME AT ME! NO STARRY-EYED FOOL IS GONNA BEAT US!
KLANK
KLANK
...
STRAW HAT!! WHERE DO YOU THINK YOU'RE GOING?!
SWUP...
WHERE?
WAAAH!!
THUD!!
SHAKE
...?!
DOOM!!!
THE SKY.
!!

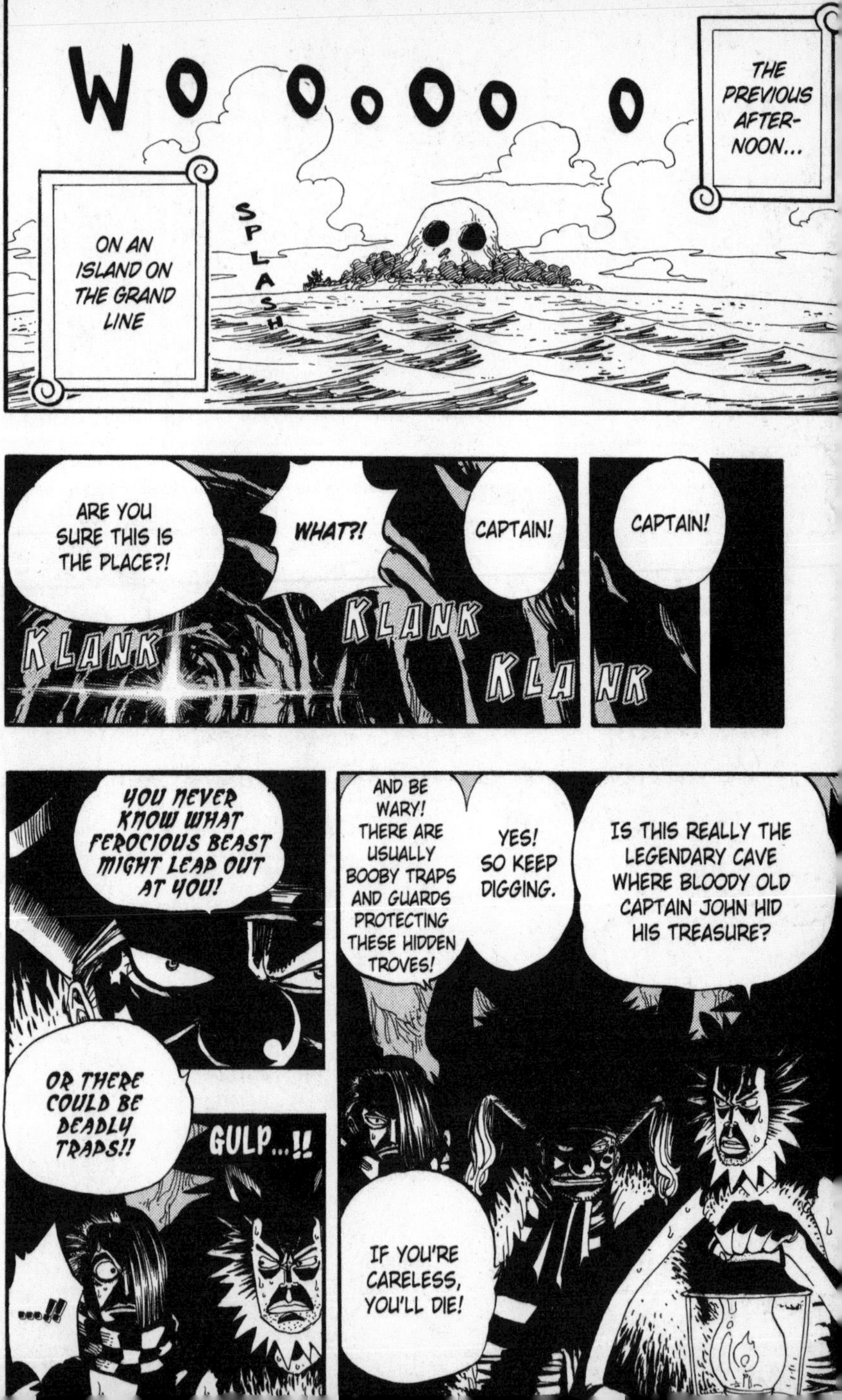
THE PREVIOUS AFTERNOON...
WOOOOOO
SPLASH
ON AN ISLAND ON THE GRAND LINE
CAPTAIN!
CAPTAIN!
WHAT?!
ARE YOU SURE THIS IS THE PLACE?!
KLANK
KLANK
KLANK
IS THIS REALLY THE LEGENDARY CAVE WHERE BLOODY OLD CAPTAIN JOHN HID HIS TREASURE?
YES! SO KEEP DIGGING.
AND BE WARY! THERE ARE USUALLY BOOBY TRAPS AND GUARDS PROTECTING THESE HIDDEN TROVES!
IF YOU'RE CARELESS, YOU'LL DIE!
YOU NEVER KNOW WHAT FEROCIOUS BEAST MIGHT LEAP OUT AT YOU!
OR THERE COULD BE DEADLY TRAPS!!
GULP...!!
...!!

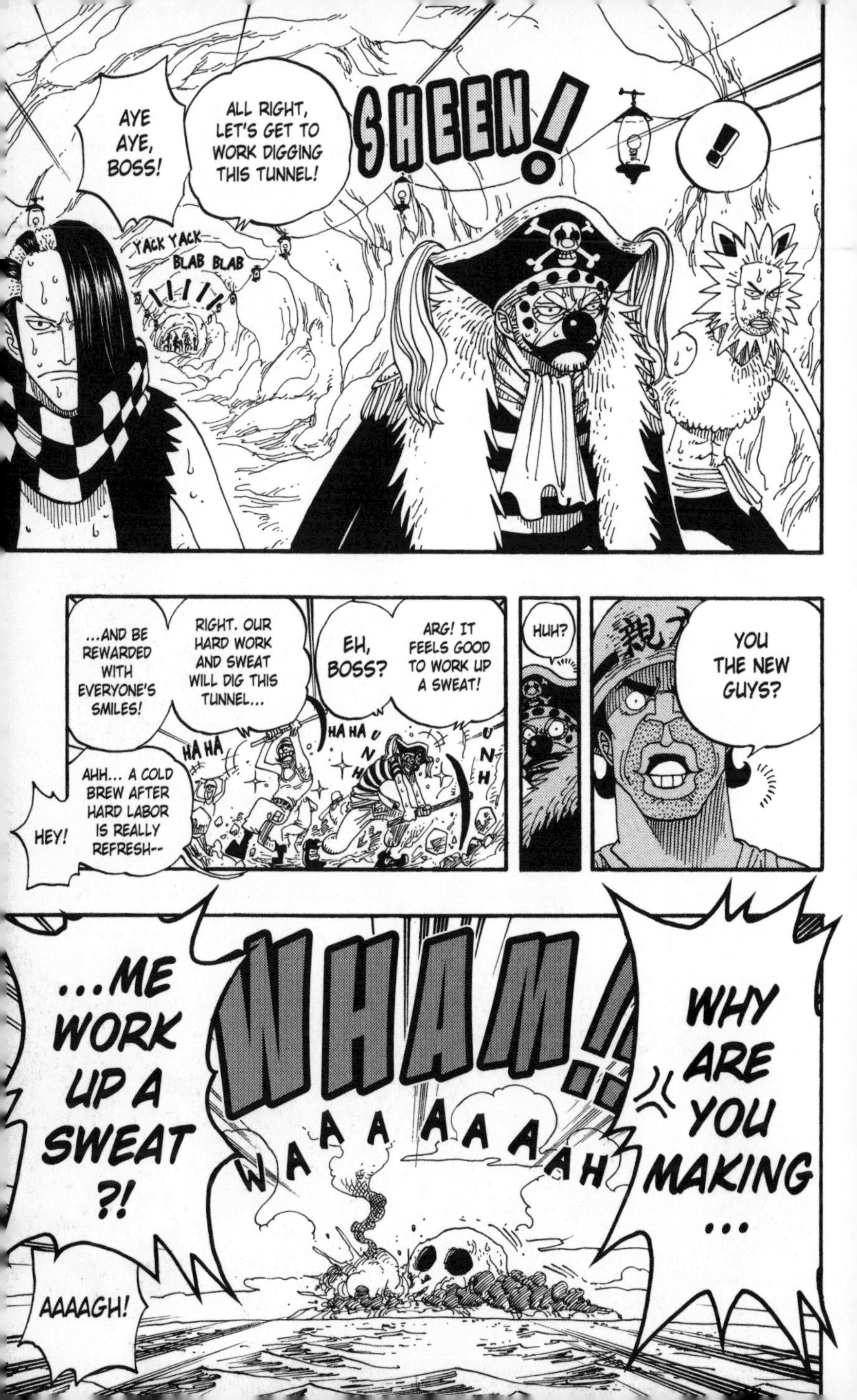
!
SHEEN!
ALL RIGHT, LET'S GET TO WORK DIGGING THIS TUNNEL!
AYE AYE, BOSS!
YACK YACK
BLAB BLAB
YOU THE NEW GUYS?
HUH?
ARG! IT FEELS GOOD TO WORK UP A SWEAT!
EH, BOSS?
RIGHT. OUR HARD WORK AND SWEAT WILL DIG THIS TUNNEL...
...AND BE REWARDED WITH EVERYONE'S SMILES!
UNH
HA HA
UNH
HA HA
AHH... A COLD BREW AFTER HARD LABOR IS REALLY REFRESH--
HEY!
WHY ARE YOU MAKING ...
WHAM!!
...ME WORK UP A SWEAT ?!
WAAAAAAAAAH
AAAAGH!

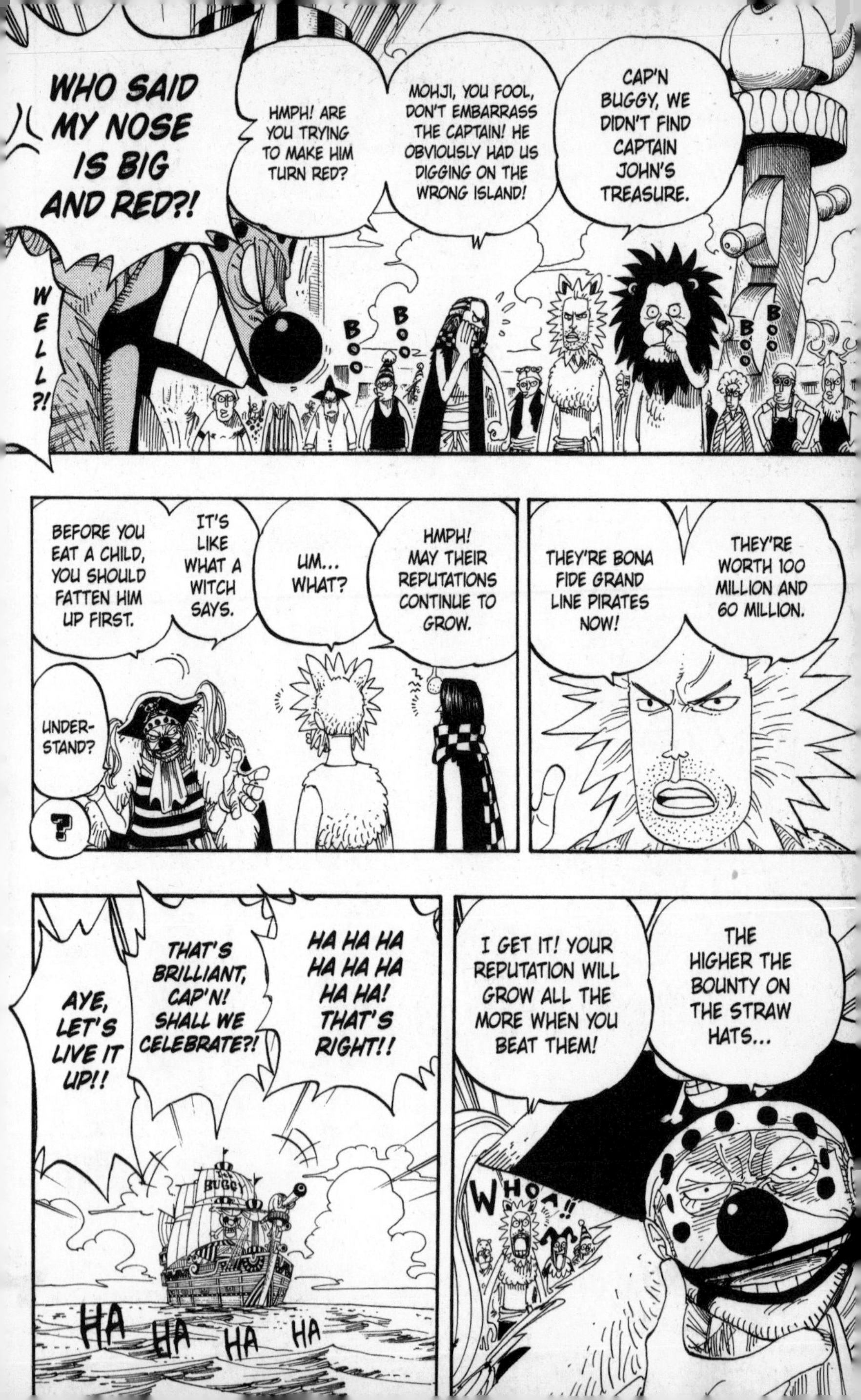
CAP'N BUGGY, WE DIDN'T FIND CAPTAIN JOHN'S TREASURE.
MOHJI, YOU FOOL, DON'T EMBARRASS THE CAPTAIN! HE OBVIOUSLY HAD US DIGGING ON THE WRONG ISLAND!
HMPH! ARE YOU TRYING TO MAKE HIM TURN RED?
WHO SAID MY NOSE IS BIG AND RED?!
BOOO
BOOO
BOOO
BOOO
WELL?!
THEY'RE WORTH 100 MILLION AND 60 MILLION.
THEY'RE BONA FIDE GRAND LINE PIRATES NOW!
HMPH! MAY THEIR REPUTATIONS CONTINUE TO GROW.
UM... WHAT?
IT'S LIKE WHAT A WITCH SAYS.
BEFORE YOU EAT A CHILD, YOU SHOULD FATTEN HIM UP FIRST.
UNDER-STAND?
?
THE HIGHER THE BOUNTY ON THE STRAW HATS...
I GET IT! YOUR REPUTATION WILL GROW ALL THE MORE WHEN YOU BEAT THEM!
WHOA!!
HA HA HA HA HA HA HA HA! THAT'S RIGHT!!
THAT'S BRILLIANT, CAP'N! SHALL WE CELEBRATE?!
AYE, LET'S LIVE IT UP!!
BUGGY
HA HA HA HA

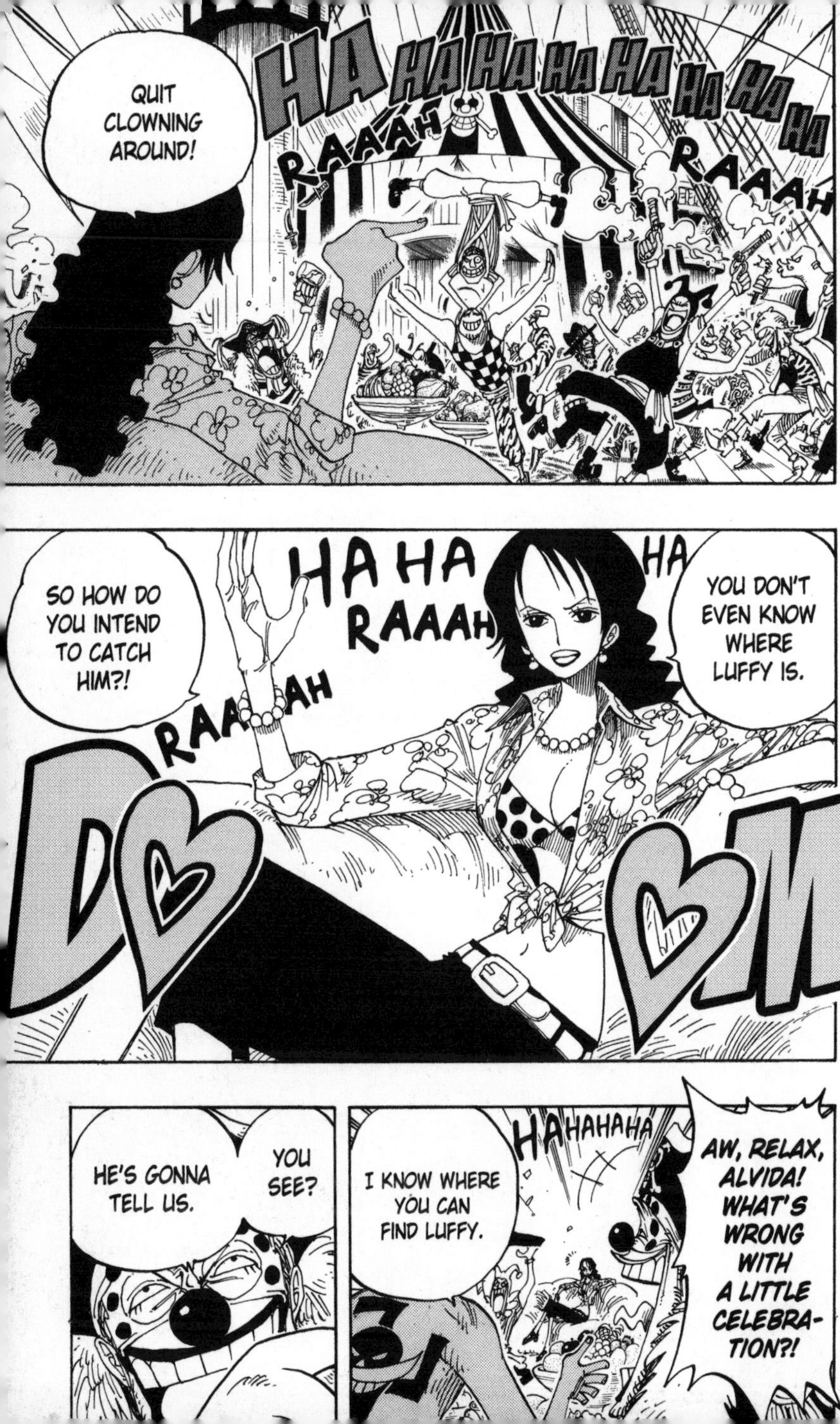
HA HA HA HA HA HA HA HA HA
RAAAH
RAAAH
QUIT CLOWNING AROUND!
YOU DON'T EVEN KNOW WHERE LUFFY IS.
HA
HA HA
RAAAH
SO HOW DO YOU INTEND TO CATCH HIM?!
RAAAH
DOOM
AW, RELAX, ALVIDA! WHAT'S WRONG WITH A LITTLE CELEBRATION?!
HAHAHAHA
I KNOW WHERE YOU CAN FIND LUFFY.
YOU SEE?
HE'S GONNA TELL US.

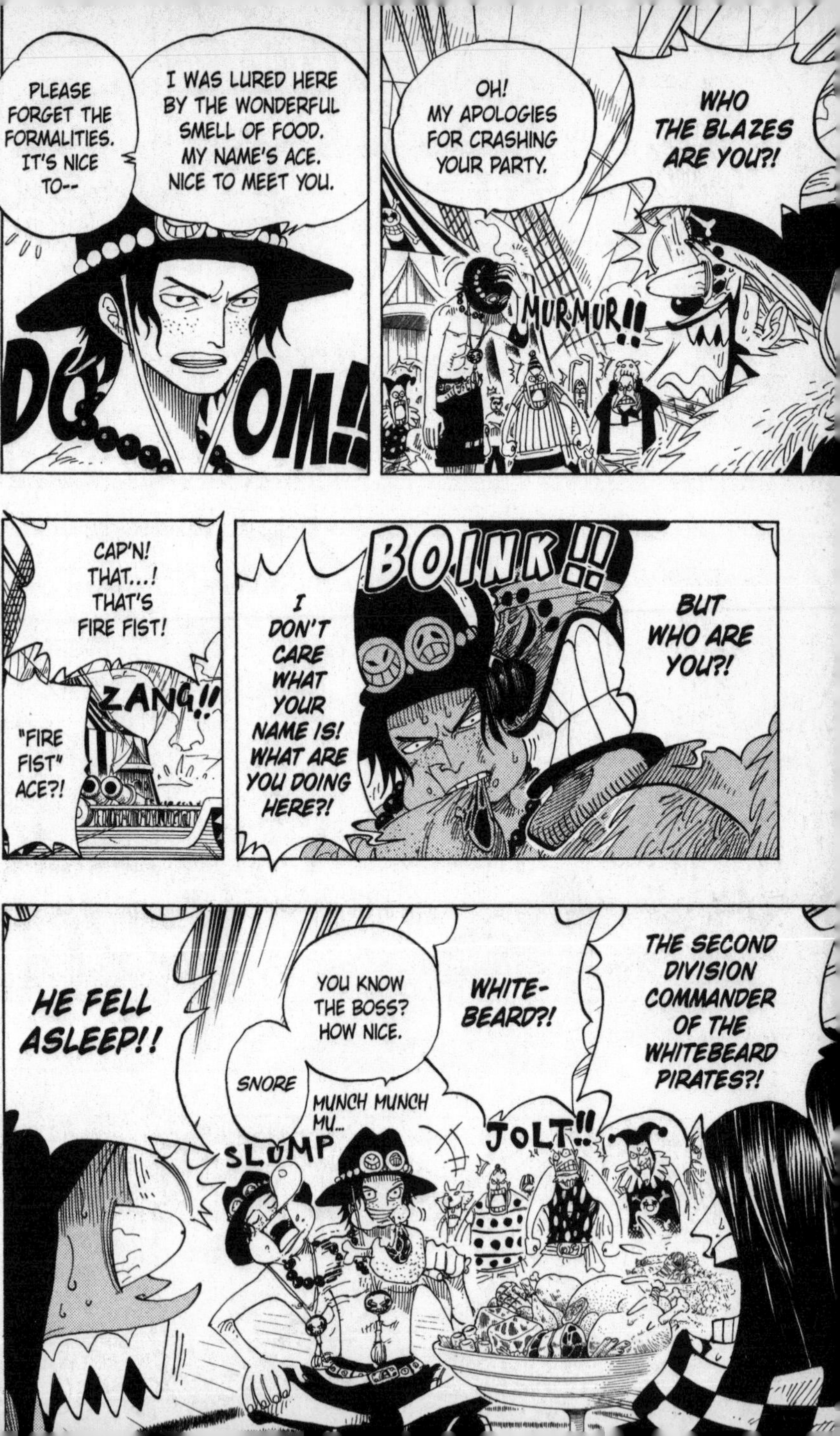
WHO THE BLAZES ARE YOU?!
OH! MY APOLOGIES FOR CRASHING YOUR PARTY.
MURMUR!!
I WAS LURED HERE BY THE WONDERFUL SMELL OF FOOD. MY NAME'S ACE. NICE TO MEET YOU.
PLEASE FORGET THE FORMALITIES. IT'S NICE TO--
DO OM!!
BOINK!!
BUT WHO ARE YOU?!
I DON'T CARE WHAT YOUR NAME IS! WHAT ARE YOU DOING HERE?!
CAP'N! THAT...! THAT'S FIRE FIST!
ZANG!!
"FIRE FIST" ACE?!
THE SECOND DIVISION COMMANDER OF THE WHITEBEARD PIRATES?!
WHITE-BEARD?!
JOLT!!
YOU KNOW THE BOSS? HOW NICE.
MUNCH MUNCH MU...
SNORE
SLUMP
HE FELL ASLEEP!!

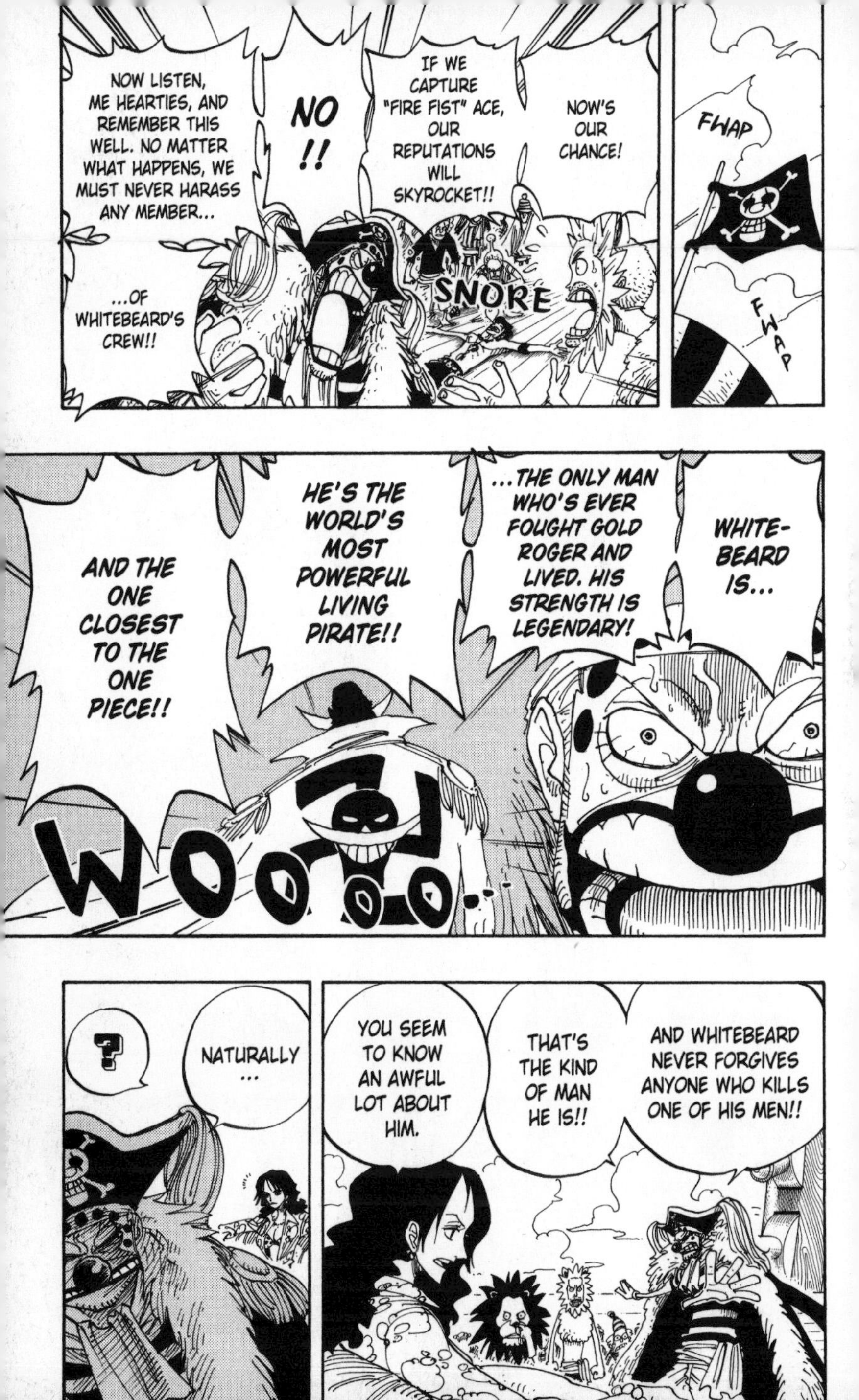
FWAP
FWAP
NOW'S OUR CHANCE!
IF WE CAPTURE "FIRE FIST" ACE, OUR REPUTATIONS WILL SKYROCKET!!
SNORE
NO !!
NOW LISTEN, ME HEARTIES, AND REMEMBER THIS WELL. NO MATTER WHAT HAPPENS, WE MUST NEVER HARASS ANY MEMBER...
...OF WHITEBEARD'S CREW!!
WHITE-BEARD IS...
...THE ONLY MAN WHO'S EVER FOUGHT GOLD ROGER AND LIVED. HIS STRENGTH IS LEGENDARY!
HE'S THE WORLD'S MOST POWERFUL LIVING PIRATE!!
AND THE ONE CLOSEST TO THE ONE PIECE!!
WOOOO...
AND WHITEBEARD NEVER FORGIVES ANYONE WHO KILLS ONE OF HIS MEN!!
THAT'S THE KIND OF MAN HE IS!!
YOU SEEM TO KNOW AN AWFUL LOT ABOUT HIM.
NATURALLY ...
?

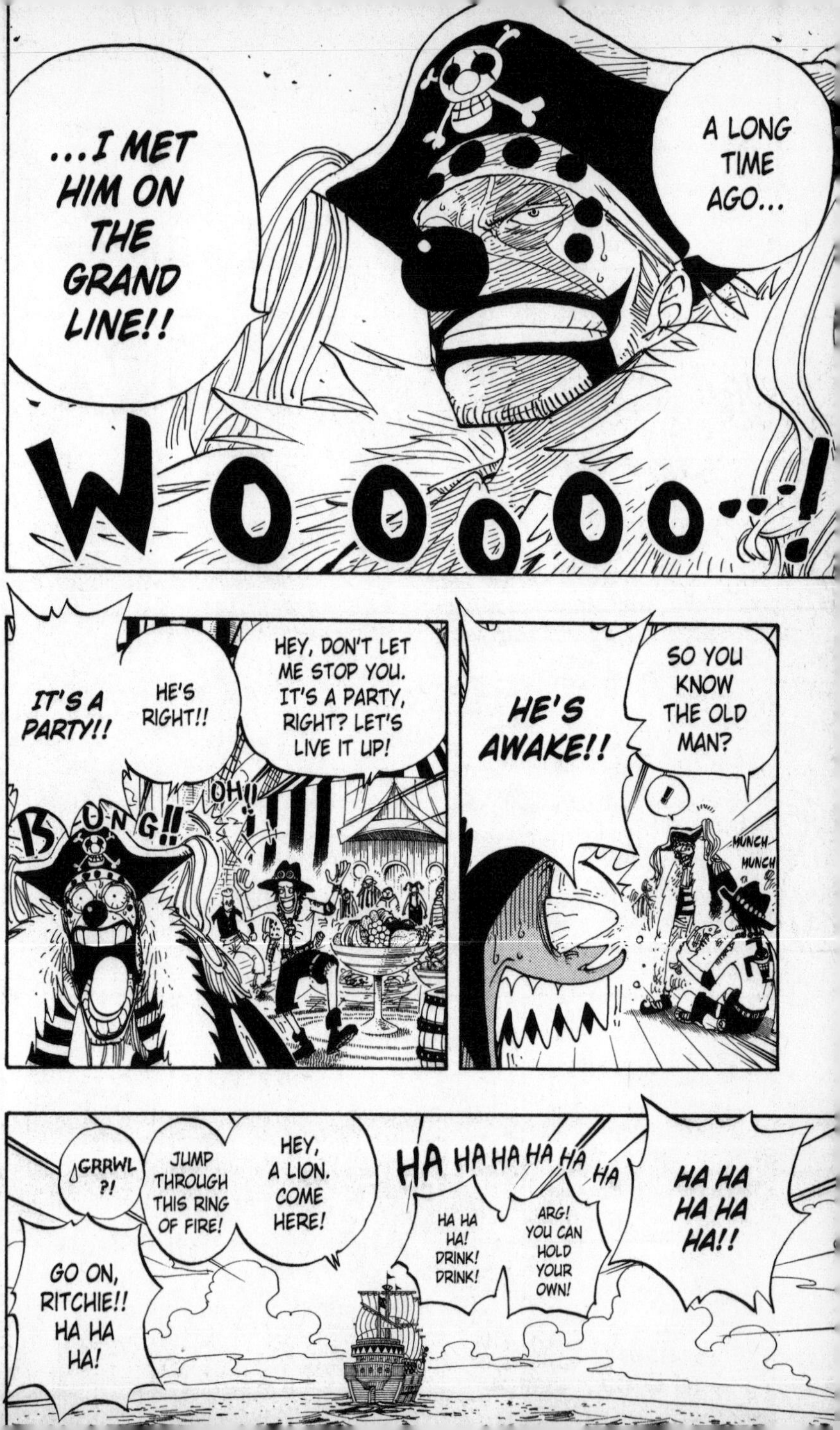
A LONG TIME AGO...
...I MET HIM ON THE GRAND LINE!!
WOOOOO...!!
SO YOU KNOW THE OLD MAN?
HE'S AWAKE!!
!
MUNCH MUNCH
HEY, DON'T LET ME STOP YOU. IT'S A PARTY, RIGHT? LET'S LIVE IT UP!
HE'S RIGHT!!
IT'S A PARTY!!
OH!!
BONG!!
HA HA HA HA HA!!
HA HA HA HA HA HA HA
ARG! YOU CAN HOLD YOUR OWN!
HA HA HA! DRINK! DRINK!
HEY, A LION. COME HERE!
JUMP THROUGH THIS RING OF FIRE!
GRRWL ?!
GO ON, RITCHIE!! HA HA HA!

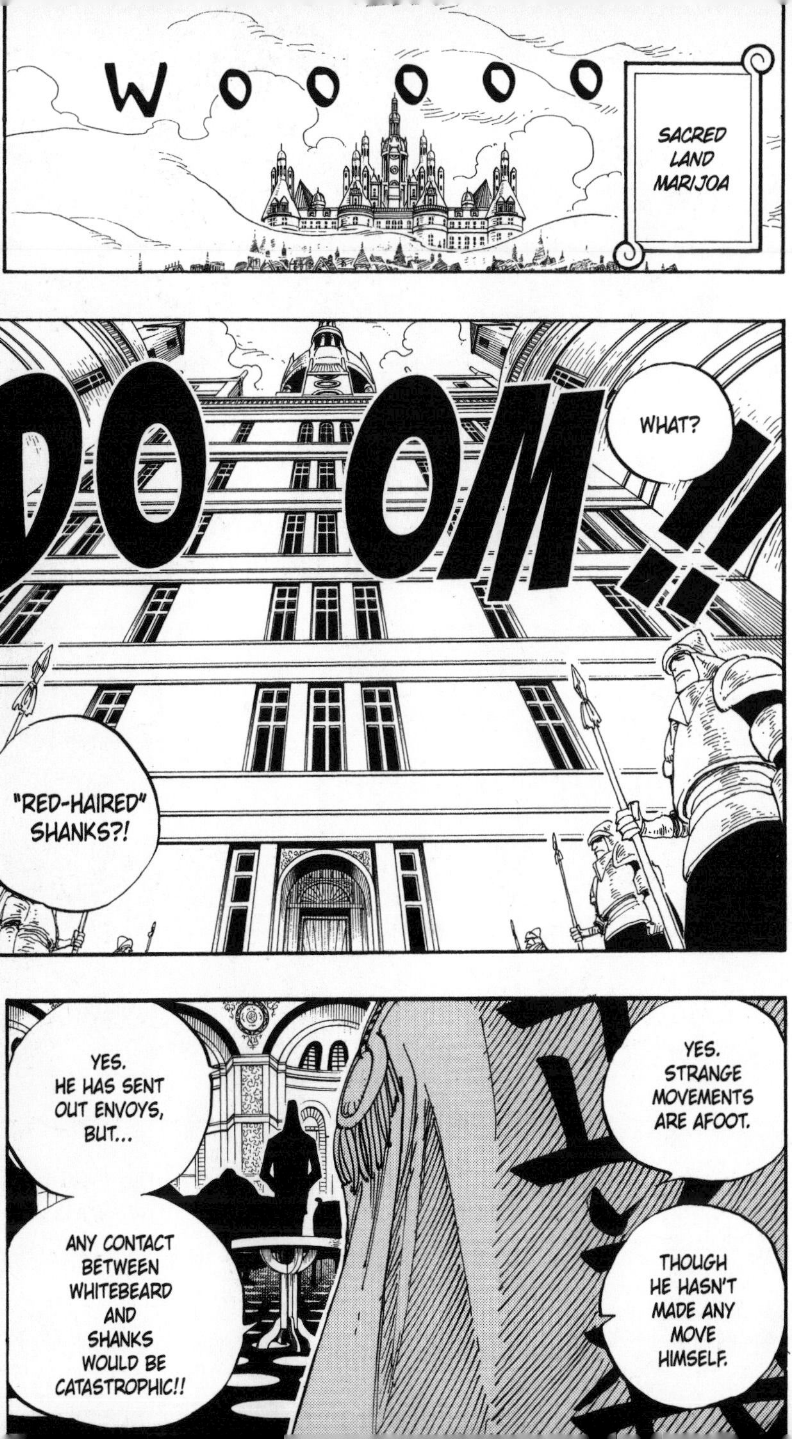
SACRED LAND MARIJOA
WOOOOO
WHAT?
DOOM!!
"RED-HAIRED" SHANKS?!
YES. STRANGE MOVEMENTS ARE AFOOT.
THOUGH HE HASN'T MADE ANY MOVE HIMSELF.
YES. HE HAS SENT OUT ENVOYS, BUT...
ANY CONTACT BETWEEN WHITEBEARD AND SHANKS WOULD BE CATASTROPHIC!!

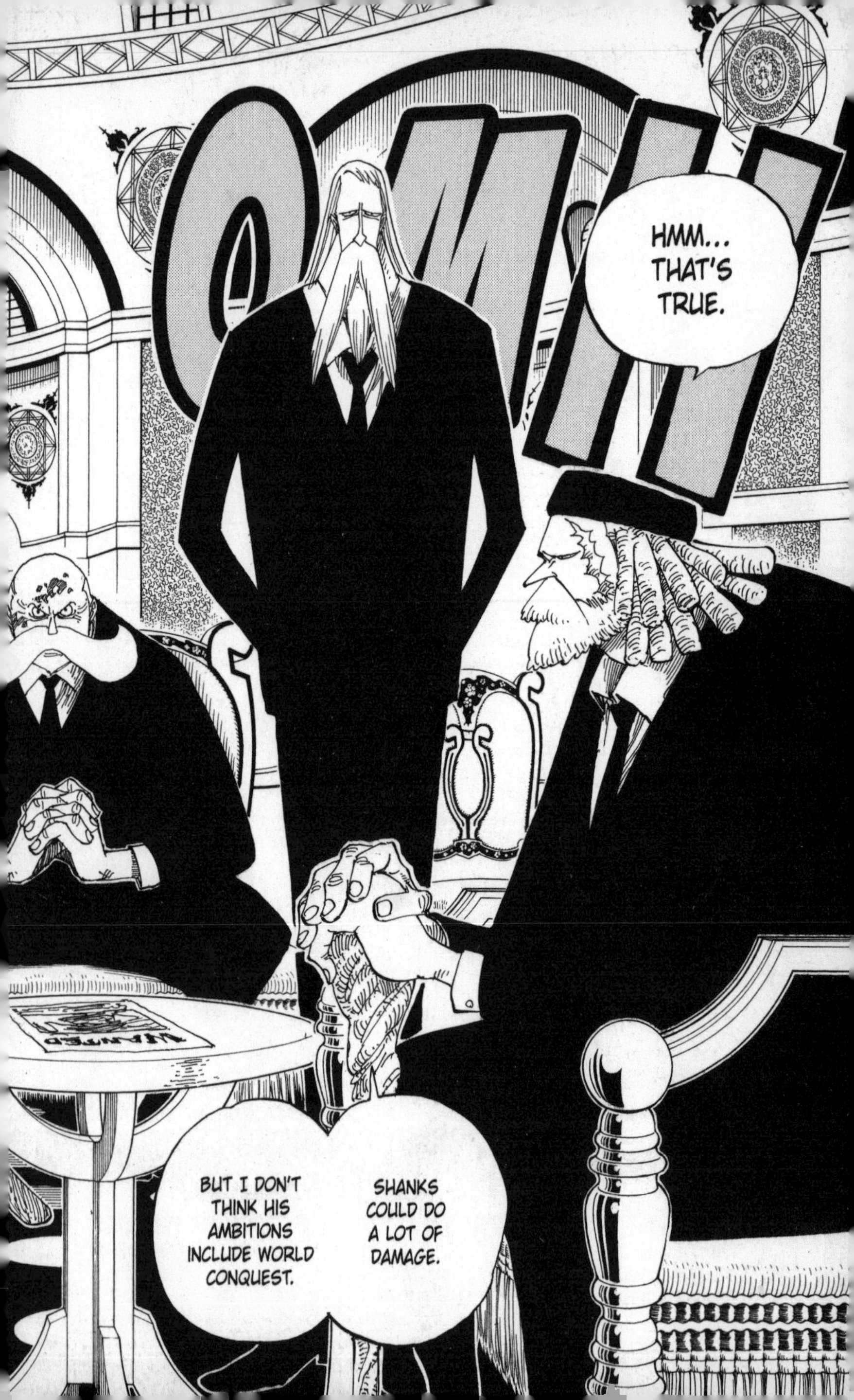
HMM... THAT'S TRUE.
SHANKS COULD DO A LOT OF DAMAGE.
BUT I DON'T THINK HIS AMBITIONS INCLUDE WORLD CONQUEST.

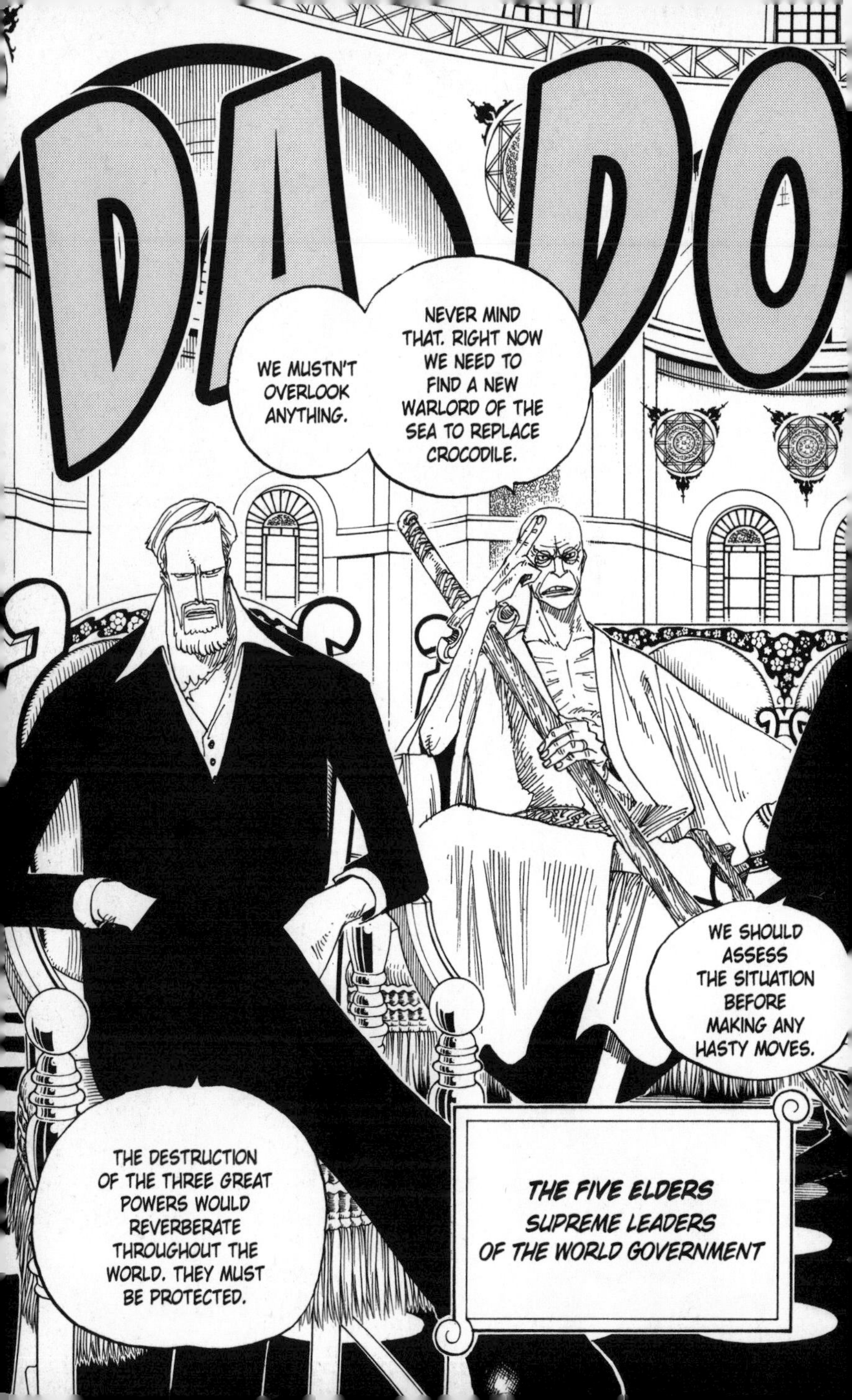
DA DO
NEVER MIND THAT. RIGHT NOW WE NEED TO FIND A NEW WARLORD OF THE SEA TO REPLACE CROCODILE.
WE MUSTN'T OVERLOOK ANYTHING.
WE SHOULD ASSESS THE SITUATION BEFORE MAKING ANY HASTY MOVES.
THE FIVE ELDERS
SUPREME LEADERS OF THE WORLD GOVERNMENT
THE DESTRUCTION OF THE THREE GREAT POWERS WOULD REVERBERATE THROUGHOUT THE WORLD. THEY MUST BE PROTECTED.

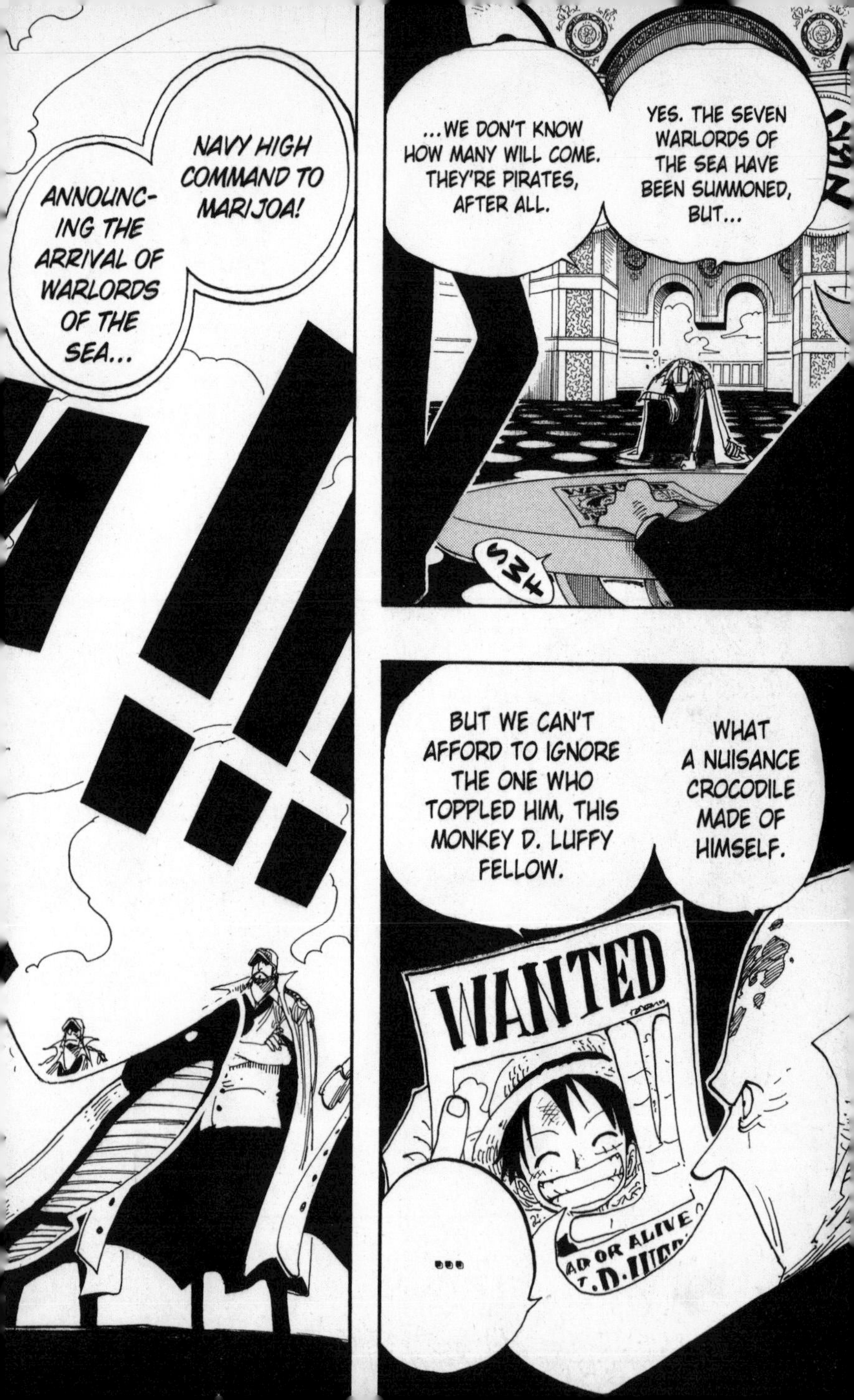
YES. THE SEVEN WARLORDS OF THE SEA HAVE BEEN SUMMONED, BUT...
...WE DON'T KNOW HOW MANY WILL COME. THEY'RE PIRATES, AFTER ALL.
WHAT A NUISANCE CROCODILE MADE OF HIMSELF.
BUT WE CAN'T AFFORD TO IGNORE THE ONE WHO TOPPLED HIM, THIS MONKEY D. LUFFY FELLOW.
WANTED
...
NAVY HIGH COMMAND TO MARIJOA!
ANNOUNCING THE ARRIVAL OF WARLORDS OF THE SEA...

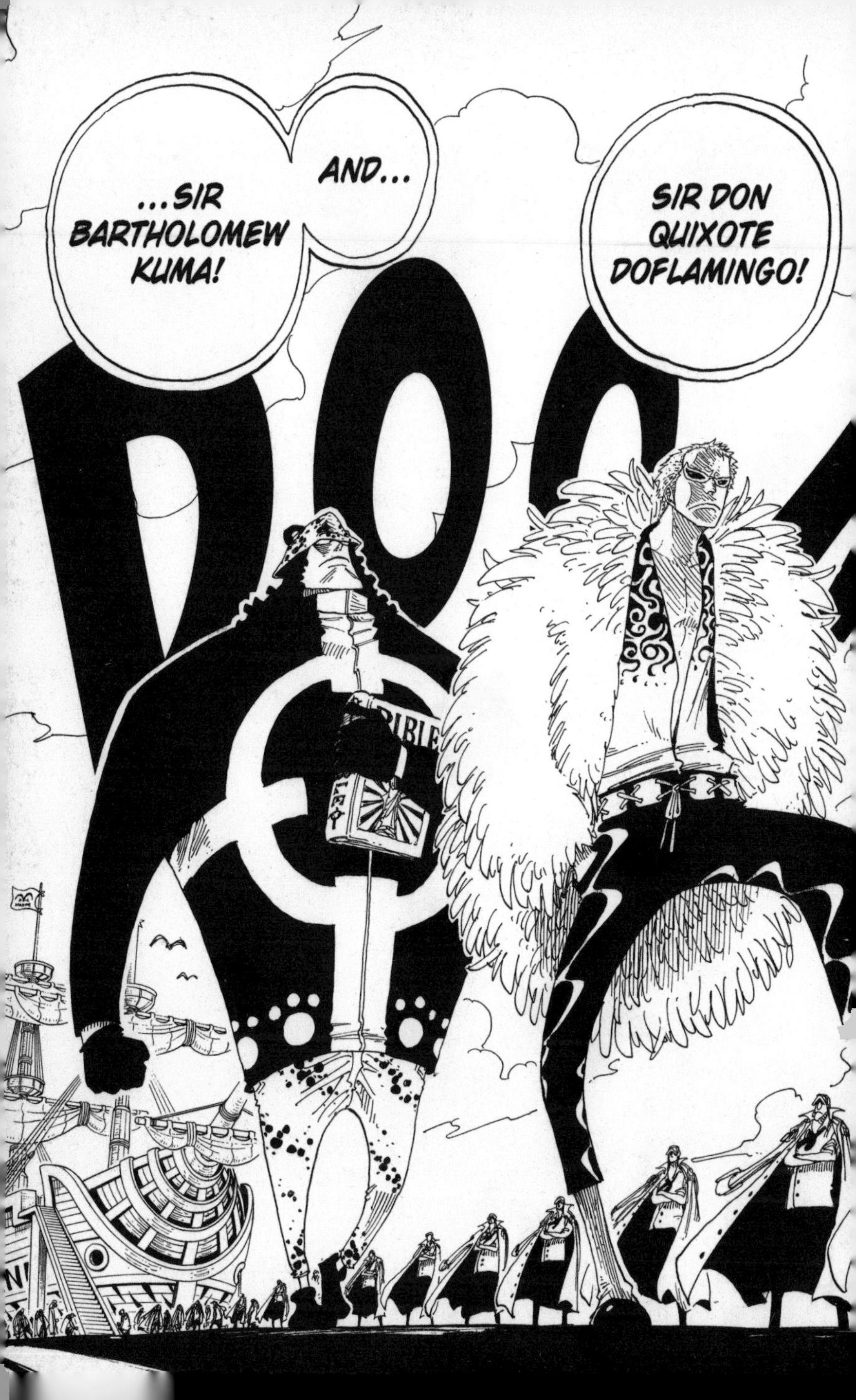

...SIR BARTHOLOMEW KUMA!
AND...
SIR DON QUIXOTE DOFLAMINGO!
DOO
BIBLE

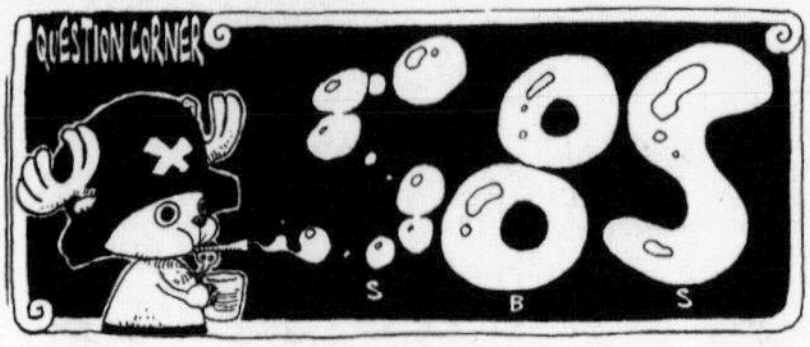
QUESTION CORNER
SBS

Oda: This is from I♡Sanji in Hokkaido. It's a compatibility test. The answers are on page 186.

Hello!♡ Yahoo!! Oda!!♡♡
I came up with a compatibility test! Please put it in your manga!♡
Time for a break, *One Piece* fans!♡

◯ Today you've come to an amusement park with Luffy and his crew. ♡ What's everybody doing? There's Luffy, Zolo, Nami, Sanji, Usopp, Chopper, Vivi, Karoo and Oda. Match them with the activities below!!

1. Eating like a pig:

2. Only riding the superfast roller coasters:

3. Watching a show with costumed characters♡:

4. Has gotten separated from the others and is lost:

5. Is with you right now:

6. Is trying an octopar (octopus parfait):

7. Enjoying things just like a regular person:

# Chapter 234:
# PLEASE REMEMBER

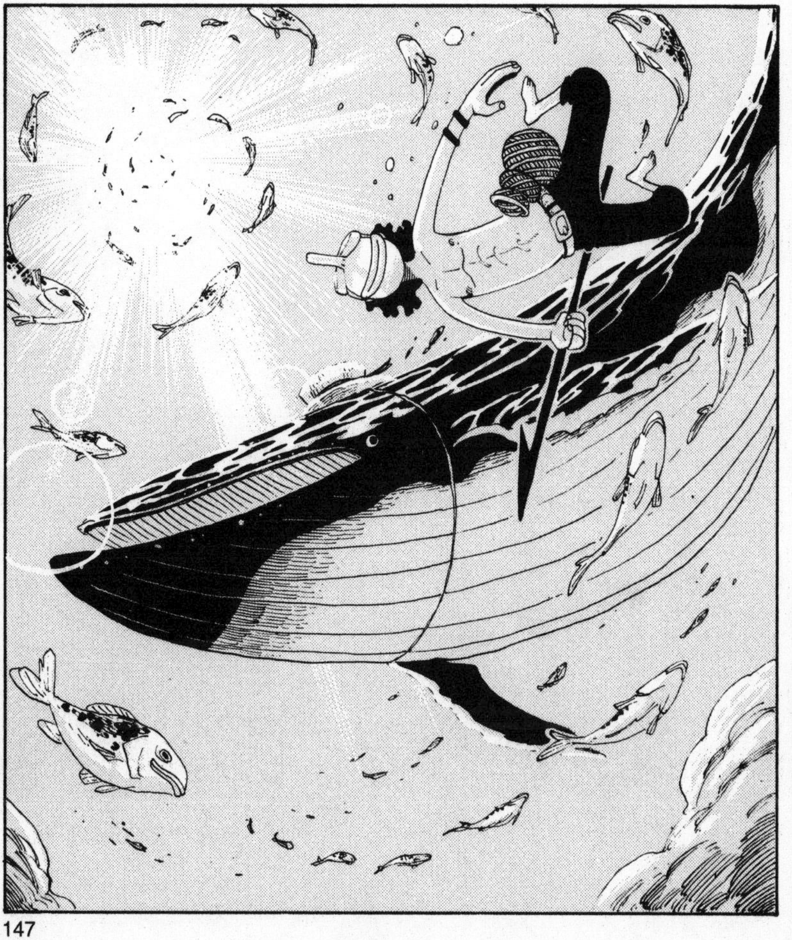

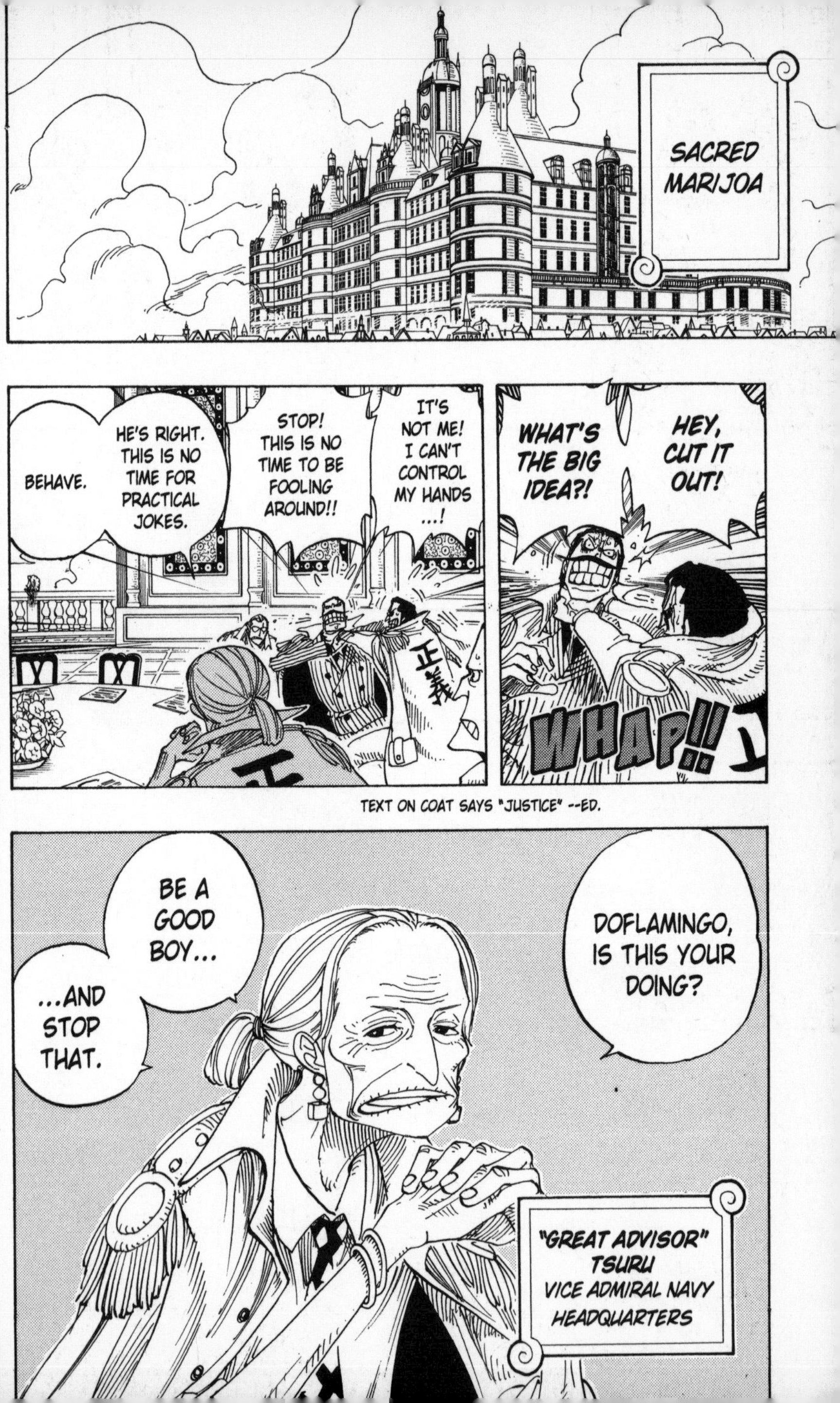
SACRED MARIJOA
HEY, CUT IT OUT!
WHAT'S THE BIG IDEA?!
WHAP!!
IT'S NOT ME! I CAN'T CONTROL MY HANDS ...!
STOP! THIS IS NO TIME TO BE FOOLING AROUND!!
HE'S RIGHT. THIS IS NO TIME FOR PRACTICAL JOKES.
BEHAVE.
TEXT ON COAT SAYS "JUSTICE" --ED.
DOFLAMINGO, IS THIS YOUR DOING?
"GREAT ADVISOR" TSURU VICE ADMIRAL NAVY HEADQUARTERS
BE A GOOD BOY...
...AND STOP THAT.

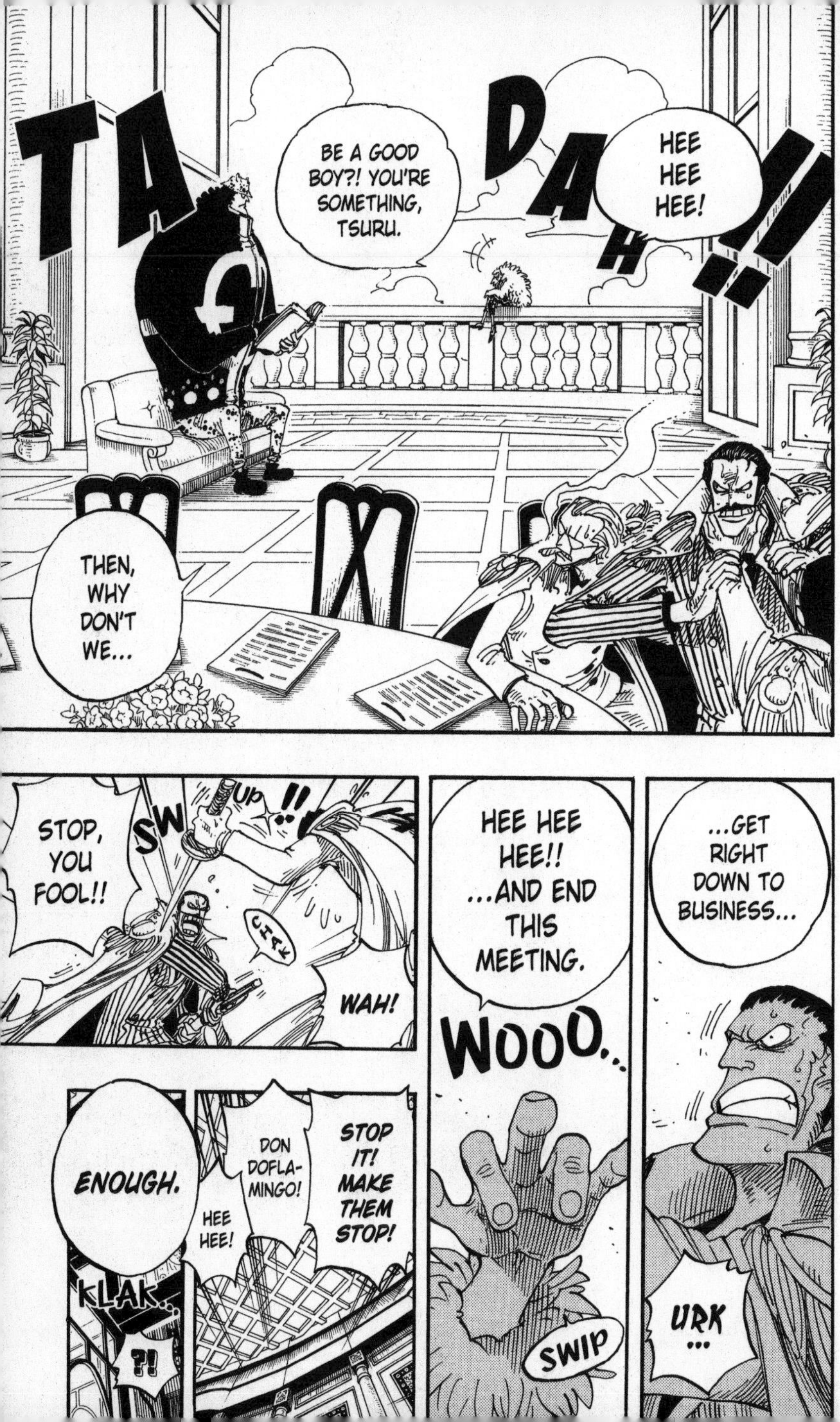
TA DAH!!
HEE HEE HEE!
BE A GOOD BOY?! YOU'RE SOMETHING, TSURU.
THEN, WHY DON'T WE...
...GET RIGHT DOWN TO BUSINESS...
URK...
HEE HEE HEE!! ...AND END THIS MEETING.
WOOO...
SWIP
SWUP!!
STOP, YOU FOOL!!
CHAK
WAH!
STOP IT! MAKE THEM STOP!
DON DOFLAMINGO!
HEE HEE!
ENOUGH.
KLAK...
?!

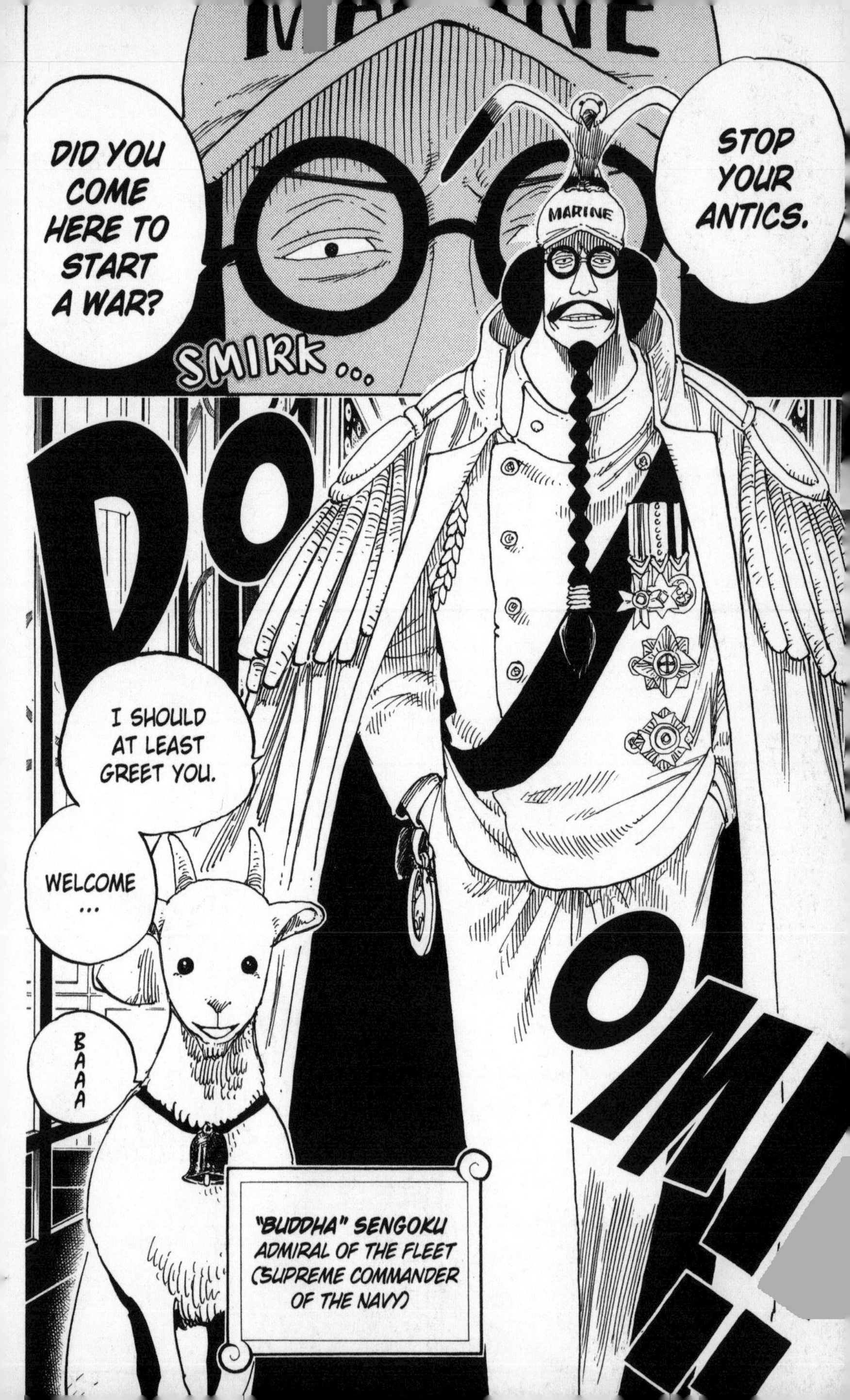
STOP YOUR ANTICS.
DID YOU COME HERE TO START A WAR?
SMIRK...
MARINE
DOOM!!
I SHOULD AT LEAST GREET YOU.
WELCOME ...
BAAA
"BUDDHA" SENGOKU
ADMIRAL OF THE FLEET
(SUPREME COMMANDER OF THE NAVY)

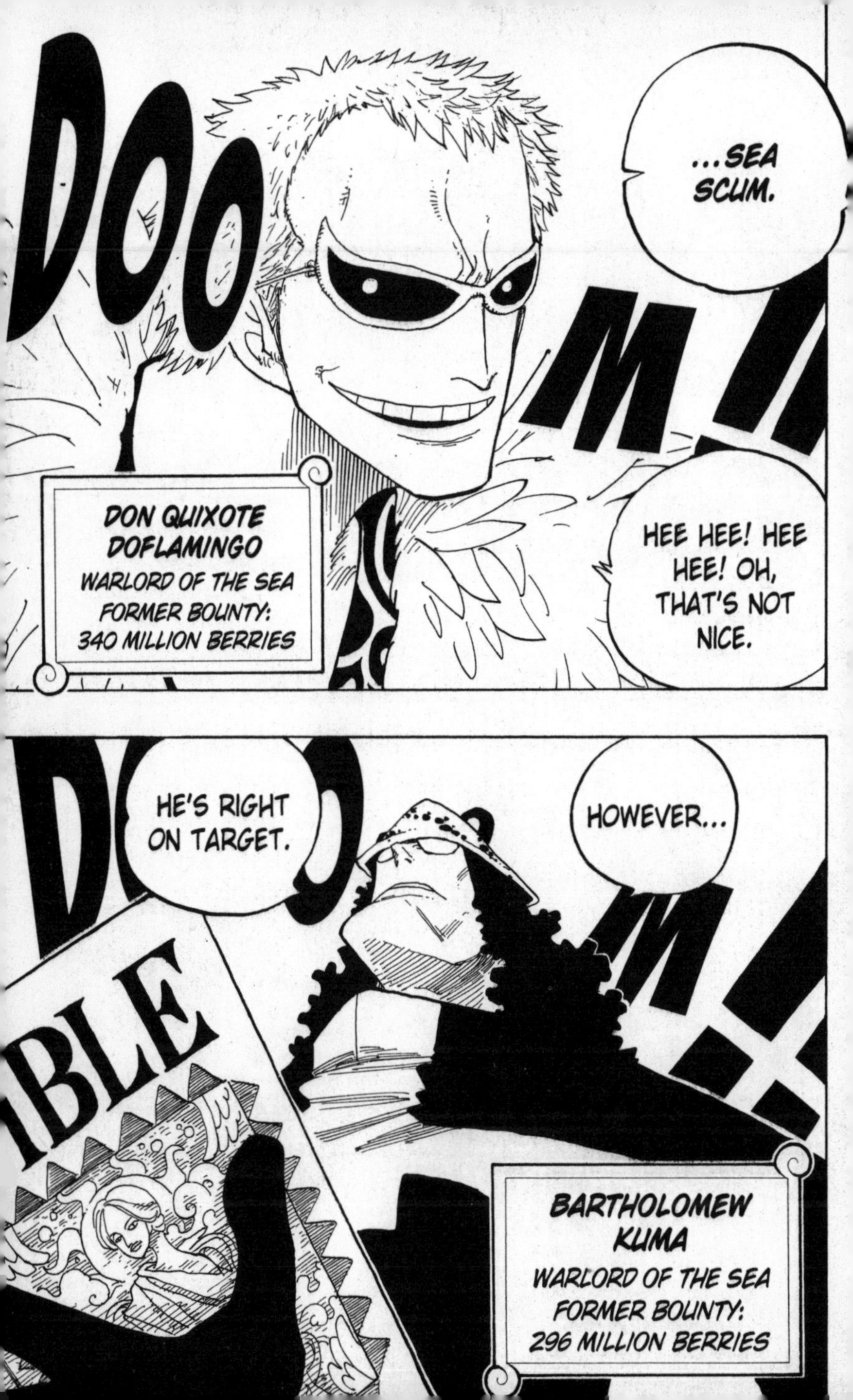
...SEA SCUM.
DOOM!!
HEE HEE! HEE HEE! OH, THAT'S NOT NICE.
DON QUIXOTE DOFLAMINGO
WARLORD OF THE SEA
FORMER BOUNTY: 340 MILLION BERRIES
HOWEVER...
HE'S RIGHT ON TARGET.
DOOM!!
IBLE
BARTHOLOMEW KUMA
WARLORD OF THE SEA
FORMER BOUNTY: 296 MILLION BERRIES

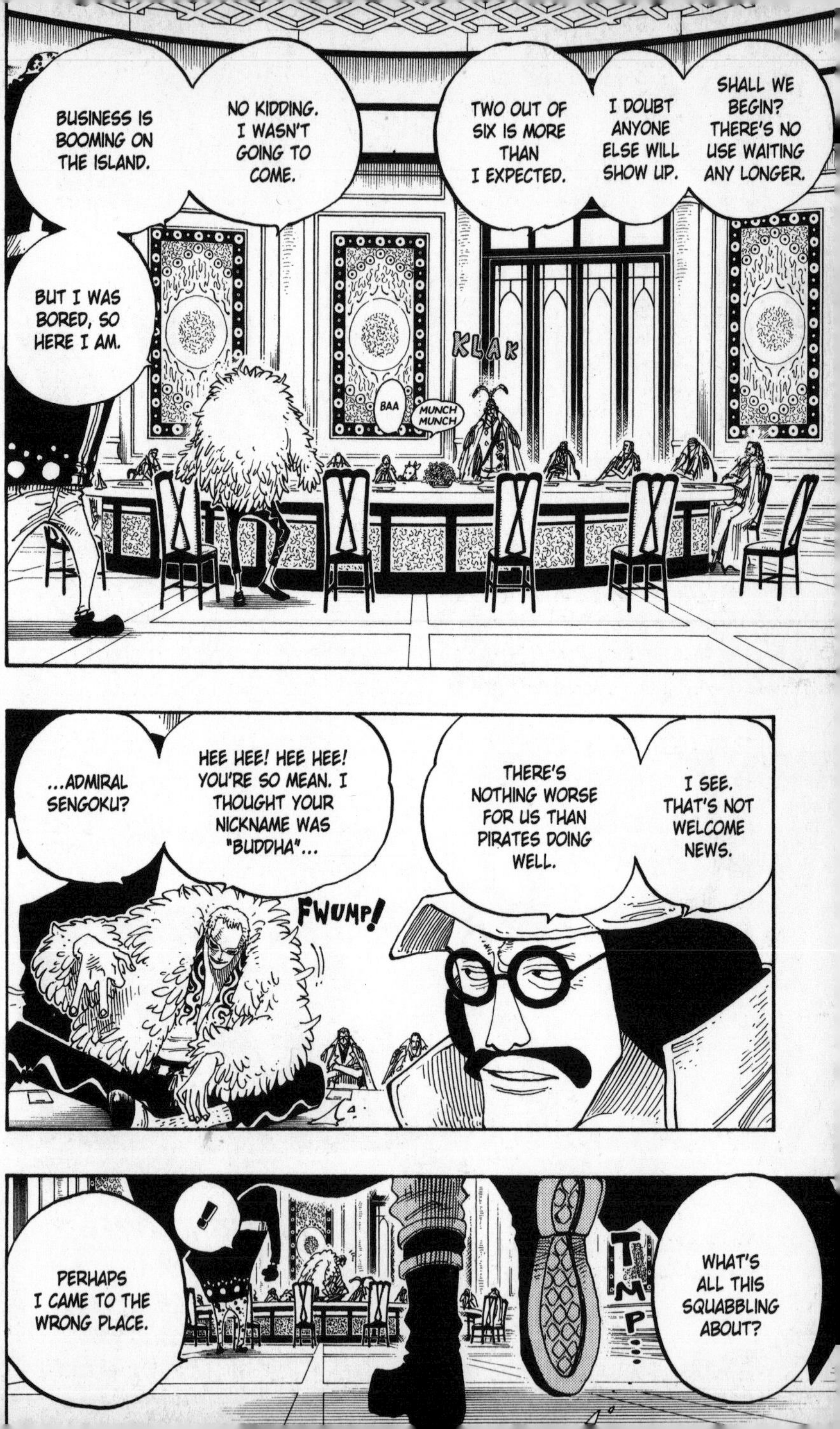
SHALL WE BEGIN? THERE'S NO USE WAITING ANY LONGER.
I DOUBT ANYONE ELSE WILL SHOW UP.
TWO OUT OF SIX IS MORE THAN I EXPECTED.
NO KIDDING. I WASN'T GOING TO COME.
BUSINESS IS BOOMING ON THE ISLAND.
KLAK
MUNCH MUNCH
BAA
BUT I WAS BORED, SO HERE I AM.
I SEE. THAT'S NOT WELCOME NEWS.
THERE'S NOTHING WORSE FOR US THAN PIRATES DOING WELL.
HEE HEE! HEE HEE! YOU'RE SO MEAN. I THOUGHT YOUR NICKNAME WAS "BUDDHA"...
...ADMIRAL SENGOKU?
FWUMP!
WHAT'S ALL THIS SQUABBLING ABOUT?
TMP...
!
PERHAPS I CAME TO THE WRONG PLACE.

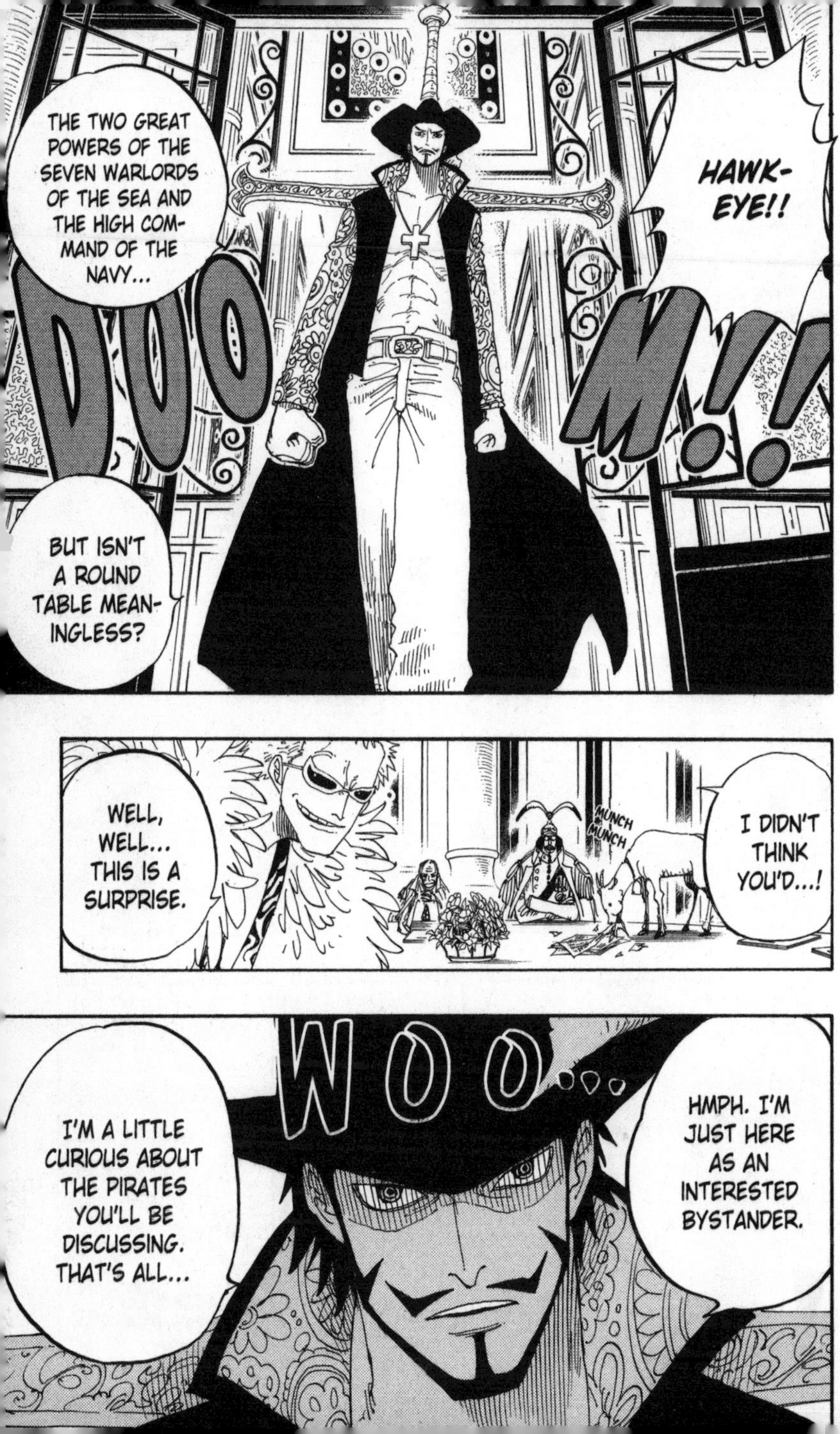
HAWK-EYE!!
THE TWO GREAT POWERS OF THE SEVEN WARLORDS OF THE SEA AND THE HIGH COM-MAND OF THE NAVY...
DUOOM!!
BUT ISN'T A ROUND TABLE MEAN-INGLESS?
I DIDN'T THINK YOU'D...!
MUNCH MUNCH
WELL, WELL... THIS IS A SURPRISE.
HMPH. I'M JUST HERE AS AN INTERESTED BYSTANDER.
WOO...
I'M A LITTLE CURIOUS ABOUT THE PIRATES YOU'LL BE DISCUSSING. THAT'S ALL...

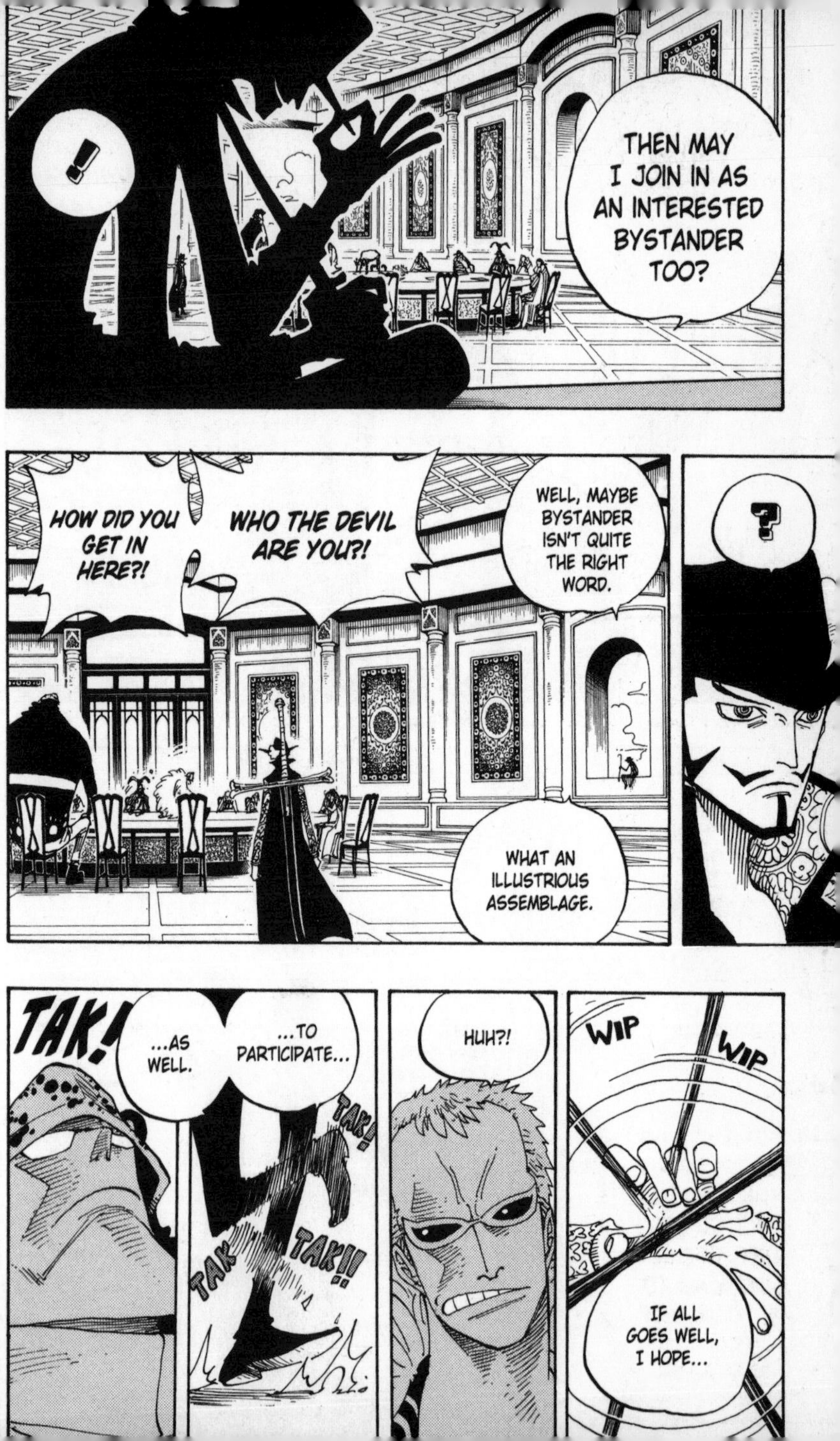
THEN MAY I JOIN IN AS AN INTERESTED BYSTANDER TOO?
!
?
WHO THE DEVIL ARE YOU?!
HOW DID YOU GET IN HERE?!
WELL, MAYBE BYSTANDER ISN'T QUITE THE RIGHT WORD.
WHAT AN ILLUSTRIOUS ASSEMBLAGE.
WIP
WIP
IF ALL GOES WELL, I HOPE...
HUH?!
...TO PARTICIPATE...
TAK!
TAK
TAK!!
TAK!
...AS WELL.

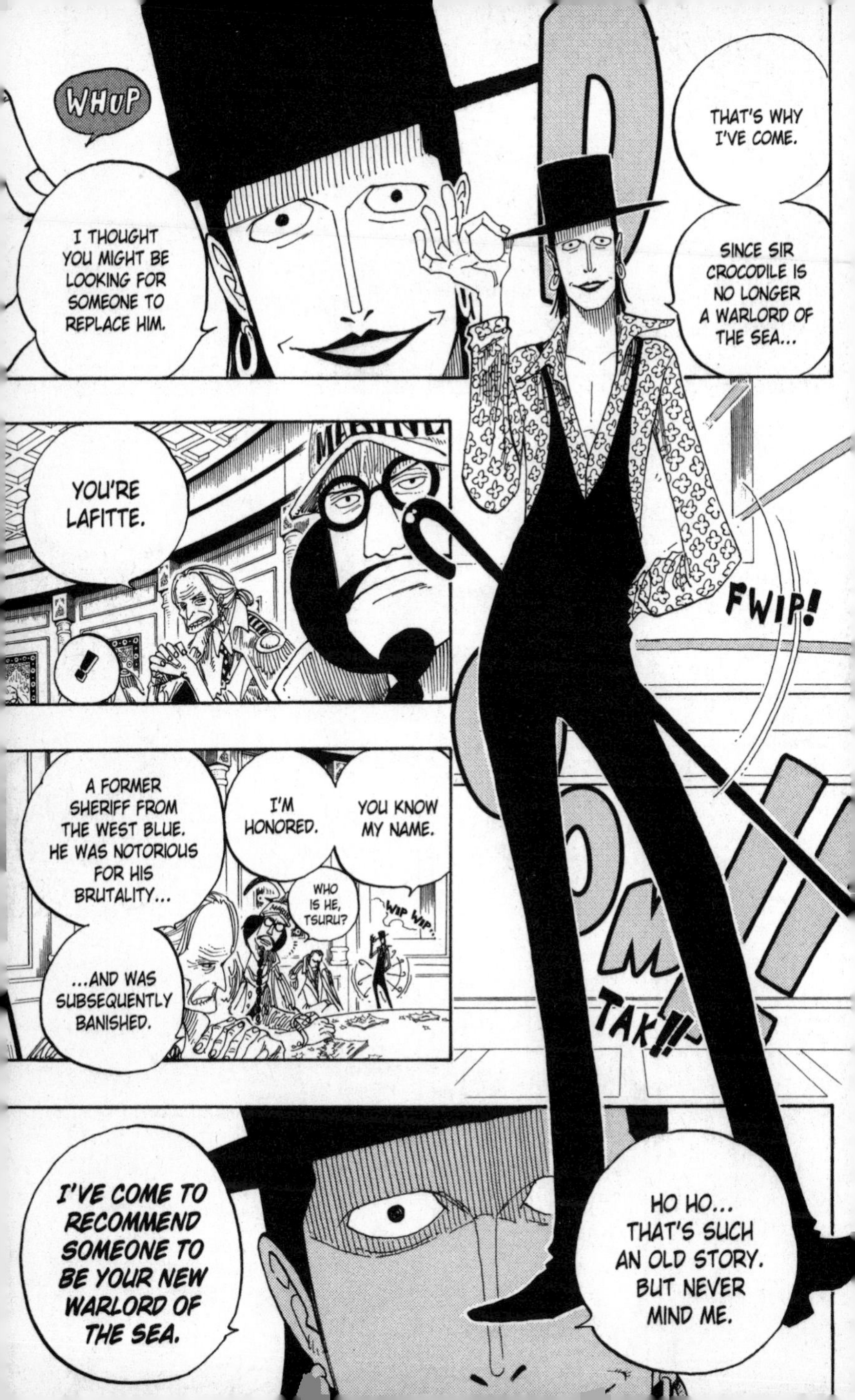
THAT'S WHY I'VE COME.
SINCE SIR CROCODILE IS NO LONGER A WARLORD OF THE SEA...
WHUP
I THOUGHT YOU MIGHT BE LOOKING FOR SOMEONE TO REPLACE HIM.
FWIP!
YOU'RE LAFITTE.
!
YOU KNOW MY NAME.
I'M HONORED.
A FORMER SHERIFF FROM THE WEST BLUE. HE WAS NOTORIOUS FOR HIS BRUTALITY...
WHO IS HE, TSURU?
WIP WIP
...AND WAS SUBSEQUENTLY BANISHED.
TAK!!
HO HO... THAT'S SUCH AN OLD STORY. BUT NEVER MIND ME.
I'VE COME TO RECOMMEND SOMEONE TO BE YOUR NEW WARLORD OF THE SEA.

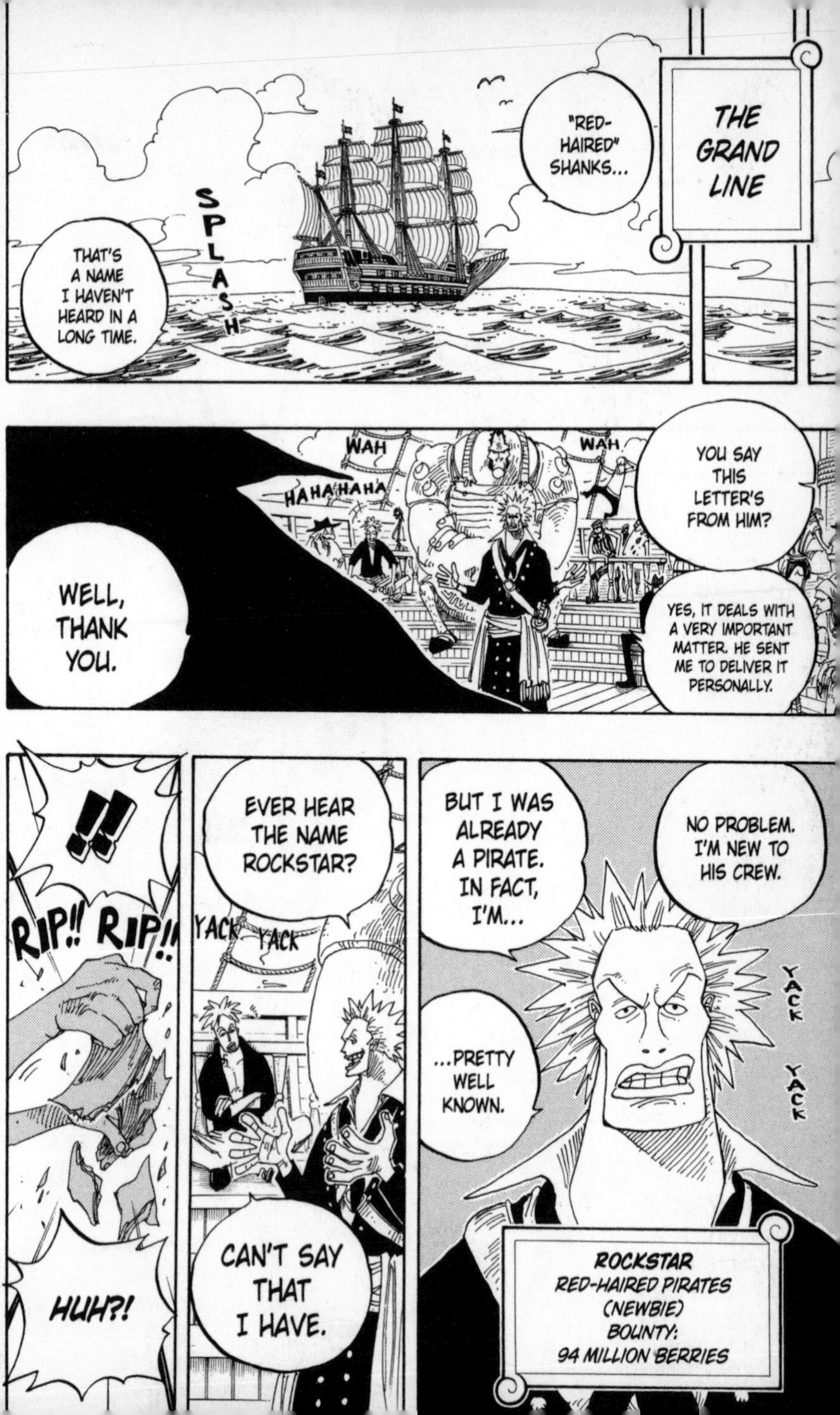
THE GRAND LINE
"RED-HAIRED" SHANKS...
SPLASH
THAT'S A NAME I HAVEN'T HEARD IN A LONG TIME.
YOU SAY THIS LETTER'S FROM HIM?
YES, IT DEALS WITH A VERY IMPORTANT MATTER. HE SENT ME TO DELIVER IT PERSONALLY.
WAH
WAH
HAHAHAHA
WELL, THANK YOU.
NO PROBLEM. I'M NEW TO HIS CREW.
BUT I WAS ALREADY A PIRATE. IN FACT, I'M...
...PRETTY WELL KNOWN.
YACK
YACK
ROCKSTAR
RED-HAIRED PIRATES
(NEWBIE)
BOUNTY:
94 MILLION BERRIES
EVER HEAR THE NAME ROCKSTAR?
YACK
YACK
CAN'T SAY THAT I HAVE.
!!
RIP!! RIP!!
HUH?!

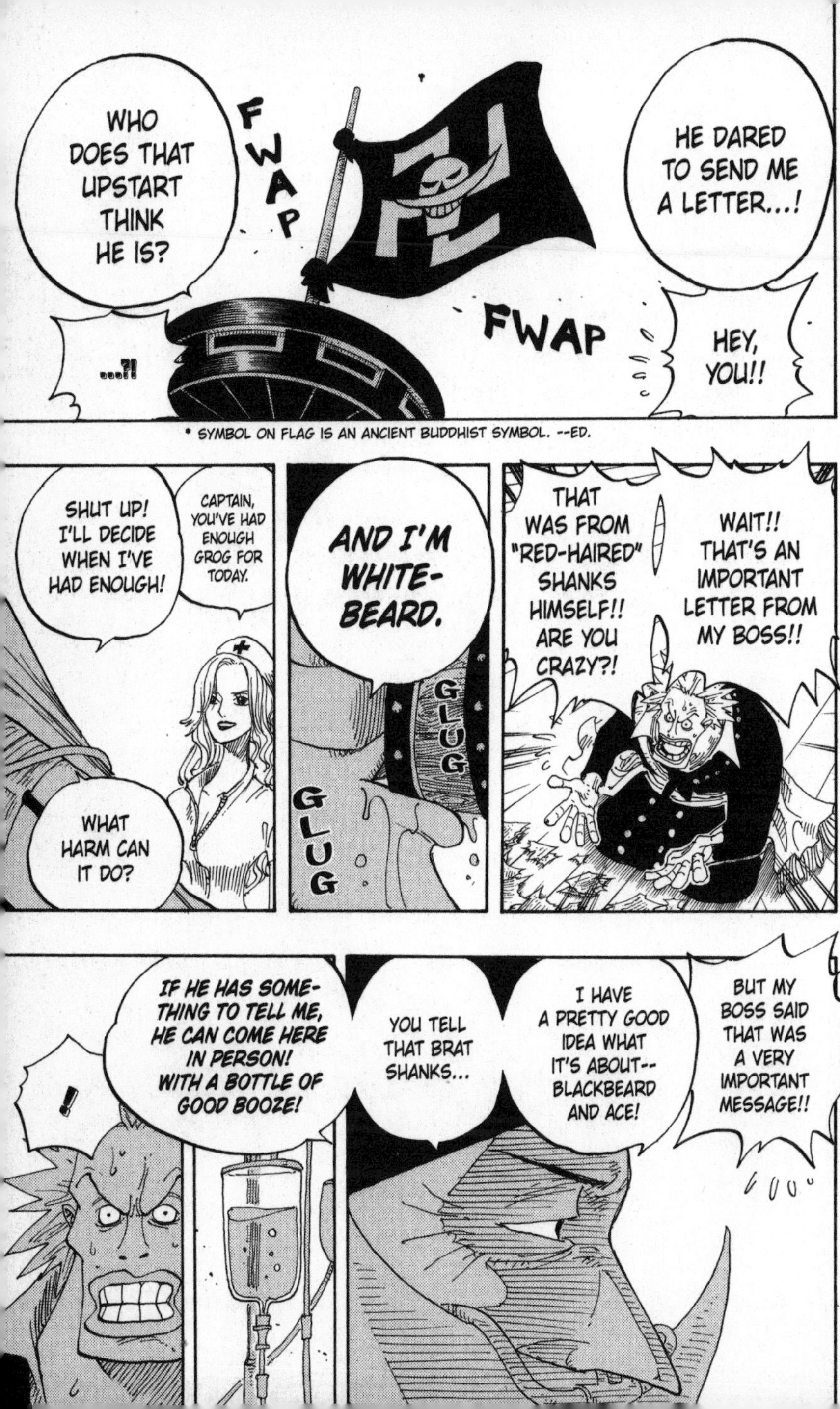
HE DARED TO SEND ME A LETTER...!
FWAP
FWAP
WHO DOES THAT UPSTART THINK HE IS?
HEY, YOU!!
...?!
WAIT!! THAT'S AN IMPORTANT LETTER FROM MY BOSS!!
THAT WAS FROM "RED-HAIRED" SHANKS HIMSELF!! ARE YOU CRAZY?!
AND I'M WHITEBEARD.
GLUG
GLUG
GLUG
GLUG
CAPTAIN, YOU'VE HAD ENOUGH GROG FOR TODAY.
SHUT UP! I'LL DECIDE WHEN I'VE HAD ENOUGH!
WHAT HARM CAN IT DO?
BUT MY BOSS SAID THAT WAS A VERY IMPORTANT MESSAGE!!
I HAVE A PRETTY GOOD IDEA WHAT IT'S ABOUT-- BLACKBEARD AND ACE!
YOU TELL THAT BRAT SHANKS...
IF HE HAS SOMETHING TO TELL ME, HE CAN COME HERE IN PERSON! WITH A BOTTLE OF GOOD BOOZE!
!

* SYMBOL ON FLAG IS AN ANCIENT BUDDHIST SYMBOL. --ED.

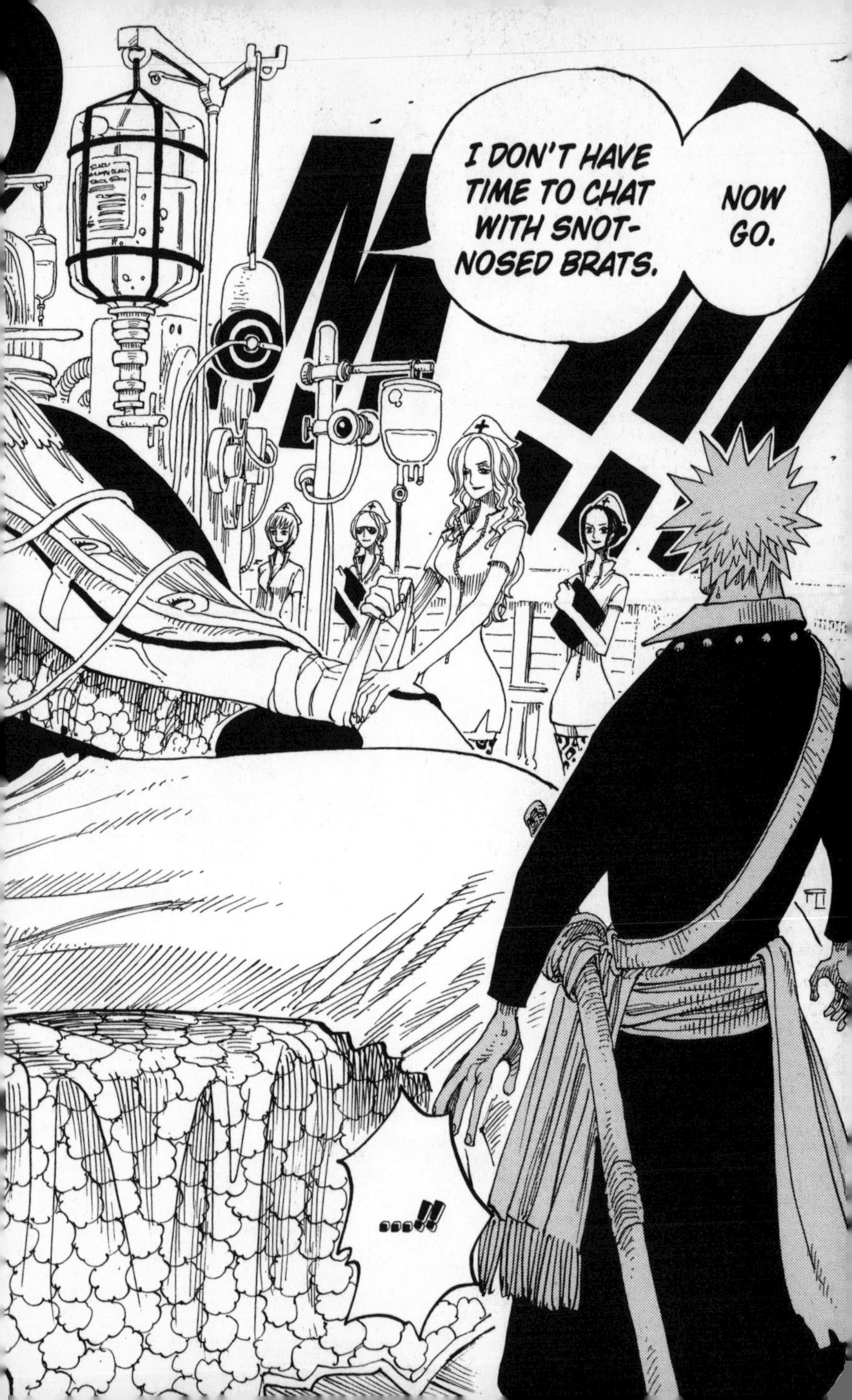
I DON'T HAVE TIME TO CHAT WITH SNOT-NOSED BRATS.
NOW GO.
...!!

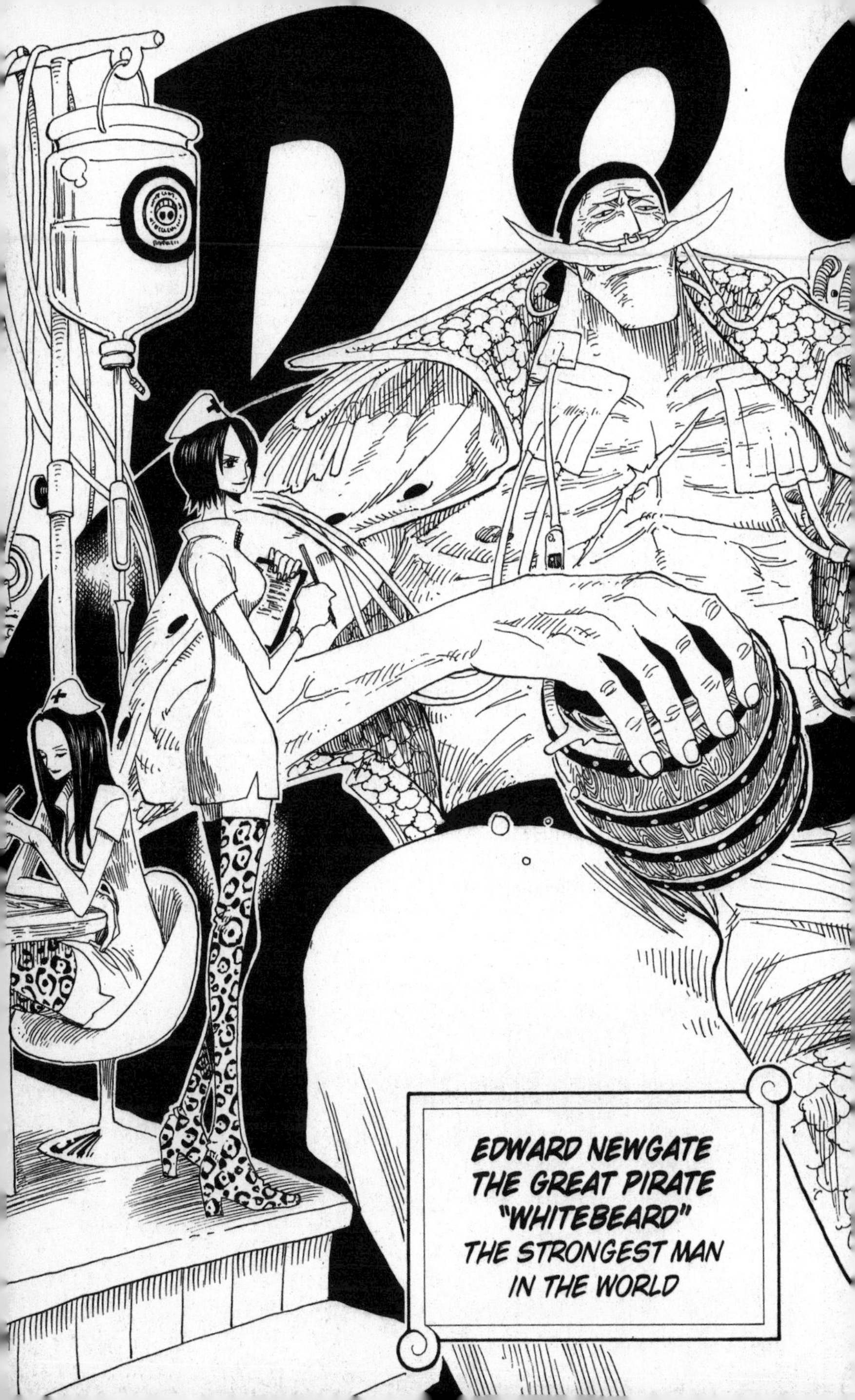
EDWARD NEWGATE
THE GREAT PIRATE
"WHITEBEARD"
THE STRONGEST MAN
IN THE WORLD

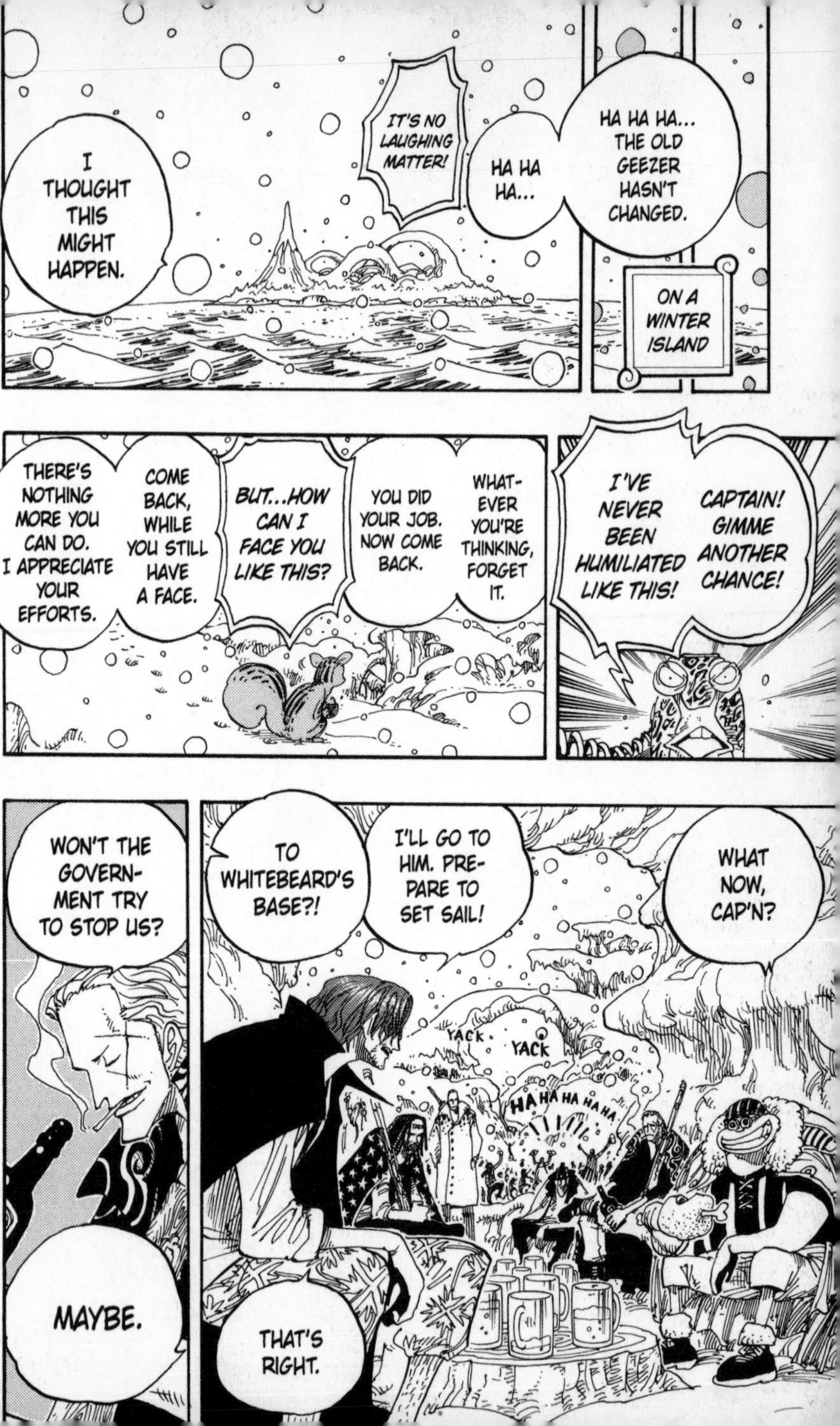
HA HA HA... THE OLD GEEZER HASN'T CHANGED.
ON A WINTER ISLAND
HA HA HA...
IT'S NO LAUGHING MATTER!
I THOUGHT THIS MIGHT HAPPEN.
CAPTAIN! GIMME ANOTHER CHANCE!
I'VE NEVER BEEN HUMILIATED LIKE THIS!
WHATEVER YOU'RE THINKING, FORGET IT.
YOU DID YOUR JOB. NOW COME BACK.
BUT...HOW CAN I FACE YOU LIKE THIS?
COME BACK, WHILE YOU STILL HAVE A FACE.
THERE'S NOTHING MORE YOU CAN DO. I APPRECIATE YOUR EFFORTS.
WHAT NOW, CAP'N?
I'LL GO TO HIM. PREPARE TO SET SAIL!
TO WHITEBEARD'S BASE?!
YACK
YACK
HA HA HA HA HA
THAT'S RIGHT.
WON'T THE GOVERNMENT TRY TO STOP US?
MAYBE.

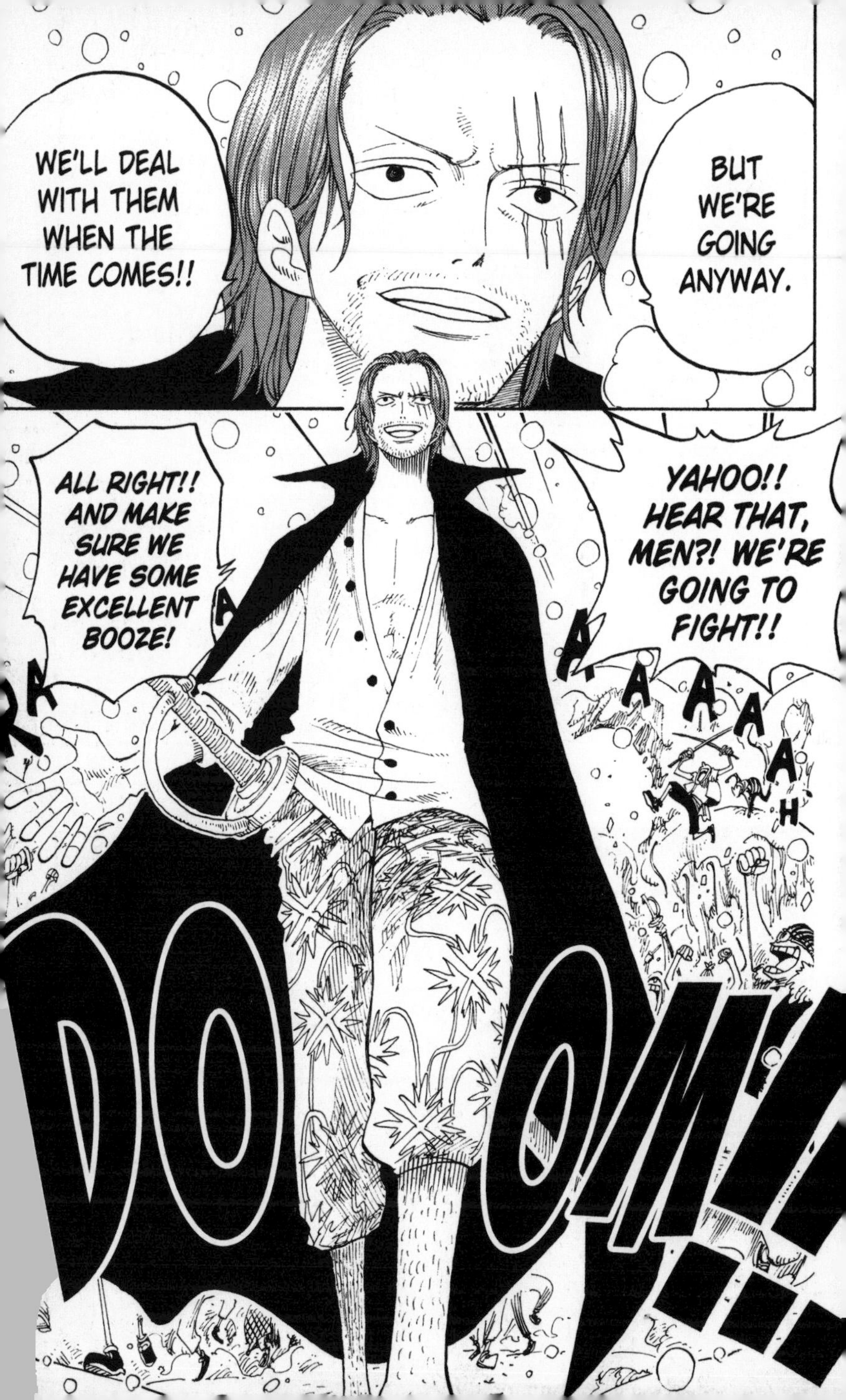
BUT WE'RE GOING ANYWAY.
WE'LL DEAL WITH THEM WHEN THE TIME COMES!!
YAHOO!! HEAR THAT, MEN?! WE'RE GOING TO FIGHT!!
ALL RIGHT!! AND MAKE SURE WE HAVE SOME EXCELLENT BOOZE!

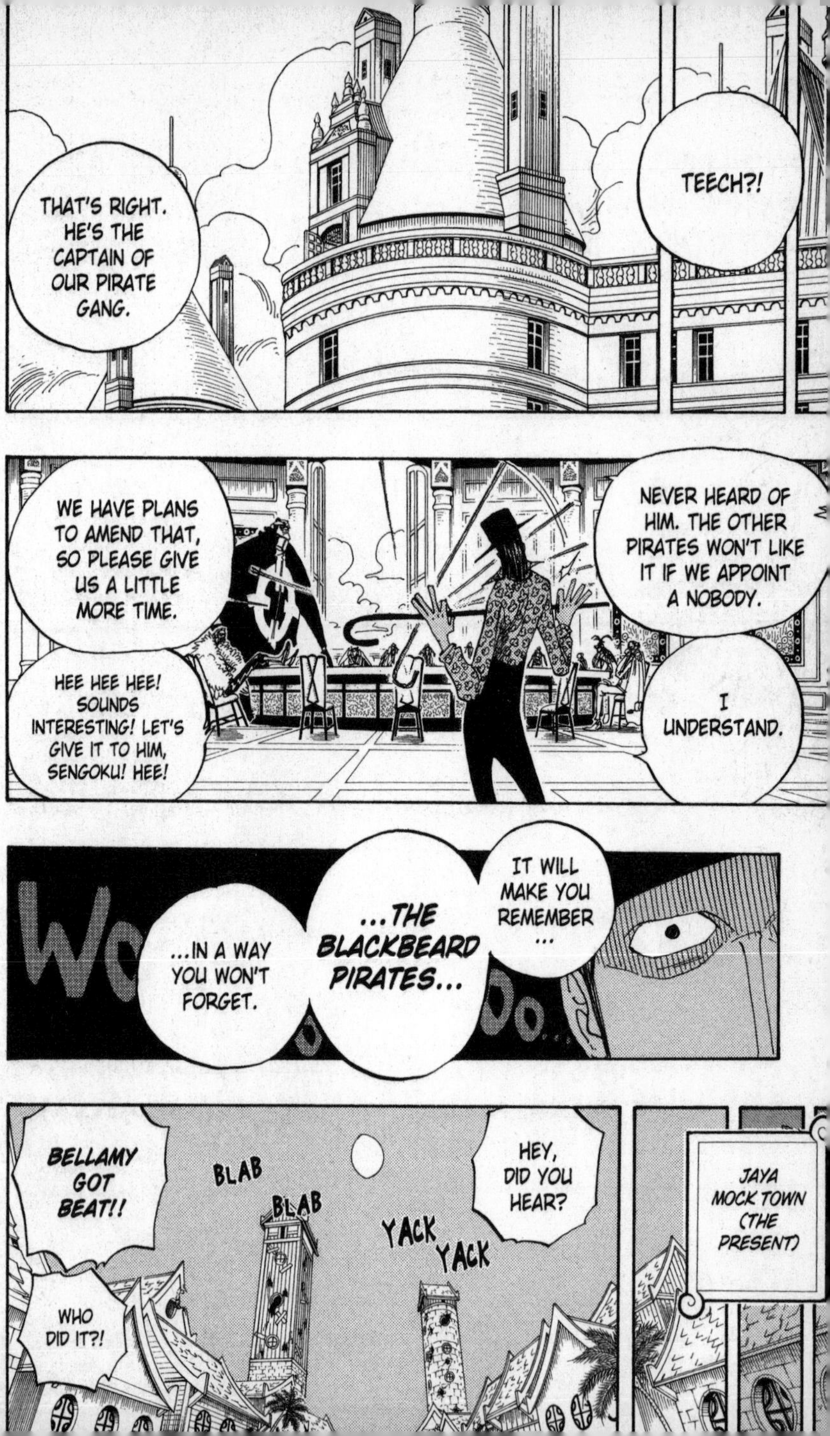
TEECH?!
THAT'S RIGHT. HE'S THE CAPTAIN OF OUR PIRATE GANG.
NEVER HEARD OF HIM. THE OTHER PIRATES WON'T LIKE IT IF WE APPOINT A NOBODY.
WE HAVE PLANS TO AMEND THAT, SO PLEASE GIVE US A LITTLE MORE TIME.
HEE HEE HEE! SOUNDS INTERESTING! LET'S GIVE IT TO HIM, SENGOKU! HEE!
I UNDERSTAND.
IT WILL MAKE YOU REMEMBER ...
...THE BLACKBEARD PIRATES...
...IN A WAY YOU WON'T FORGET.
JAYA MOCK TOWN (THE PRESENT)
HEY, DID YOU HEAR?
YACK YACK
BLAB BLAB
BELLAMY GOT BEAT!!
WHO DID IT?!

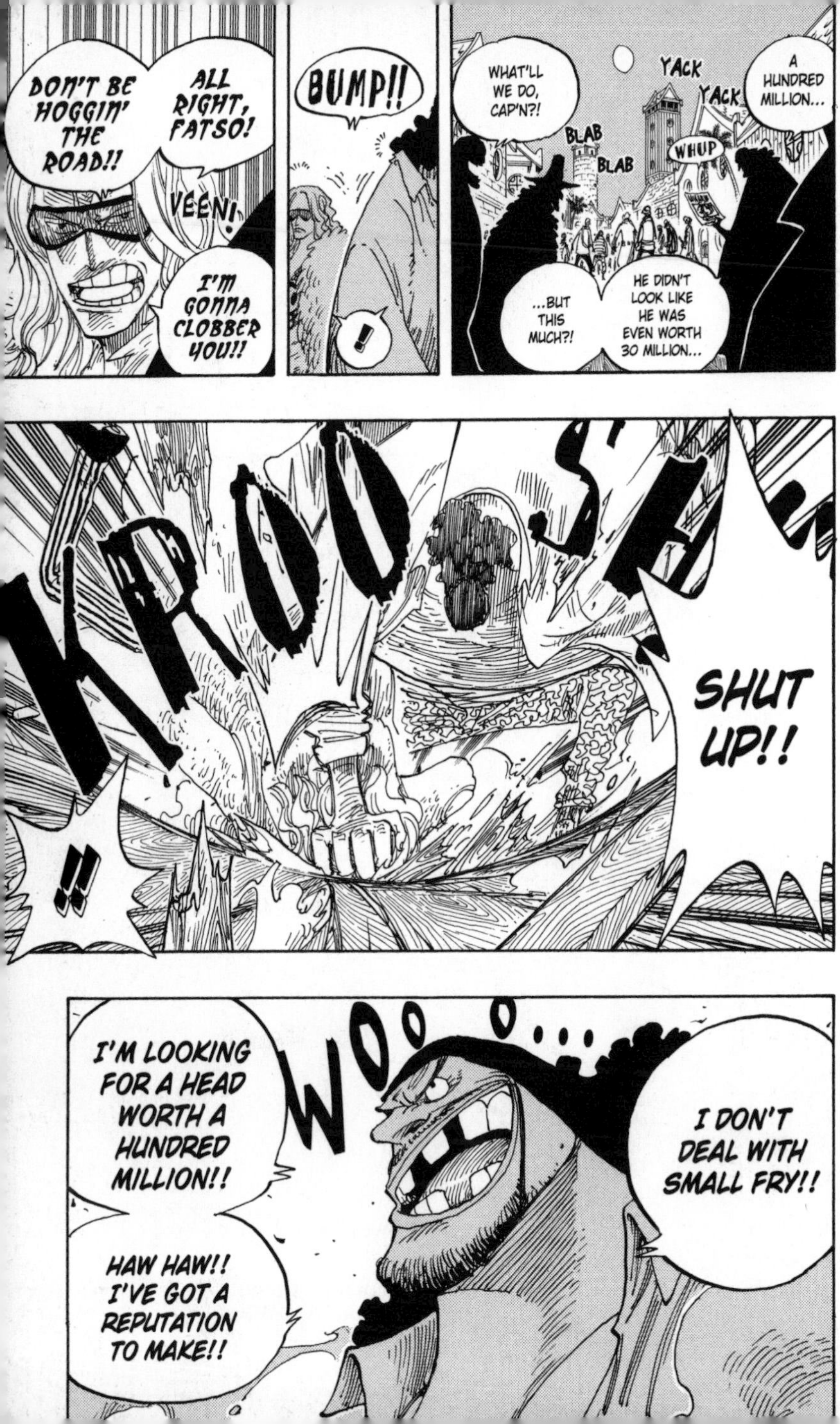
A HUNDRED MILLION...
YACK
YACK
WHAT'LL WE DO, CAP'N?!
BLAB
BLAB
WHUP
HE DIDN'T LOOK LIKE HE WAS EVEN WORTH 30 MILLION...
...BUT THIS MUCH?!
BUMP!!
!
ALL RIGHT, FATSO!
DON'T BE HOGGIN' THE ROAD!!
VEEN!
I'M GONNA CLOBBER YOU!!
SHUT UP!!
KRROOSH
!!
WOO O...
I DON'T DEAL WITH SMALL FRY!!
I'M LOOKING FOR A HEAD WORTH A HUNDRED MILLION!!
HAW HAW!! I'VE GOT A REPUTATION TO MAKE!!

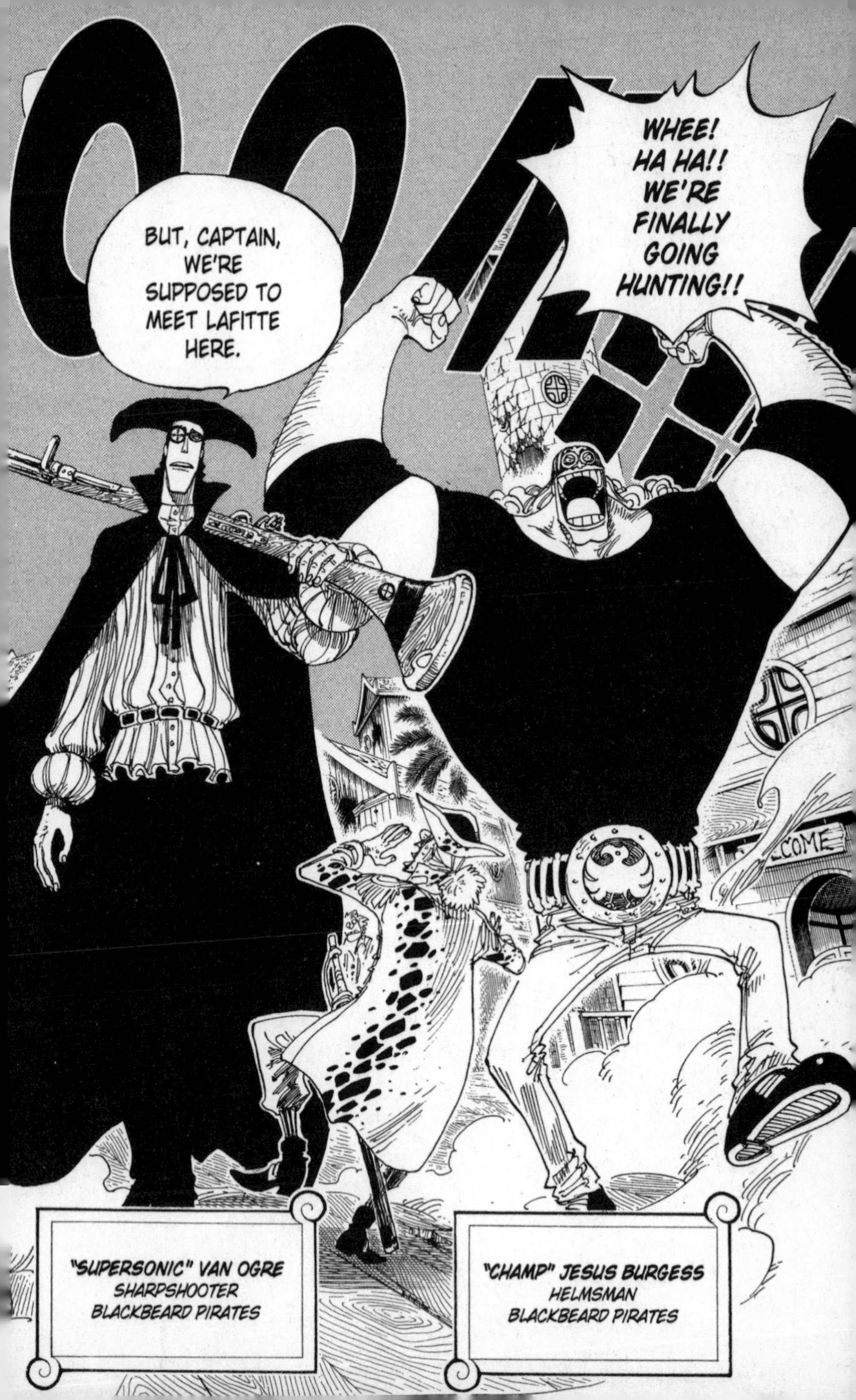
WHEE! HA HA!! WE'RE FINALLY GOING HUNTING!!
BUT, CAPTAIN, WE'RE SUPPOSED TO MEET LAFITTE HERE.
...COME
"CHAMP" JESUS BURGESS
HELMSMAN
BLACKBEARD PIRATES
"SUPERSONIC" VAN OGRE
SHARPSHOOTER
BLACKBEARD PIRATES

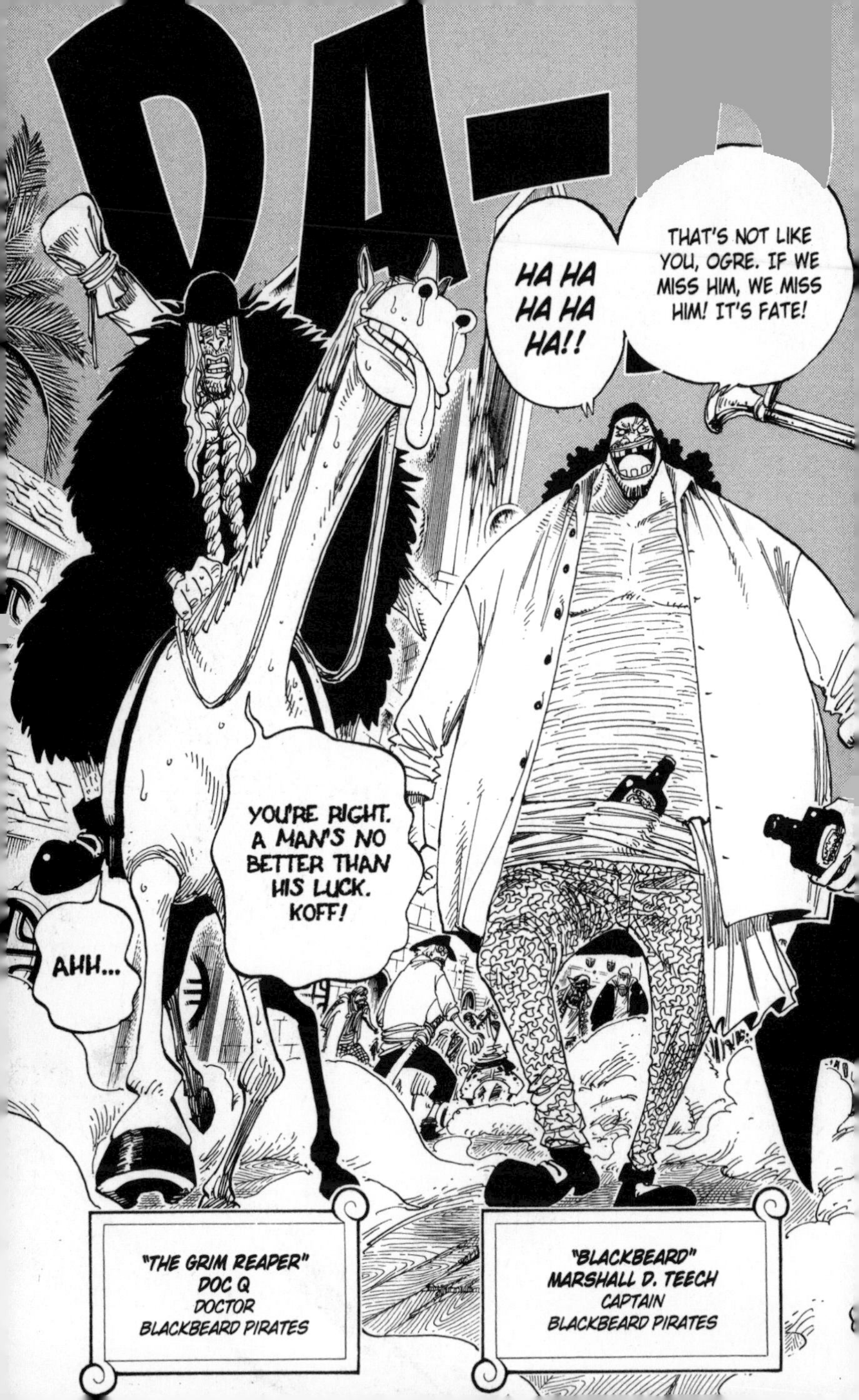
DA-
THAT'S NOT LIKE YOU, OGRE. IF WE MISS HIM, WE MISS HIM! IT'S FATE!
HA HA HA HA HA!!
YOU'RE RIGHT. A MAN'S NO BETTER THAN HIS LUCK. KOFF!
AHH...
"BLACKBEARD" MARSHALL D. TEECH CAPTAIN BLACKBEARD PIRATES
"THE GRIM REAPER" DOC Q DOCTOR BLACKBEARD PIRATES

QUESTION CORNER
S
B
S

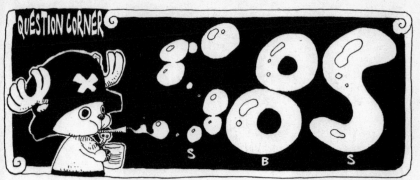

Q: Where is Vira? First it was the scene of a coup d'état in volume 11, then the wild town in chapter 228. What's going on there?

A: Well, well... That's very shrewd of you. Vira was a thriving town back in Noland's day 400 years ago, but presently, because of the many revolutions that have happened there, it has become a dangerous place. So, instead of asking what's going on in Vira, maybe one should ask what's going on in the world? And I believe you'll soon begin to understand. It's a small nation on the Grand Line, smaller than Alabasta. But I wouldn't go there on vacation.

THE WORLD SURE IS IN TURMOIL.
THERE WAS ANOTHER COUP D'ÉTAT IN VIRA.
FWUP!

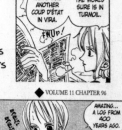

◆ VOLUME 11 CHAPTER 96

AMAZING... A LOG FROM 400 YEARS AGO.
"THE AGE OF KAIEN 1120, JUNE 21. CLEAR SKIES. SAILED FROM THE LIVELY TOWN OF VIRA.
FWIP
Log book

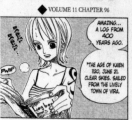

◆ THIS VOLUME CHAPTER 228

Q: Oda Sensei, I saw the *One Piece* movie *Chopper's Kingdom on the Island of Strange Animals*. It was so good. And I was surprised to see you in *Soccer King of Dreams*, the short feature that was shown with it. By the way, Oda Sensei, do you really look like that?

A: Yes.

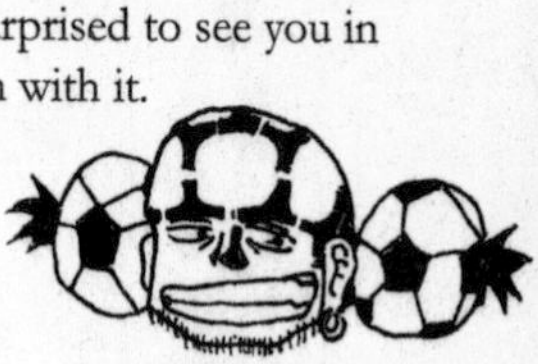

Q: Hello, Oda Sensei. I was watching *One Piece* recently and realized for the first time that Sanji has hair on his legs. For some reason I thought that blond leg hair wasn't as noticeable. I'm a big Sanji fan, but I don't really like his hairy legs. Please do something, Oda Sensei.

--From the Heart

A: But Sanji's really hairy. And Chopper's really hairy too. That's it for the Question Corner! See you in the next volume!

# Chapter 235:
# THE KNOCK UP STREAM

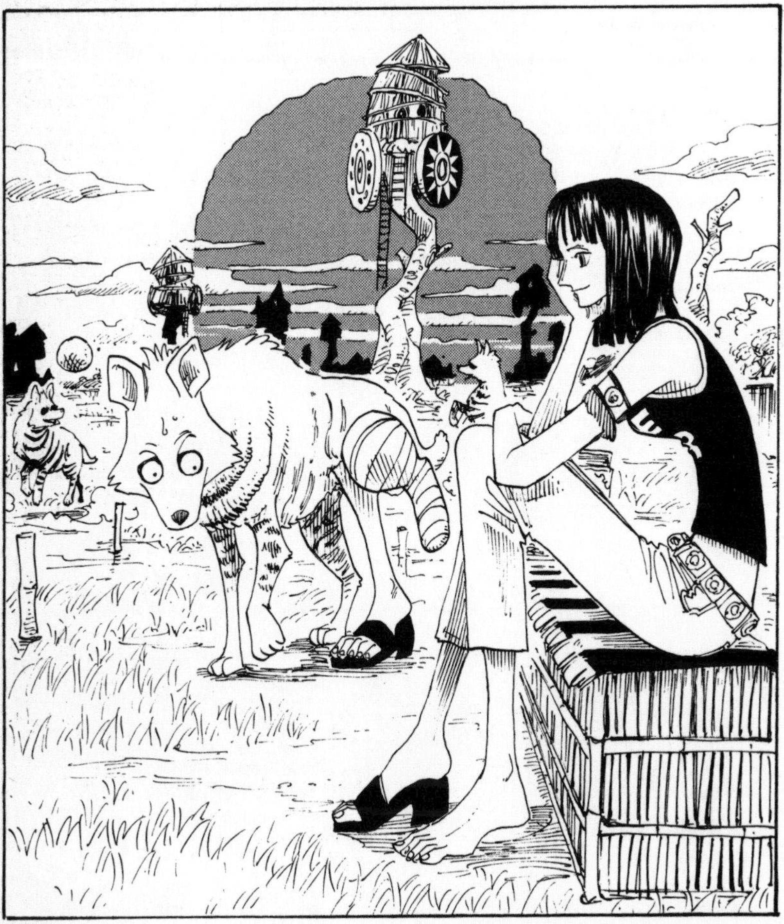

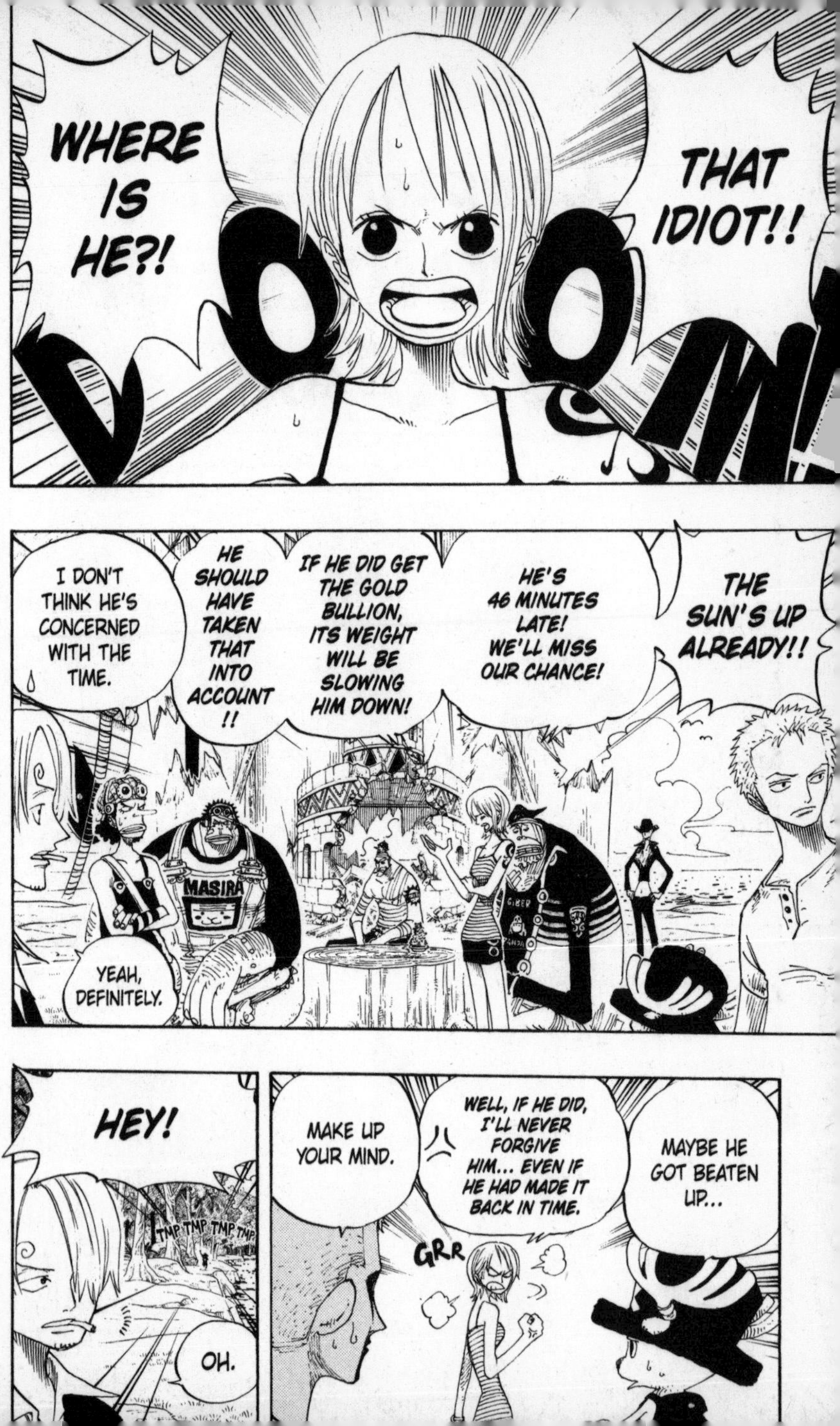
THAT IDIOT!!
WHERE IS HE?!
THE SUN'S UP ALREADY!!
HE'S 46 MINUTES LATE! WE'LL MISS OUR CHANCE!
IF HE DID GET THE GOLD BULLION, ITS WEIGHT WILL BE SLOWING HIM DOWN!
HE SHOULD HAVE TAKEN THAT INTO ACCOUNT!!
I DON'T THINK HE'S CONCERNED WITH THE TIME.
YEAH, DEFINITELY.
MAYBE HE GOT BEATEN UP...
WELL, IF HE DID, I'LL NEVER FORGIVE HIM... EVEN IF HE HAD MADE IT BACK IN TIME.
MAKE UP YOUR MIND.
GRR
HEY!
TMP TMP TMP TMP
OH.

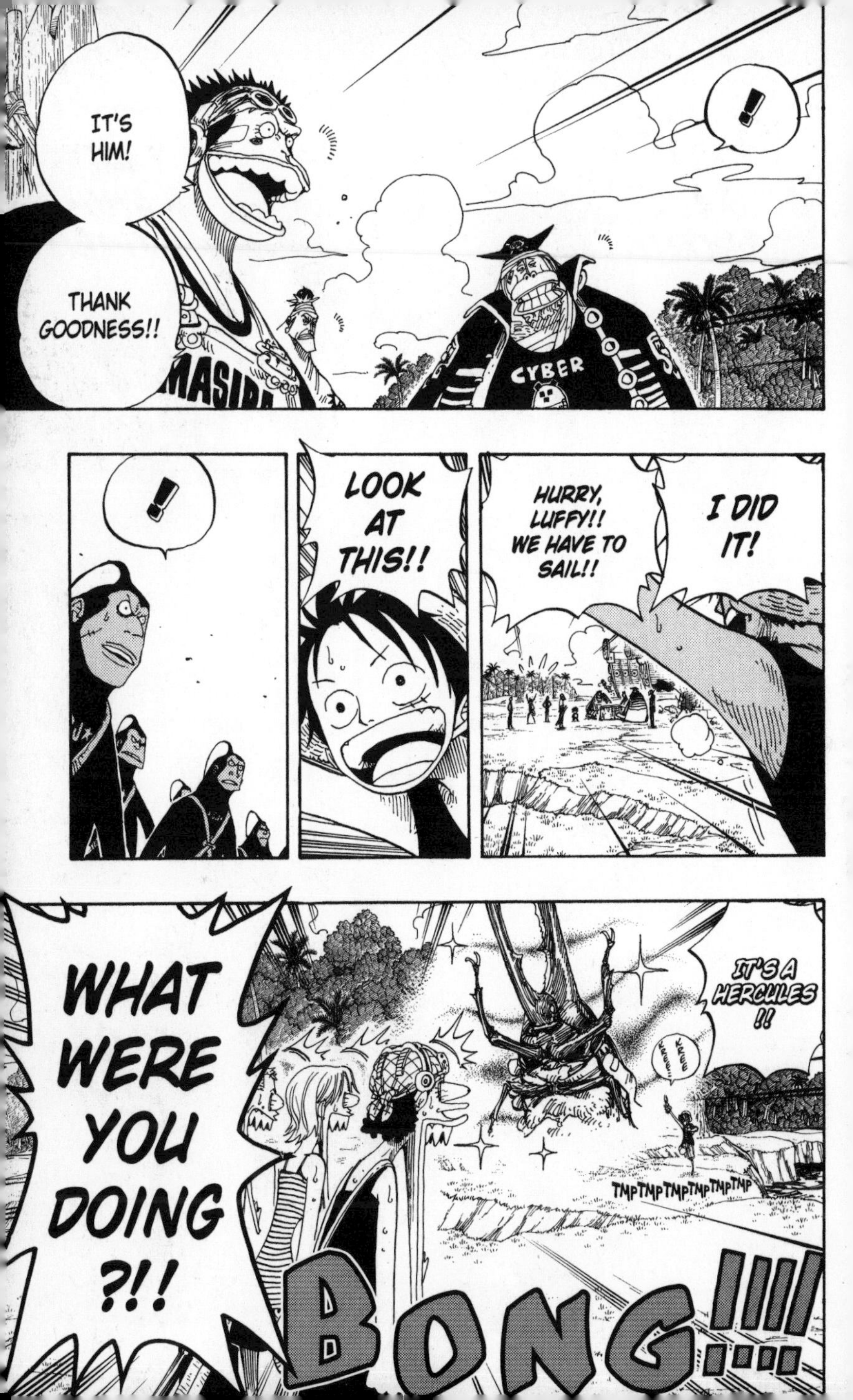
!
IT'S HIM!
THANK GOODNESS!!
MASIRA
CYBER
I DID IT!
HURRY, LUFFY!! WE HAVE TO SAIL!!
LOOK AT THIS!!
!
IT'S A HERCULES!!
TMPTMPTMPTMPTMPTMP
WHAT WERE YOU DOING?!!
BONG!!!!

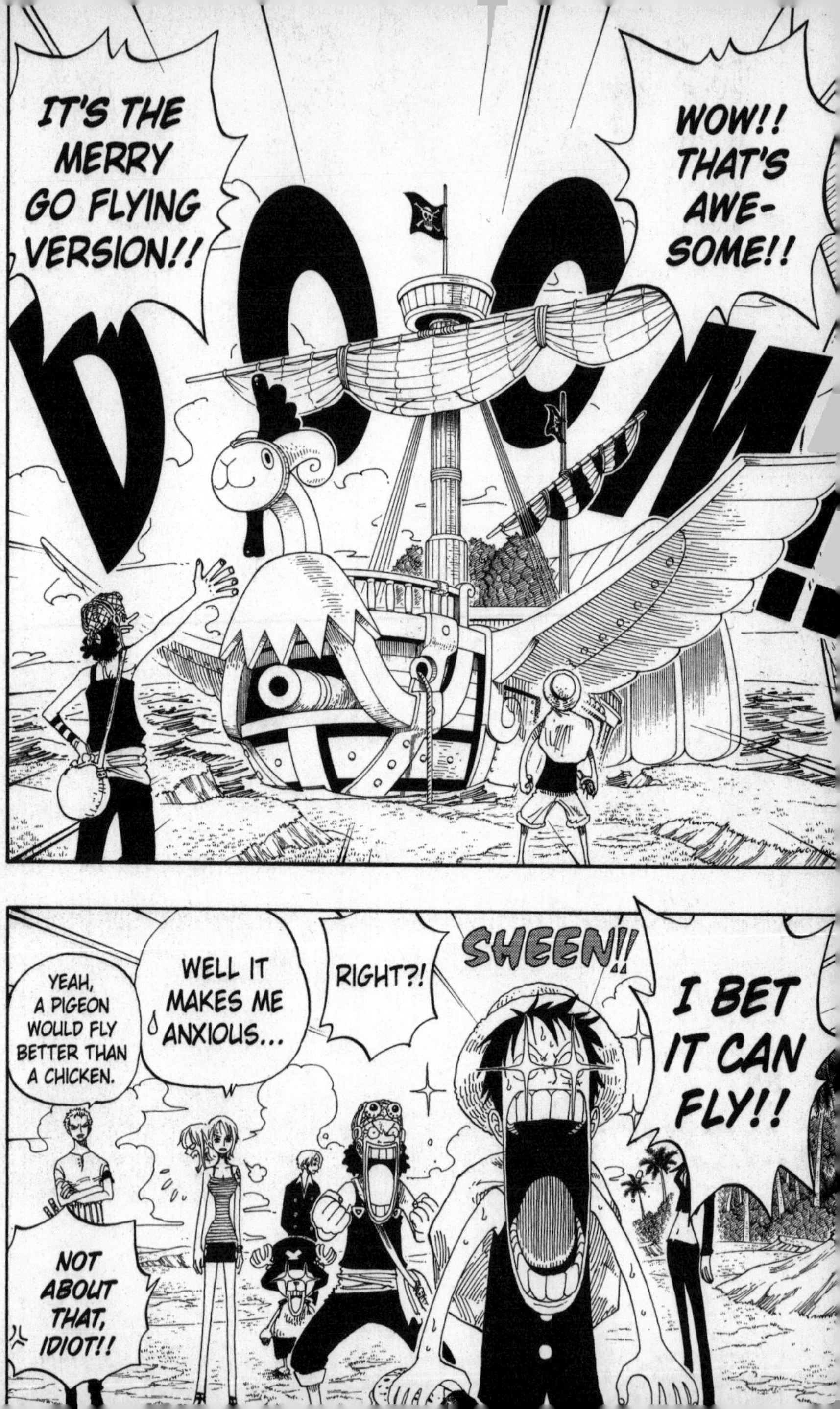
WOW!! THAT'S AWE-SOME!!
DOOM!!
IT'S THE MERRY GO FLYING VERSION!!
SHEEN!!
I BET IT CAN FLY!!
RIGHT?!
WELL IT MAKES ME ANXIOUS...
YEAH, A PIGEON WOULD FLY BETTER THAN A CHICKEN.
NOT ABOUT THAT, IDIOT!!

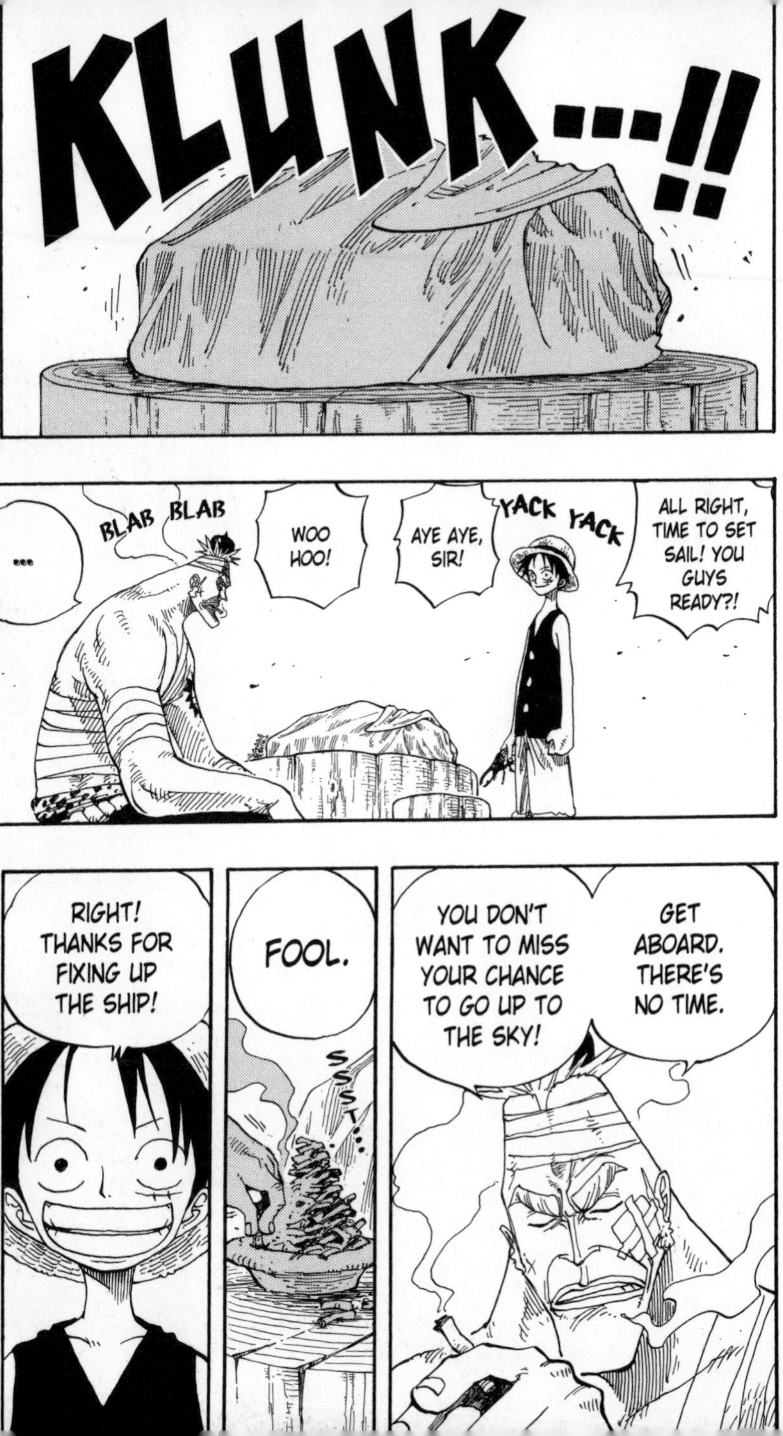
KLUNK...!!
ALL RIGHT, TIME TO SET SAIL! YOU GUYS READY?!
YACK YACK
AYE AYE, SIR!
WOO HOO!
BLAB BLAB
...
GET ABOARD. THERE'S NO TIME.
YOU DON'T WANT TO MISS YOUR CHANCE TO GO UP TO THE SKY!
FOOL.
SSST...
RIGHT! THANKS FOR FIXING UP THE SHIP!

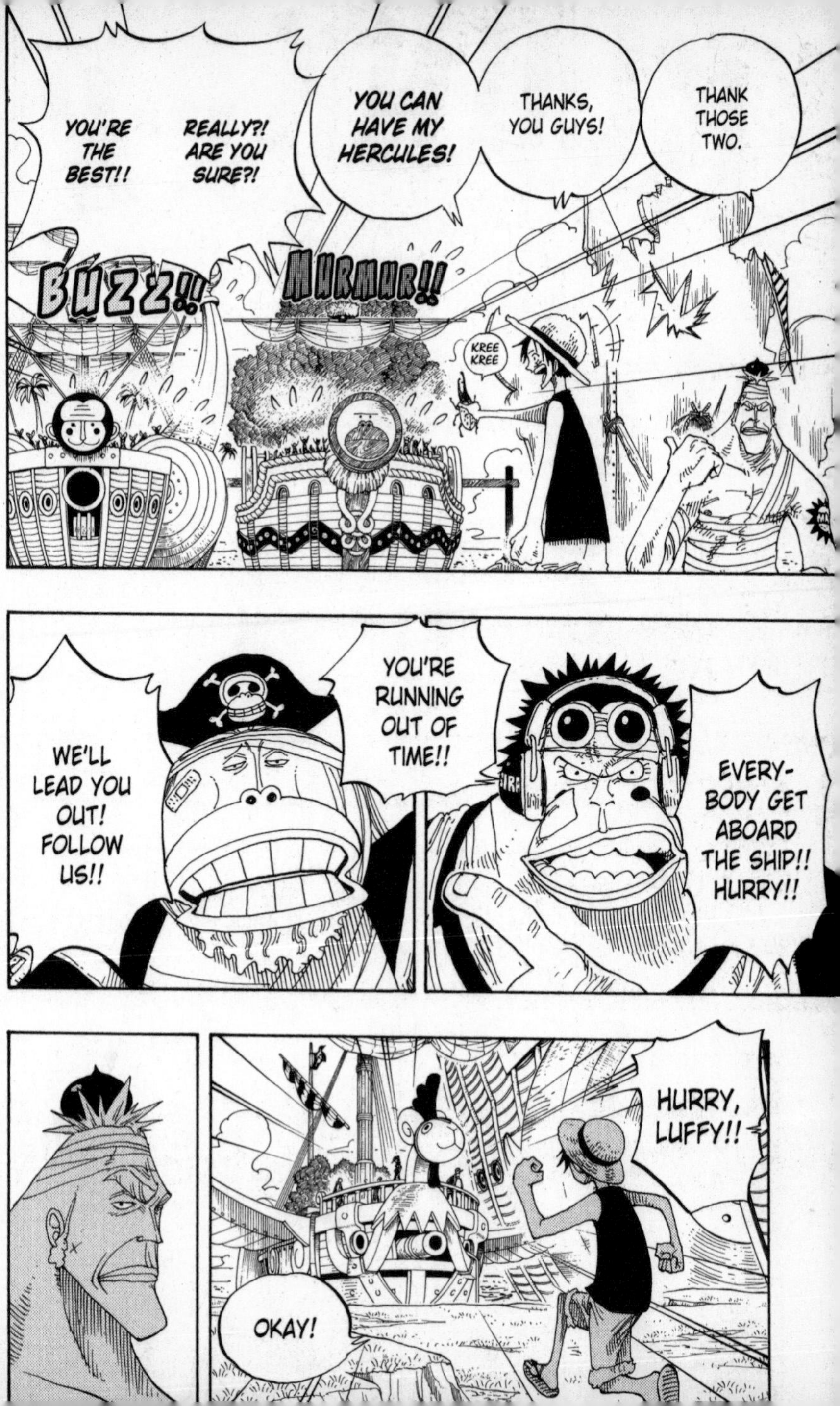
THANK THOSE TWO.
THANKS, YOU GUYS!
YOU CAN HAVE MY HERCULES!
REALLY?! ARE YOU SURE?!
YOU'RE THE BEST!!
KREE KREE
MURMUR!!
BUZZ!!
EVERY-BODY GET ABOARD THE SHIP!! HURRY!!
YOU'RE RUNNING OUT OF TIME!!
WE'LL LEAD YOU OUT! FOLLOW US!!
HURRY, LUFFY!!
OKAY!

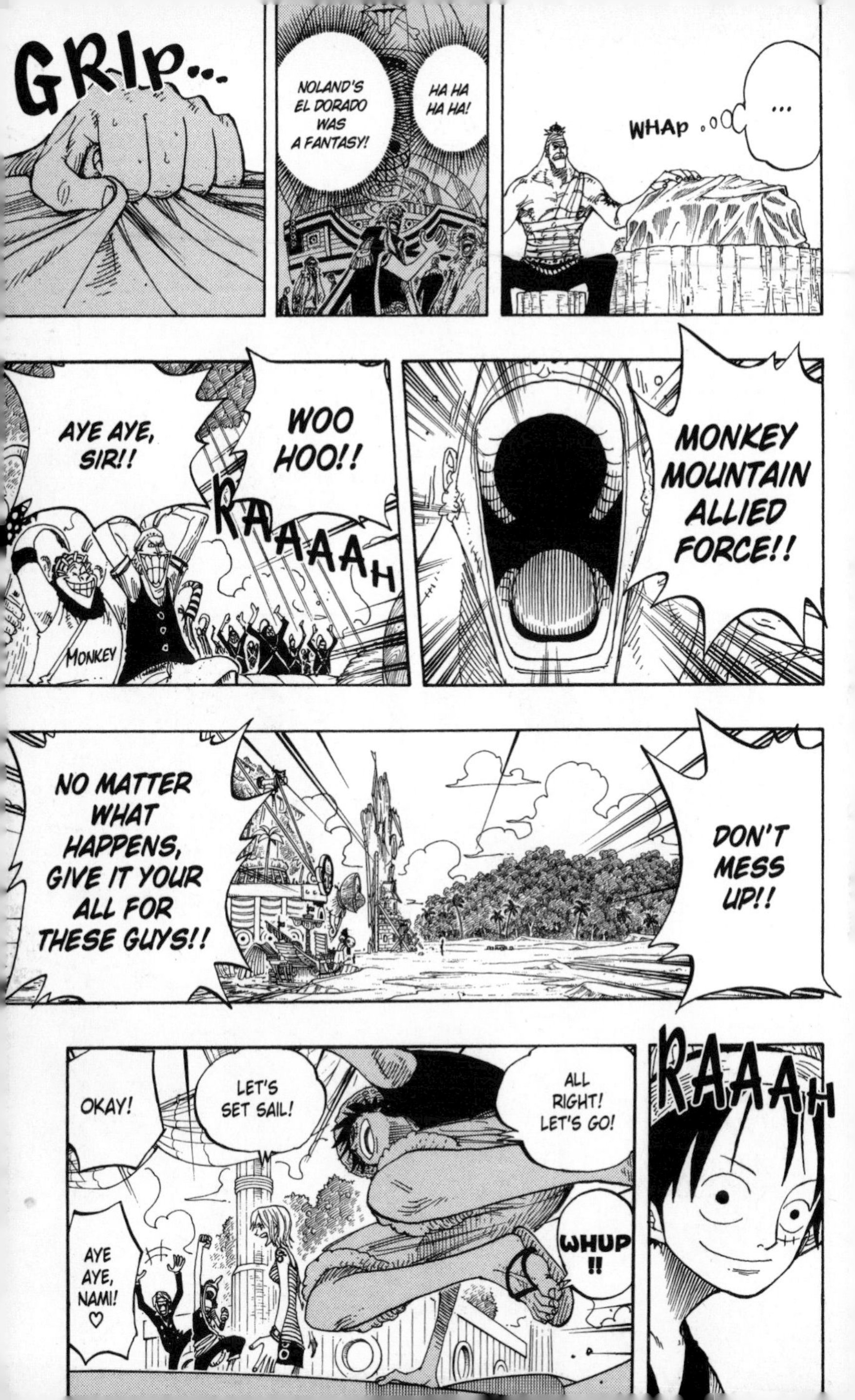

...
WHAp
HA HA HA HA!
NOLAND'S EL DORADO WAS A FANTASY!
GRIP...
MONKEY MOUNTAIN ALLIED FORCE!!
WOO HOO!!
AYE AYE, SIR!!
RAAAAAH
MONKEY
DON'T MESS UP!!
NO MATTER WHAT HAPPENS, GIVE IT YOUR ALL FOR THESE GUYS!!
RAAAH
ALL RIGHT! LET'S GO!
LET'S SET SAIL!
OKAY!
WHUP!!
AYE AYE, NAMI! ♡

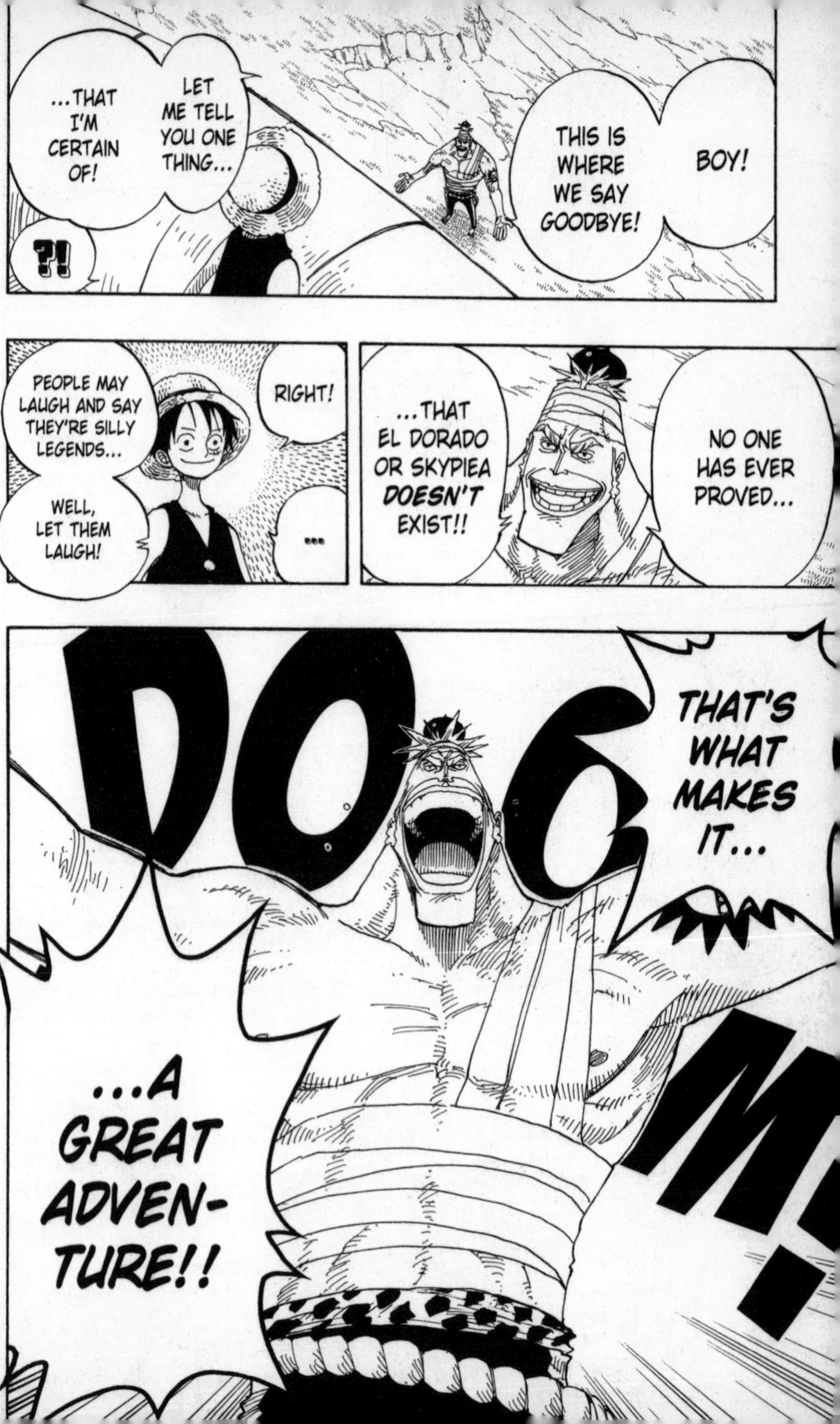
BOY!
THIS IS WHERE WE SAY GOODBYE!
LET ME TELL YOU ONE THING...
...THAT I'M CERTAIN OF!
?!
NO ONE HAS EVER PROVED...
...THAT EL DORADO OR SKYPIEA *DOESN'T* EXIST!!
RIGHT!
PEOPLE MAY LAUGH AND SAY THEY'RE SILLY LEGENDS...
...
WELL, LET THEM LAUGH!
DOGM!
THAT'S WHAT MAKES IT...
...A GREAT ADVEN-TURE!!

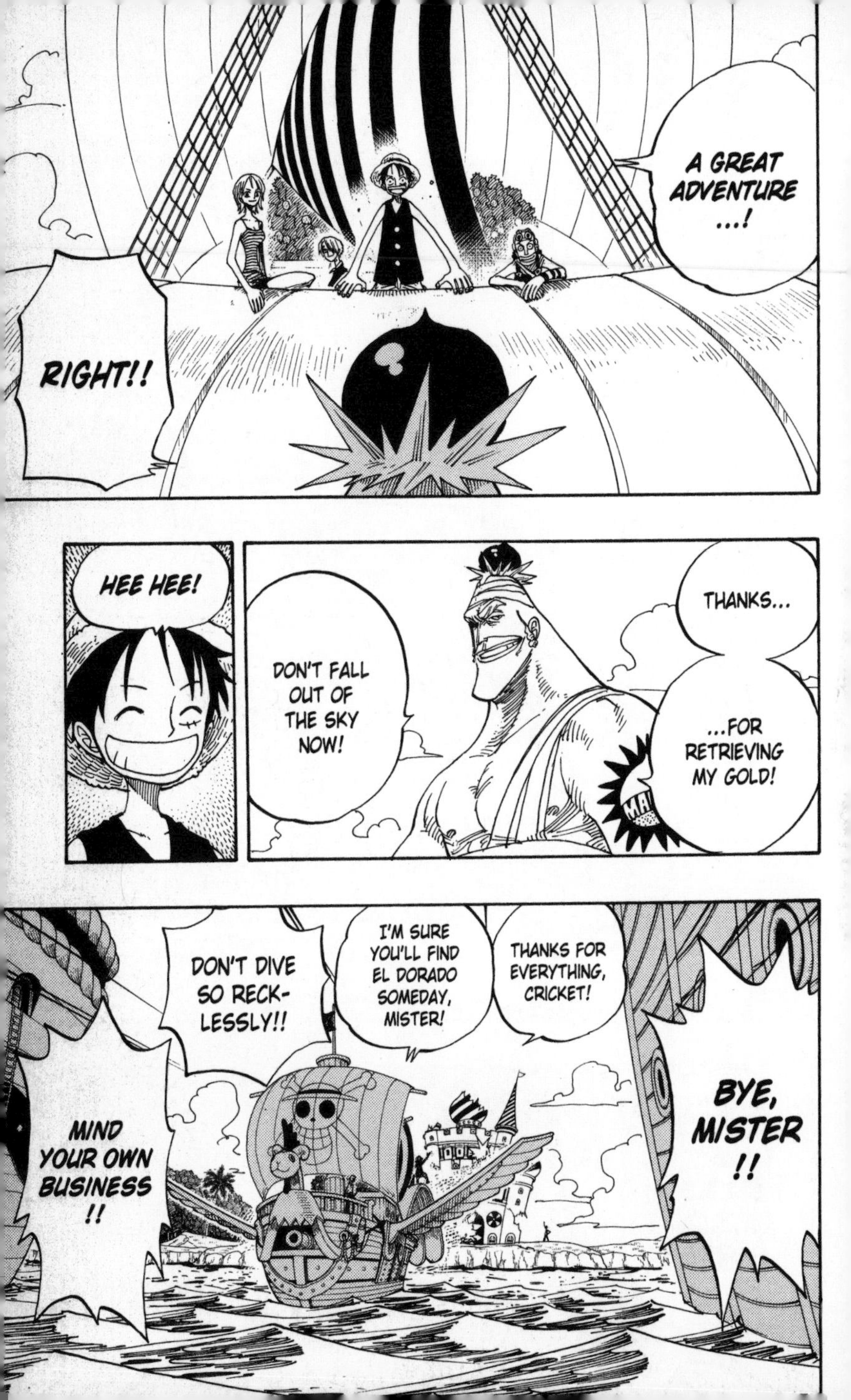
A GREAT ADVENTURE ...!
RIGHT!!
THANKS...
...FOR RETRIEVING MY GOLD!
DON'T FALL OUT OF THE SKY NOW!
HEE HEE!
THANKS FOR EVERYTHING, CRICKET!
I'M SURE YOU'LL FIND EL DORADO SOMEDAY, MISTER!
DON'T DIVE SO RECK-LESSLY!!
BYE, MISTER !!
MIND YOUR OWN BUSINESS !!

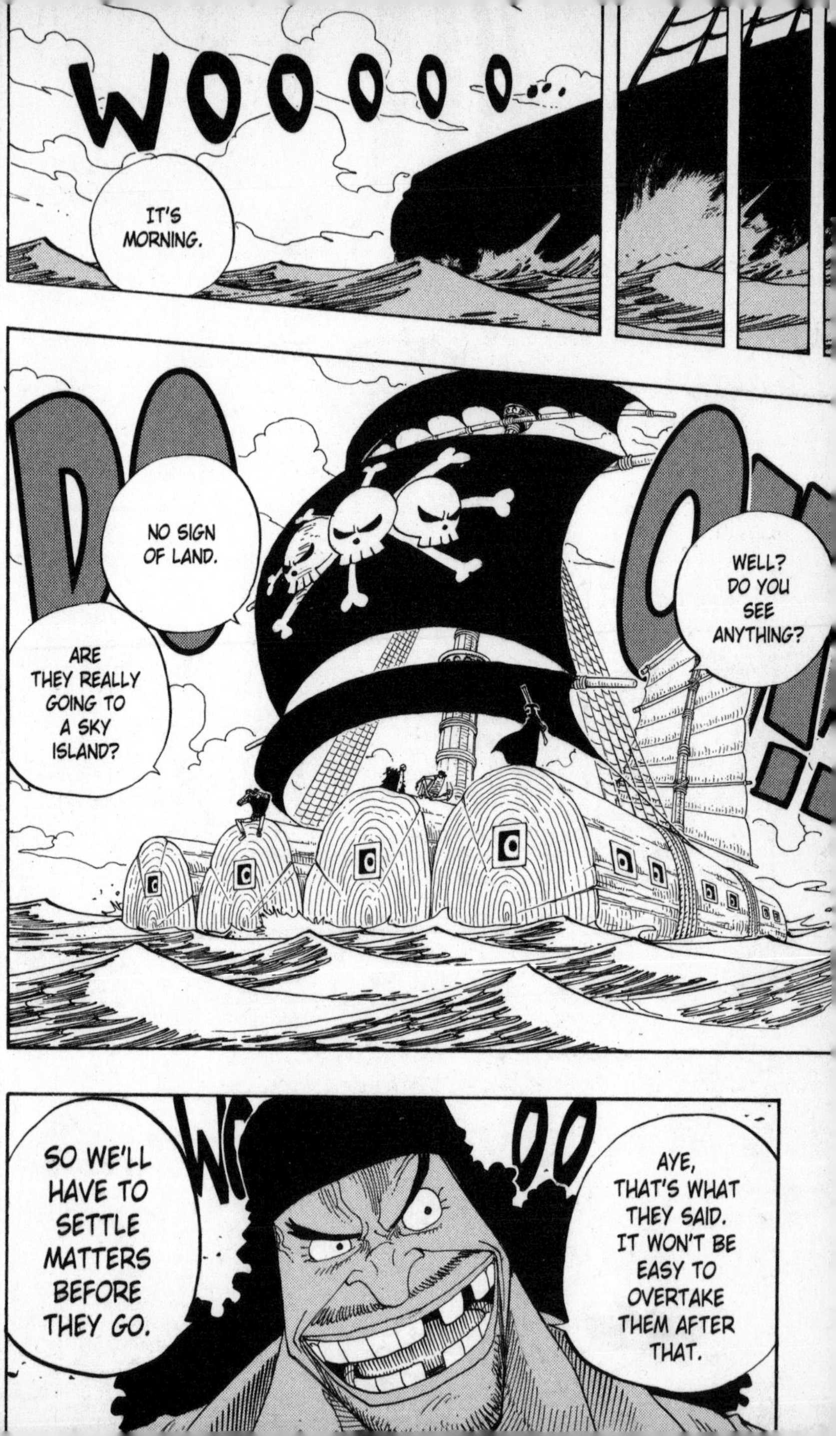
WOOOOO...
IT'S MORNING.
WELL? DO YOU SEE ANYTHING?
NO SIGN OF LAND.
ARE THEY REALLY GOING TO A SKY ISLAND?
AYE, THAT'S WHAT THEY SAID. IT WON'T BE EASY TO OVERTAKE THEM AFTER THAT.
SO WE'LL HAVE TO SETTLE MATTERS BEFORE THEY GO.

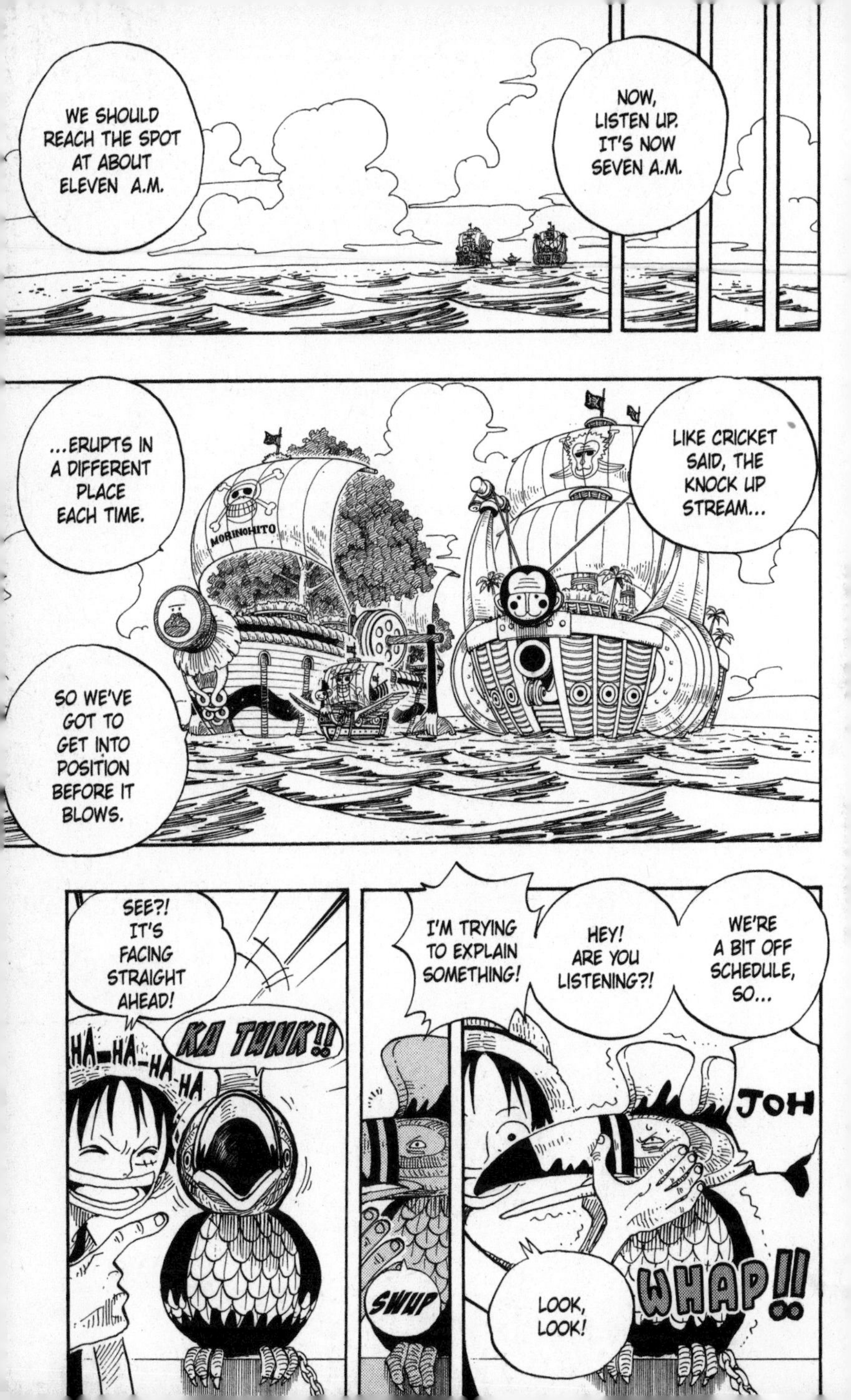
NOW, LISTEN UP. IT'S NOW SEVEN A.M.
WE SHOULD REACH THE SPOT AT ABOUT ELEVEN A.M.
LIKE CRICKET SAID, THE KNOCK UP STREAM...
...ERUPTS IN A DIFFERENT PLACE EACH TIME.
MORINOHITO
SO WE'VE GOT TO GET INTO POSITION BEFORE IT BLOWS.
WE'RE A BIT OFF SCHEDULE, SO...
HEY! ARE YOU LISTENING?!
I'M TRYING TO EXPLAIN SOMETHING!
JOH
WHAP!!
LOOK, LOOK!
SWUP
SEE?! IT'S FACING STRAIGHT AHEAD!
KA TUNK!!
HA-HA-HA-HA-HA

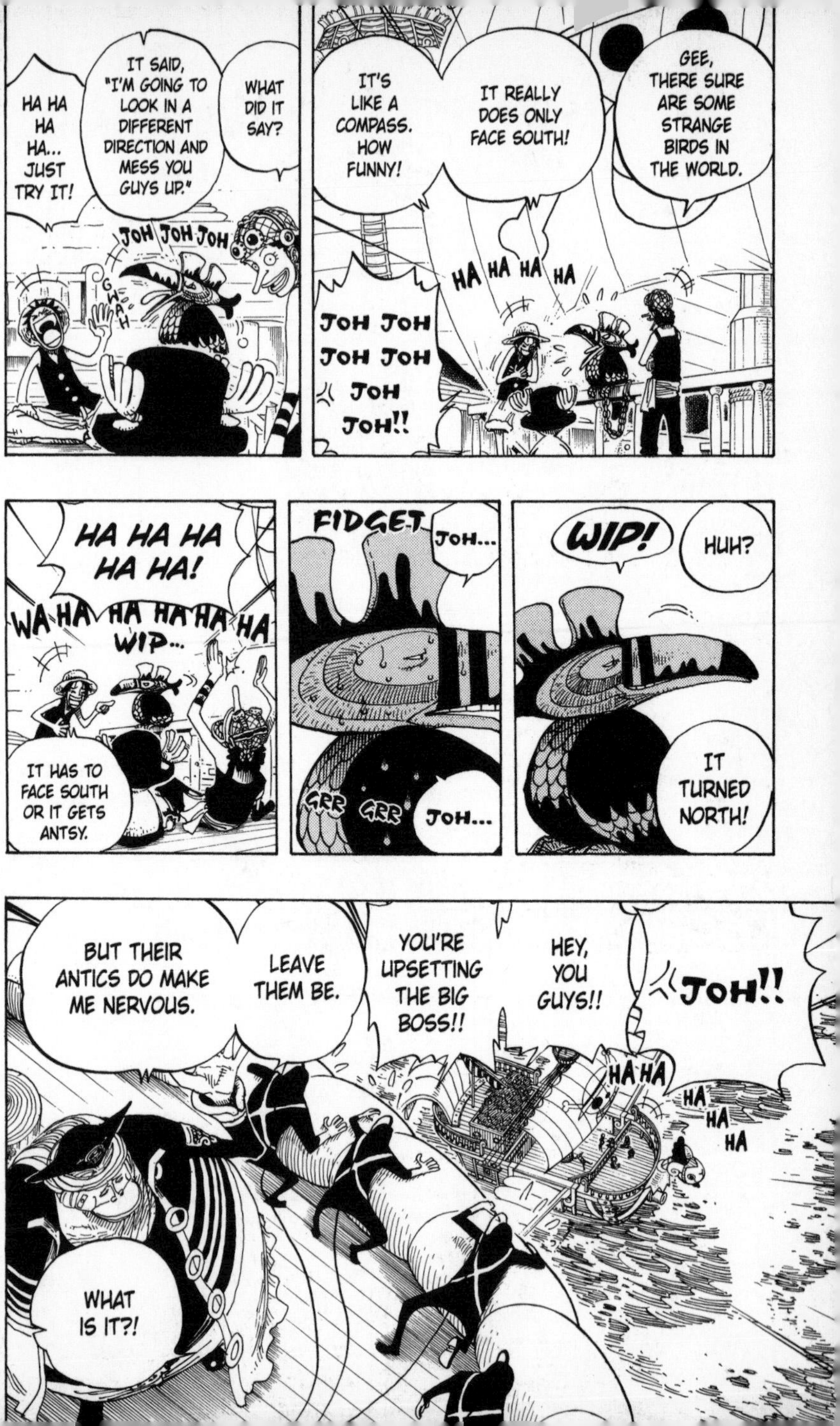
GEE, THERE SURE ARE SOME STRANGE BIRDS IN THE WORLD.
IT REALLY DOES ONLY FACE SOUTH!
IT'S LIKE A COMPASS. HOW FUNNY!
HA HA HA HA
JOH JOH JOH JOH JOH JOH!!
WHAT DID IT SAY?
IT SAID, "I'M GOING TO LOOK IN A DIFFERENT DIRECTION AND MESS YOU GUYS UP."
HA HA HA HA... JUST TRY IT!
JOH JOH JOH
GWAH
HUH?
WIP!
IT TURNED NORTH!
JOH...
FIDGET
GRR GRR
JOH...
HA HA HA HA HA!
WA HA HA HA HA HA
WIP...
IT HAS TO FACE SOUTH OR IT GETS ANTSY.
JOH!!
HEY, YOU GUYS!!
YOU'RE UPSETTING THE BIG BOSS!!
HA HA HA HA HA
LEAVE THEM BE.
BUT THEIR ANTICS DO MAKE ME NERVOUS.
WHAT IS IT?!

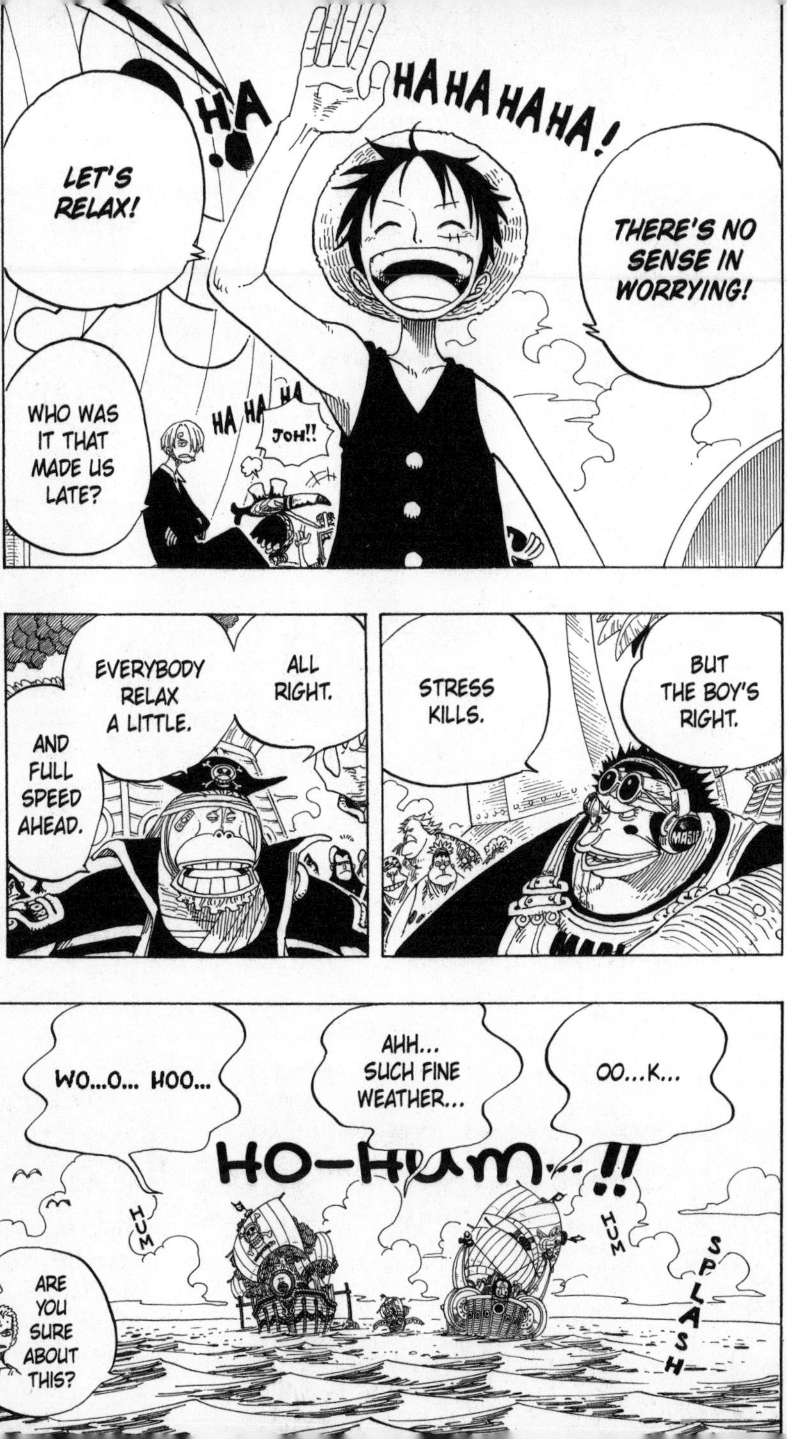
THERE'S NO SENSE IN WORRYING!
HA HAHAHAHAHA!
LET'S RELAX!
WHO WAS IT THAT MADE US LATE?
HA HA HA
JOH!!
BUT THE BOY'S RIGHT.
STRESS KILLS.
ALL RIGHT.
EVERYBODY RELAX A LITTLE.
AND FULL SPEED AHEAD.
OO...K...
AHH... SUCH FINE WEATHER...
WO...O... HOO...
HO-HUM...!!
HUM
SPLASH
HUM
ARE YOU SURE ABOUT THIS?

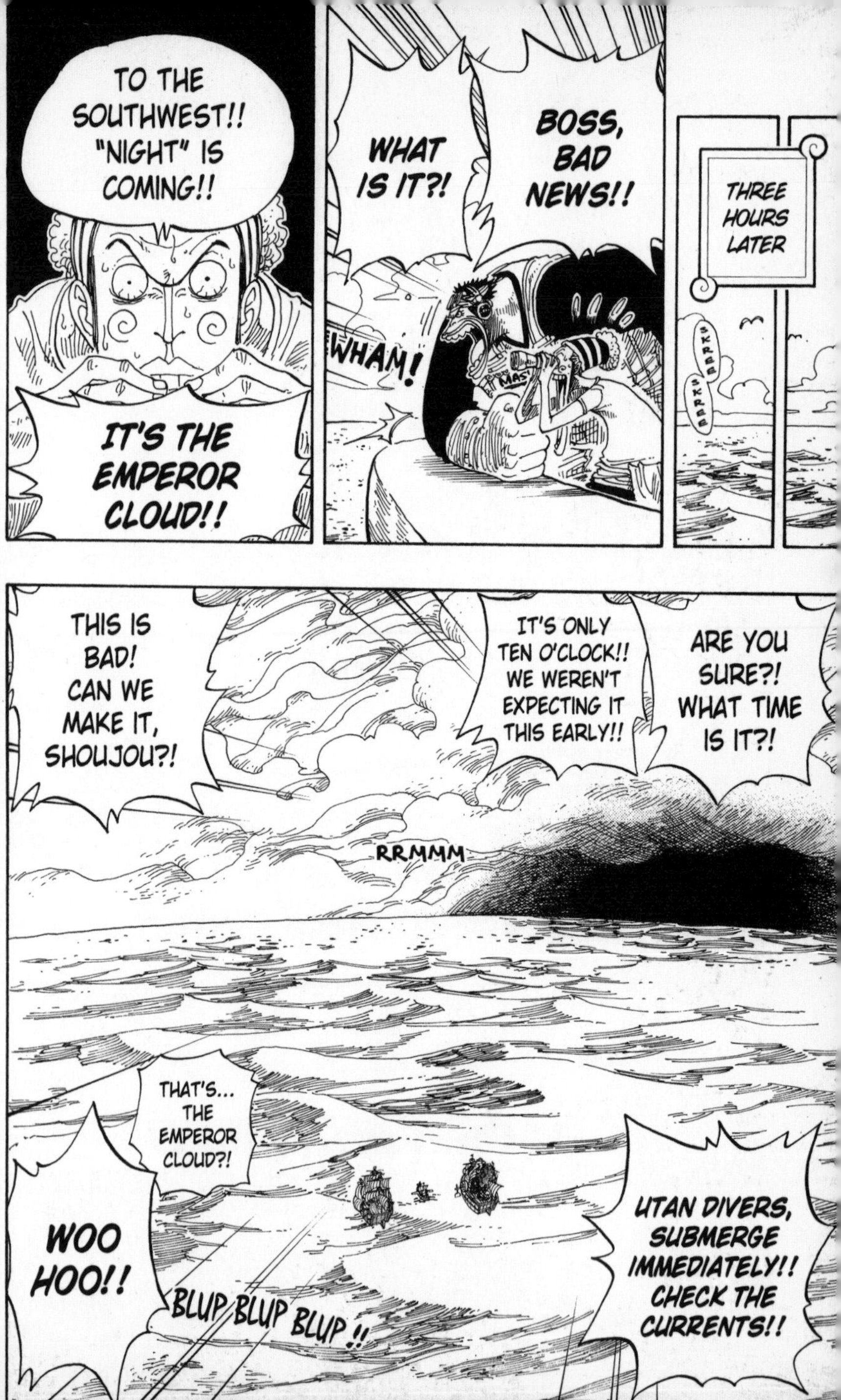
THREE HOURS LATER
SKREE
SKREE
BOSS, BAD NEWS!!
WHAT IS IT?!
WHAM!
TO THE SOUTHWEST!! "NIGHT" IS COMING!!
IT'S THE EMPEROR CLOUD!!
ARE YOU SURE?! WHAT TIME IS IT?!
IT'S ONLY TEN O'CLOCK!! WE WEREN'T EXPECTING IT THIS EARLY!!
THIS IS BAD! CAN WE MAKE IT, SHOUJOU?!
RRMMM
UTAN DIVERS, SUBMERGE IMMEDIATELY!! CHECK THE CURRENTS!!
THAT'S... THE EMPEROR CLOUD?!
WOO HOO!!
BLUP BLUP BLUP!!

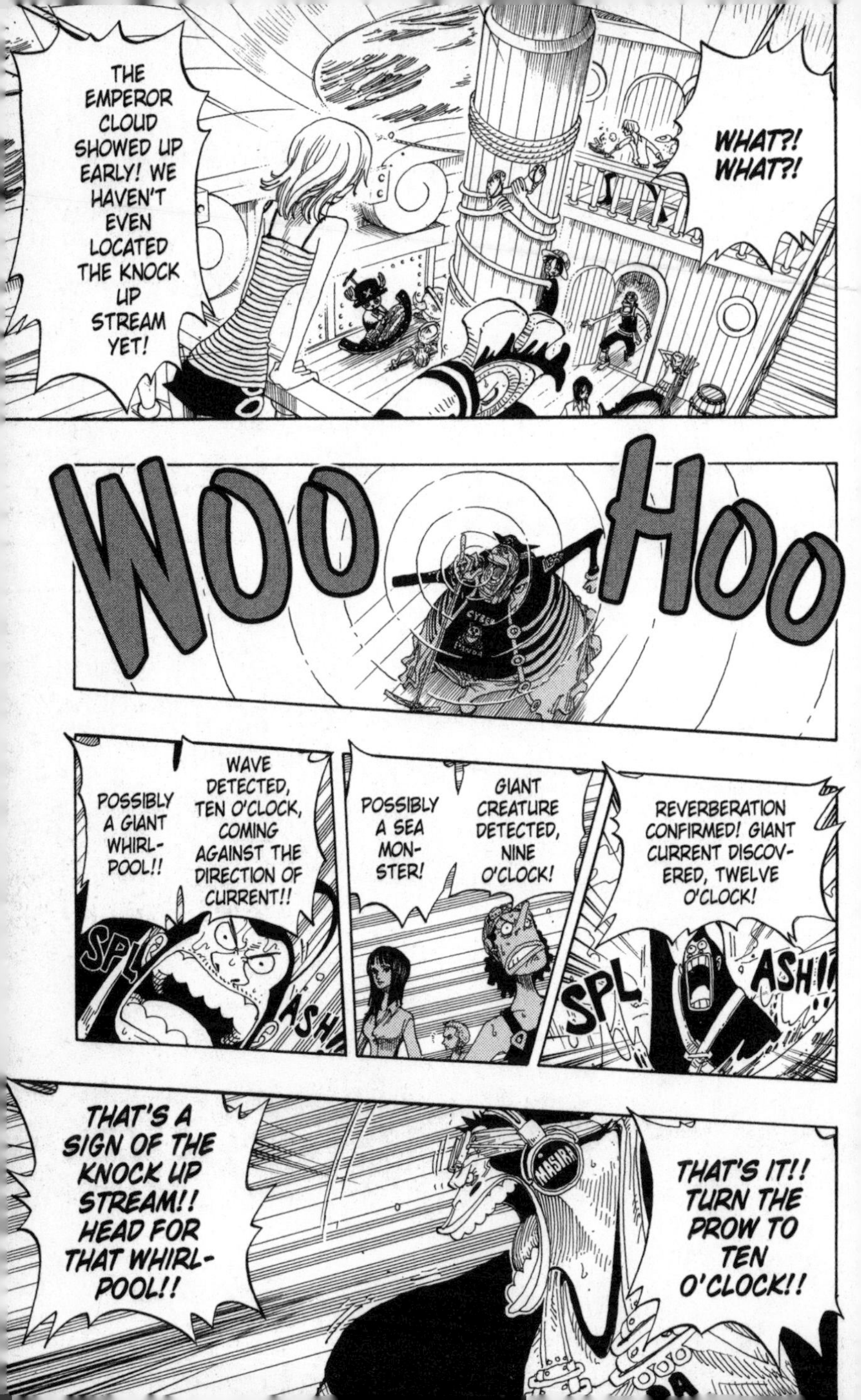
WHAT?! WHAT?!
THE EMPEROR CLOUD SHOWED UP EARLY! WE HAVEN'T EVEN LOCATED THE KNOCK UP STREAM YET!
WOO-HOO
REVERBERATION CONFIRMED! GIANT CURRENT DISCOV-ERED, TWELVE O'CLOCK!
SPLASH!!
GIANT CREATURE DETECTED, NINE O'CLOCK!
POSSIBLY A SEA MON-STER!
WAVE DETECTED, TEN O'CLOCK, COMING AGAINST THE DIRECTION OF CURRENT!!
POSSIBLY A GIANT WHIRL-POOL!!
SPLASH
THAT'S IT!! TURN THE PROW TO TEN O'CLOCK!!
THAT'S A SIGN OF THE KNOCK UP STREAM!! HEAD FOR THAT WHIRL-POOL!!

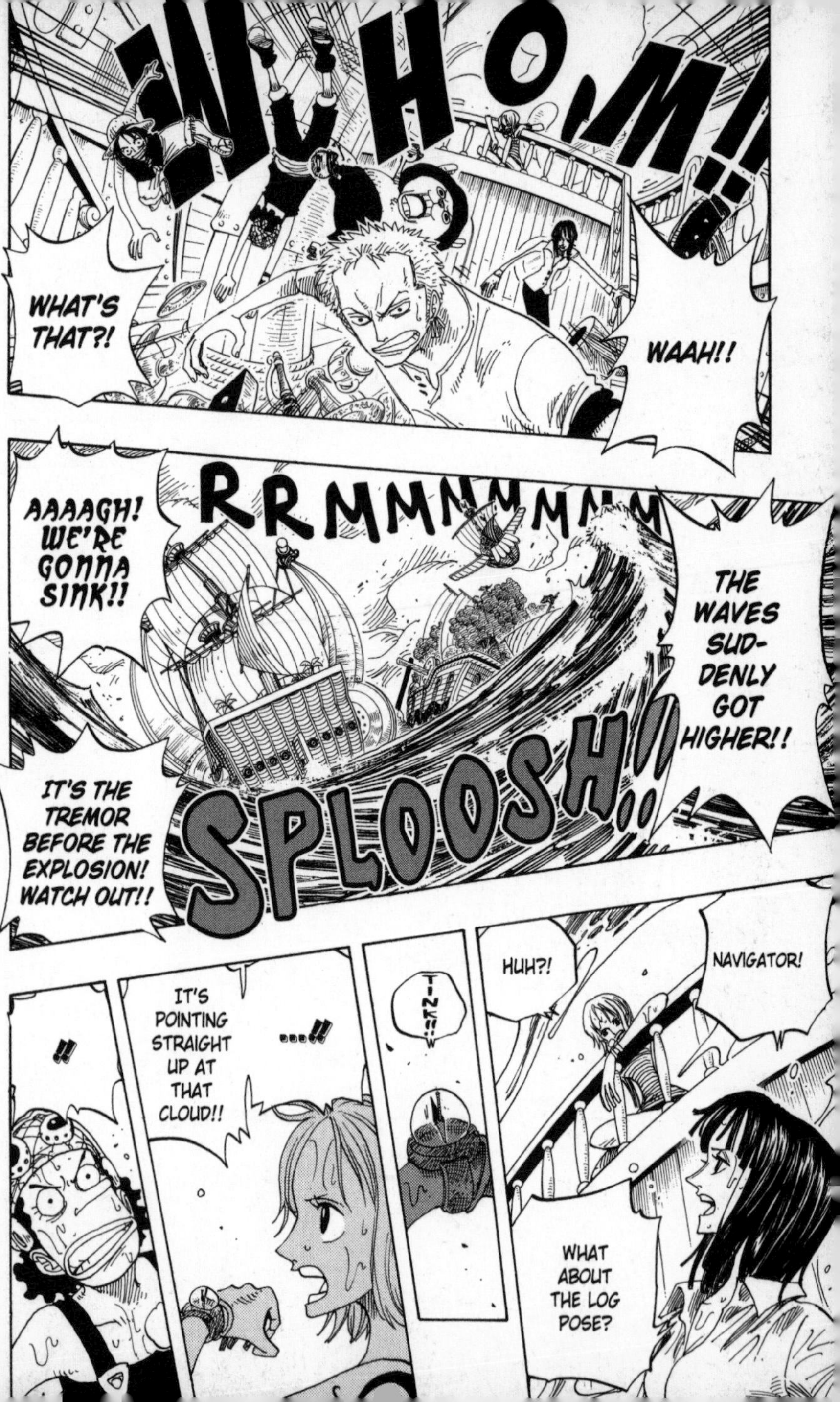
WHOM!!
WAAH!!
WHAT'S THAT?!
RRMMMMMMM
THE WAVES SUD- DENLY GOT HIGHER!!
AAAAGH! WE'RE GONNA SINK!!
SPLOOSH!!
IT'S THE TREMOR BEFORE THE EXPLOSION! WATCH OUT!!
NAVIGATOR!
HUH?!
WHAT ABOUT THE LOG POSE?
TINK!!
...!!
IT'S POINTING STRAIGHT UP AT THAT CLOUD!!
!!

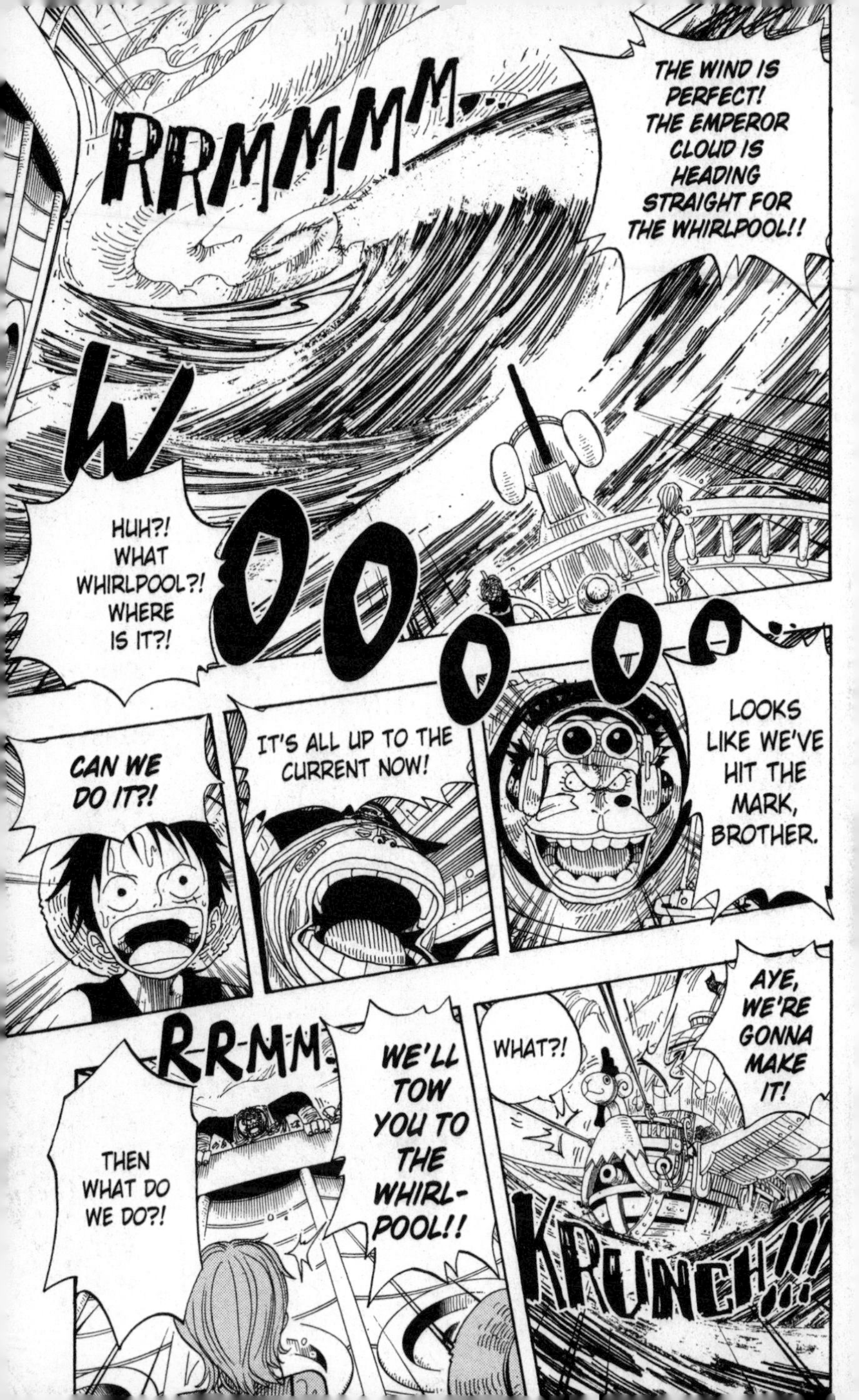
THE WIND IS PERFECT! THE EMPEROR CLOUD IS HEADING STRAIGHT FOR THE WHIRLPOOL!!
RRMMMMM...
WOOOOO...
HUH?! WHAT WHIRLPOOL?! WHERE IS IT?!
LOOKS LIKE WE'VE HIT THE MARK, BROTHER.
IT'S ALL UP TO THE CURRENT NOW!
CAN WE DO IT?!
AYE, WE'RE GONNA MAKE IT!
WHAT?!
KRUNCH!!!
WE'LL TOW YOU TO THE WHIRL-POOL!!
R-R-MM...
THEN WHAT DO WE DO?!

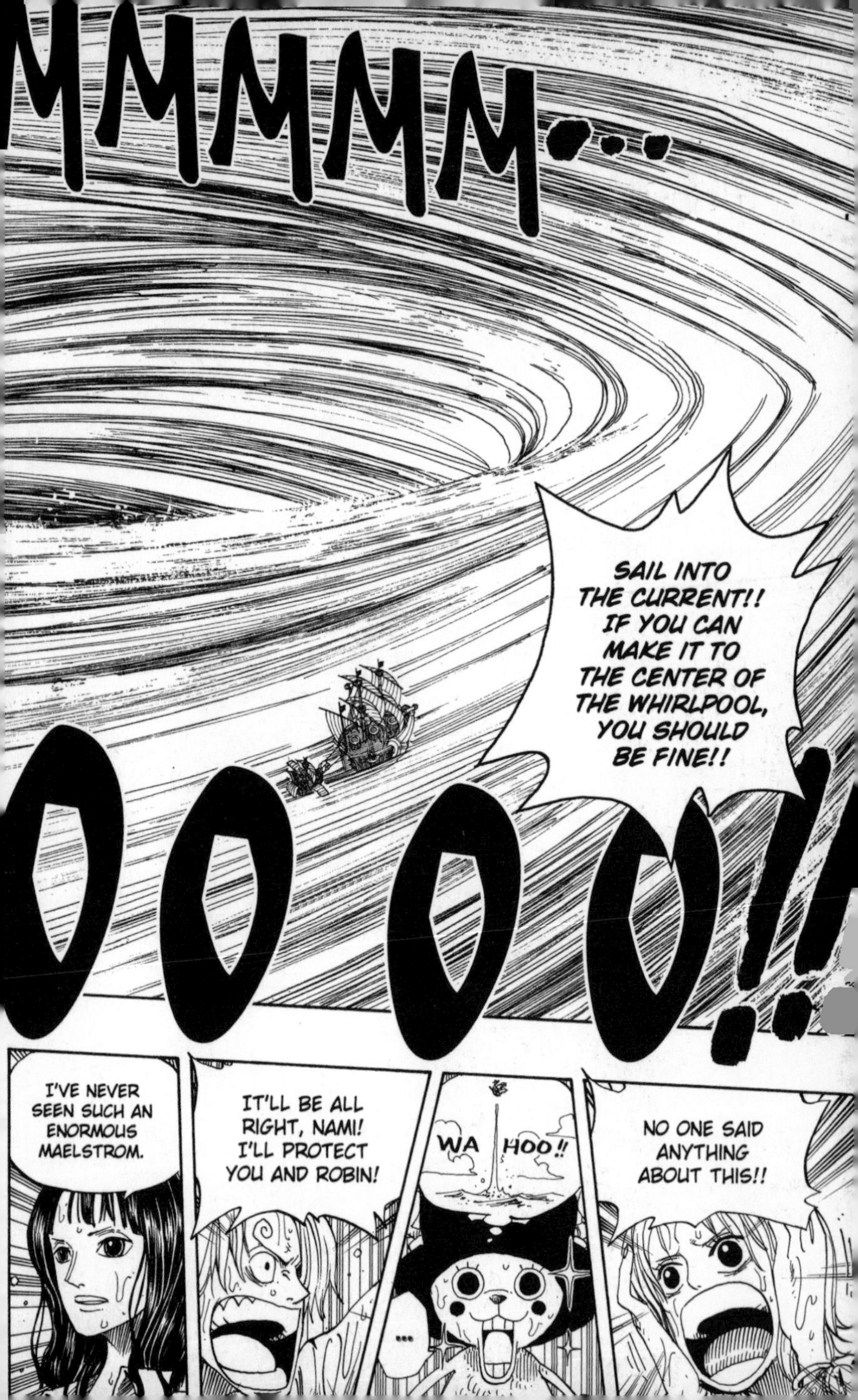
MMMMM...
SAIL INTO THE CURRENT!! IF YOU CAN MAKE IT TO THE CENTER OF THE WHIRLPOOL, YOU SHOULD BE FINE!!
OOOO!!
NO ONE SAID ANYTHING ABOUT THIS!!
WA HOO!!
IT'LL BE ALL RIGHT, NAMI! I'LL PROTECT YOU AND ROBIN!
I'VE NEVER SEEN SUCH AN ENORMOUS MAELSTROM.

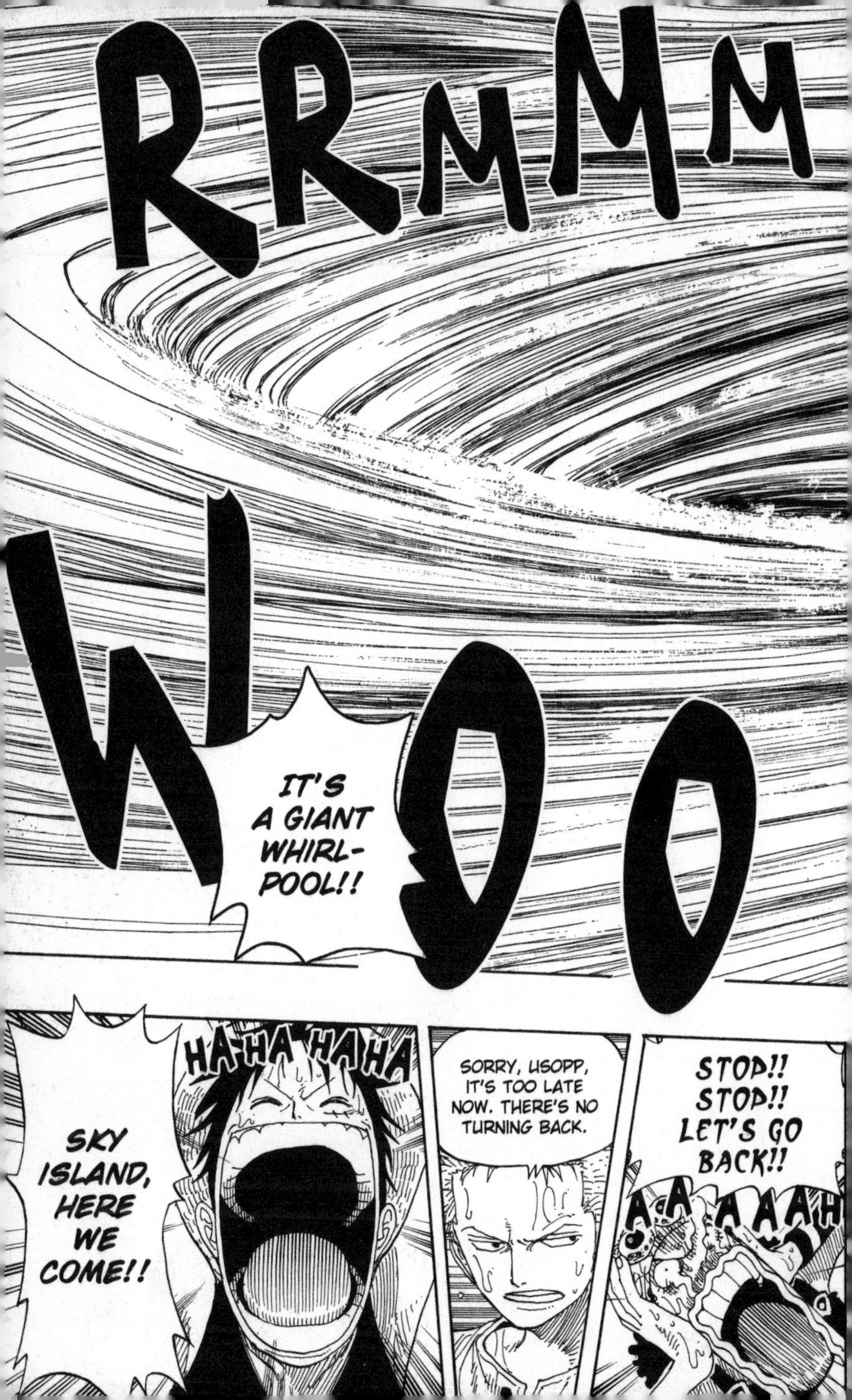
RRMMM
WOO
IT'S A GIANT WHIRL-POOL!!
STOP!! STOP!! LET'S GO BACK!!
AAAAAH
SORRY, USOPP, IT'S TOO LATE NOW. THERE'S NO TURNING BACK.
HAHA HAHA
SKY ISLAND, HERE WE COME!!

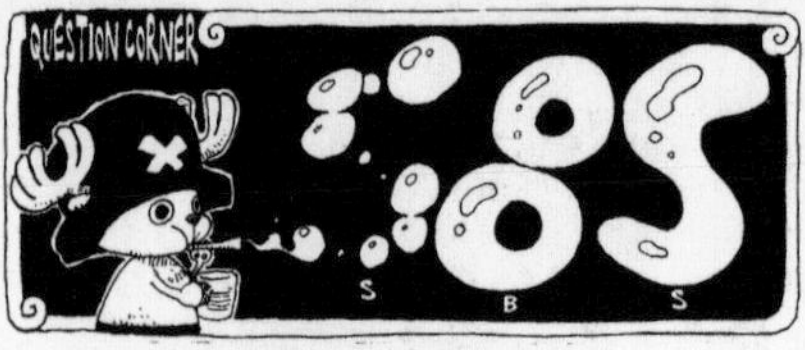
QUESTION CORNER
SBS

Oda: Don't peek!
Here are the answers!

For the compatibility
test from page 146

Here are the answers for the compatibility test!!
This test will tell you how you feel about your friends who are like Luffy and his crew.

1 → Although you think this person is a bit silly, you love him or her anyway. ♡♡

2 → You are very compatible with this type of person. You should try talking to this person. ♡

3 → You don't get along with this type at all. Best to avoid them.

4 → This person is bound to become a dear friend. Do you rely on this type of person the most?

5 → You always look down on this person, but when the two of you are alone, your attitude changes. Open your eyes!!

6 → When your good friends aren't around, you find yourself killing time with this person. That's not good.

7 → It may not be obvious, but this person and you are almost perfect for each other. Going out with this person on days that contain the number three will certainly increase your chances for love!!

# Chapter 236:
# THE SHIP SAILS TO THE SKY

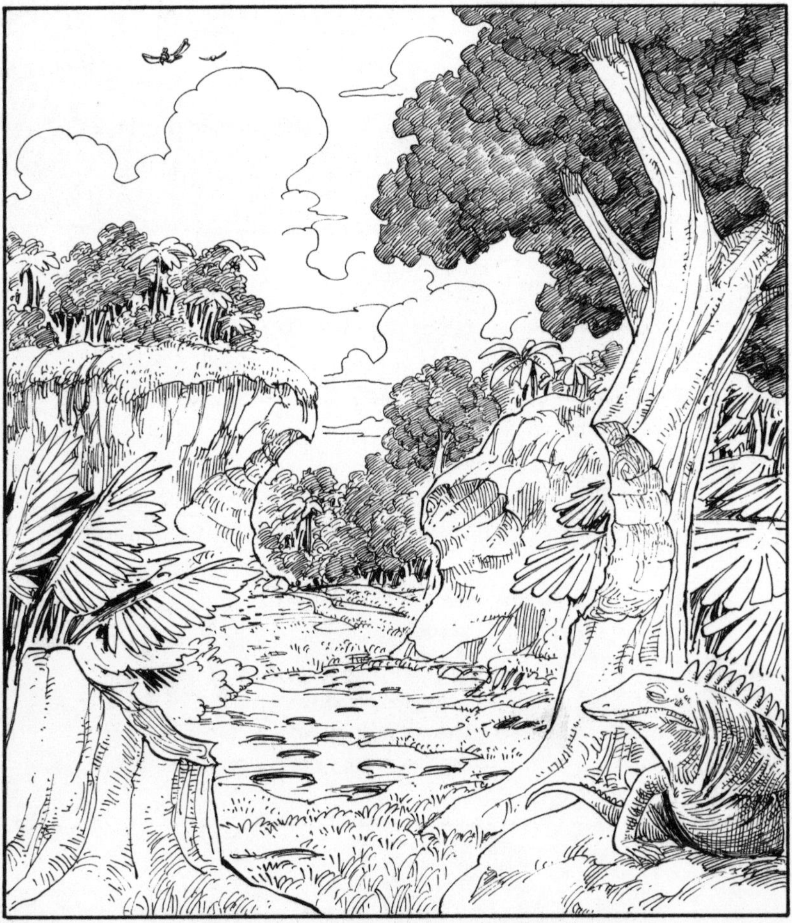

CHAPTER TITLE PAGE SERIES #5:
"I WOULDN'T DIE EVEN IF YOU KILLED ME"

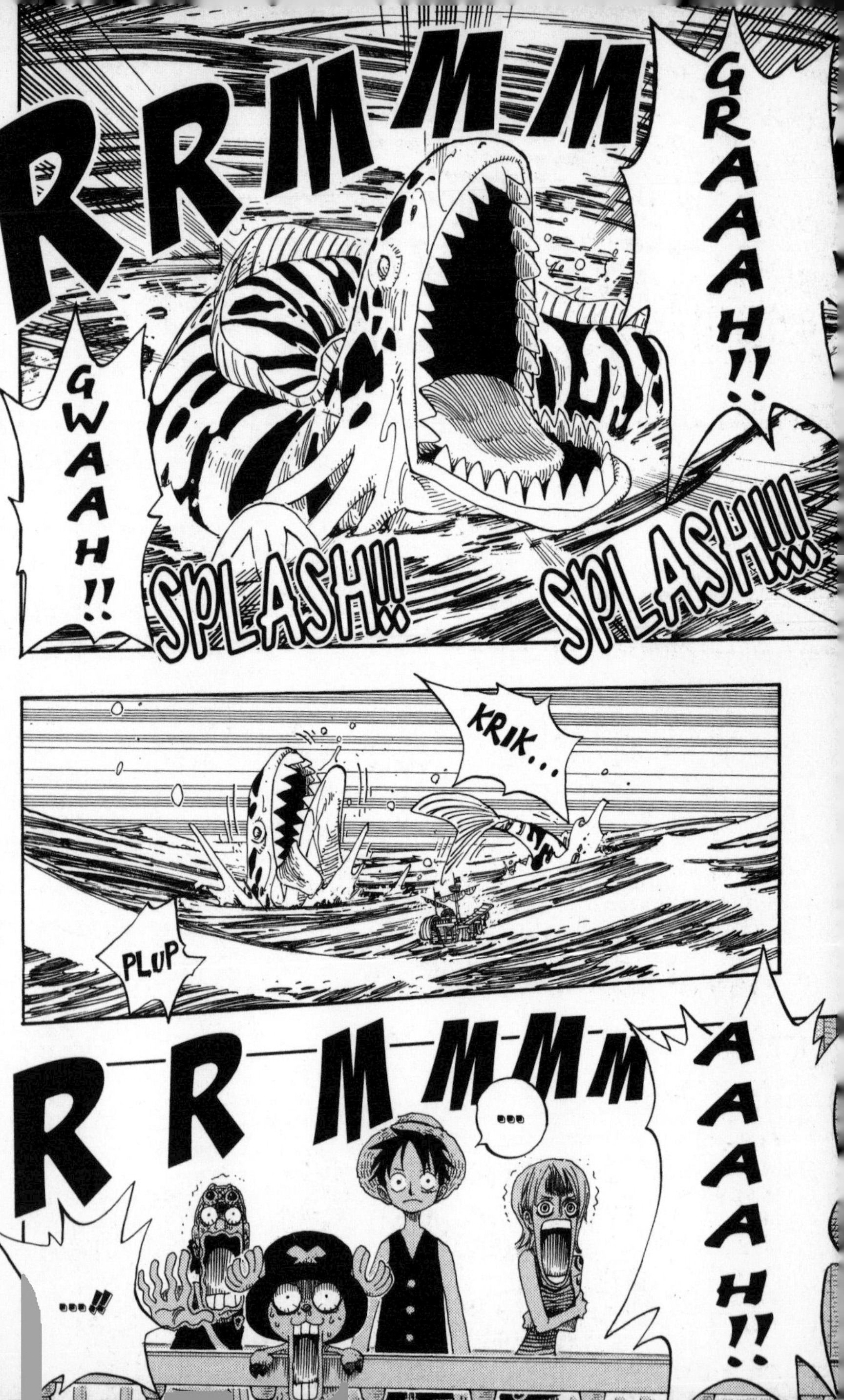
GRAAAH!!
RRMMMM
SPLASH!!!
GWAAAH!!
SPLASH!!
KRIK...
PLUP
AAAAAH!!
RRMMMMM
...
...!!

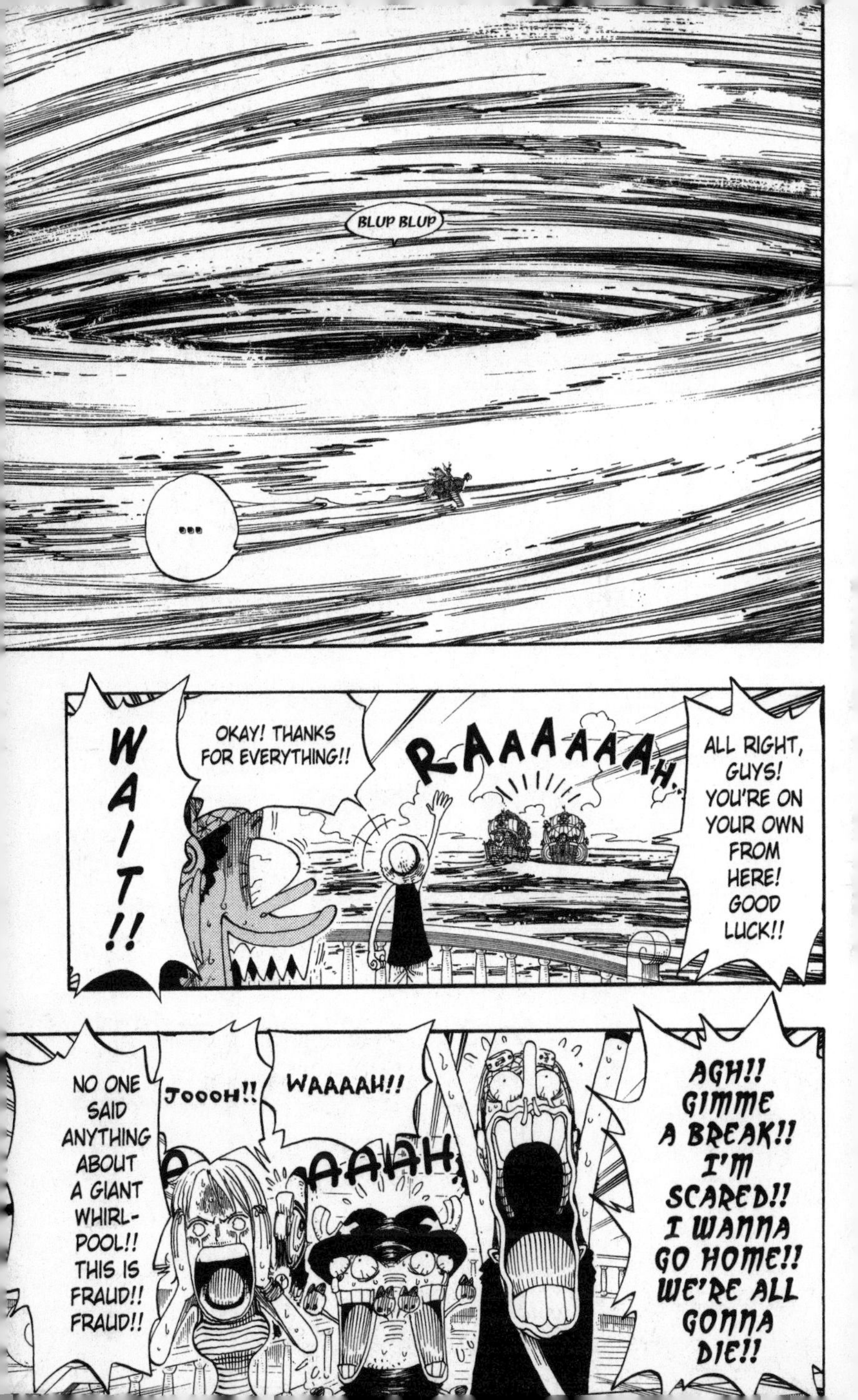
BLUP BLUP
...
ALL RIGHT, GUYS! YOU'RE ON YOUR OWN FROM HERE! GOOD LUCK!!
RAAAAAAH
OKAY! THANKS FOR EVERYTHING!!
WAIT!!
AGH!! GIMME A BREAK!! I'M SCARED!! I WANNA GO HOME!! WE'RE ALL GONNA DIE!!
WAAAAH!!
AAAH
JOOOH!!
NO ONE SAID ANYTHING ABOUT A GIANT WHIRLPOOL!! THIS IS FRAUD!! FRAUD!!

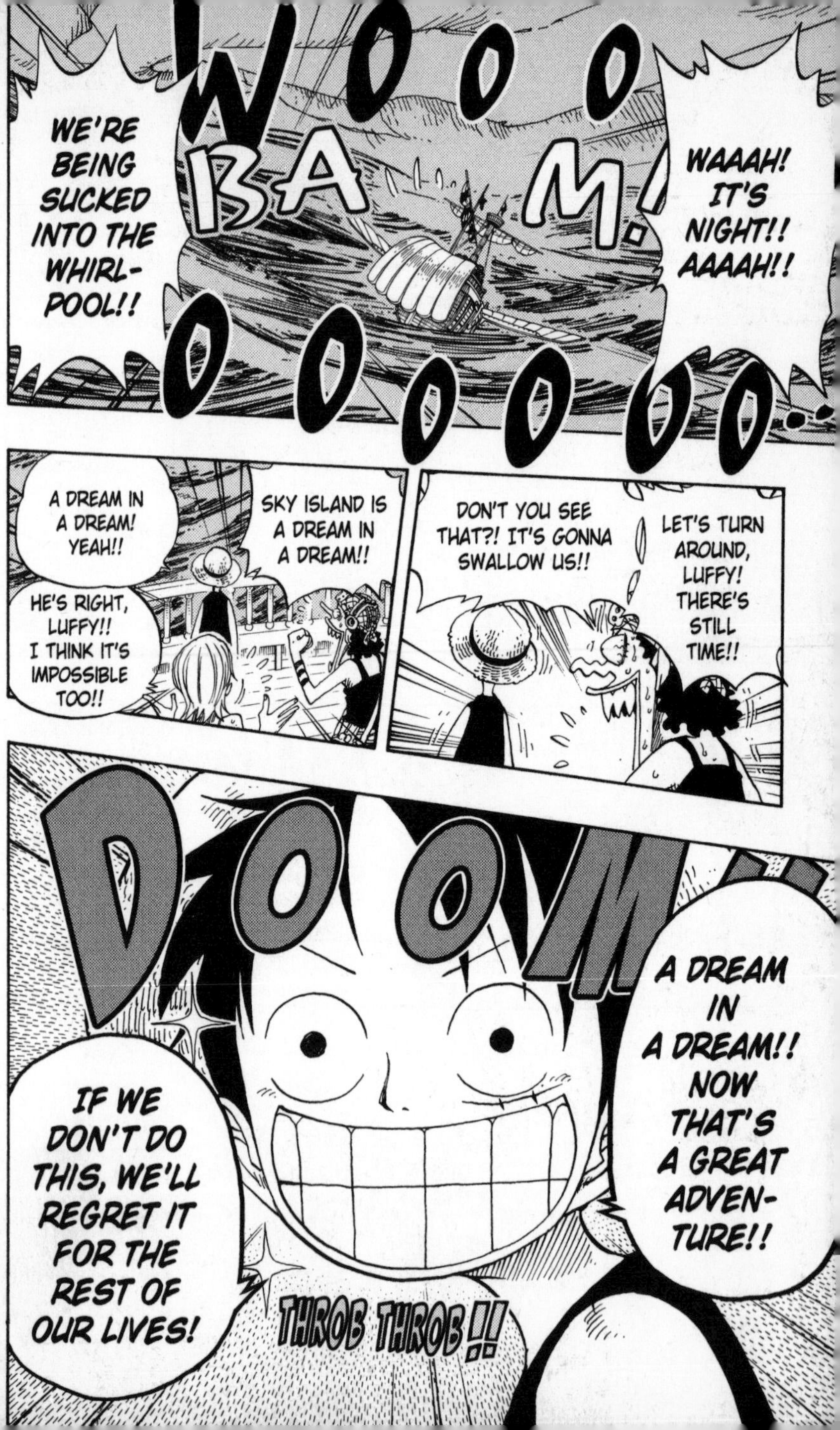
WOOO BAM! OOOOOOO..
WAAAH! IT'S NIGHT!! AAAAH!!
WE'RE BEING SUCKED INTO THE WHIRL-POOL!!
LET'S TURN AROUND, LUFFY! THERE'S STILL TIME!!
DON'T YOU SEE THAT?! IT'S GONNA SWALLOW US!!
SKY ISLAND IS A DREAM IN A DREAM!!
A DREAM IN A DREAM! YEAH!!
HE'S RIGHT, LUFFY!! I THINK IT'S IMPOSSIBLE TOO!!
DOOM!!
A DREAM IN A DREAM!! NOW THAT'S A GREAT ADVEN-TURE!!
IF WE DON'T DO THIS, WE'LL REGRET IT FOR THE REST OF OUR LIVES!
THROB THROB!!

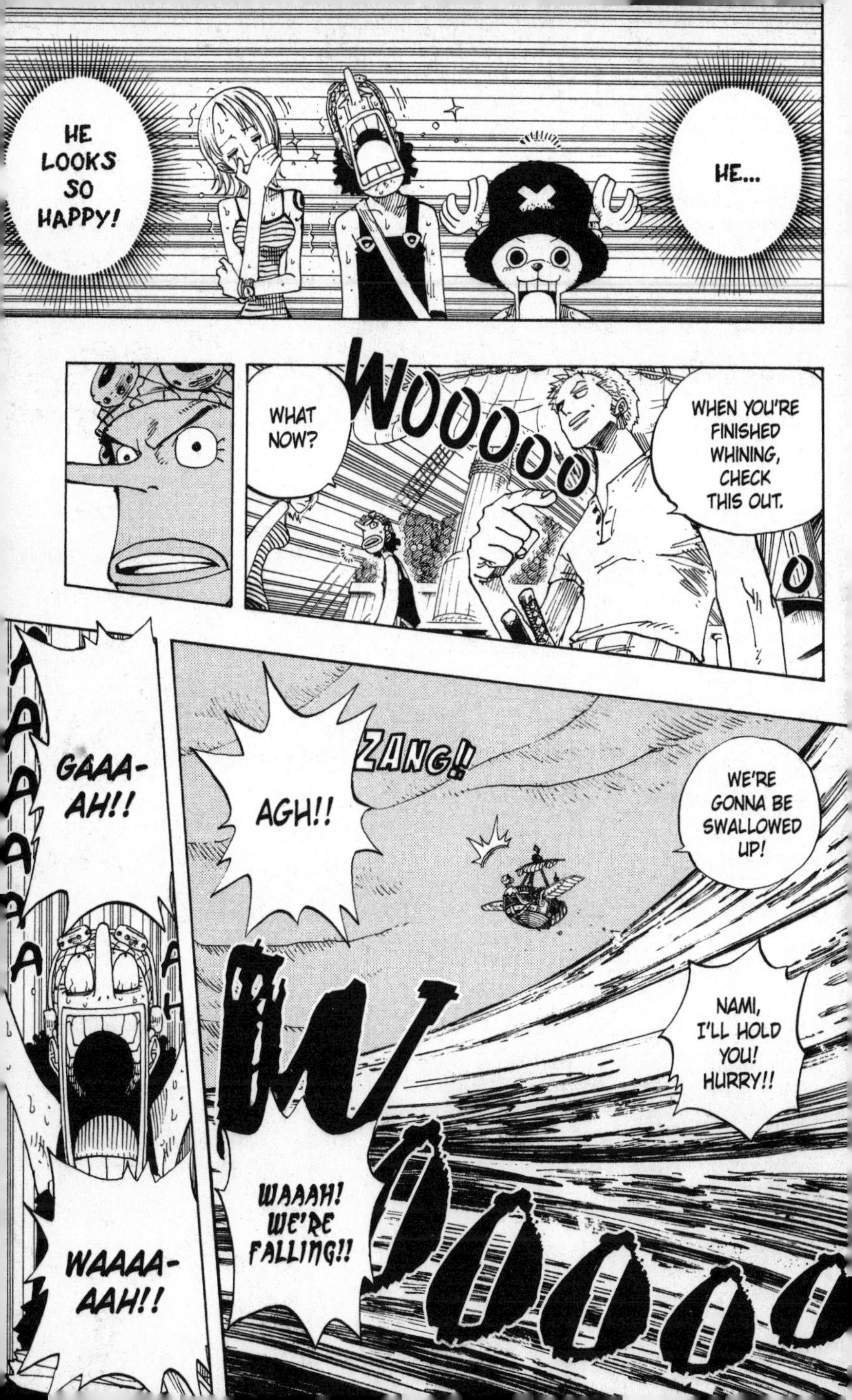
HE...
HE LOOKS SO HAPPY!
WHEN YOU'RE FINISHED WHINING, CHECK THIS OUT.
WOOOOOO
WHAT NOW?
WE'RE GONNA BE SWALLOWED UP!
ZANG!!
AGH!!
NAMI, I'LL HOLD YOU! HURRY!!
WAAAH! WE'RE FALLING!!
GAAAA-AH!!
WAAAA-AAH!!

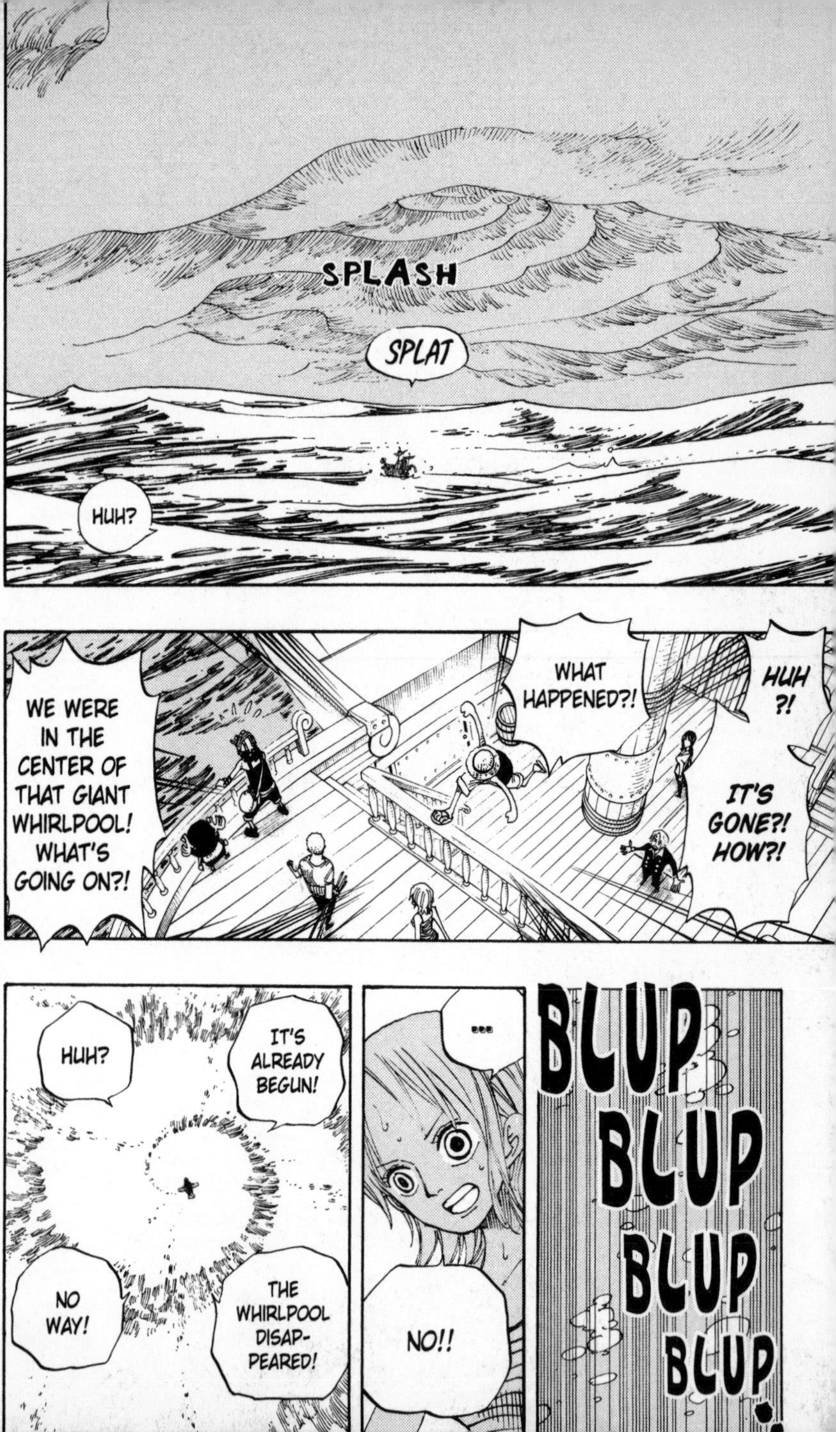
SPLASH
SPLAT
HUH?
HUH ?!
IT'S GONE?! HOW?!
WHAT HAPPENED?!
WE WERE IN THE CENTER OF THAT GIANT WHIRLPOOL! WHAT'S GOING ON?!
BLUP
BLUP
BLUP
BLUP
...
NO!!
IT'S ALREADY BEGUN!
HUH?
THE WHIRLPOOL DISAP-PEARED!
NO WAY!

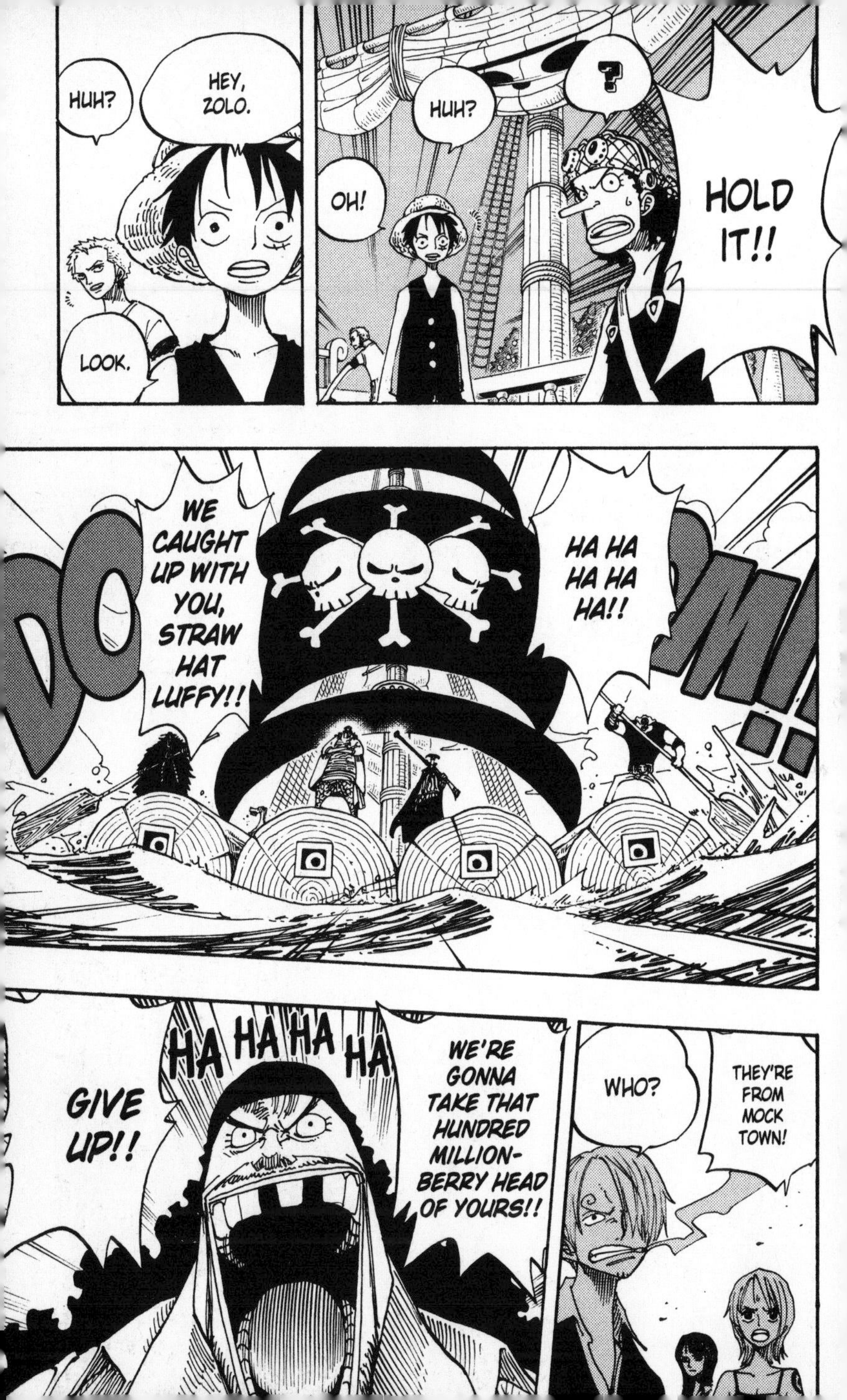
HOLD IT!!
?
HUH?
OH!
HEY, ZOLO.
HUH?
LOOK.
HA HA HA HA HA!!
WE CAUGHT UP WITH YOU, STRAW HAT LUFFY!!
DO
M!!
THEY'RE FROM MOCK TOWN!
WHO?
WE'RE GONNA TAKE THAT HUNDRED MILLION-BERRY HEAD OF YOURS!!
HA HA HA HA HA
GIVE UP!!

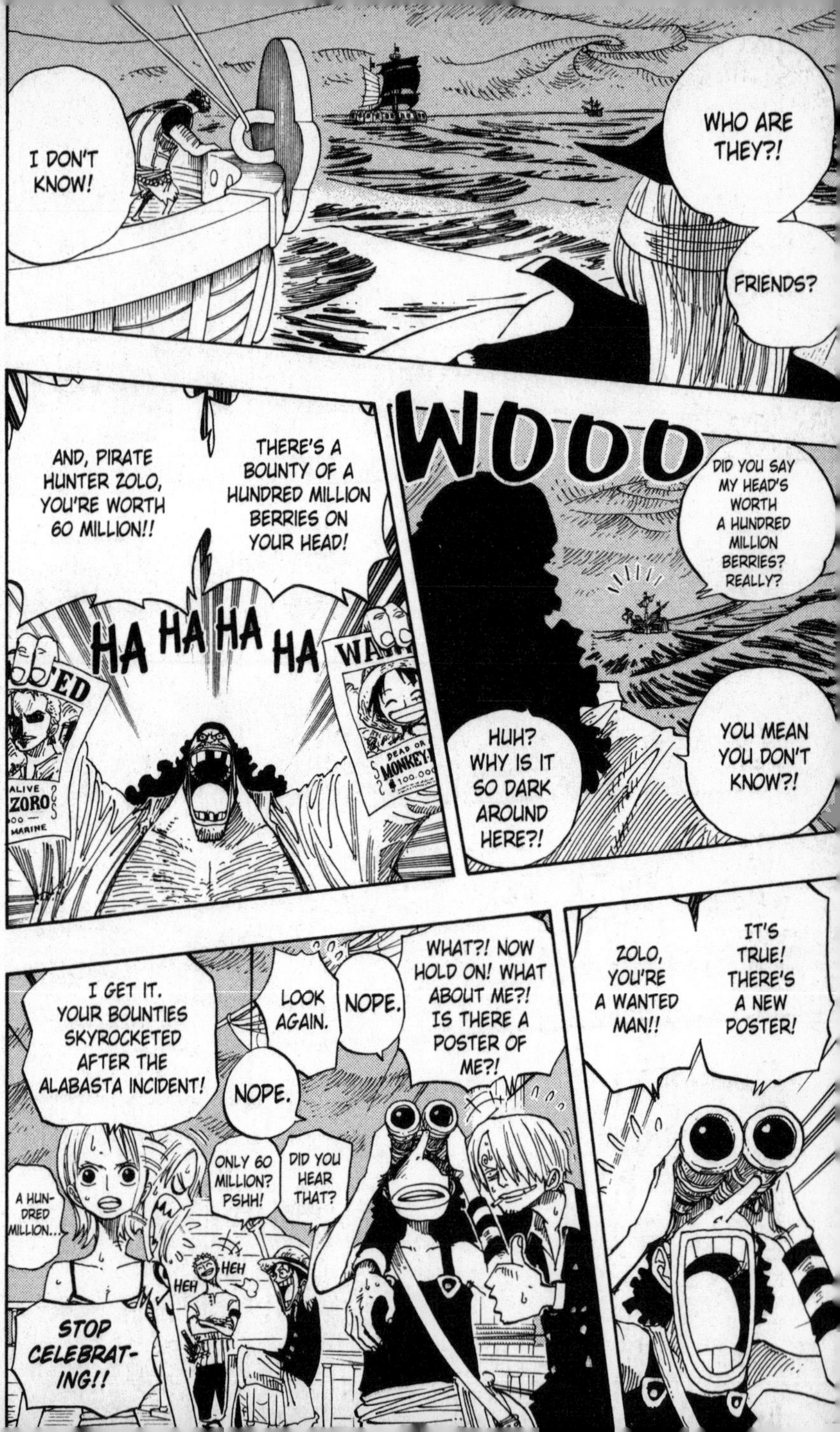
WHO ARE THEY?!
FRIENDS?
I DON'T KNOW!
WOOO
DID YOU SAY MY HEAD'S WORTH A HUNDRED MILLION BERRIES? REALLY?
YOU MEAN YOU DON'T KNOW?!
HUH? WHY IS IT SO DARK AROUND HERE?!
THERE'S A BOUNTY OF A HUNDRED MILLION BERRIES ON YOUR HEAD!
AND, PIRATE HUNTER ZOLO, YOU'RE WORTH 60 MILLION!!
HA HA HA HA
IT'S TRUE! THERE'S A NEW POSTER!
ZOLO, YOU'RE A WANTED MAN!!
WHAT?! NOW HOLD ON! WHAT ABOUT ME?! IS THERE A POSTER OF ME?!
NOPE.
LOOK AGAIN.
NOPE.
I GET IT. YOUR BOUNTIES SKYROCKETED AFTER THE ALABASTA INCIDENT!
DID YOU HEAR THAT?
ONLY 60 MILLION? PSHH!
HEH
HEH
A HUNDRED MILLION...
STOP CELEBRATING!!

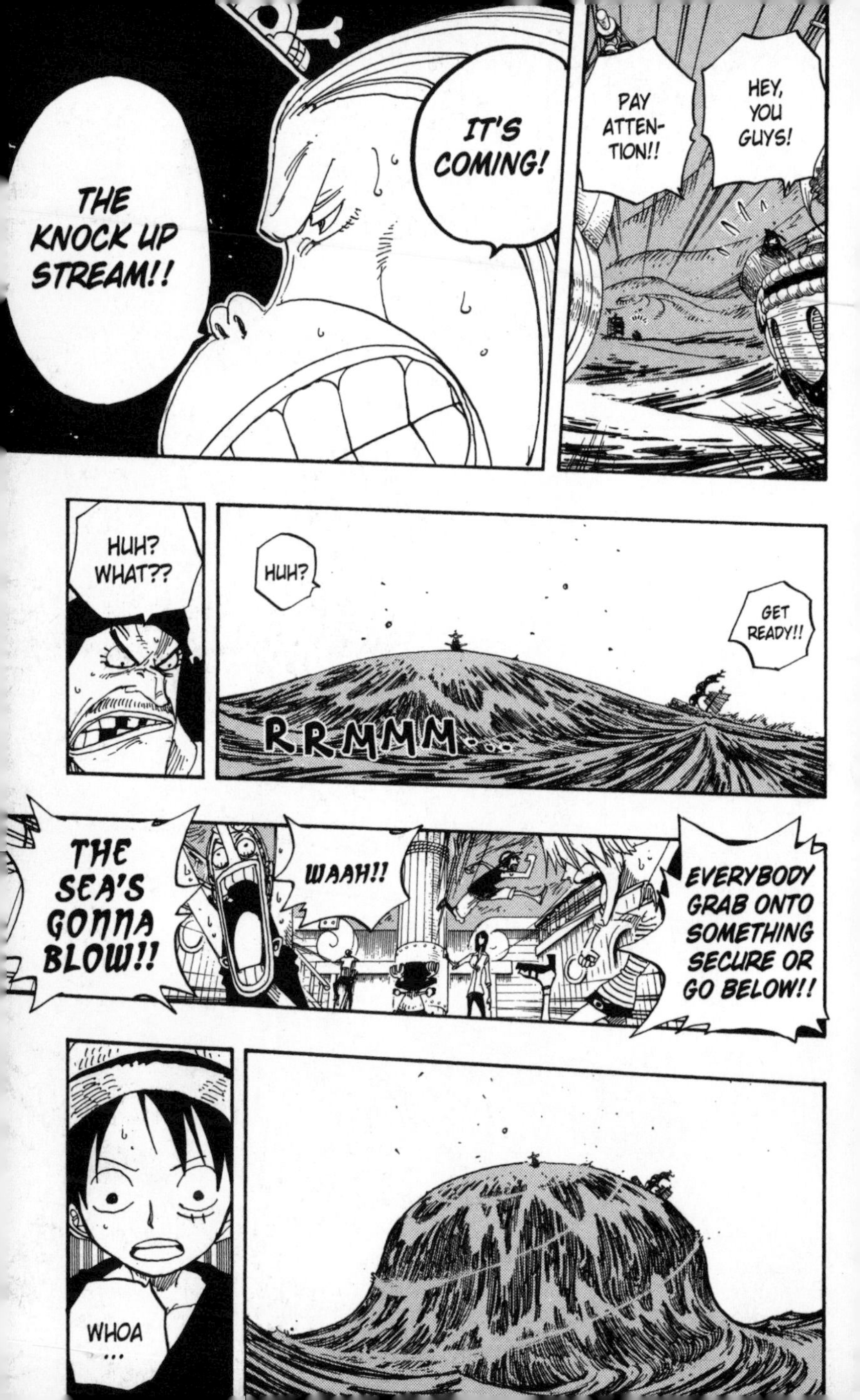
HEY, YOU GUYS!
PAY ATTEN-TION!!
IT'S COMING!
THE KNOCK UP STREAM!!
GET READY!!
HUH?
RRMMM...
HUH? WHAT??
EVERYBODY GRAB ONTO SOMETHING SECURE OR GO BELOW!!
WAAH!!
THE SEA'S GONNA BLOW!!
WHOA...

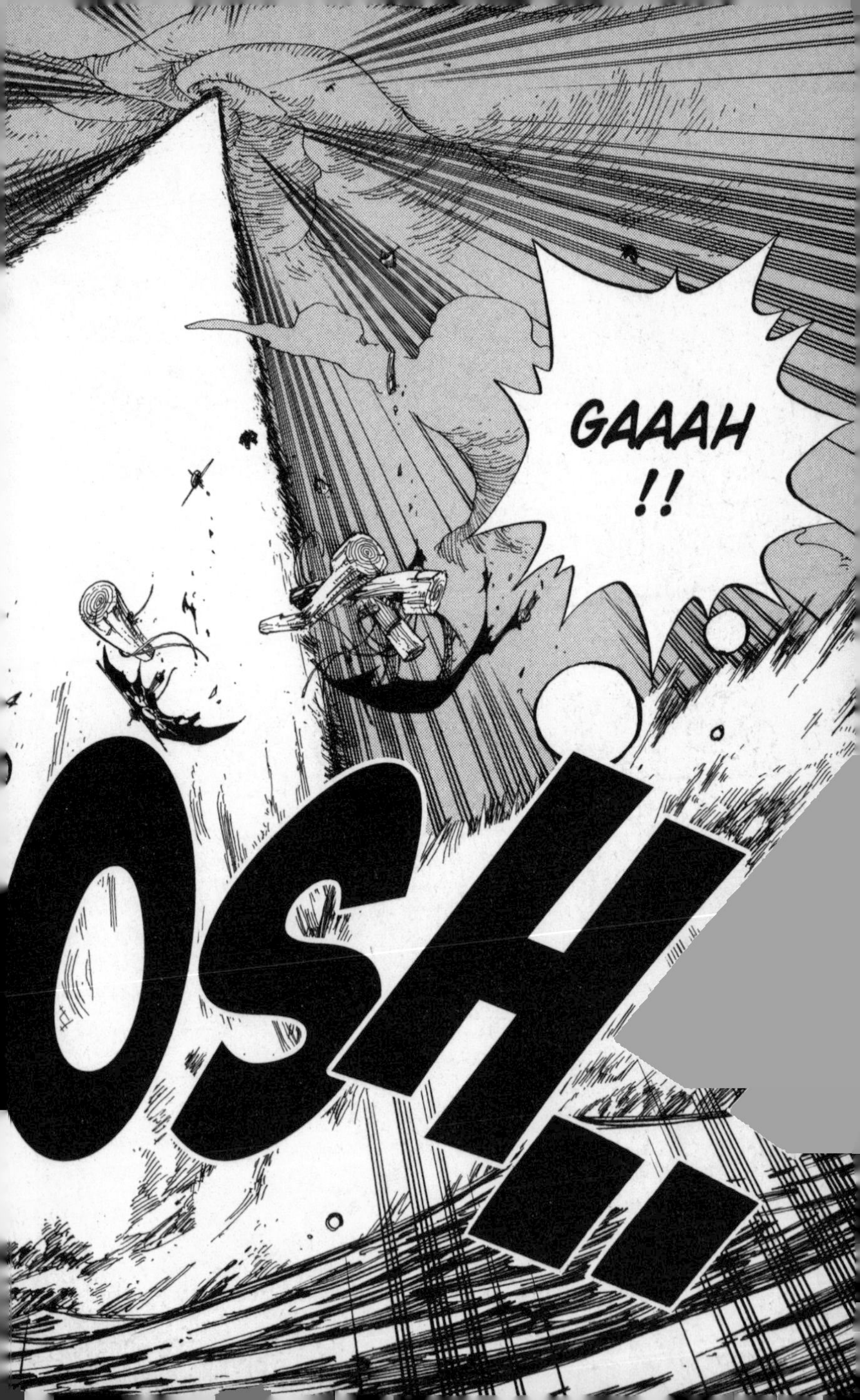
GAAAH !!
OSH!!

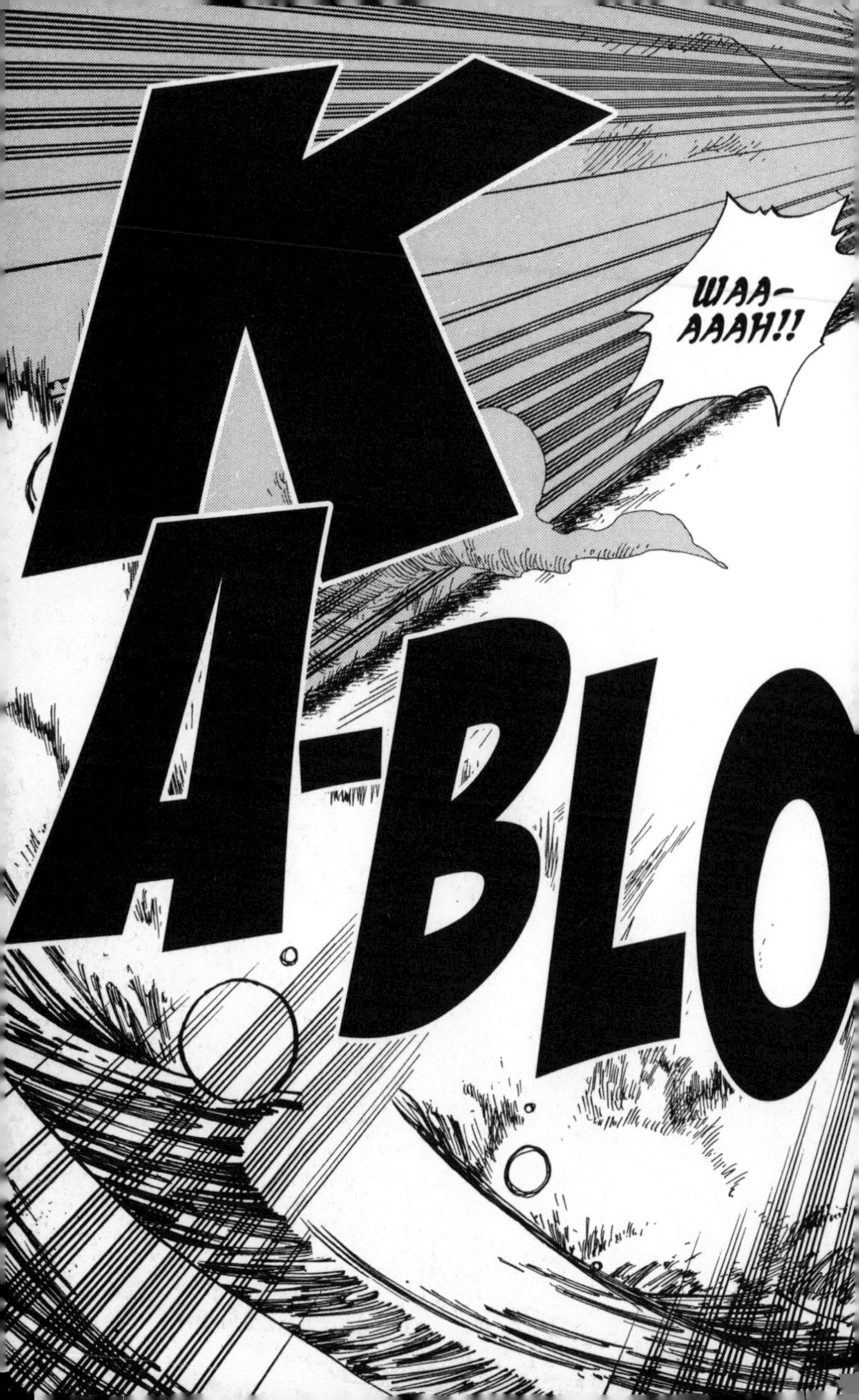
WAA-AAAH!!
KA-BLO

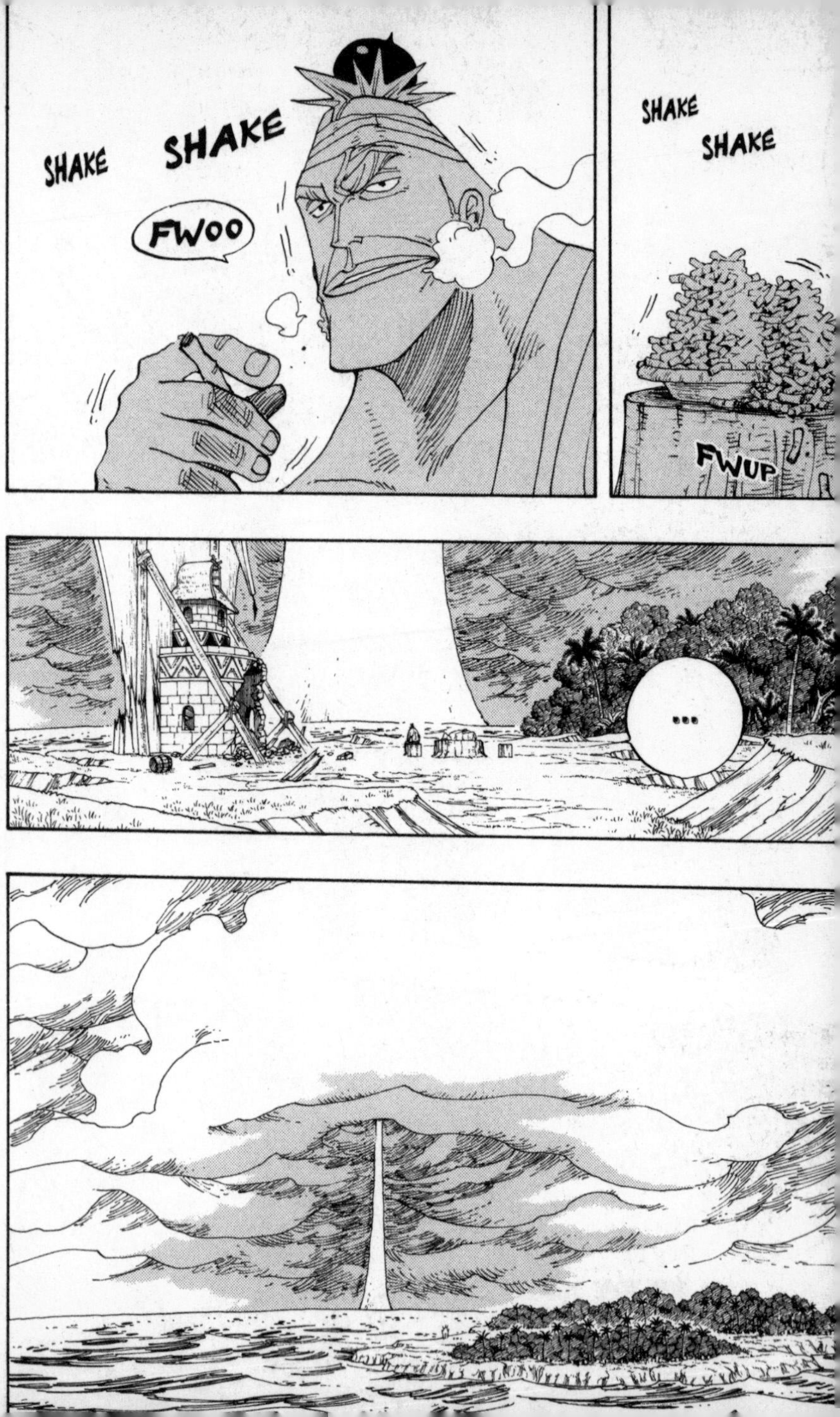
SHAKE
SHAKE
FWUP
SHAKE
SHAKE
FWOO
...

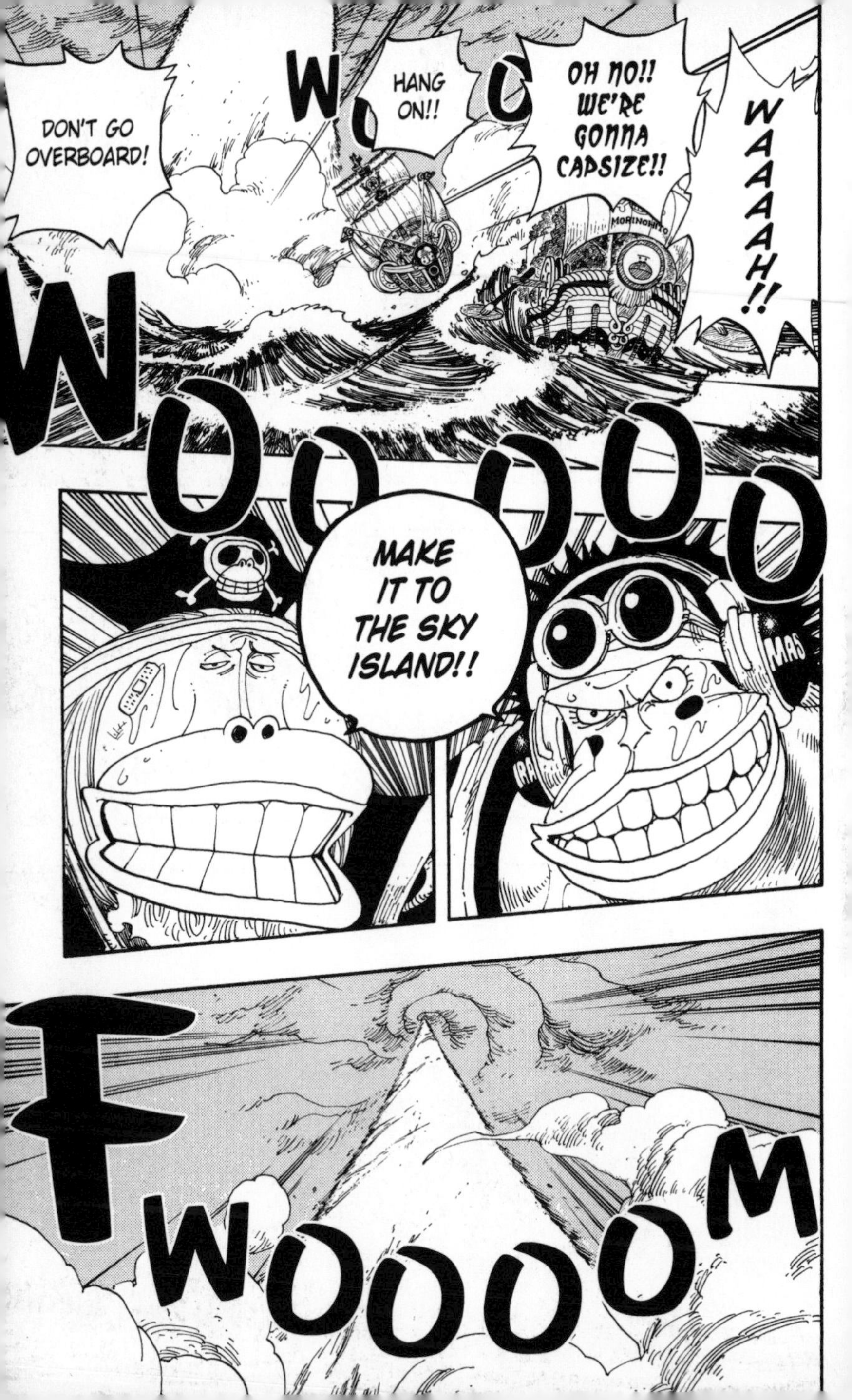
WAAAAAH!!
OH NO!! WE'RE GONNA CAPSIZE!!
HANG ON!!
DON'T GO OVERBOARD!
WOOOOOO
MAKE IT TO THE SKY ISLAND!!
FWOOOOOM

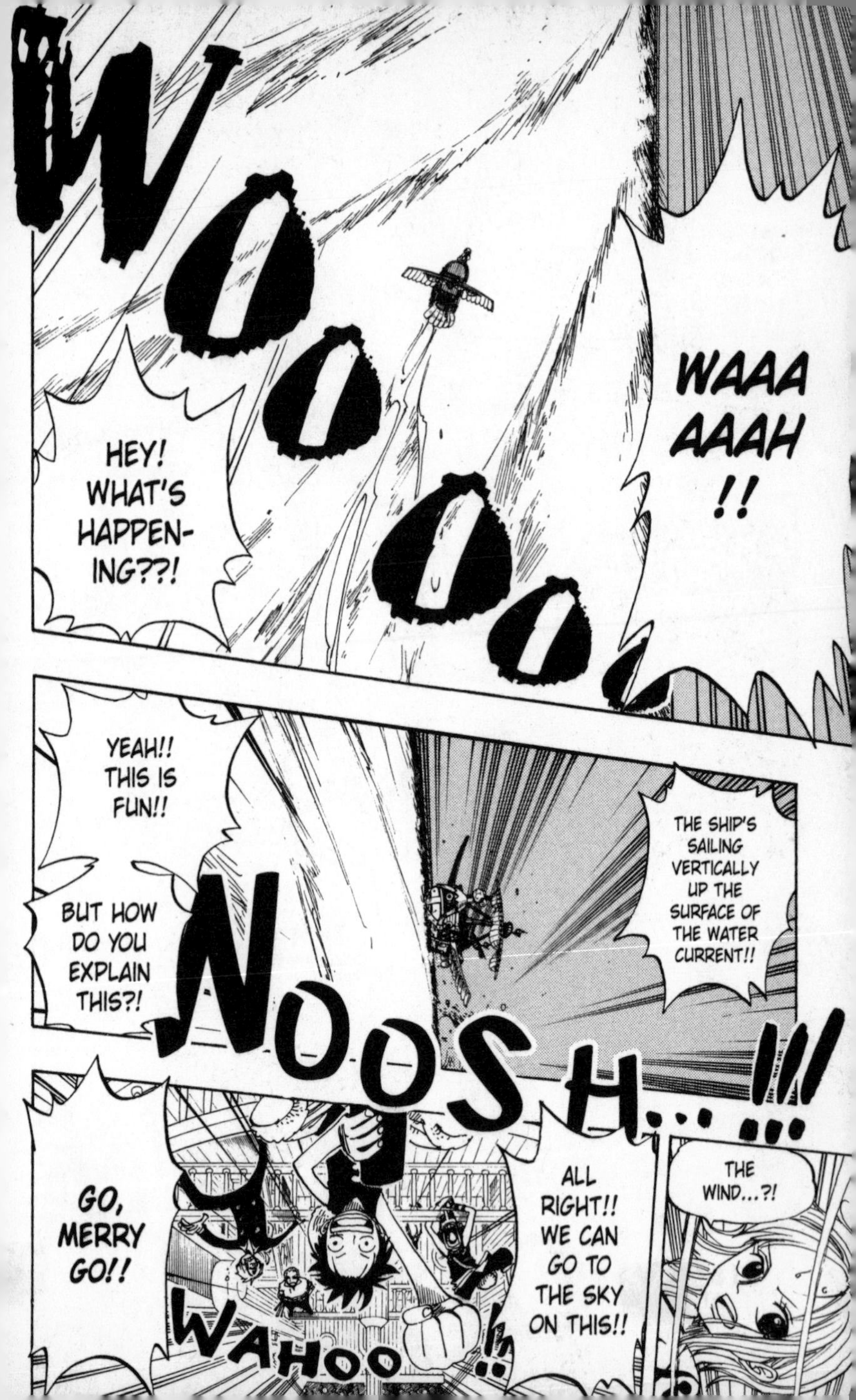
WAAA AAAH!!
WOOOO...
HEY! WHAT'S HAPPENING??!
THE SHIP'S SAILING VERTICALLY UP THE SURFACE OF THE WATER CURRENT!!
YEAH!! THIS IS FUN!!
BUT HOW DO YOU EXPLAIN THIS?!
WOOSH...!!!
THE WIND...?!
ALL RIGHT!! WE CAN GO TO THE SKY ON THIS!!
GO, MERRY GO!!
WAHOO!!

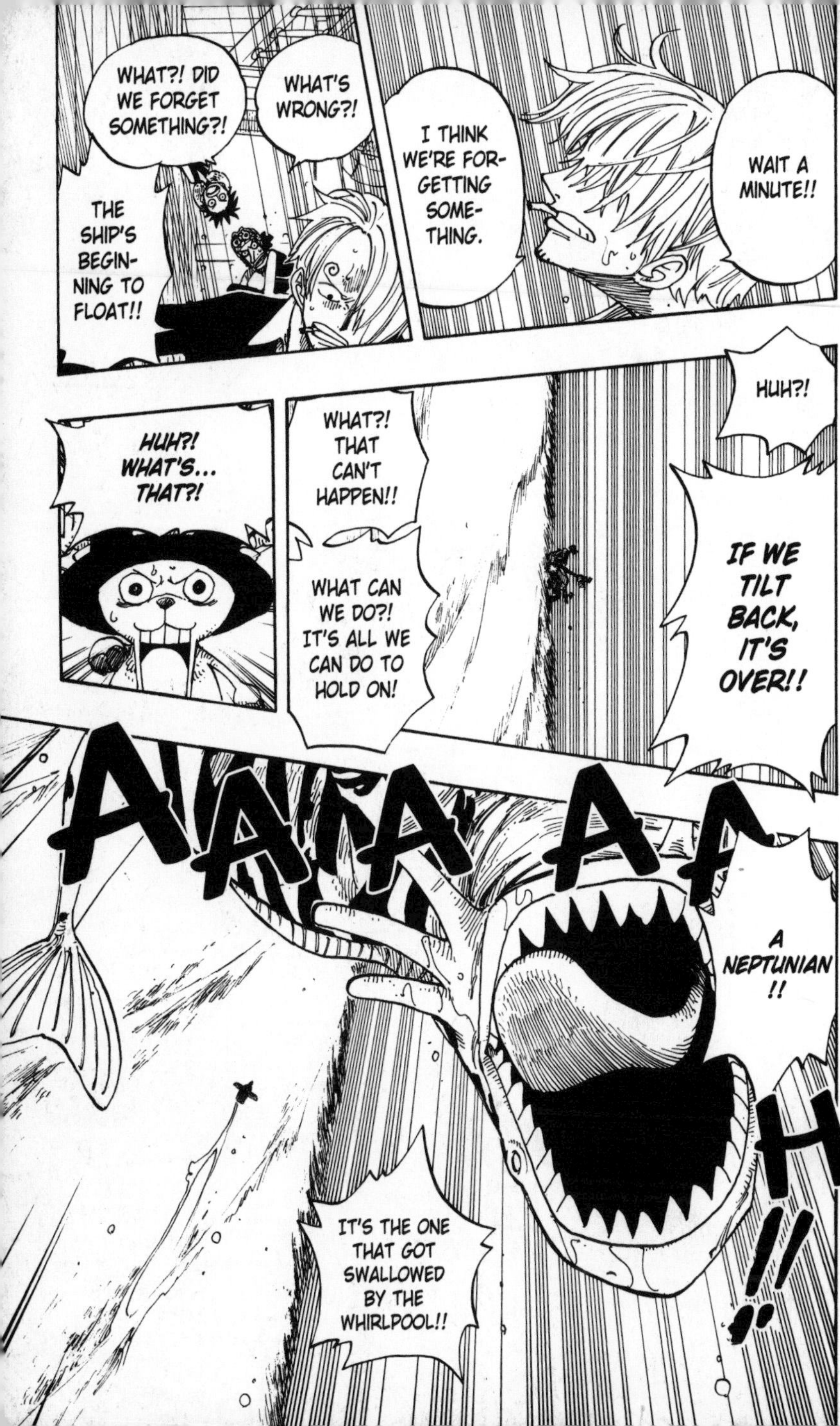
WAIT A MINUTE!!
I THINK WE'RE FOR-GETTING SOME-THING.
WHAT'S WRONG?!
WHAT?! DID WE FORGET SOMETHING?!
THE SHIP'S BEGIN-NING TO FLOAT!!
HUH?!
IF WE TILT BACK, IT'S OVER!!
WHAT?! THAT CAN'T HAPPEN!!
WHAT CAN WE DO?! IT'S ALL WE CAN DO TO HOLD ON!
HUH?! WHAT'S... THAT?!
AAAAAAH!!
A NEPTUNIAN!!
IT'S THE ONE THAT GOT SWALLOWED BY THE WHIRLPOOL!!

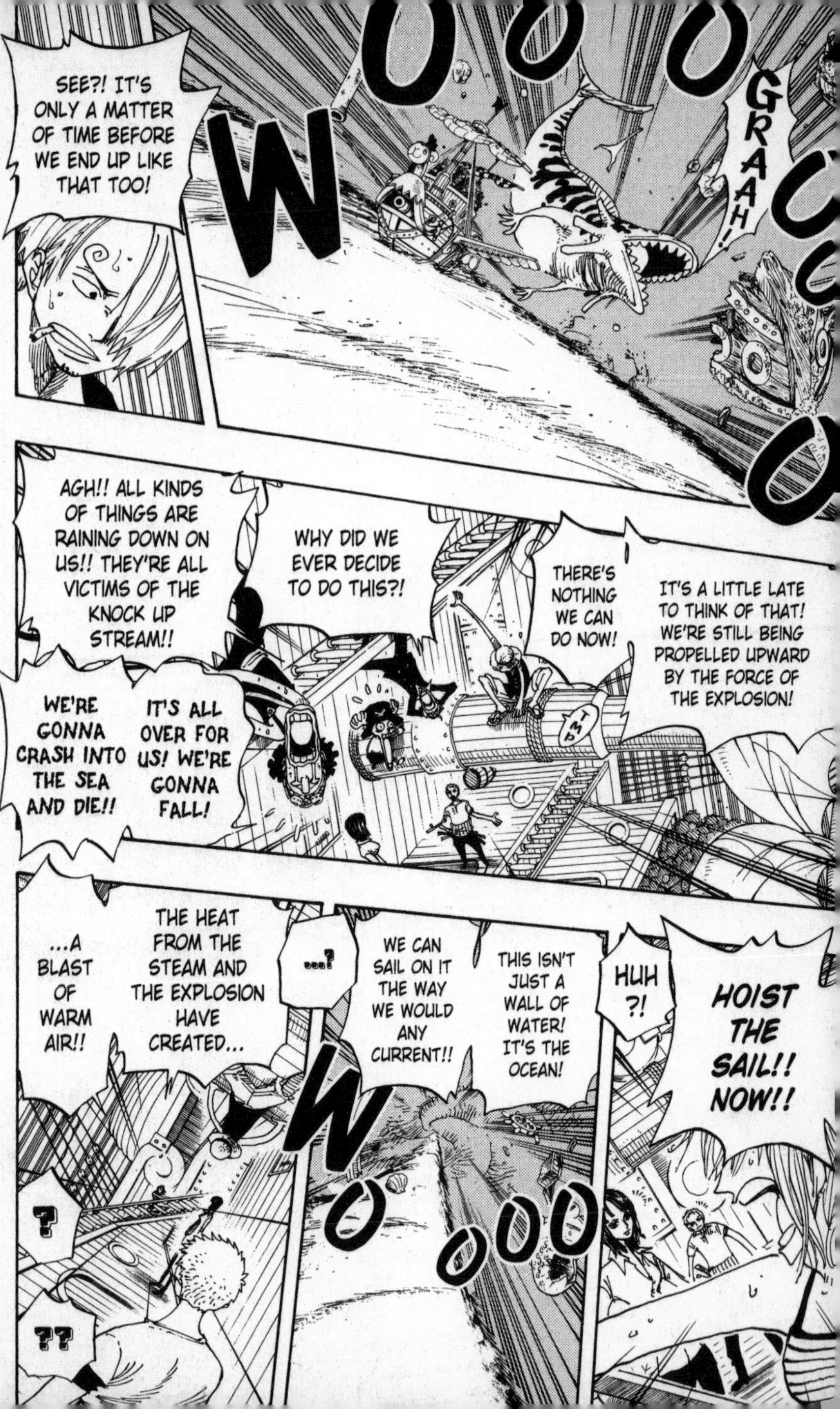
WOOOOO
GRAAH!
SEE?! IT'S ONLY A MATTER OF TIME BEFORE WE END UP LIKE THAT TOO!
IT'S A LITTLE LATE TO THINK OF THAT! WE'RE STILL BEING PROPELLED UPWARD BY THE FORCE OF THE EXPLOSION!
THERE'S NOTHING WE CAN DO NOW!
TMP
WHY DID WE EVER DECIDE TO DO THIS?!
AGH!! ALL KINDS OF THINGS ARE RAINING DOWN ON US!! THEY'RE ALL VICTIMS OF THE KNOCK UP STREAM!!
IT'S ALL OVER FOR US! WE'RE GONNA FALL!
WE'RE GONNA CRASH INTO THE SEA AND DIE!!
HOIST THE SAIL!! NOW!!
HUH?!
THIS ISN'T JUST A WALL OF WATER! IT'S THE OCEAN!
WE CAN SAIL ON IT THE WAY WE WOULD ANY CURRENT!!
...?
WOOOOO
THE HEAT FROM THE STEAM AND THE EXPLOSION HAVE CREATED...
...A BLAST OF WARM AIR!!
?
??

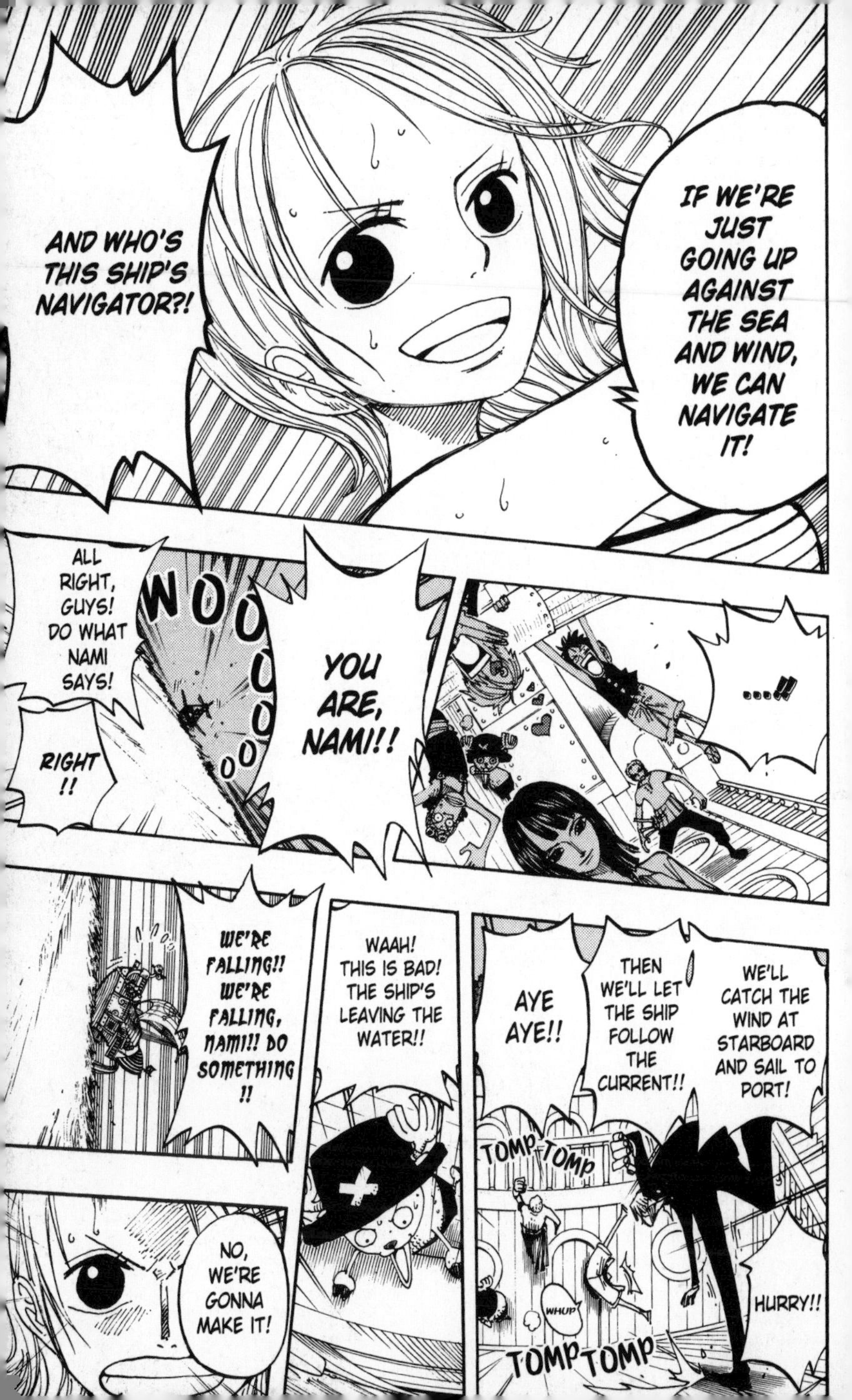
IF WE'RE JUST GOING UP AGAINST THE SEA AND WIND, WE CAN NAVIGATE IT!
AND WHO'S THIS SHIP'S NAVIGATOR?!
...!!
YOU ARE, NAMI!!
WOOOOOOO
ALL RIGHT, GUYS! DO WHAT NAMI SAYS!
RIGHT!!
WE'LL CATCH THE WIND AT STARBOARD AND SAIL TO PORT!
THEN WE'LL LET THE SHIP FOLLOW THE CURRENT!!
AYE AYE!!
TOMP TOMP
WHUP
HURRY!!
TOMP TOMP
WAAH! THIS IS BAD! THE SHIP'S LEAVING THE WATER!!
WE'RE FALLING!! WE'RE FALLING, NAMI!! DO SOMETHING!!
NO, WE'RE GONNA MAKE IT!

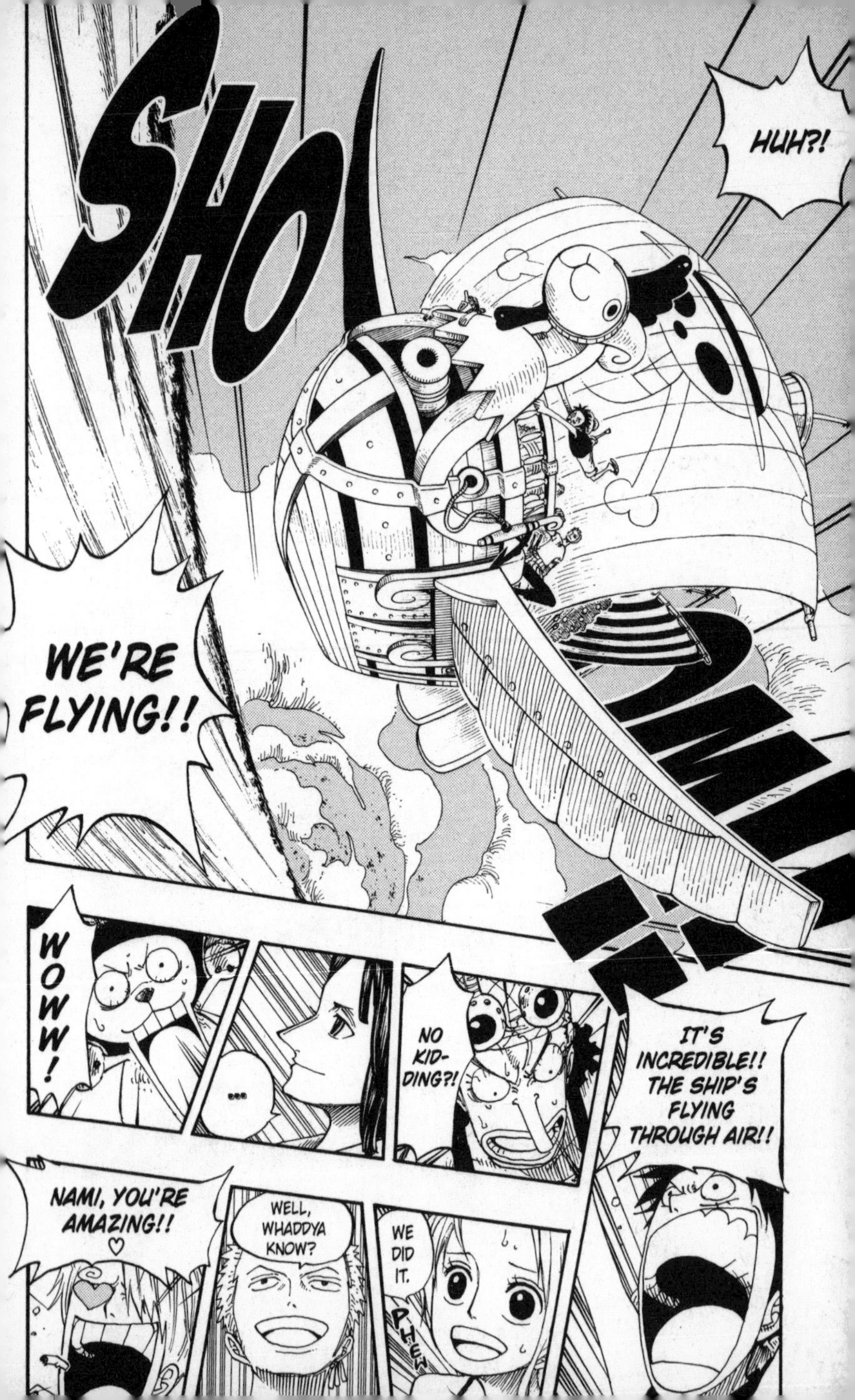
HUH?!
SHO
WE'RE FLYING!!
IT'S INCREDIBLE!! THE SHIP'S FLYING THROUGH AIR!!
NO KID-DING?!
...
WOWWW!
WE DID IT.
PHEW
WELL, WHADDYA KNOW?
NAMI, YOU'RE AMAZING!! ♡

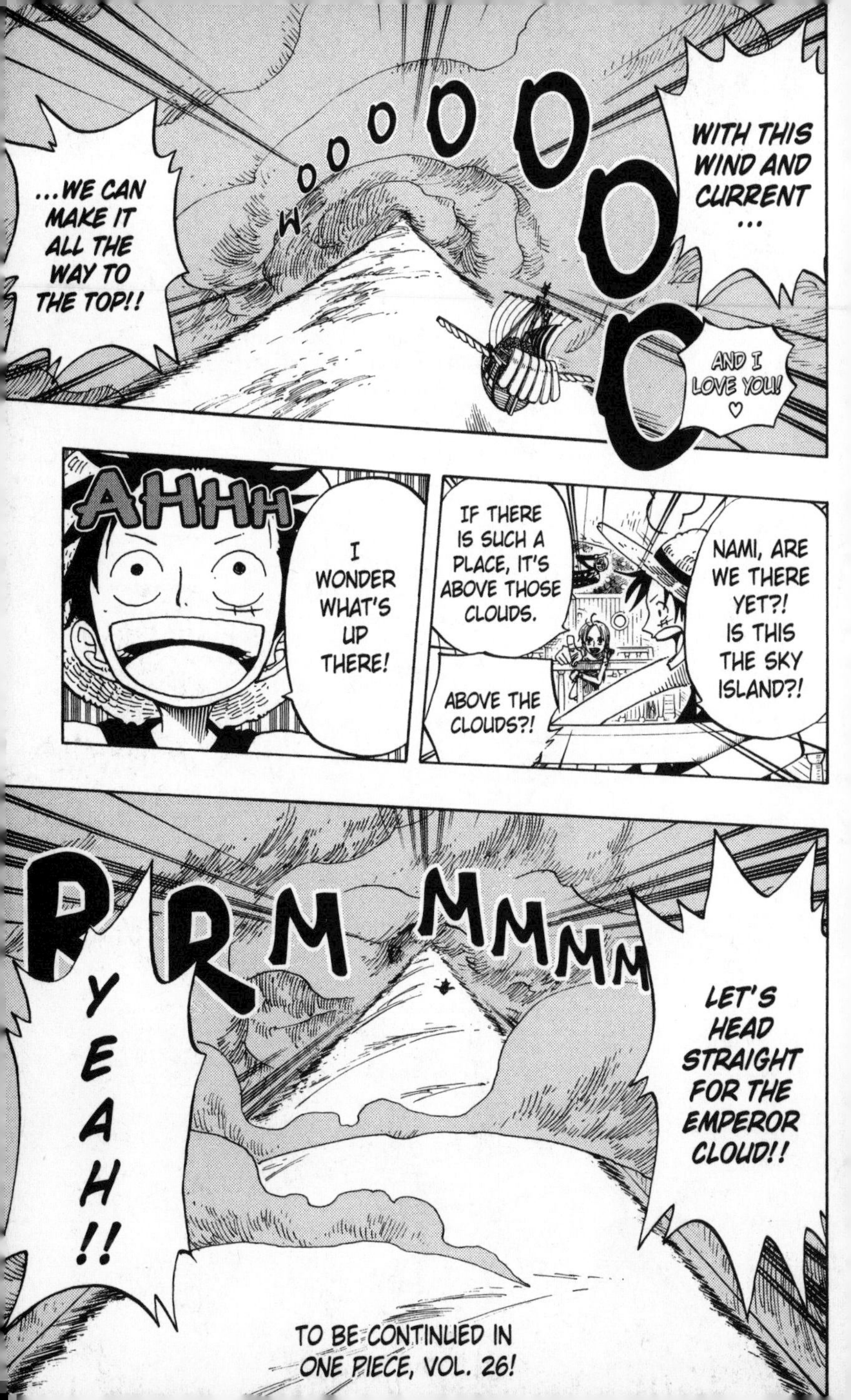
WITH THIS WIND AND CURRENT...
AND I LOVE YOU! ♡
WOOOOOOOC
...WE CAN MAKE IT ALL THE WAY TO THE TOP!!
NAMI, ARE WE THERE YET?! IS THIS THE SKY ISLAND?!
IF THERE IS SUCH A PLACE, IT'S ABOVE THOSE CLOUDS.
ABOVE THE CLOUDS?!
AHHH
I WONDER WHAT'S UP THERE!
LET'S HEAD STRAIGHT FOR THE EMPEROR CLOUD!!
YEAH!!
RRMMMMMM

TO BE CONTINUED IN ONE PIECE, VOL. 26!

# COMING NEXT VOLUME:

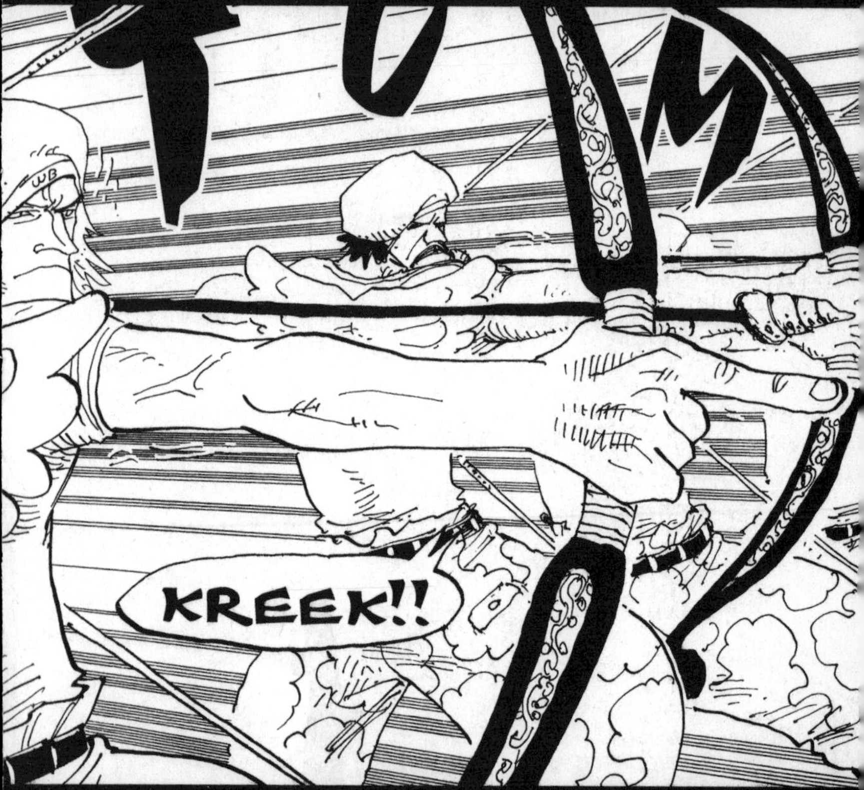
KREEK!!

The Straw Hats have made it to the ocean in the sky, but not everything is as angelic as they had imagined. Charged with illegal entry, they're being pursued by not only the Skypiea Police, but all the other inhabitants of the sky too! Who knew that illegal immigration was such a treacherous felony? Even if the Straw Hats want to leave, will these outlaws be allowed to leave in peace?!

**ON SALE NOW!**

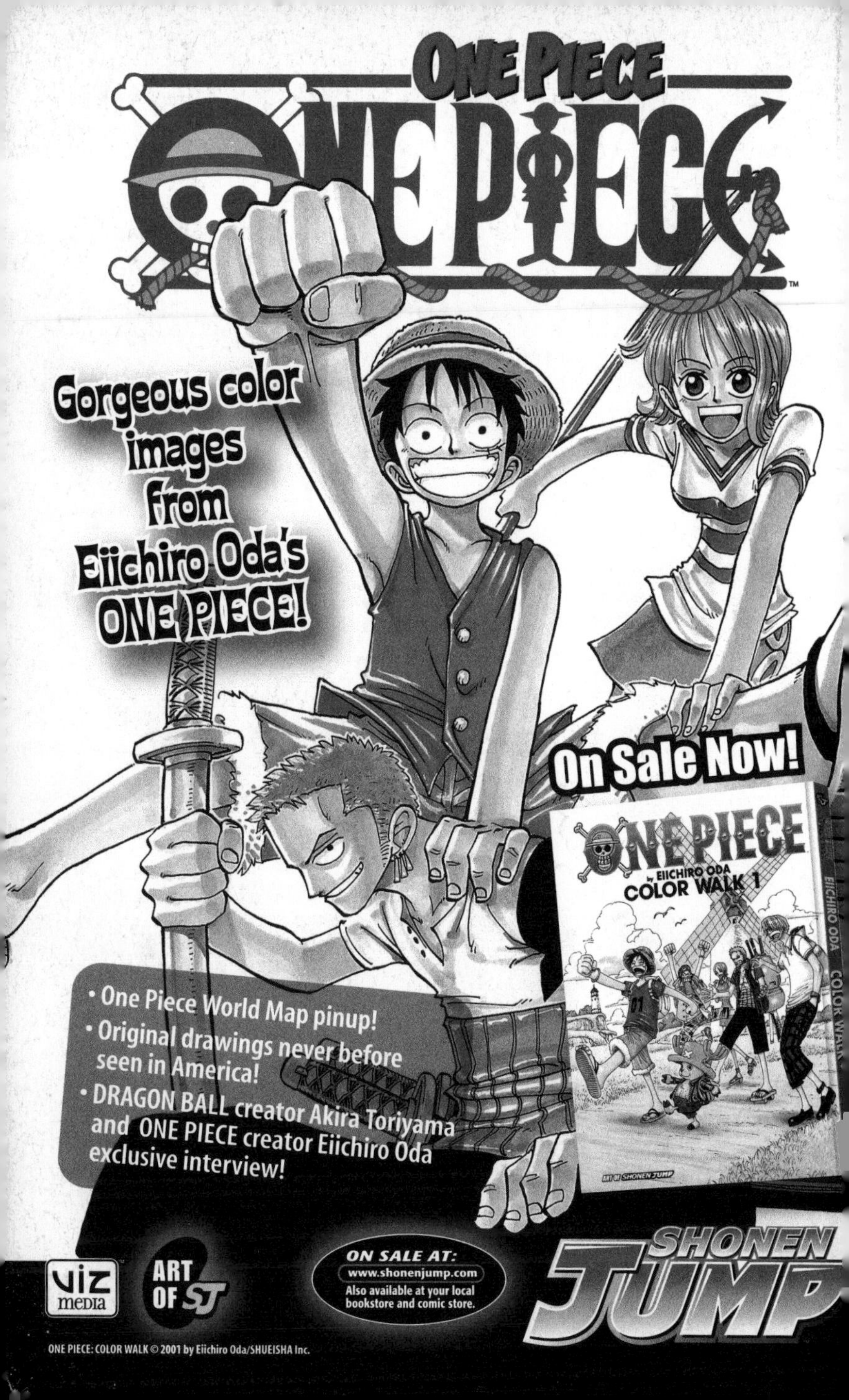

ONE PIECE
ONE PIECE
Gorgeous color images from Eiichiro Oda's ONE PIECE!
On Sale Now!
ONE PIECE by EIICHIRO ODA COLOR WALK 1
EIICHIRO ODA COLOR WALK
ART OF SHONEN JUMP
• One Piece World Map pinup!
• Original drawings never before seen in America!
• DRAGON BALL creator Akira Toriyama and ONE PIECE creator Eiichiro Oda exclusive interview!
viz media
ART OF SJ
ON SALE AT:
www.shonenjump.com
Also available at your local bookstore and comic store.
SHONEN JUMP
ONE PIECE: COLOR WALK © 2001 by Eiichiro Oda/SHUEISHA Inc.